THE SEXUAL PREDATOR

LEGAL ISSUES • CLINICAL ISSUES •

SPECIAL POPULATIONS

Volume II

Edited by
Anita Schlank, Ph.D.

Civic Research Institute
4478 U.S. Route 27 • P.O. Box 585 • Kingston, NJ 08528

Copyright © 2001

By Civic Research Institute, Inc.
Kingston, New Jersey 08528

The information in this book is not intended to replace the services of a trained legal professional. Civic Research Institute, Inc. provides this information without advocating the use of or endorsing the issues, theories, precedent, guidance, resources, practical materials or programs discussed herein. Any application of the issues, theories, precedent, guidance, resources, practical materials or programs set forth in this book is at the reader's sole discretion and risk. The authors, editors, contributors and Civic Research Institute, Inc. specifically disclaim any liability, loss or risk, personal or otherwise, which is incurred as a consequence, directly or indirectly, of the use and application of any of the contents of this book.

All rights reserved. This book may not be reproduced in part or in whole by any process without written permission from the publisher.

Printed in the United States of America

Library of Congress Cataloging in Publication Data
The sexual predator/Anita Schlank

ISBN 1-887554-14-9

Library of Congress Control Number 2001 135002

Acknowledgments

I would like to offer my deepest gratitude to the authors of the individual chapters and also give grateful acknowledgment to the following people for their work on both volumes in this series: Art Rosenfeld, Publisher and Deborah Launer, Editorial Director of Civic Research Institute; and Fran Stevens, copy editor. I would also like to thank all of the staff at MSOP for their hard work, and the following people for their continuing personal support: Craig Nelson, Janice Marques, Connie Isaac, Jeanne Morrow, Bill Plum, John Bergman, "Piggy" Gardner, Robin Lagerquist, Chris Mitchell, Jim Haaven, Barbara Schwartz, Joanne Fairfield, and Rick Harry. Finally, I would like to thank my family. (Unfortunately, however, it's another one that doesn't have a "coffee table book" type of title—so don't worry, you're not expected to read this one, either.)

About the Authors

John Bergman, M.A., R.D.T., M.T./B.C.T.
Mr. Bergman is a registered dramatherapist and master teacher in dramatherapy. He is the Founding Director of Geese Theatre, a company based both in England and in the United States, and conducts dramatherapy with sexual offenders, violent offenders, chemical abusers, and juvenile offenders in treatment programs located in many different countries. Mr. Bergman has also authored many articles and book chapters on the use of dramatherapy with offenders.

Pamela Bidelman, M.S.W., L.I.C.S.W.
Ms. Bidelman is a licensed independent clinical social worker who has worked in the Minnesota Department of Human Services sex offender treatment programs since 1977. She holds a master's degree in social work from the University of Minnesota. Currently, Ms. Bidelman works in the Minnesota Sex Offender Program, a program for civilly committed sexual offenders located in Moose Lake and St. Peter.

Edward A. Delgado-Romero, Ph.D.
Dr. Delgado-Romero is a licensed psychologist in the state of Florida. He is currently the assistant director at the University of Florida's Counseling Center, where he supervises clinical services.

Joanne Fairfield, C.Q.S.W.
Ms. Fairfield has a certificate of qualification in social work (British equivalent of an L.I.C.S.W.), and has worked in the sexual abuse field since 1983. She has worked with both sexual offenders and survivors of sexual abuse. She is currently the Assistant Clinical Director of the Minnesota Sex Offender Program, a program for civilly committed sexual offenders located in Moose Lake and St. Peter.

James Haaven, M.A.
Mr. Haaven received his master's degree in behavioral science-psychology from Pacific Lutheran University in Tacoma, Washington. He has worked clinically with developmentally disabled sex offenders for twenty-one years. He currently directs the Social Rehabilitation Unit at Oregon State Hospital in Salem, Oregon.

Rick Harry, C.O.O., M.S.O.P.
Mr. Harry received his bachelor's degree in psychology from the University of Minnesota. He has worked since 1969 in a variety of administrative and management positions in programs for mentally ill, chemically dependent, and developmentally disabled populations. He is currently the Chief Operating Officer for the Moose Lake Regional State Operated Services, which administers twenty residential and nonresidential state operated programs in northeastern Minnesota. He is also responsible for the administrative direction of the Minnesota Sex Offender Program at Moose Lake and St. Peter.

Amy K. Heesacker, Ph.D.
Dr. Heesacker is a licensed psychologist in the state of Florida. She works at the University of Florida as a therapist and instructor as well as working in private practice. She has been conducting juvenile and adult sex offender evaluations for the past three years.

Harry M. Hoberman, Ph.D., L.P.
Dr. Hoberman is the director of the PACIFICA Center for Psychological and Psychiatric Services. He is in the private practice of clinical and forensic psychology. He is also a clinical assistant professor of psychiatry at the University of Minnesota Medical School. He serves as a consultant to district courts in Minnesota in the area of civil commitments and has served as a court-appointed examiner or as an expert witness for the petitioner in over forty civil commitment proceedings.

Eric S. Janus, J.D.
Mr. Janus is a professor of law at William Mitchell College of Law, St. Paul, Minnesota, where he has taught full-time since 1984. He received his doctorate in law from Harvard Law School and his bachelor's degree from Carleton College. Mr. Janus has written two books, *Law and Mental Health Professionals*: *Minnesota* (APA 1994, Supp. 1998) (with Mickelsen and Sanders) and *Civil Commitment in Minnesota* (2d ed., Butterworth, 1991). His recent publications on mental health law appear in a number of law reviews, including *Indiana Law Review*; *Psychology,Public Policy & Law*; *Stanford Law & Policy Review*; and *Northwestern University Law Review*, and address contemporary legal approaches to preventing and predicting sexual violence.

Ken Kozlowski, J.D., M.L.S.
Mr. Kozlowski received his bachelor's degree in communications from the University of Akron, his master's degree in library science from Kent State University, and his doctorate in law from Cleveland-Marshall College of Law. He worked as an associate librarian at the Cleveland, Ohio based law firm of Squire, Sanders & Dempsey from 1987-1992, and at the Cleveland Law Library Association from 1992-1997. He currently holds the position of Head of Public Services at the Zimmerman Law Library at the University of Dayton School of Law. Mr. Kozlowski is a contributing editor for the following publications: *Community Corrections Report*, *Journal of Offender Monitoring, Campus Safety & Student Development*, and *Sex Offender Law Report*.

Roxanne Lieb, M.P.A.
Ms. Lieb is the Director of the Washington State Institute for Public Policy, a nonpartisan think tank. The Institute has published several research papers related to sex offense policy, including reviews of state laws on sex offender registration, sexual predator statutes, and community notification.

Janice K. Marques, Ph.D.
Dr. Marques is Chief of Program Development and Evaluation for the California Department of Mental Health. She has worked for over twenty years in the field of

sexual abuse as a clinician, researcher, program developer, and consultant. She trained at the University of Washington with G. Alan Marlatt and was a pioneer in adapting his relapse prevention model for use with sex offenders. In California, she designed and directed the Sex Offender Treatment and Evaluation Project (SOTEP), a rigorous longitudinal study of the effectiveness of intensive cognitive-behavioral treatment in reducing reoffense among rapists and child molesters. She is a past president of the Association for the Treatment of Sexual Abusers (ATSA) and a recipient of that organization's Significant Achievement Award.

Craig Nelson, Ph.D.
Dr. Nelson is currently the Executive Director of Atascadero State Hospital in California. He has previously served as a clinical psychologist, director of research, program director, and clinical administrator at that facility. He received his undergraduate training in psychology from the University of Iowa and his master's degree and doctorate in clinical psychology from Kent State University. Dr. Nelson previously served as the treatment director of California's Sex Offender Treatment and Evaluation Project (SOTEP), and he has published widely in the area of sex offender treatment and assessment. He is a recipient of the William T. Rossiter Award from the California Forensic Mental Association and is a member of the Board of Directors of the Association for the Treatment of Sexual Abusers (ATSA).

Randy K. Otto, Ph.D.
Dr. Otto is a licensed psychologist and diplomate in forensic psychology (ABFP). He is an associate professor in the Department of Mental Health Law & Policy at the University of South Florida, and he has a private practice limited to forensic evaluation. Dr. Otto is a member of the Board of Directors of the American Board of Forensic Psychology and the Executive Committee of the American Psychology-Law Society. He serves on the editorial boards of *Law & Human Behavior*, *Behavioral Sciences & the Law*, *Psychological Assessment*, and the *Journal of Threat Assessment*.

John Petrila, J.D., L.L.M.
Mr. Petrila is Chairman of the Department of Mental Health Law and Policy at the Florida Mental Health Institute. He holds joint appointments as professor in the University of South Florida College of Public Health and School of Social Work. He is co-author of three books, including *Psychological Evaluations for the Courts* (2d ed., Guilford Press, 1997), and of more than fifty other articles, monographs, and book chapters on mental disability law and policy. Mr. Petrila was formerly Director of Forensic Services in the Missouri Department of Mental Health and General Counsel and Deputy Commissioner in the New York Office of Mental Health. He was the 1999 recipient of the Saleem Shah award from the Forensic Division of the National Association of State Mental Health Program Directors for his contributions to forensic mental health.

William Plum, L.A.D.C.
Mr. Plum, a licensed alcohol and drug counselor, is Director of Outpatient

Programming and Training Director for the Center for Alcohol and Drug Treatment in Duluth, Minnesota. Mr. Plum was formerly a trainer for the Hazelden Foundation, and he has consulted with chemical dependency programs throughout the United States and in several countries, including Finland and Russia.

Anita Schlank, Ph.D., L.P.
Dr. Schlank received her doctorate in clinical psychology from the University of Nebraska-Lincoln, as part of the Forensic Psychology Specialty Track of the Law and Psychology Program. She is a licensed psychologist and has worked with sexual offenders since 1986. Dr. Schlank is currently the clinical director of the Minnesota Sex Offender Program, a treatment program for civilly committed sexual offenders located in Moose Lake and St. Peter. She is also past president of the Minnesota Chapter of the Association for the Treatment of Sexual Abusers.

Ted Shaw, Ph.D.
Dr. Shaw is a licensed psychologist in private practice in Florida, where he holds the contract for face-to-face evaluations under the Sexually Violent Predator Act. In addition, he supervises the treatment of more than 300 adult sex offenders. He has designed and operated both residential and outpatient juvenile and adult sex offender treatment programs since 1985. He was the first president of the Florida Association for the Treatment of Sexual Abusers (FATSA) and has served on the ATSA Ethics Committee since 1991.

David Thornton, Ph.D.
Dr. Thornton spent twenty-five years working in English corrections. He specializes in the design of risk assessment and treatment procedures for sexual and violent offenders. Currently (January 2001), he heads the Programs Unit in the national headquarters of the English Prison Service. The unit is responsible for treatment programs provided in over 100 prisons. He has developed risk assessment systems that are widely used in England by police forces, probations and prison services, and forensic health services. With Karl Hanson, he developed the Static-99, a static prediction scale that is widely used in civil commitment assessment.

Introduction

The argument used to be "Should they stay or should they go?", but now it appears that despite legal, clinical, and financial concerns, sexually violent predator (SVP) statutes are here to stay. Approximately twenty states have now adopted this type of legislation, and several programs have reached the point of releasing the first offenders back into the community after successful program completion. Still, the debates surrounding this controversial issue continue. Civil libertarians are now focusing on specific elements of the SVP statutes, hoping at least to narrow the scope of those selected for further detainment. Attention is being focused on both the quality of treatment that is being made available to the detainees and the effectiveness of the release process. An article in the February 2, 2000 *Milwaukee Journal Sentinel* outlines the manner in which these areas can overlap. The article describes how a sexual predator was ordered to remain indeterminately confined in a state hospital; this occurred one day after the state's Department of Health and Family Services was found to be in contempt of court for failing to find local housing for that same offender. The article goes on to describe how more than one hundred sites refused to allow this offender to reside in their buildings, prompting the court to direct the program to build its own halfway house.

This second volume in the Sexual Predator series provides recognition of the complexity of issues still faced by legal experts and clinicians involved with the assessment, court proceedings, and provision of treatment for those who are civilly committed. Part 1 highlights the change in direction of the legal challenges to the SVP statutes, which in the past have been called "a misguided attempt to solve a serious problem" (Bilbrey, 1999). Part 2 focuses on the administrative and clinical issues that surface following the initial steps of implementation of a treatment program for civilly committed offenders. And finally, Part 3 illustrates the importance of shedding the one-size-fits-all approach to treatment, showing that offenders often present with complicated histories that require modifications of standard treatment modalities. Whether the offender comes to treatment as a juvenile, with a developmental disability, or with a history of chemical dependency, the clinical challenges remains the same: to provide the patient effective and comprehensive sex offender treatment while ensuring the safety and protection of society. This book examines some of these very difficult issues.

References

Bilbrey, R. (1999, Nov.-Dec). Civil commitment of sexually violent predators: A misguided attempt to solve a serious problem. *Journal of the Missouri Bar, 55,* 321–329.

Sink, L. (2000, Feb. 2). Molester won't be freed, *Milwaukee Journal Sentinel*, available online at www.jsonline.com/news/state/feb00/oldpred02r020100.asp.

Table of Contents

Acknowledgments iii
About the Authors v
Introduction ix

PART 1: LEGAL ISSUES

Chapter 1: Sex Offender Commitments and the "Inability to Control"—Developing Legal Standards and a Behavioral Vocabulary for an Elusive Concept

"Inability to Control": The Search for a Definition 1-2
The Legal Context 1-3
Criteria for a Legal Standard for Inability to Control 1-4
    The Inability-to-Control Judgment Must Be Grounded on Observation 1-4
    The Standard Contains a Normative Component 1-5
    The Standard Must Meet the Legal Standards Required by the Constitution 1-5
        A Narrow Class of Persons Eligible for Commitment 1-5
        A Justification for Civil Commitment 1-6
        Criminal Interstitiality 1-7
        Jurisprudence of Difference 1-7
Distinguishing and Discarding Concepts 1-8
    Involuntary and Reflexive Responses 1-8
    Volitional Dysfunction 1-8
    Caused Behavior 1-8
    Inability to Do Otherwise 1-9
A Proposed Typology of Inability to Control 1-10
    Self-Regulation 1-10
    Classifying Inability to Control 1-10
Application to Sex Offenders 1-12
    The Strong Impulses Model 1-12
        Impulsivity; Antisocial Personality 1-12
        Addictive Disorders 1-13

The Problem of Offender Acquiescence to Impulses 1-14
　　　The Impaired Self-Regulation Model 1-17
　　　　　"Self-Regulation" Defined 1-17
　　　　　Key Ingredients 1-17
　　　　　Requisite Physical and Mental Strength 1-18
　　　Self-Regulation in the Sexual Offending Context 1-18
　　　Meeting the Constitutional Criteria 1-20
　　　The Character/Personality Model 1-21
Conclusion 1-22

Chapter 2: Professional Standards for Civil Commitment Programs

Constitutional and Treatment Issues 2-2
　　　Legal Context 2-3
　　　Clinical Context 2-4
Relevant Guidelines and Standards 2-5
　　　General Resources 2-5
　　　State Guidelines 2-5
　　　Professional Guidelines 2-5
Requirements of the *Turay* Injunction 2-6
The Professional Standards 2-7
　　　Staff Training and Supervision 2-8
　　　　　Properly Trained Staff and Clinical Supervision 2-8
　　　　　Staffing Structure and Roles 2-8
　　　　　Consistency in Treatment Planning 2-8
　　　Treatment Components and Measures of Progress 2-9
　　　　　Individual and Comprehensive Treatment Plans 2-9
　　　　　Components Provided in Institutional Programs 2-10
　　　　　Monitoring and Feedback 2-10
　　　　　Identifiable Phases and Conditional Release 2-10
　　　Treatment Environment 2-11
　　　　　Nonpunitive Treatment Environments 2-12
　　　　　Adequate Space 2-12
　　　　　Staff Behavior 2-12
　　　　　Consistently Enforced Policies 2-12
　　　　　Residents' Grievances 2-13
　　　　　Residents Who Refuse Treatment 2-13
　　　Program Review and Oversight 2-13
　　　　　Internal Review Procedures 2-14
　　　　　External Oversight 2-14
Summary and Conclusions 2-15

Chapter 3: Admissibility of Expert Testimony in Sexually Violent Predator Proceedings

Introduction 3-2
Evidentiary Requirements 3-3
    The *Frye* Rule 3-3
    The *Daubert* Rule 3-4
    Federal Rules of Evidence 3-5
Evidentiary Challenges to Expert Clinical Testimony 3-5
    Assessment Methods 3-6
        Clinical Assessment 3-6
        Anamnestic Assessment 3-6
        Guided or Structured Clinical Assessment 3-6
    Actuarial and Adjusted Actuarial Assessments 3-7
        Arguments Against Adjusted Estimates 3-7
        Perceived Reliability 3-8
        Use in SVP Assessments 3-8
Statutory Requirements and Challenges to Expert Clinical Testimony 3-8
    History of Sexual Offending 3-9
        "Sexual Nature" of Nonsexual Offense 3-9
        Expert's "Special Knowledge" Requirement 3-10
    Presence of a Mental Disorder That Is Causally Related to
        Sex Offending 3-11
    Lack of Control 3-13
        Modified Lack of Control Standard 3-13
        State's Burden of Proof 3-14
    Risk for Sexual Reoffending 3-14
        Issue of Expert's Ability to Assess Risk 3-14
        No Assessment Approach Considered Illegal 3-14
        Minnesota's Structured Approach 3-15
        Attacks on Expert Testimony 3-17
    Florida's Rejection of Actuarial Instruments 3-19
        Use of *Frye* Test to Determine Exclusion 3-19
        Scrutiny of "Scientific Principle" 3-20
    Getting Beyond the Appearances of Scientific Judgment 3-20
Summary and Conclusions 3-21

Chapter 4: In the Wake of *Hendricks*—States Seem Committed to SVP Programs

The Broad Reach of *Hendricks* 4-2
United States Supreme Court 4-3

Circuit and District Courts ... 4-5
    First Circuit ... 4-5
    Second and Third Circuits ... 4-5
    Fourth Circuit ... 4-6
    Fifth Circuit ... 4-7
    Sixth and Seventh Circuits ... 4-7
    Eighth Circuit ... 4-7
    Ninth Circuit ... 4-8
    Tenth, Eleventh, and D.C. Circuits ... 4-9
State Court Decisions ... 4-9
    Alabama ... 4-9
    Arizona ... 4-10
    California ... 4-10
    Illinois ... 4-11
    Indiana ... 4-11
    Kansas ... 4-12
    Massachusetts ... 4-13
    Michigan ... 4-14
    Minnesota ... 4-14
    Missouri ... 4-15
    New Jersey ... 4-15
    Washington ... 4-16
    Wisconsin ... 4-17
    Other States ... 4-18
        Colorado ... 4-18
        Connecticut ... 4-18
        District of Columbia ... 4-18
        Florida ... 4-18
        Kentucky ... 4-18
        Maine ... 4-18
        Montana ... 4-18
        Nebraska ... 4-18
        New York ... 4-19
        North Dakota ... 4-19
        Ohio ... 4-19
        Oregon ... 4-19
        Pennsylvania ... 4-19
        South Dakota ... 4-19
        Texas ... 4-19
        Vermont ... 4-19

    Virginia 4-19
Conclusion 4-19

PART 2: CLINICAL ISSUES

Chapter 5: Treatment Programs for Sexually Violent Predators—A Review of States

Introduction 5-2
Treatment Standards 5-3
Population Characteristics 5-3
    Previous Treatment 5-4
    Multiple Diagnoses; Personality Disorders 5-5
Program Settings 5-6
    Secure Psychiatric Hospital 5-6
    Mental Health Facility Within a Prison 5-6
    Free-Standing Secure Facility 5-8
Staffing 5-9
    Staff Levels and Patterns 5-9
        Psychiatric Hospitals 5-9
        Free-Standing Facility 5-9
        Prison-Based Program 5-11
    Training and Expertise 5-11
        Cohesion of Treatment Team 5-11
        Cost of Staffing 5-11
Treatment Programming 5-12
    Cognitive-Behavioral Approaches 5-12
    Medications 5-13
    Behavior Therapy 5-13
    Assessment 5-14
    Treatment Planning 5-15
    Program Phases 5-15
    Ancillary Treatment Programming 5-15
    Special Populations 5-15
Residential Management Issues 5-16
    Resistance to Treatment 5-16
    Harassment of Staff 5-17
    Strategies to Minimize Difficulties 5-17
    Resident Advocacy 5-18
State Provisions for Least Restrictive Alternative 5-18
    Transition to Outpatient Setting 5-19

Community Notification Issues 5-20
Types of LRA Facilities 5-20
Summary 5-21

Chapter 6: Civil Commitment of Dangerous, Personality-Disordered Offenders—Developing a Model

Introduction 6-1
The Concept of Dangerous Severe Personality Disorder 6-2
Risk Assessment Methodologies Relevant to DSPD 6-3
    Actuarial Instruments 6-3
    Case Formulations 6-3
    Structured Clinical Judgment 6-4
Assessing Personality Disorder for DSPD 6-4
Assessing the Link to Risk 6-5
A Possible Process 6-5
    1. Actuarial Classification Based on Widely Available Data to
       Serve as a Screen for High-Risk Offenders 6-5
    2. Specialist Instrument-Based Risk Classification 6-7
    3. Preliminary Assessment of Personality Disorder and
       Its Link to Risk 6-8
    4. First Tribunal Hearing 6-8
    5. Residential Assessment 6-9
    6. Second Tribunal Hearing 6-9
    7. Release 6-9
        Prior Record/Current Behavior Scales 6-10
        Psychometric Tests 6-10
Reflections 6-11

Chapter 7: Civil Commitment Programs—Administrative Concerns

Introduction 7-1
Program Location—Urban or Rural? 7-2
    Site Requirements 7-2
    Medical Issues 7-3
    Recruitment 7-3
    Resident Services 7-3
    Contact With Local Government 7-4
Staffing Levels 7-4
    Security and Treatment Requirements 7-4
    Direct Care Staff 7-5
    Professional Care Staff 7-5
    Administrative Staff 7-5

Staff Recruitment and Training 7-6
    Direct Care and Support Staff 7-6
    Professional Staff 7-7
    New Employee/Refresher Training 7-7
    Boundary Issues 7-9
Program Jurisdiction 7-10
    The MSOP Experience 7-10
    Dual Jurisdiction Issues 7-10
Summary and Directions for the Future 7-11

Chapter 8: Using Drama Therapy to Uncover Genuineness and Deception in Civilly Committed Sexual Offenders

The Therapist's Lodestone 8-2
A Lifetime of Secrecy and Deception 8-3
    Deception and Attachment 8-3
    The Implicit "Dangerous World" Theory of Mind 8-4
Discordant Lying and Agents of Change 8-4
Experiential Therapies 8-5
    The Action Forum for Struggle 8-6
    Design of Drama Therapy Sessions 8-7
Classic Presentations of the Nongenuine Self: Butting Into the
  Offender's Map 8-8
    The Overly Intellectualized Client 8-8
    The Detached and Passive Client 8-8
    The Overly Compliant Client 8-8
    The Indignant, Outraged, Rigid, and Morally Righteous Client 8-9
    The Reality of Play 8-10
    Modified Confrontation 8-10
    The Adult Rapist 8-11
The Sense of Genuineness 8-12
    Elements of a Successful Drama Therapy Session 8-12
    Remaking Meaning 8-14

Chapter 9: Working With Nonoffending Partners

Why Work With Nonoffending Partners? 9-2
Impact on Partner of Discovery of the Abuse 9-3
    As an Individual 9-4
    On Relationship With Offender 9-4
    On Relationship With Victim 9-5
    On Relationship With Victim's Siblings 9-6
    On Relationship With Friends and Community 9-6

    Financial Concerns 9-6
    Support Services 9-7
The Integrated Treatment Model 9-7
    Program Philosophy 9-7
    When Is This Treatment Approach Appropriate? 9-7
    Framework and Goals 9-8
    Why Use a Cognitive-Behavioral Treatment Model? 9-8
        Modeling 9-10
        Respondent Conditioning 9-10
        Instrumental Conditioning 9-11
    A Gradual Process 9-11
Assessment of Nonoffending Partners 9-11
Group Work for Nonoffending Partners 9-15
    Group Work, Part A 9-16
        Address the Impact of Offending 9-16
        Increase Understanding of Victim Dynamics 9-16
        Increase Understanding of Offender Dynamics 9-16
        Provide an Alternative Model/Framework 9-18
    Group Work, Part B 9-19
        Learn to Identify and Challenge Cognitive Distortions 9-19
        Learn to Identify and Resist Grooming Strategies 9-19
        Introduce the Relapse Prevention Model and
            Learn to Identify Cues 9-21
        Develop Partner and Victim Alert Lists 9-22
        Develop a Support Network 9-22
    Group Work, Part C1 9-22
Dyadic Work 9-22
    Assessing Readiness for Joint Work 9-23
    Joint Work, Part C2 9-23
        Communication and Information 9-23
        Practice Skills 9-24
        Addressing Unresolved Issues 9-24
Therapist's Role 9-24
Summary 9-25

Chapter 10: Transition—Challenges for the Offender and the Community
The Need for Gradual, Controlled Transition 10-1
    Internal Risk Factors 10-2
    External Risk Factors 10-2
    Housing Issues 10-3
Aftercare Issues 10-3

Stakeholders 10-4
    Victim and Victim Advocates 10-4
    Policy-Makers 10-5
    County Government 10-5
    The Media 10-6
    The Sex Offender 10-6
    The Treatment Program 10-7
Transition and Technology 10-7
Ethical Issues 10-8
Summary 10-9

Chapter 11: Dangerousness and Sex Offenders—Assessing Risk for Future Sex Offenses

The Three Basic Factors Governing Commitment 11-3
    Role of the Mental Health Professional 11-3
    Constitutional Basis for Mental Health Professionals' Role ... 11-4
Definitional Issues: Just What Is It That Is Being Predicted? 11-5
Relative Ability of Mental Health Professionals to Predict
    Dangerousness for Legal Matters 11-6
Prediction of Dangerousness, General Criminal and Violent Recidivism 11-7
Evidentiary Standards for Admissibility of Expert Witness Testimony 11-8
    Admissibility of Expert Testimony 11-9
    The *Daubert* Standard 11-9
Statistical Aspects of Prediction 11-10
    Significance of Base Rate 11-11
    ROC Analysis 11-12
    The Confidence Interval 11-13
The Methodology of Prediction of Future Dangerousness 11-13
    Unstructured ("Pure") Clinical Judgment 11-13
    Structured or Guided Clinical Judgment 11-14
    Pure Actuarial Methods 11-15
        Limitations 11-16
        Specificity Problem 11-17
    Actuarial Plus Expert Modifiers—Adjusted Actuarial Methods 11-17
Elements and Issues Involved in the Methodology of Risk Prediction 11-18
    Population Sample Variables 11-18
    Predictor Variables—Identifying and Defining Potential
        Risk Factors 11-19
    Criterion Variables—Identifying and Defining Sex Offense
        Recidivism 11-20
            Self-Reports and Collateral Sources 11-20

Processes in the Justice System 11-20
Number of Actual Offenses 11-21
Police and Parole Office Records 11-21
No Correlation Between Variable and Potential Offense 11-22
Length of Follow-Up Period 11-22
Survival Analysis 11-22
Types of Sex Offenders 11-23
Increased Recidivism With Increased Follow-Up Period 11-23
The Base Rate of Sexual Offense Recidivism 11-24
Obtaining Information for Risk Assessment 11-25
Individual and Combinations of Risk Factors That Differentiate
Recidivists 11-25
Static and Historical Factors 11-26
Deviancy and Psychopathy 11-26
Meta-Analysis 11-27
Dynamic Risk Factors 11-28
Two General Types of Risk Factors 11-29
Specific Risk Assessment Measures and Guidelines 11-30
The Psychopathy Checklist—Revised 11-30
Inter-Rater Reliability 11-30
Meta-Analysis 11-30
Psychopathy and Recidivism 11-31
PCL Screening Version 11-31
Misuse of PCL-R 11-32
The ASSESS-LIST 11-32
Violence Risk Appraisal Guide (VRAG) 11-33
Violent Behavior Predictions 11-34
Limitations 11-35
Minnesota Sex Offender Screening Tool (MnSOST) 11-35
Rapid Risk Assessment for Sexual Offense Recidivism
(RRASOR) 11-37
Sex Offender Risk Appraisal Guide (SORAG) 11-39
Minnesota Sex Offender Screening Tool—Revised (MnSOST-R) 11-40
Structured Anchored Clinical Judgment (SACJ/SACJ-Min) 11-42
Static-99 11-43
Sex Offender Need Assessment Rating (SONAR) 11-44
Structured Risk Assessment (SRA) 11-45
Historical Clinical Risk Management-20 11-46
Sexual Violence Rating Scale 11-47
Risk for Sexual Violence Protocol (RSVP) 11-48

    Relationships Among the Different Recidivism Measures 11-48
Communicating Information Regarding the Level of Risk of
    Future Dangerousness 11-50
Conclusion 11-50

PART 3: SPECIAL POPULATIONS

Chapter 12: Implications of Sexually Violent Predator Laws for Youthful Offenders

Overview 12-1
Brief Review of the Development of SVP Laws 12-2
Assessment of Dangerousness 12-3
    Traditional Assessment Tools 12-3
    Juvenile Data 12-4
Housing Issues 12-4
Quality of Treatment 12-5
Financial Implications of Civil Commitment 12-6
    Specific Costs 12-6
    Political Capital 12-8
Summary 12-9

Chapter 13: The Challenge of Treating the Sex Offender With Developmental Disabilities

Elements of the Challenge 13-1
    Safety and Management Issues 13-2
    Population Characteristics 13-2
Assessment Considerations 13-5
    Interview/Sexual History 13-5
    Psychometric Testing 13-6
    Plethysmograph 13-7
    Abel Assessment for Sexual Interest 13-7
Treatment Approaches 13-8
    Overall Strategies 13-8
        Milieu/Motivation 13-8
        Effective Teaching 13-9
        Community Transition 13-10
    Specific Components 13-11
        Adapting the DDSO's Relapse Prevention Model 13-11
        Approach Skills—The "New Me" 13-13

   Avoidance Skills—"What-to-Dos" 13-14
   Medication 13-15
Civil Commitment Programs 13-16
Summary 13-17

Chapter 14: Sex Offender and Chemical Dependency Treatment
Introduction 14-1
Philosophy (Program Statement) 14-1
   Core Clinical Concepts 14-2
   Sex Offender-Specific CD Model 14-3
CA Component Design 14-3
   Assessment and Education 14-5
   Recovery Structure and Support System 14-5
   Application of the Relapse Prevention Model 14-6
   Transition Issues and Aftercare Planning 14-7
Conclusion 14-8

Appendices
Appendix 1, Bibliography A-1

Table of Acronyms T-1
Table of Cases and Statutes T-3

Index I-1

Part 1

Legal Issues

While the legal arguments surrounding the overall constitutionality of the SVP statutes appear to be dwindling, concerns over several factors specific to those laws still remain. In particular, legal experts have raised questions regarding expert testimony, risk assessment, adequacy of treatment, and the manner in which one assesses an offender's ability to control his behavior. This section provides an in-depth analysis of the legal issues that remain at the center of the civil commitment debate.

In the first chapter, Eric Janus discusses the elusive concept of "inability to control" one's behavior. He points out the while many court opinions have focused on this finding being a prerequisite for commitment, there is a lack of consistency among both clinicians and legal experts regarding how to identify and measure one's ability to control behavior. He also offers suggestions for the future.

Recent cases have also focused on the availability and quality of treatment offered in civil commitment programs. In Chapter 2, Janice Marques uses her experience as a court-ordered Special Master to review the quality of treatment provided by one program. She proposes professional standards of treatment for all civil commitment programs for sex offenders.

There have been continuing concerns raised in court proceedings regarding the reliability and validity of both clinical testimony and the various assessment instruments used by examiners. Most recently, considerable attention has been directed toward new risk assessment tools. These revised tools are now believed to have evolved to the point of being able to specifically predict sexually violent recidivism. In Chapter 3, John Petrila and Randy Otto discuss evidentiary standards for scientific testimony, with a particular focus on risk assessment tools.

Finally, in Chapter 4, Ken Kozowlski provides a detailed summary of court cases that have been decided around the country since the pivotal *Kansas v. Hendricks* decision, in which the U.S. Supreme Court decided that commitment under Kansas's Sexually Violent Predator Act is civil in nature and, therefore, not punitive. Since this decision states have been passing SVP legislation at a rapid pace, and more than 260 cases have cited *Hendricks* as an authority on the subject of commitment, in both SVP and non-SVP cases.

Chapter 1

Sex Offender Commitments and the "Inability to Control"—Developing Legal Standards and a Behavioral Vocabulary for an Elusive Concept

by Eric S. Janus, J.D.*

"Inability to Control": The Search for a Definition 1-2
The Legal Context 1-3
Criteria for a Legal Standard for Inability to Control 1-4
    The Inability-to-Control Judgment Must Be Grounded on
        Observation 1-4
    The Standard Contains a Normative Component 1-5
    The Standard Must Meet the Legal Standards Required
        by the Constitution 1-5
        A Narrow Class of Persons Eligible for
            Commitment 1-5
        A Justification for Civil Commitment 1-6
        Criminal Interstitiality 1-7
        Jurisprudence of Difference 1-7
Distinguishing and Discarding Concepts 1-8
    Involuntary and Reflexive Responses 1-8
    Volitional Dysfunction 1-8
    Caused Behavior 1-8

---

    * The author served as co-counsel in extended litigation challenging Minnesota's sex offender commitment statutes. Thanks to Bernard Nodzon for his assistance in preparing this manuscript.

    Inability to Do Otherwise 1-9
A Proposed Typology of Inability to Control 1-10
    Self-Regulation 1-10
    Classifying Inability to Control 1-10
Application to Sex Offenders 1-12
    The Strong Impulses Model 1-12
        Impulsivity; Antisocial Personality 1-12
        Addictive Disorders 1-13
    The Problem of Offender Acquiescence to Impulses 1-14
    The Impaired Self-Regulation Model 1-17
        "Self-Regulation" Defined 1-17
        Key Ingredients 1-17
        Requisite Physical and Mental Strength 1-18
    Self-Regulation in the Sexual Offending Context 1-18
    Meeting the Constitutional Criteria 1-20
    The Character/Personality Model 1-21
Conclusion 1-22

"INABILITY TO CONTROL": THE SEARCH FOR A DEFINITION

For the past 60 years, courts have asserted that the use of "preventive detention" is safely limited to a small group of persons with a particular form of "mental disorder"—an "inability to control" their dangerous impulses. In its 1997 *Hendricks* decision, the U.S. Supreme Court reconfirmed the vitality of this limit, repeatedly emphasizing inability to control as the central factor that supported the constitutionality of Kansas's sexually violent predator commitment law (the Sexually Violent Predator Act, or SVPA).[1]

Yet there is good evidence that the inability-to-control concept lacks substance. Not one court has offered a useful definition of this concept in the sex offender commitment context. Commentators have for years criticized the concept, arguing that it has no empirical, observable foundation and is based on unstructured moral guesswork.[2] Philosophers have long argued about what it means to say that a given person could, or could not, have acted otherwise than he did.[3]

The problematic nature of the inability-to-control concept means that it cannot function very effectively as a constitutional limit on civil commitment. In practice, the concept is used in a conclusory manner. Its vagueness is a sure sign that courts are unable—or more likely, unwilling—to assert clear legal standards for commitment.

My purpose in writing this chapter is to provide some tools and vocabulary for talking about inability to control more precisely. If courts articulate their inability-to-control standards with some clarity, there will be less arbitrariness and more accountability in sex offender commitments. Two kinds of clarity are required. First, the concept needs anchoring in the law. We must determine which features inability to control must display in order to perform its constitutional role in validating sex offender commitment laws. Second, it must be anchored in the real world. When a mental health professional assesses an individual for inability to control, what sorts of things should he or she look for? What sort of judgments should he make? And what can we learn from the literature about how sex offenders fit into the definition of inability to control?

What we will learn is that many, perhaps most, sex offenders might sensibly be said to exhibit *some* form of inability to control their behavior. After all, these are offenders who have repeatedly *failed* to conform their conduct to important social norms. But if the inability-to-control concept is to perform its constitutional role, it will be a significantly narrower concept and will exclude the vast majority of sex offenders.

THE LEGAL CONTEXT

When courts hold sex offender commitments to be constitutional, they almost always allude, more or less directly, to the concept of inability to control. Thus it seems clear that in some form, inability to control is part of the constitutional underpinnings for sex offender commitments. It is somewhat more difficult to tease out the constitutional reasons for this central role.

Hendricks provides the most authoritative statement on the role of inability to control. In *Hendricks*, the Supreme Court upheld the constitutionality of Kansas's commitment law, and in doing so, the justices alluded repeatedly to inability to control. In a typical reference, the majority opinion stated that the Kansas law is constitutional because it requires a "mental disorder" that "narrows the class of persons eligible for confinement to those who are unable to control their dangerousness."[4] In another key passage, the Court alluded to "the existence of a 'mental abnormality' or 'personality disorder' that makes it difficult, if not impossible, for the person to control his dangerous behavior."[5]

In *Hubbart v. Superior Court,*[6] the California Supreme Court specifically noted that California's commitment law requires proof of an "inability" to control dangerous behavior, and, for that reason, is consistent with Hendricks:

> The statute then "links that finding [of dangerousness]" to a currently diagnosed mental disorder characterized by the *inability-to-control* dangerous sexual behavior. (*Hendricks*, . . . 521 U.S. 346, 358.) This formula permissibly circumscribes the class of persons eligible for commitment under the Act.[7]

The Minnesota Supreme Court has taken varied approaches to inability to control. In 1939, the court held that the state's sex offender commitment law could be applied only to those who exhibited "utter lack of power to control" their sexual behaviors.[8] On review of *Pearson*, the U.S. Supreme Court held that allowing commitments for less severe conditions "might render [the Act] of doubtful validity."[9]

In 1994, when the Minnesota Supreme Court was again called on to pass on the constitutionality of this statute, it reaffirmed the vitality of the *Pearson* "utter lack of power to control" test, calling the condition a "volitional dysfunction which grossly impairs judgment and behavior with respect to the sex drive."[10] In its 1999 *Linehan* decision, however, while the Minnesota court acknowledged that *Hendricks* established inability to control as a constitutional hallmark for sex offender commitment laws, it held that the only showing required was a demonstration of "inadequate control."[11]

The Washington Supreme Court described the typical subject for sex offender commitments using the language of compulsion and attempts to control behavior.[12] And most recently, the Kansas Supreme Court reversed a commitment on the grounds that the trial judge had failed to instruct the jury that inability to control was a constitutional prerequisite for commitment.[13]

The inability-to-control rubric has shaped the law of police power confinements for nearly sixty years.[14] For example, when Congress adopted a sex offender commitment law in 1948, it carefully crafted the law to reflect the inability-to-control test of *Pearson*.[15] Despite the long history of reliance on inability to control in the constitutional analysis, courts have almost never provided any guidance on what the concept means and how inability to control is to be assessed. It is common for courts to rely on conclusory professional testimony, and on testimony about past criminal behaviors, without in either case explaining either the behavioral or the legal theories underlying their findings.[16] Without substantially greater clarity, the inability-to-control test is too vague to provide any real limits on sex offender commitments. This leaves the constitutionality of commitment laws in doubt. As Justice Kennedy warned in his *Hendricks* concurrence:

> [I]f it were shown that mental abnormality is too imprecise a category to offer a solid basis for concluding that civil detention is justified, our precedents would not suffice to validate it.[17]

CRITERIA FOR A LEGAL STANDARD FOR INABILITY TO CONTROL

In this section, I set out three criteria that any legal standard for inability to control should meet:

1. The judgment of inability to control must be grounded on observation.

2. The standard for judgment must contain more than simple factual inference; it must include a *normative*, or value, judgment.

3. The standard must meet the legal standards required by the Constitution.

The Inability-to-Control Judgment Must Be Grounded on Observation

Inability to control is a construct which is, at least arguably, based on two negatives: that a person has no ability to refrain from (to not do) certain actions. It is a commonplace that proving a "negative" is difficult, and like all similar concepts, inability to control must be ascertained by inference—it cannot be directly observed. Nonetheless, the judgment about inability to control must be grounded on observations.

Observations may be of two sorts. Some may be observations of behavior (or reports of behavior) and others may be psychological facts, ascertained through interview and testing of the sort normally relied upon by mental health professionals.

The Standard Contains a Normative Component

Certain sets of observations will support the conclusion that a person lacks the ability to control his or her actions. But the conclusion is not a simple factual inference; it also includes a normative, or value, judgment. An example will demonstrate the difference. If we observe a person perform a certain task—say, balance her checkbook—we are entitled to conclude that she has the ability to balance a checkbook. "Ability" is a construct, but it can be inferred directly from observed behavior. A judgment of "inability" is similar in one way: it too must be inferred from observation. A key observation in this inference will be information about how hard the person *tried* at the task before *giving up*. If she tried "hard enough," then we conclude that she could not (lacked the capacity) rather than simply would not. The judgment about what level of effort is "enough" is a normative or value judgment. The judgment of incapacity is essentially a judgment of excuse; that is, the normative judgment has to do with how hard we expect a person to try before we will excuse her nonperformance as beyond her control and, therefore, not her fault.[18]

The complexity of the incapacity judgment means that its multiple strands must be teased apart in the legal context. This is necessary so that decisions that are essentially normative are not delegated sub rosa to mental health professionals. Thus, a valid definition of inability to control should specify the inference rules that mental health professionals use and should distinguish fact-based judgments from the normative or moral judgments that inform the incapacity characterization.

The Standard Must Meet the Legal Standards Required by the Constitution

The discussion so far has focused on producing a judgment about incapacity that is based on facts, clearly articulated inference rules, and distinctly stated moral or normative judgments. In addition, the judgment of inability to control must meet the legal standards required by the Constitution. This means that the standard must grow out of the constitutional role that inability to control plays in the constitutional justification of sex offender commitments.

As mentioned above, ascertaining the legal standards for inability to control is problematic, because the courts have avoided any substantive discussion of the legal theory underlying inability to control. My reading of the cases, and of commentary on the cases, suggests that an inability-to-control standard must meet two criteria to perform its requisite constitutional role.[19] The standard must narrow the class of persons eligible for civil commitment, and it must justify civilly committing these persons.

A Narrow Class of Persons Eligible for Commitment. Courts have made clear that civil commitment is not—and must not become—the primary means of dealing with antisocial behavior. That role is reserved for the criminal justice system. As the Minnesota Supreme Court put it:

> Substantive due process forecloses the substitution of preventive detention schemes for the criminal justice system, and the judiciary has a constitution-

al duty to intervene before civil commitment becomes the norm and criminal prosecution the exception.[20]

Further, of the two constitutional pillars for civil commitment (mental disorder and dangerousness), it is clearly the mental disorder element that must serve this narrowing function. Since criminal activity by definition poses a danger, it is only the mental disorder element that can narrow the civil commitment group. In *Hendricks*, the Supreme Court emphasized this role for mental disorder:

> The precommitment requirement of a "mental abnormality" or "personality disorder" is consistent with the requirements of these other statutes that we have upheld in that it narrows the class of persons eligible for confinement to those who are unable to control their dangerousness.[21]

Note that this "narrowing" criterion does not help explain why any *particular* group (say, mentally disordered dangerous people) is eligible for commitment. Its function is to insure that only a small group can get committed. To the extent that a given definition of inability to control would allow the commitment of a large group of dangerous persons, that definition would fail this constitutional test.

How narrow should the commitment category be in order to meet constitutional muster? As a beginning benchmark, courts can look at the actual practice of states with sex offender commitment laws. In these states, commitments range between 1 percent and 6 percent of released sex offenders.[22] Thus, as a rough guide, definitions of inability to control that would apply to more than 6 percent of sex offenders would exceed the narrowing function that marks the de facto outer limit of civil commitment in the United States.

A Justification for Civil Commitment. Second, the definition of inability to control must serve to *justify* civil commitment.[23] That is, the inability-to-control definition must provide the explanation for why the commitment group can be civilly committed, whereas the vast majority of others, including others who are similarly dangerous, cannot be. The Supreme Court has twice alluded to this role for the mental disorder element. In *Hendricks*, the Court said:

> This admitted lack of volitional control, coupled with a prediction of future dangerousness, *adequately distinguishes* Hendricks from other dangerous persons who are perhaps more properly dealt with exclusively through criminal proceedings.[24]

And in *Foucha*, the Court struck down the state's use of civil commitment, in part because:

> [T]he State does not explain why its interest would not be vindicated by the ordinary criminal processes involving charge and conviction, the use of enhanced sentences for recidivists, and other permissible ways of dealing with patterns of criminal conduct.[25]

The identification of a "justifying" element of inability to control is the most difficult aspect of the analysis. Essentially, the mental disorder element must support an explanation for treating the commitment group differently from non-mentally disordered, but equally dangerous, persons who may not constitutionally be locked up for preventive detention. What kind of "mental disorder" justifies taking away rights that people without the disorder have as a matter of course?

Two distinct approaches can tie the notion of mental disorder to a justification for civil commitment. I call them the principle of "criminal interstitiality" and the "jurisprudence of difference."[26]

Criminal Interstitiality. Under the principle of criminal interstitiality, civil commitment is justified as a tool to address antisocial violence to the extent that it addresses violence that is unreachable by the criminal law. In this context, this means violence that is excused because the actor has a serious mental illness. This violence is "interstitial" to the criminal system—it falls into an area that the state cannot reach through the criminal law. The state's interest in self-defense is enough to justify the state in using an alternate system to address the violence. Thus, one constitutional standard for inability to control would be the standard for criminal nonresponsibility. Some jurisdictions incorporate a "volitional" standard for criminal excuse; others do not, and rely instead on a "cognitive" standard. In any event, under this theory, only those individuals whose inability to control would excuse them from liability for their sexual crimes would meet the constitutional standards for commitment.

This standard also is congruent with the "narrowing" criterion, in that it retains the primary position in the social control effort for the criminal law. It is not irrelevant to note that most of the men who have been committed as sex offenders have been held liable for their criminal behavior and would thus not qualify under such a standard for commitment.[27]

Jurisprudence of Difference. The second possible way to connect mental disorder with a constitutional justification for civil commitment rests on the assignment of a degraded civil status to a class of persons who are "different" in some critical way from the norm. We are accustomed, for example, to according "incompetent" people a different (and diminished) set of civil rights—they are often deprived, for example, of the right to make their own decisions about important life events. To the extent that inability to control is a marker for a similar sort of status—one that results in a diminished civic personhood—then the diminished set of rights accorded to the targets of civil commitment might be justifiable. For example, free will is thought to be an essential characteristic of human beings. To the extent that inability to control and free will are viewed as incompatible ascriptions, then inability to control would mark diminished personhood.

Baumeister et al. place self-regulation at the center of the notion of "self."[28] "No cognitive, motivational, emotional, or behavioral theory about the self can pretend to be complete without addressing the issue of self-regulation."[29] Similarly, Eshete characterizes "freedom" in the philosophical sense as "self-mastery."[30] Thus, a serious dysfunction of the capacity for self-control marks a serious defect in the moral self and thus may justify diminished status for the individual.

To think about it another way, if a person lacks the capacity to control his antisocial behavior, one can say that his essence is "dangerousness"—it flows inexorably from who he is, rather than being the result of personal choice or environmental conditions. But an individual whose essence is "dangerousness" is different in kind from the norm, which we assume entails choice and, hence, responsibility for evil actions.[31]

In sum, inability to control will meet one of the justificatory criteria if it either excuses the actor from criminal liability or places him or her in a status of degraded personhood. Clearly, both of these are normative judgments, which need to be made based on standards articulated by courts of law.

DISTINGUISHING AND DISCARDING CONCEPTS

Before proposing a typology of inability to control, I want to distinguish and discard several ideas about it that are either inapplicable or unhelpful in our context. We can then move on with greater clarity to a usable definition of the concept.

Involuntary and Reflexive Responses

First, there are several types of behavior that are beyond the control of the individual in trivial ways that ought not to interest us in this discussion. Thus, the kind of behavior that is the subject of sex offender commitments is not accidental or "automatic" (like sleepwalking). Nor does it, like a blink, involve a reflexive response to an external stimulus.[32] Nor is it "involuntary" like laughter, anger, shame, and fear.[33] Rather, it is clearly under the conscious control of the individual and, more to the point, is intentional action by the person.[34] If inability to control is to have any applicability to our legal context, then it must refer to actions that are not simply reflexive or automatic. As I shall develop below, I believe that the most fruitful way of talking about inability to control is as an impairment of an individual's ability to regulate his or her own behavior.

Volitional Dysfunction

Next, I want to discard three concepts which, though commonly used especially in legal contexts, are unclear and confusing. Since we can discuss inability to control without using these concepts, we ought to avoid their use. First, I propose that we discard the notion of volition and not focus on volitional dysfunction.[35] "Volition" is a confused concept with no agreed-on meaning. To some it refers to the psychological function that "executes" the person's intention or choice. Morse shows clearly that in most cases where we want to say that a person lacks control, that function is unimpaired.[36] That is, the person does indeed execute what he or she intends or chooses. Alternatively, "volition" may be a synonym for "intention," in which case it again has little or no applicability to our interest, since intent arises in all sexual offending.[37] Finally, some authorities define volition as "the capacity to exercise choice or will"[38] or the "act or the power of making a choice, or decision; will."[39] This, in turn, might refer to two separate ideas: the person's ability to choose otherwise, which is a complicated concept that adds no clarity to the discussion, or the notion of strength of will, or willpower. This is a more useful concept, understandable to all from everyday usage. Instead of using the opaque term "volition," we ought to speak directly about the sort of strength we call "willpower."

Caused Behavior

Second, we should not use the concept of "caused behavior" as a defining characteristic of inability to control, as this concept is often confused for the latter. It is assumed that if certain behavior is "caused" by a given psychological condition, then the person had no "control" over the behavior. But this approach proves too much. All human behavior is "caused," but we nonetheless insist that humans have control over their behavior, at least in general. It may be that we will want to say that certain kinds of "caused" behavior evidence inability to control, such as a behavior "caused" by a particular kind of mental disorder. But then the real work will be done by our characterization of the mental disorder, not by the attribution of "causation." And just as being "caused" does not make behavior beyond an individual's control, so too being "caused" by a mental disorder does not ipso facto justify that ascription:[40]

> [T]he fact that an individual's presentation meets the criteria for a DSM-IV diagnosis does not carry any necessary implication regarding the individual's degree of control over the behaviors that may be associated with the disorder. Even when diminished control over one's behavior is a feature of the disorder, having the diagnosis in itself does not demonstrate that a particular individual is (or was) unable to control his or her behavior at a particular time.[41]

The American Psychiatric Association's Task Force on the Use of Psychiatric Diagnoses in the Legal Process emphasizes the disconnect between mental disorder and the inability to control behavior:

> It is rare for mental disorders to be associated with incapacities which obviate the possibility that the patient can make more than one behavioral response to a situation. Because some element of choice (however difficult that choice may be) is usually present, it is rarely correct to talk about behavioral symptoms as "involuntary" or "beyond the patient's control."[42]

Inability to Do Otherwise

Finally, we need to address, at least briefly, the concept of "could not have done otherwise." It is often said that a person does not have the ability to control his behavior unless he could have behaved otherwise than he did.[43] The concept of an ability to act otherwise is just as opaque as the inability-to-control concept; it has essentially the same meaning and adds no clarity to any discussion. It should not be used in any discussion of inability to control that attempts to gain clarity. Nonetheless, the phrase can offer an insight into the kind of evidence that supports the inability-to-control judgment. When we make this judgment, we make it within a set of givens, what we might call auxiliary assumptions.

To understand this, recall the famous story of Martin Luther: "Here I stand," Luther said. "I can do no other."[44] Of course, this is a not a situation in which anyone would conclude that Luther could not control his behavior. Quite the opposite—he was in perfect control of his behavior. Nonetheless, we are prepared to credit Luther's own account that he could not have chosen otherwise.

This seeming paradox holding that Luther could control his behavior even though he could not have chosen other than he did, reflects shifting auxiliary assumptions. The premise that Luther was in control of his behavior—was exercising free will—reflects our judgment that people are responsible for (have the ability to shape) their personalities and character. The statement that he could not do otherwise, on the other hand, reflects a narrowing of context. We are saying that *given his personality, values, and beliefs*, Luther could not have chosen otherwise. Thus, the judgment of whether a person "could have chosen otherwise" will depend on what the auxiliary assumptions are—how large the context for the decision is. I will discuss this further below.

A PROPOSED TYPOLOGY OF INABILITY TO CONTROL

Self-Regulation

Before proposing a typology of inability to control, it is useful to set out two underlying concepts about self-regulation:

1. *Parallel and complex processes.* Human beings are complex organisms who have parallel psychological processes occurring. Although we tend to talk as if a "person" has only one "self," it is clear, both from our subjective experience and from the perspective of psychologists, that we harbor parallel and often competing processes.[45] As Pinker puts it: "Self-control is unmistakably a tactical battle between parts of the mind."[46] Thus, one part of a person may "want" to engage in sexually inappropriate behavior, while another part "wants" to avoid it.

2. *Hierarchy of processes.* We use different language depending on which of our parallel wants prevails. If the offender's avoidance impulse wins, then we say that he was able to "control" or regulate his sexual impulse. If his sexual impulse wins, we characterize this as a failure of self-control; we rarely say that the person successfully controlled his impulse to act responsibly. This suggests that we rank the parallel and competing processes in a hierarchy. Inherent in the discourse of inability to control is the notion that certain desires are "higher" than others.[47]

Thus, when we talk about regulating or controlling ourselves, what we mean is that the "higher" processes prevail over the lower.[48] This explains how we can say that a person is "unable" to regulate her own behavior despite the fact that it is her brain, and in fact her mind, that is sending electrical signals (brain) and intentions (mind) to her limbs.

In the limited space of this chapter, I do not intend to explore what the nature of this hierarchy of values is.[49] It may be that this notion has deep philosophical roots,[50] or that the valuing of certain kinds of processes over others is an arbitrary social construct, or that it is adaptive in some evolutionary sense and hence a part of the "normal" or "natural" psychology of humans.[51] All I am asserting here is that the question of ability to control oneself appears to have to do with the individual's ability to govern or regulate his or her behavior according to "higher" processes.

Classifying Inability to Control

Having set this background, I now propose a typology of inability to control. I suggest that we mean one of three things when we say that a person lacks the ability to control his or her behavior. The first two types arise out of the existence of parallel and competing processes within a person, which is why I refer to them as "bifurcated self" theories of inability to control.

1. *Type 1 incapacity—The "strong urges" paradigm.* This paradigm focuses on the strength of the uncontrolled impulse and posits that it is so strong that it cannot be resisted. This type is akin to the "irresistible impulse" concept that has influenced criminal excuse theory in the past[52] and that characterizes outdated psychoanalytic models of the sex offender.[53]

2. *Type 2 incapacity—The impaired self-regulation model.* This paradigm focuses on a person's skills and strength of self-regulation. It posits that the self-regulatory capacity is inadequate to control the impulse.

3. *Type 3—The character model.* This model is a unified self theory that we can describe as character- or personality-based. On this theory, the person's behavior is so central to his or her character or personality that we are prepared to say that he or she could not have acted differently.

Types 1 and 2 are in a sense two different perspectives on the same phenomenon. The meanings they convey, however, differ in three important ways. First, there is a suggestion that the portion of the process that each focuses on is deficient or abnormal or disordered. Thus, the irresistible impulse model posits that even a person of normal ability could not resist the abnormally strong impulse, while the impaired self-regulation model does not necessarily suggest that the impulse is abnormally strong. Second, the type 1 model, but not the type 2, is generally discussed as if it refers to an "objective" standard—the point of reference is the "normal" capacity to resist, not the particular individual's. Third, the type 1 model carries with it a stronger cachet of excuse—in part because of the "objective" connotation, but also because we tend to think of impulses as arising involuntarily, whereas we tend to hold people responsible for the level of proficiency at self-regulation that they have developed in their lifetimes.[54] Thus, whether a person's failure to control gets characterized as a strong impulse or a weak control mechanism depends, I suggest, a great deal on whether we are prepared to excuse his or her behavior.

Type 3, which I call character- or personality-based inability to control, posits that because a person's behavior is so based on his nature or personality, he cannot act differently than he does. But as the Martin Luther example above shows, this is a very problematic formulation because it applies to many of the actions of normal people.

A modified approach to this theory would apply the ascription of inability to control only where an individual's personality or constitution is somehow abnormal. Some older theories of criminality, for example, viewed criminal behavior as inevitably arising from certain types of (abnormal) personalities.[55]

But "mental disorder" as a general category is not sufficient to ascribe inability to control to an individual. Psychiatrically, "mental disorder" is not a concept that entails a loss of ability to control.[56] Nor does "mental disorder" automatically provide an excuse for criminal behavior.[57] Further, even though research now suggests that aggressive behavior has a significant degree of heritability, "other factors such as choice and volition are more important in explaining behavior" and "we must allow for the salient ability of humans, as compared to other species, to shape and choose their environments—in effect to use free will—in order to cope with and compensate for the pre-existing vulnerabilities."[58]

"Mental disorders" are not, however, irrelevant to the determination of inability to control. A mental disorder may involve impairments of the various capacities that help a person exercise self-regulation. It is at that *functional* level that our attention should be directed.

APPLICATION TO SEX OFFENDERS

How these three typologies, or models, above might be applied to sex offenders must be explored in more detail. There is an important caveat in doing this, however: sexual offending, and sex offenders, are heterogeneous.[59] Further, although some researchers propose typologies for sexual offenders,[60] there is no claim that all individuals who exhibit some characteristics of a category share all of them. Thus, ascriptions of inability to control for an individual offender ought to be made based not on diagnostic or descriptive category membership, but on individualized observation of that individual.

The Strong Impulses Model

In what is perhaps the most stereotypical view of sexual violence, the offender is seen as driven by strong and ultimately uncontrollable sexual urges.[61] Thorne and Haupt, writing in 1966, described rapists as characterized by the "standard psychoanalytic interpretation of high sex drive repressed from consciousness by strong Super Ego and resulting in episodes of failure of impulse control associated with intense conflict and guilt."[62] The Washington Supreme Court described the sex offenders who are subject to civil commitment using similar language:

> [They experience] recurrent, repetitive, and compulsive urges and fantasies to commit rapes. These offenders attempt to control their urges, but the urges eventually become so strong that they act upon them, commit rapes, and then feel guilty afterwards with a temporary reduction of urges, only to have the cycle repeat again. This [is a] cycle of ongoing urges, attempts to control them, breakdown of those attempts, and recurrence of the sex crime.[63]

In a similar vein, Brooks characterizes the proper subjects of civil commitment as limited to sex offenders exhibiting "uncontrollable pathological rape." "[A] rapist selected for civil commitment," he argues, "should have a recurrent, compulsive urge and a pathological need to repetitively carry out psychologically driven rape."[64]

Impulsivity; Antisocial Personality. The strong impulses paradigm describes at best only one type of sexual offending; other types of offending are inconsistent with this model. Researchers attempting to produce typologies of sex offenders have helped to put the notion of strong sexual urges in perspective. Knight identifies four primary motivations for sexual offending: opportunity, pervasive anger, sexual gratification, and vindictiveness.[65] These motivations "appear to be related to enduring behavioral patterns that distinguish particular groups of offenders."[66] Only one relates to sexual urges, although two others relate to other sorts of impulses (anger and vindictiveness). "Opportunity" compels "sexual assaults [that] appear to be impulsive predatory acts that are controlled more by situational and contextual factors . . . than by sexual fantasy or explicit anger at women."[67]

Similarly, Prentky differentiates between offending characterized by "lifestyle impulsivity" and offending involving "frequent uncontrollable sexual urges, preoccupation with gratification of sexual needs, multiple paraphilias, a high sexual drive, obsessional thinking about sex, and detailed offense planning."[68] He points out that the former, lifestyle impulsivity, is highly correlated with antisocial behavior and recidivism, and that the latter is "less clearly associated with reoffense risk."[69]

Berlin draws the same distinction between child molesters who act out of "aberrant sexual drive" and those who act "because of a generally antisocial attitude or because of malicious disregard for the well-being of others."[70]

The typology of sex offenders Hudson et al. developed includes types that are inconsistent with the strong urges paradigm[71] and makes distinctions between "appetitively driven" offense pathways and "impaired-regulation" models of offending.[72] The most frequent type they describe does not fit into the strong urges paradigm because it entails a positive attitude toward offending, involves explicit decisions to offend, arises out of a basically happy affective state and, after the offense, concludes with a commitment (to self) to continue the offending behavior. This description does not fit with the typical "strong urges" model because there is no growing internal pressure to act, no attempts to control, and no regret or feeling bad afterwards. Rather than representing an impaired ability to control behavior, this pathway, in Hudson et al.'s description, represents an example of "expert" or skilled performance.[73]

In contrast, the second most common pathway in Hudson et al.'s study is more consistent with the strong urges paradigm. It arises out of negative affect (feeling bad), covert planning (rather than explicit planning), negative evaluation of the offending behavior, and resolve not to offend in the future.

Paraphilia in the DSM-IV definition is characterized by "recurrent, intense sexual urges, fantasies, or behaviors . . . [that] cause clinically significant distress or impairment in social, occupational, or other important areas of functioning."[74] This definition accommodates intense "urges" but could be satisfied by "intense behaviors" as well, and says nothing about failed attempts to control the urges.[75] Closer to the mark of the stereotypical model is "impulse control disorder" whose essential feature "is the failure to resist an impulse, drive, or temptation to perform an act that is harmful to the person or to others."[76] The DSM-IV requires that "[t]he individual feels an increasing sense of tension or arousal before committing the act and then experiences pleasure, gratification, or relief associated with the activity."[77] Schneider adds: "Following the sexual acting out, there may or may not be regret, self-reproach, or guilt."[78] Nothing in the DSM definition of Impulse Control Disorder requires a finding of "inability," rather than simply "failure," to control.

Addictive Disorders. Even more central to the stereotypical strong impulses model is the notion of "sexual addiction." Addictive disorders are generally held to be characterized by three central features, described by Schneider as loss of control, continuation despite adverse consequences, and preoccupation or obsession."[79] Sexual offending is sometimes compared to or characterized as an addictive process.[80] In fact, the classic definition of addiction sounds very much like the strong urges paradigm of sexual offending and commonly is thought to involve a loss of control over behavior.[81] It is also thought to involve intense urges that the addict is "unable" to control or resist. Heyman points out that addiction is described in diagnostic manuals as "out of control" or "compulsive."[82] In the context of drug use, he writes that these phrases mean

> that drug use persists despite a wide array of ensuing legal, medical, and social problems; and that after periods of abstinence, however long, addicts relapse. In other words, according to authoritative clinical opinion, addiction is not simply frequent drug use, it is loss of control over drug use.[83]

Ivey and Simpson assessed the "subjective meaning of child abuse from the perpetrators' perspective."[84] They say that pedophiles are "obsessed by sexual fantasies about children and feel compelled to engage in opportunity-seeking and risk-taking behavior in order to fulfill their compulsive desire to have sexual contact with children."[85] They describe pedophilic behavior as having an "addictive quality" characterized by unsuccessful "attempts to curb" the pedophilic behavior.[86] Carnes asserts that "a prototypical case of the incestuous father" involves "sexual addiction."[87] He asserts, though without citation of research support, that "many abusers are sex addicts."[88] He describes the "sexual addict" as "no longer able to manage or control" his "sick relationship to sexual behavior."[89] "The individual is drawn into an addictive cycle of sexual preoccupation, ritualization, compulsiveness, and despair that is self-perpetuating and eventually takes over the person's life."[90]

The Problem of Offender Acquiescence to Impulses

How shall we evaluate a claim that a particular person's sexual urges are so strong that he or she "cannot control" them? Of course, this inquiry must start with an examination of the subjective or phenomenological experiences of the offender. Relevant evidence is how strongly the urge or compulsion is felt and how hard the offender tried to resist.

But for two main reasons, these subjective reports can only be the beginning. First, there are credibility issues.[91] Offenders may be expected to shape their reports of these subjective data to serve their own interests. But here is a paradoxical twist. The normal "bias" in self-reporting is to minimize responsibility by disclaiming the ability to control. In their study of convicted rapists, for example, Scully and Marolla found that 83 percent of their subjects viewed themselves as "nonrapists." More than half of those, while admitting their involvement, "explained themselves and their acts by appealing to forces beyond their control, forces which reduced their capacity to act rationally and thus compelled them to rape."[92]

Second, we must make a judgment about whether the urge should be characterized *as a constitutional matter* as one that an individual "could not" have resisted. When it comes to sexual offending, commentators are uniformly dubious about characterizing sexual impulses as "irresistible." They point out that other people resist similar impulses or that the particular individual resists at some times.[93] This sort of analysis emphasizes the "objective" view of uncontrollability.[94] Further, commentators point out that the behavior in question is, after all, under the control of the individual.

As Baumeister et al. put it with respect to the unsuccessful dieter: "Someone may claim that she cannot control her eating, but do her jaws really move up and down to chew the food against her will?"[95]

But this point is a bit unfair. No one claims that acting according to a very strong impulse is somehow automatic or not under the intentional control of the individual. Much more to the point is the third response, put forth by Baumeister et al., that acquiescence is a central feature of failure to resist strong impulses:

> Although it is very difficult to obtain decisive empirical data regarding the issue of acquiescence, we suspect that acquiescence is the norm, not the exception. It is rare that human behavior is the result of inner forces that the person is entirely helpless to stop or control.[96]

> Popular concepts of self-regulation failure depict people becoming overwhelmed by irresistible impulses that they are powerless to control. . . . A more accurate view may be that people do feel that their strength is depleted and their capacity overwhelmed, and so they decide to give up trying to control themselves. Then they go on and take an active role in indulging their impulses.[97]

Of course, the mere fact that there is acquiescence does not mean that the inability-to-control ascription is inapposite. Rather, the presence of acquiesce simply highlights what I have argued earlier, that the standard for a judgment of inability to control contains a heavily normative, or moral, judgment. Baumeister et al. remind us that resisting strong urges and impulses takes strength; one must "try" and exert effort. A person might be

> merely tired, rather than fully exhausted, and in such circumstances, the person may choose to allow self-regulation to fail, because the tiredness makes the exertion of self-control that much more unappealing. The person does not wish to put forth the effort that would be required for successful self-regulation.[98]

The question presented here, then, is: How much effort do we expect a person to exert before we say that his violent and abusive acts were beyond his control? Morse makes a similar though not identical argument, asking how much pain we expect a person to endure before we judge his "giving in" as beyond his control.[99] The answer, clearly, is that we expect him to exert maximum effort to avoid sexual violence. It seems clear that *any acquiescence* by an individual ought to negate the inability-to-control ascription when the impulse in question leads to sexual violence. As Baumeister et al. conclude, there is "abundant evidence that self-regulatory failure is something that people actively acquiesce in, and that therefore should not excuse violent, addictive, delinquent, or other socially undesirable actions."[100]

Writing in the context of drug addiction, Heyman makes an argument that is at its core similar: addiction is a preference rather than a disease. He refers to the "long-standing debate whether addiction is best classified as an involuntary state, for example, a disease, or a voluntary state, that is, a preference."[101] Advocates of a disease model of addiction characterize it as involuntary: "The loss of control signifies a victim state that reflects an alteration of brain function by alcohol or drugs that is not under the conscious volitional control of the individual."[102]

Heyman disputes the disease theory, concluding that "the behaviors that comprise addiction are voluntary even though their net consequences are aversive."[103] He argues that addictive behaviors result from "bookkeeping schemes"—i.e., choice mechanisms—that operate at a more local rather than overall level.[104] As the contingencies and consequences change, so too does the relative effectiveness of local versus overall "value functions."[105] He concludes: "[T]he idea that addiction is a choice, albeit a less than optimal one, implies that addicts should be helped to make better decisions and not excused as helpless victims of a disease."[106] Addiction is best understood not as "involuntary," disease-like behavior, but rather the consequence of an individual's preferences or choices, made according to a value calculus that is local rather than "overall."

Heyman's view of addictive behavior is consistent with that of a number of sexual violence researchers. For example, Herman puts forth an addiction model of sexual violence, stating "one can not assume that [a sex offender] has any reliable internal motivation for change. The offender may have lost effective control of his behavior . . ."[107] But she states that offenders have not lost "moral and legal responsibility" for their behavior, and emphasizes that "both compulsive and opportunistic offenders are keenly sensitive to external controls" such as "vigorous enforcement of existing criminal laws."[108]

Marshall et al.'s view is in accord:

> It is our view that sexual offenders are not suffering from any disease and that their behavior is not out of their control . . . . In fact, it is clear from an examination of the behavior of these men that their offending is very well controlled.[109]

Pithers, as well, agrees:

> Offenders are informed that urges do not control behavior. Rather, giving in to an urge is an active decision, an intentional choice for which he is responsible.[110]

Should courts make the moral or normative judgment that sexual abuse that fits the "strong urges" paradigm is properly described as "beyond the control" of the individual? Baumeister et al. warn against this conclusion, arguing that it is imperative that people be

> exhorted to regard their behavior as controllable whenever possible. If the view prevails that self-regulation failure is something that happens to an individual and excuses his or her subsequent behavior, then gradually the culture itself will become a context that supports—and in a powerful sense encourages—such failures.[111]

Lamb, writing specifically in the context of sexual and domestic abuse, argues that "men's lack of control over their sex drive" is "the dominant discourse of sexuality widely believed and accepted in our culture."[112] "This vision of male sexuality makes it appear as if choice is overwhelmed by urge."[113] She warns against this view: "We as onlookers collude in this transformation to passivity when we begin to see the perpetrator as object rather than subject of his acts."[114] As Scully and Marolla argue, the "irresistible impulse" model of rape "has contributed to the vocabulary of motive that rapists use to excuse and justify their behavior."[115]

The Impaired Self-Regulation Model

A second model for inability to control focuses on the process by which human beings regulate their own behavior. Incapacity describes deficits in the self-regulatory process rather than the "irresistible" strength of urges or impulses. The study of self-regulation is well developed and provides a vocabulary for describing and assessing deficits in self-control. The most common approach to sex offender treatment—relapse-prevention, cognitive-behavioral approach—makes use of self-regulation concepts, and a number of researchers are applying a more extensive self-regulation model to sexual offending in general.[116]

"Self-Regulation" Defined. "Self-regulation," a term akin to "self-control," is "any effort by a human being to alter its own responses."[117] "Self-regulation prevents [the] normal or natural response from occurring, and substitutes another response (or lack of response) in its place."[118] Humans have "multiple processes or levels of action"[119] that operate simultaneously or in parallel.[120] Self-regulation results in one process "overriding" another, and thus assumes that these parallel processes are in competition with each other.[121]

The concept of self-regulation assumes a hierarchy among the multiple processes. Self-regulation occurs when a "higher" process overrides a "lower" one. "When the reverse happens, it is *failure* of self-regulation."[122] "Higher" processes involve "longer time spans, more extensive networks of meaningful associations and interpretations, and more distal or abstract goals."[123] Thus, the concept of self-regulation entails a normative component, a differential valuing of the multiple processes of the human being. There is no assumption that the "lower" processes are not intentional or controlled by the individual. Rather, they are the "normal or natural" responses of the person and thus will be exhibited in the absence of the "effort" at self-control.[124]

Key Ingredients. The self-regulatory model posits three important ingredients for self-regulation: First, we must have standards, "abstract concepts of how things should be."[125] "When standards are unclear, ambiguous, lacking, or conflicting, self-regulation will be less effective."[126] Second, we need a self-monitoring mechanism.[127] People must "pay attention to what they are doing."[128] Third, people must have some way of "operating on themselves in order to bring about the desired changes or responses."[129] Competition among potential responses is an important feature of the model, and people may experience this competition as an "inner conflict."[130]

The areas in which self-regulation can fail mirror the key ingredients above. "[T]here can be a problem with knowing the standards, a problem with monitoring the self, or a problem with making the self conform to them."[131] "Empirical evidence supports the view that self-regulation is severely hampered by conflicting standards."[132] Ineffective self-monitoring is a prominent cause of failure[133] which can produce behavior that reflects "impulses and feelings that would normally be held in check."[134] Alcohol or drug use reduces self-awareness, the "essence of the monitoring function," and thus results in self-regulation failure.[135]

Requisite Physical and Mental Strength. The impaired self-regulation model involves a concept of strength akin to the "commonsense concept of willpower."[136] It is not simply that the "stronger" of two competing processes wins. Rather, this sort of strength "involves both mental and physical exertion."[137] That is, it takes energy to monitor oneself and make oneself conform to one's own standards.

The required energy may be limited; a person may lack the requisite strength in several different ways. He or she may be "chronically weak," with an underdeveloped self-regulatory capacity. Such a person should be able to strengthen this capacity over time.[138] The energy may also become depleted over time. A person may become exhausted because he has had to confront stressful or demanding circumstances.[139] Or, as discussed above, the impulse that should be controlled may be so strong that even a person of normal strength could not resist it.[140]

Self-Regulation in the Sexual Offending Context

Ward and Hudson use a theory of self-regulation in the context of sexual offending,[141] identifying three styles of "dysfunctional self-regulation." First, an individual may simply fail to regulate his behavior, referred to as underregulation.[142] Second, he or she may *mis*regulate—choose strategies of regulation that "backfire and ultimately result in a loss of control."[143] The third style, in contrast, involves *effective* self-regulation. It is the individual's choice of goals and "associated values and beliefs" that lead to sexual aggression, rather than a failure of self-regulation.[144]

The authors trace the sequence of events that can lead to sexual offending. First, some event in the person's life triggers "the emergence of a desire for offensive sex or maladaptive activities and emotions associated with these desires."[145] The "impulse" that is triggered need not be a "sexual" urge. It could be "happiness, curiosity, sexual arousal, anxiety, and anger."[146]

From this point, Ward and Hudson identify four main patterns of sexual offending:

1. *The avoidant-passive pathway.* The "avoidant-passive pathway is characterized by both the desire to avoid sexual offending and the failure to actively attempt to prevent this from happening."[147] This involves underregulation. These individuals attempt to manage their desire for abusive sex through "denial or simple and ineffective attempts to distract themselves."[148]

2. *The avoidance-active pathway.* The "avoidance-active" pathway involves an active attempt to avoid sexual offending.[149] However, the techniques the individual uses are ineffective and paradoxically "increase the probability of an offense occurring."[150] These individuals "possess the ability to plan, monitor, and evaluate their behavior, but lack knowledge concerning the likely effectiveness of the coping response selected."[151]

3. *The approach-automatic pathway.* The "approach-automatic" pathway involves behavior that "is relatively impulsive and only planned in a rudimentary way; it is basically a mirror image of the avoidant-passive relapse process in that the goals and the associated strategies are unlikely to be under attentional control and are activated by situational features."[152]

4. *The approach-explicit pathway.* The fourth pathway is called "approach-explicit" and involves "conscious, explicit planning and well-crafted strategies that result in a sexual offense."[153] This pathway involves competent self-regulation but "inappropriate, harmful" goals, standards and attitudes.[154]

In both of the "approach" pathways, part of what leads to harmful self-regulation is inappropriate standards for behavior. In their study of rapists, Scully and Marolla found that a significant portion of the men sought to *justify* their sexual violence. The researchers concluded that "convicted rapists have learned the attitudes and actions consistent with sexual aggression against women."[155] These men raped "because their value system provided no compelling reason not to do so. When sex is viewed as a male entitlement, rape is no longer seen as criminal."[156]

Ward and Hudson discuss the mechanisms by which self-regulation fails. Though their level of analysis is more detailed than a discussion here allows, the following quotation is instructive for the lessons it teaches. The authors give this description of the avoidant-passsive pathway to reoffending:

> Offenders who are following the avoidant-passive pathway will be struggling with conflicting goals at this point. The contact, or anticipated contact, with a victim will activate goals linked to offending behavior, and they are likely to be experiencing increasing sexual arousal. The offender may attempt to disguise his real intentions, probably through a narrowing of attention or a movement down to a lower level of behavioral control, probably the program level. The result of control at this more concrete level is that behavior is more automatic and "mindless" and likely to reflect well-rehearsed or habitual sequences of action. The functional autonomy of control at this level means that self-evaluative processes are effectively disengaged.[157]

The points to be made here are that it is possible to take apart or deconstruct the processes of sexual offending and identify their component parts and, having done so, to identify the aspects of behavior that impede self-regulation. Here, for example, it is the well-rehearsed and "automatic" or "mindless"[158] nature of the behavior, coupled with the disengagement of the self-evaluative functioning that contributes to the failure of self-regulation. Finally, this kind of deconstruction helps expose the legal question, which is whether this form of self-regulation failure meets the constitutional requirements for civil commitment.

Ward and Hudson also discuss the abstinence violation effect (AVE). This is the reaction that some people experience when they are trying to refrain from an undesirable behavior (abusive sex, drinking, etc.) but commit a "lapse," or step, that places them closer to relapse. The authors point out that if the offender identifies an internal cause for the lapse, such as lack of willpower or weak personality, "there is little reason to expend energy and he is, therefore, more likely to relapse and offend sexually."[159] Baumeister et al. make the same point:

> [I]f the person attributes the lapse to internal, stable, and global factors that are perceived to be uncontrollable (e.g., there is a lack of willpower or the person has a disease), then the probability of relapse is heightened. The person perceives that there is little reason to continue trying to control what is uncon-

trollable, or the person concludes that he does not have the necessary skills to control behavior.[160]

One of the consequences of the AVE, say Ward and Hudson, is that individuals "give up attempting to control their behavior."

A major cause of some sex offenders' impaired self-control is their impulsivity. Knight and Prentky identify one of the four main motivations for rape as "opportunistic," in which "the sexual assault appears to be an impulsive, typically unplanned, predatory act, controlled more by contextual and immediately antecedent factors than by any obvious protracted or stylized sexual fantasy."[161] Knight and Prentky's measure for stable, trait-like impulsivity—lifestyle impulsivity—is highly predictive of sexual reoffense.[162] They point out that this construct is related to the DSM-IV Antisocial Personality Disorder and Hare's Checklist of Psychopathy.[163] It is defined as a "pervasive and enduring pattern of poor impulse control and irresponsible behavior."[164]

Meeting the Constitutional Criteria

Do deficits in self-regulation meet the constitutional standard for inability to control? As described early in this chapter, to meet constitutional standards, an individual's inability to control must satisfy two criteria: it must be of the sort that is applicable only to a *narrow* segment of people whose dangerousness might qualify them for civil commitment, and it must *justify* the use of civil commitment, "*adequately distinguish[ing]* [the individual] from other dangerous persons who are perhaps more properly dealt with exclusively through criminal proceedings."[165]

As a general matter, the kinds of self-regulatory failure that characterize sexual offending do not narrow the group eligible for civil commitment, and do not provide a means of distinguishing sex offenders from the great mass of other criminals. In fact, the impulsivity that marks many sex offenders is the hallmark of general criminality. Further, though the consequences of self-regulatory failure among sex offenders are horrendous, the mechanisms involved may not differ *in kind* from the garden-variety failures that impair people's ability to obey the law, quit smoking, lose weight, stop gambling, or achieve any difficult, long-horizon goal. As Baumeister et al. observe, "Self-regulation failure has been implicated as possibly the single greatest cause of destructive, illegal, and antisocial behavior."[166]

It is worth emphasizing that self-regulatory failure *identifies* sex offenders with other criminals. Knight and Prentky report that the proportion of sex offenders who exhibit impulsivity is high—40 percent in their study—which was "consistent with previous research."[167] They show that their measure for stable, trait-like impulsivity—lifestyle impulsivity—is highly predictive of future sexual reoffending.[168] But the very same trait, life-style impulsivity, is a "relatively robust predictor of reoffense risk across domains of criminal behavior."[169]

More generally, one of the most widely accepted general theories of criminality, that of Gottfredson and Hirschi, argues that criminality arises from an underlying deficit in self-control.[170] Poor self-control is widely thought to be a "stable and robust predictor of reoffending among the general criminal population."[171] As Baumeister et al. point out, "[T]he most important generalization about crime and criminality is that they arise from lack of self-control. Most crimes are impulsive actions, and most criminals exhibit broad and multifaceted patterns of lacking self-control."[172] Substantial research shows that the majority of incarcerated criminals are diagnosable either with antisocial personality disorder[173] or attention deficit hyperactivity disorder,[174] both of which are centrally characterized by impulsivity.

In short, the kind of self-regulatory failure that characterizes many sex offenders does not distinguish them from the general criminal population, but rather is a unifying feature of criminality. We do not excuse people whose antisocial behavior arises from a lack of self-control; this is precisely what we condemn in the criminal justice system. This sort of self-control problem does not mark sex offenders as different in kind from other humans, but as suffering from the kinds of weaknesses that are inherent in being human.

The Character/Personality Model

It remains to consider what I have called the type 3 model of inability to control, the character- or personality-based model. Let us consider a sex offender who falls into Ward and Hudson's approach-explicit category, an offender who desires to continue abusive sex and actively plans for it. How should we classify this person with respect to control capacity?

There are two sound reasons for refusing to ascribe an inability to control. First, this person exhibits self-regulation skills rather than a self-regulation deficit. He has characteristics that we associate with deliberate, under-control behavior, such as careful planning[175] and explicit decision making. Second, because he *desires* to continue offending, there is an absence of evidence from which one could conclude that he lacks the capacity to control his behavior. Since he has *not yet tried hard to stop*, we have no basis for judging whether he could refrain from offending if he tried "hard enough." The only potential basis for ascribing an inability to control to this person is that his offending is so much a part of his personality, so ingrained in his values and personal goals, that he "could not act otherwise."

This is, of course, a rhetorical move that could be made with anyone at any time. We are all, after all, who we are. If we say that the pedophile lacks the ability to control his behavior because his behavior is determined by his personality, then we must say that we *all* lack that ability. This is a dangerous rhetorical move because it undercuts the general assumption of free will and moral responsibility, absolving the individual of responsibility for his or her own character.

Most thoughtful commentators reject this move. We hold people responsible even when (especially when) they act "in character" because we judge that their current character—and hence their current behavior—is a consequence of choices they have made. People who lack the internal strength to alter their behavior "could build up their strength over time by practicing self-control or learning to regulate themselves effectively."[176] Discussing "sexual predators" in his popular-press book *Obsession*, John Douglas reflects this common understanding of sex offender behavior. On the one hand, he writes, "The sexual predator commits his individual crimes in the way he does because it is what he must do to satisfy himself. It's who and what he is—the proverbial case of the leopard not being able to change his spots."[177] But two pages later, he says of the same people, they have "made choices, rather than being hapless victims of adverse environments."[178]

The point is that we make inability-to-control judgments in a particular context, using a particular set of auxiliary assumptions, or specifications of the "givens," when questioning whether someone could have chosen otherwise. The legal question this presents is: in what context is the inability-to-control judgment to be made? I suggest that in our society, we generally make inability-to-control judgments in a fairly wide context. We generally hold people responsible for their character and personality and for developing the strength of character to control their impulses.[179]

CONCLUSION

Inability to control is not a concept that is hopelessly beyond the reach of a rational judicial process. What is needed are three concrete steps to cut through the fog. First, we need to stop using opaque and confusing terms such as "volition" and "cause." Second, we need to focus attention on the basic psychological processes that comprise self-regulation. Third, we need to recognize that ascribing inability to control to a person means making normative and legal judgments. Having observed and described the mechanisms by which self-regulation fails to prevent sexual violence *in a particular individual*, courts must determine whether this form of dysfunction justifies the conclusion that the individual was *unable* to control his behavior.

To meet clear constitutional standards, courts must insure that their formulation of inability to control is a narrow one. A careful, concrete assessment of the self-regulatory failure that leads to sexual offending will show that much of it is identical to that which characterizes the general criminal population. A definition of inability to control that sweeps so broadly cannot pass constitutional muster.

In setting the threshold for attaching the authoritative legal label of "inability to control," courts will do well to keep in mind that this ascription may contribute to a "subculture of violence . . . [that] does support and reinforce the belief that violent impulses cannot be resisted or controlled."[180] It also likely contributes to the "dominant discourse of uncontrollable male sexuality."[181] As the inability-to-control metaphor gains currency, men who aim to refrain from sexual abuse may "re-evaluate their goals and decide that they lack the ability to refrain from further sexual abuse and therefore continue offending."[182]

A broad and careless use of the inability-to-control rubric undercuts the constitutional legitimacy of sex offender commitments and supports the outmoded and excuse-laden idea that male sexual impulses are beyond their control.

Footnotes

[1] Kan. Stat. Ann. § 59-29a01 (1994). *See* Kansas v. Hendricks, 521 U.S. 346 (1997).

[2] *See* Richard J. Bonnie, "The Moral Basis of the Insanity Defense," 69 *A.B.A.J.* 194, 196 (1983).

[3] *See* Laura Waddell Ekstrom, *Free Will: A Philosophical Study* 21 (2000).

[4] Hendricks, *supra* note 1, at 358.

[5] Id.

[6] 969 P.2d 584 (Cal. 1999).

[7] Hubbart, 969 P.2d at 597 (emphasis added).

[8] *See* Minnesota ex rel. Pearson v. Probate Court of Ramsey County, 205 Minn. 545, 555, 297 N.W. 297, 302 (1939).

[9] Minnesota ex rel. Pearson v. Probate Court of Ramsey County, 309 U.S. 270, 274 (1940).

[10] In re Blodgett, 510 N.W.2d 910, 915 (Minn. 1994), *cert. denied*, 513 U.S. 849 (1994).

[11] In re Linehan, 594 N.W.2d 867, 872 (Minn. 1999).

[12] In re Young, 857 P.2d 989, 1002 (Wash. 1993).

[13] In re Crane, No. 82,080, 2000 WL 966703, at *6 (Kan. July 14, 2000).

[14] The weight of academic scholarship confirms that the *Pearson* limits are constitutionally based. *See* "Developments in the Law: Civil Commitment," 87 *Harv. L. Rev.* 1190, 1233–1234 (1974) (stating "police power commitment standards would appear to be unconstitutionally overbroad unless mental illness is interpreted to mean a condition which induces substantially diminished criminal responsibility"); Robert F. Schopp, "Sexual Predators and the Structure of the Mental Health System: Expanding the Normative Focus of Therapeutic Jurisprudence," 1 *Psychol. Pub. Pol'y & L.* 161, 181 (1995) (noting commitment for "social control" is justified only for mental illnesses "undermining the capacity to direct . . . conduct within the constraints of . . . criminal justice system); Bruce J. Winick, "Ambiguities in the Legal Meaning and Significance of Mental Illness," 3 *Psychol. Pub. Pol'y & L.* 34, 538 (1995) (declaring "for the purpose of commitment to a psychiatric hospital, a condition must be capable of so impairing functioning that the individual is unable to engage in rational decision making or to control his or her behavior"); Allen E. Buchanan & Daniel W. Brock, *Deciding for Others: The Ethics of Surrogate Decision Making* 329 (1989) (stating "If the dangerous mentally ill are justifiably [involuntarily committed], it must be because they are not capable of responsibly controlling their behavior that is dangerous to others as required by criminal prohibitions. . . . [T]he requirement should be understood to be that persons' mental illness causes them to be both dangerous to others and not in control of nor thus responsible for their dangerous behavior as required under the criminal law.").

[15] *See* S. Rep. No. 1377, at 6 (1948) (restricting commitment to those who are dangerous "because of their lack of power to control their sexual impulses").

[16] *See* Eric S. Janus, "Sex Offender Commitments: Debunking the Official Narrative and Revealing the Rules-in-Use," 8 *Stan. L. & Pol'y Rev.* 71, 71–74 (1997).

[17] Kansas v. Hendricks, *supra* note 1, at 373 (1997).

[18] *See* Stephen J. Morse, "Culpability and Control," 142 *U. Pa. L. Rev.* 1587, 1588 (1994).

[19] Eric S. Janus, "Foreshadowing The Future of *Kansas v. Hendricks*: Lessons from Minnesota's Sex Offender Commitment Litigation," 92 *Nw. U. L. Rev.* 1279, 1288 (1998).

[20] In re Linehan, 557 N.W.2d 171, 181 (Minn. 1996).

[21] Hendricks, *supra* note 1, at 358.

[22] *See* Eric S. Janus & Nancy Walbeck, "Sex Offender Commitments in Minnesota: A Descriptive Study of Second Generation Commitments," 18 *Behav. Sci. & L.* 343, 348 (2000); Samuel Jan Brakel & James L. Cavanaugh, "Of Psychopaths and Pendulums: Legal and Psychiatric Treatment of Sex Offenders in the United States," 30 *N.M. L. Rev.* 69, 81 (2000).

[23] *See* Robert F. Schopp, "Sexual Predators and the Structure of the Mental Health System: Expanding the Normative Focus of Therapeutic Jurisprudence," 1 *Psychol. Pub. Pol'y & L.* 161, 169 (1995); Robert F. Schopp & Barbara J. Sturgis, "Sexual Predators and Legal Mental Illness for Civil Commitment," 13 *Behav. Sci. & L.* 437, 445 (1995).

[24] Hendricks, *supra* note 1, at 360 (emphasis added).

[25] Foucha v. Louisiana, 504 U.S. 71, 81 (1992).

[26] *See* Eric S. Janus, "Toward a Conceptual Framework for Assessing Police Power Commitment Legislation: A Critique of Schopp's and Winick's Explications of Legal Mental Illness," 76 *Neb. L. Rev.* 1, 35 (1997); Eric S. Janus, "Hendricks and the Moral Terrain of Police Power Civil Commitment," 4 *Psychol. Pub. Pol'y & L.* 297, 313 (1998).

[27] *See, e.g.,* Janus & Walbeck, *supra* note 22, at 350.

[28] Roy F. Baumeister et al., *Losing Control: How and Why People Fail at Self-Regulation* 6 (1994).

[29] Id.

[30] *See* Andreas Eshete, "Character, Virtue and Freedom," 57 *Philosophy* 495, 497 (1982).

[31] *See generally* Sharon Lamb, *The Trouble With Blame: Victims, Perpetrators & Responsibility* (1996).

[32] *See* Gene M. Heyman, "Resolving the Contradictions of Addiction," 19 *Behav. & Brain Sci.* 561, 561 (1996).

[33] *See* Steven Pinker, *How the Mind Works* 546 (1997); Robert M. Adams, "Involuntary Sins," XCIV *Phil. Rev.* 3, no. 1 at 3 (1985).

[34] *See* Morse, *supra* note 18, at 1588.

[35] *Cf.* In re Blodgett, *supra* note 10; In re Crane, *supra* note 13.

[36] Morse, *supra* note 18, at 1617.

[37] *See, e.g.,* George MacDonald Fraser, *Flashman at the Charge* (1990), in which narrator Colonel Harry Flashman writes of the run-up to the great Charge of the Light Brigade: "[S]uddenly, without the slightest volition on my part, there was the most crashing discharge of wind, like the report of a mortar . . . 'Can you not contain yourself, you disgusting fellow?' [says Cardigan]." To which Flashman replies: "My lord, I cannot help it—it is the feverish wind, you see." Fraser at 102.

[38] In re Crane, *supra* note 13.

[39] George S. Howard & Christine G. Conway, "Can There Be an Empirical Science of Volitional Action?", *Am. Psychologist*, Nov. 1986, at 1241, 1242.

[40] Further, the notion that given behavior is "caused" by a mental disorder is itself an extremely problematic conclusion to draw. *See, e.g.,* Virginia Adige Hiday, "Understanding the Connection Between Mental Illness and Violence," 20 *Int'l J.L. & Psychiatry* 399, 412 (1997).

[41] *See* American Psychiatric Association, *Diagnostic and Statistical Manual of Mental Disorders* xxiii (4th ed. 1994) [hereinafter DSM-IV].

[42] Seymour L. Halleck, M.D. et al., "The Use of Psychiatric Diagnoses in the Legal Process: Task Force Report of the American Psychiatric Association," 20 *Bull. Am. Acad. Psychiatry & L.* 481, 493 (1992).

[43] *See* Ekstrom, *supra* note 3, at 21.

[44] Daniel C. Dennett, *Elbow Room: The Varieties of Free Will Worth Wanting* 133 (1983).

[45] Baumeister et al., *supra* note 28, at 7.

[46] Pinker, *supra* note 33, at 419.

[47] Charles S. Carver & Michael F. Scheier, "Principles of Self-Regulation: Action and Emotion," in 2 *Handbook of Motivation and Cognition: Foundations of Social Behavior* 12 (Richard M. Sorrentino & E. Troy Higgins eds., 1996).

[48] Baumeister et al., *supra* note 28, at 8.

⁴⁹ *See generally* Morse, *supra* note 18.

⁵⁰ Eshete, *supra* note 30, at 498 (arguing that "The condition for the possibility of self-mastery is to be found in the ordering of desires.").

⁵¹ Baumeister et al., *supra* note 28, at 7.

⁵² *See* Judith A. Morse & Gregory K. Thoreson, "*United States v. Lyons*: Abolishing the Volitional Prong of the Insanity Defense," 60 *Notre Dame L. Rev.* 177 (1984).

⁵³ *See* Robert A. Prentky & Raymond A. Knight, "Classifying Sexual Offenders: The Development and Corroboration of Taxonomic Models," in *The Handbook of Sexual Assault: Issues, Theories, and Treatment of the Offender* 27, 27–28 (W.L. Marshall et al. eds., 1990) [hereinafter Prentky & Knight I]; Robert A. Prentky & Raymond A. Knight, "Identifying Critical Dimensions for Discriminating Among Rapists," 59 *J. Consulting & Clinical Psychol.* 643, 643 (1991) [hereinafter Prentky & Knight II].

⁵⁴ *See* Baumeister et al., *supra* note 28, at 6. *But see* Lamb, *supra* note 31, at 92 on holding people responsible for their emotions.

⁵⁵ *See* Stephen Jay Gould, *The Mismeasure of Man* 124 (Norton 1981) (referring to Lambroso's theory "born criminals cannot escape their inherited taint").

⁵⁶ *See* DSM-IV, *supra* note 41, at 165.

⁵⁷ Abraham Rudnick & Amihay Levy, "Personality Disorders and Criminal Responsibility: A Second Opinion," 17 *Int'l J.L. & Psychiatry* 409, 411 (1994); Stephen Rachlin et al., "The Volitional Rule, Personality Disorders and the Insanity Defense," 14 *Psychiatric Annals* 139, 140 (1984).

⁵⁸ David Goldman & Diana H. Fishbein, "Genetic Bases for Impulsive and Antisocial Behaviors—Can their Course Be Altered?", in *The Science, Treatment and Prevention of Antisocial Behaviors* 9-1, 9-13 (Diana H. Fishbein ed., 2000).

⁵⁹ *See supra* note 53.

⁶⁰ *See generally* Prentky & Knight I, *supra* note 53 (surveying both offender and nonoffender sexual aggression research for evidence about which dimensions should be included in multivariate models that attempt to discriminate rapists from nonrapists); Stephen M. Hudson et al., "Offense Pathways in Sexual Offenders," 14 *J. Interpersonal Violence* 779 (1999) (classifying sexual offenders into three major pathways of offenses).

⁶¹ *See* Diana Scully & Joseph Marolla, "Convicted Rapists' Vocabulary of Motive: Excuses and Justifications," 31 *Social Probs.* 530, 530 (1984) (criticizing the characterization, since 1925, of "irresistible impulse" and "disease of the mind" as the causes of rape).

⁶² Frederick C. Thorne & T.D. Haupt, "The Objective Measurement of Sex Attitudes and Behavior in Adult Males," 22 *J. Clinical Psychol.* 395, 402 (1966).

⁶³ In re Young, *supra* note 12.

⁶⁴ Alexander D. Brooks, "The Constitutionality and Morality of Civilly Committing Violent Sexual Predators," 15 *U. Puget Sound L. Rev.* 709, 732 (1992).

⁶⁵ *See* Raymond A. Knight, "Validation of a Typology for Rapists," 14 *J. Interpersonal Violence* 303, 311 (1999).

⁶⁶ Id.

⁶⁷ Id.

⁶⁸ *See* Letter from Robert Prentky, Massachusetts Treatment Center, to Eric S. Janus, Professor of Law at William Mitchell College of Law (undated) (on file with author).

[69] Id.

[70] *See* Fred S. Berlin, "Special Considerations in the Psychiatric Evaluation of Sexual Offenders Against Minors," in *Critical Issues in American Psychiatry and the Law*, vol. 4 (R. Rosner & H. I. Schwartz eds., 1989).

[71] *See* Hudson et al., *supra* note 60, at 793.

[72] Id.

[73] Id.

[74] Jennifer Schneider & Richard Irons, "Differential Diagnosis of Addictive Sexual Disorders Using the DSM-IV," 3 *Sexual Addiction & Compulsivity* 7, 10 (1996).

[75] Id.

[76] Id.

[77] Id.

[78] Id.

[79] Schneider & Irons, *supra* note 74, at 16.

[80] Judith Lewis Herman, "Sex Offenders: A Feminist Perspective," in *The Handbook of Sexual Assault: Issues, Theories, & Treatment of the Offender* 177, 184 (W.L. Marshall et al. eds., 1990).

[81] Herman, *supra* note 80, at 185.

[82] *See* Gene M. Heyman, "Resolving the Contradictions of Addiction," 19 *Behav. & Brain Sciences* 561, 561 (1996).

[83] Id.

[84] Gavin Ivey & Peta Simpson, "The Psychological Life of Paedeophiles: A Phenomenological Study," 28 *S. Afr. J. Psychol.* 15 (1998).

[85] Ivey & Simpson, *supra* note 84, at 17.

[86] Ivey & Simpson, *supra* note 84, at 19.

[87] Patrick J. Carnes, "Sexual Addiction," in *The Incest Perpetrator: A Family Member No One Wants to Treat* 126, 126–127 (Anne L. Horton et al. eds., 1990).

[88] Carnes, *supra* note 87, at 127.

[89] Carnes, *supra* note 87, at 128.

[90] Carnes, *supra* note 87, at 129.

[91] *See* Hudson et al., *supra* note 60, at 782.

[92] *See* Scully & Marolla, *supra* note 61, at 541–542; *see also* Baumeister et al., *supra* note 28, at 232 (stating "the perpetrators of violence may prefer to describe their aggressive impulses as strong rather than to describe themselves as weak"); Lamb, *supra* note 31, at 65 (noting "[T]he legal system encourages people to describe violent impulses as uncontrollable, because more lenient penalties are used.").

[93] Lamb, *supra* note 31, at 67–69.

[94] *See* Baumeister et al., *supra* note 28, at 232 (stating "If, as we have suggested, that belief is objectively false—in other words, if violence can indeed usually be controlled and overridden—then people must allow themselves to be carried away by such impulses in order to act on them.").

[95] Baumeister et al., *supra* note 28, at 134.

[96] Baumeister et al., *supra* note 28, at 30.

[97] Baumeister et al., *supra* note 28, at 247.

[98] Baumeister et al., *supra* note 28, at 30.

[99] *See* Morse, *supra* note 18, at 1588.

[100] Baumeister et al., *supra* note 28, at 251.

[101] *See* Gene M. Heyman, "Resolving the Contradictions of Addiction," 19 *Behav. & Brain Sciences* 561, 562 (1996).

[102] Heyman, *supra* note 101, at 565 (quoting N. Miller & J. Chappel, "History of the Disease Concept," 21 *Psychiatric Annals* 196, 197 (1991)).

[103] Heyman, *supra* note 101, at 574.

[104] Heyman, *supra* note 101, at 571.

[105] Id.

[106] Heyman, *supra* note 101, at 573.

[107] Herman, *supra* note 80, at 185.

[108] Herman, *supra* note 80, at 188.

[109] W.L. Marshall et al., "Present Status and Future Directions," in *Handbook of Sexual Assault: Issues, Theories, & Treatment of the Offender* 389, 391 (W.L. Marshall et al. eds., 1990).

[110] William D. Pithers, "Relapse Prevention with Sexual Aggressors: A Method for Maintaining Therapeutic Gain and Enhancing External Supervision," in *Handbook of Sexual Assault: Issues, Theories, & Treatment of the Offender* 343, 345 (W.L. Marshall et al., eds., 1990).

[111] Baumeister et al., *supra* note 28, at 251.

[112] Lamb, *supra* note 31, at 76.

[113] Id.

[114] Lamb, *supra* note 31, at 78.

[115] Scully & Marolla, *supra* note 61, at 542.

[116] *See* Hudson et al., *supra* note 60, at 794.

[117] Baumeister et al., *supra* note 28, at 7.

[118] Id.

[119] Id.

[120] Baumeister et al., *supra* note 28, at 8.

[121] Id.

[122] Id. (emphasis in original).

[123] Id.

[124] Baumeister et al., *supra* note 28, at 7.

[125] Baumeister et al., *supra* note 28, at 9.

[126] Id.

[127] Id.

[128] Id.

[129] Id.

[130] Id.

[131] Baumeister et al., *supra* note 28, at 14.

[132] Baumeister et al., *supra* note 28, at 15.

[133] Id.

[134] Baumeister et al., *supra* note 28, at 16.

[135] Baumeister et al., *supra* note 28, at 17.

[136] Id.

[137] Id.

[138] Baumeister et al., *supra* note 28, at 19.

[139] Id.

[140] *See* Baumeister et al., *supra* note 28, at 20.

[141] Tony Ward & Stephen M. Hudson, "A Self-Regulation Model of Relapse Prevention," in *Remaking Relapse Prevention With Sex Offenders: A Sourcebook* 79, 80 (Richard D. Laws et al., eds., 2000).

[142] Ward & Hudson, *supra* note 141, at 84.

[143] Id.

[144] Id.

[145] Ward & Hudson, *supra* note 141, at 88.

[146] Ward & Hudson, *supra* note 141, at 89.

[147] Ward & Hudson, *supra* note 141, at 91.

[148] Id.

[149] Ward & Hudson, *supra* note 141, at 92.

[150] Id.

[151] Id.

[152] Id.

[153] Id.

[154] Ward & Hudson, *supra* note 141, at 93.

[155] Scully & Marolla, *supra* note 61, at 530.

[156] Scully & Marolla, *supra* note 61, at 542.

[157] Ward & Hudson, *supra* note 141, at 94.

[158] Hudson uses the term "automatic" to refer to "well-scripted" sequences of behavior. Charles S. Carver and Michael F. Scheier point out that even such "automatic" behaviors are under the control of the individual. *See* Charles S. Carver & Michael F. Scheier, "Principles of Self-Regulation: Action and Emotion," in 2 *Handbook of Motivation and Cognition: Foundations of Social Behavior* 1, 10 (Tory Higgins & Richard M. Sorrentino eds., 1990).

[159] Hudson et al., *supra* note 60, at 78.

[160] Baumeister et al., *supra* note 28, at 141.

[161] Prentky & Knight I, *supra* note 53, at 44.

[162] Prentky & Knight II, *supra* note 53, at 649.

[163] Prentky & Knight II, *supra* note 53, at 648.

[164] Id.

[165] Hendricks, *supra* note 1, at 360 (emphasis added).

[166] Baumeister et al., *supra* note 28, at 12.

[167] Prentky & Knight II, *supra* note 53, at 648.

[168] *See* Prentky & Knight II, *supra* note 53, at 649.

[169] Id.

[170] *See* Daniel A. Krauss et al., "Beyond Prediction to Explanation in Risk Assessment Research: A Comparison of Two Explanatory Theories of Criminality and Recidivism," 23 *Int'l J.L. & Psychiatry* 91, 98 (2000).

[171] Robert J. McGrath, "Sex Offender Risk Assessment and Disposition Planning: A Review of Empirical and Clinical Findings," 35 *Int'l J. Offender Therapy & Comp. Criminology* 328, 338 (1991).

[172] Baumeister et al., *supra* note 28, at 11–12.

[173] *See* Stephen D. Hart et al., "The Psychopathy Checklist: An Overview for Researchers and Clinicians" 103, 105, in 8 *Advances in Psychological Assessment* (J. Rosen & P. McReynolds eds., 1991) (stating that 75–80 percent of criminals are diagnosable with antisocial personality disorder); Rosalie Wells, "A Fresh Look at the Muddy Waters of Psychopathy," 63 *Psychol. Rep.* 843, 846 (1988) (80 percent); James S. Wulach, "Diagnosing the DSM-III Antisocial Personality Disorder," 14 *Prof. Psychol.: Res. & Prac.* 330 (1983) (75–80 percent); P.J. Clayton et al., "Psychiatric Disorders and Criminality," 227 *J.A.M.A.* 641–642 (1974) (90 percent of felons have a "psychiatric disorder"; 70 percent are "sociopathic").

[174] Wendy Richardson, "Criminal Behavior Fueled by Attention Deficit Hyperactivity Disorder and Addiction," in *The Science, Treatment and Prevention of Antisocial Behaviors* 18-2 (Diana H. Fishbein ed., 2000).

[175] Prentky et al. state that planning the offense is one of the most frequent precursors to offenses by child molesters, being exhibited by 73 percent of the sample in one study. *See* Robert A. Prentky et al., *Child Sexual Molestation: Research Issues* (U.S. Department of Justice, June 1997) at 8.

[176] Baumeister et al., *supra* note 28, at 33. *Cf.* David Ballard et al., "A Comparative Profile of the Incest Perpetrator: Background Characteristics, Abuse History, and Use of Social Skills," in *The Incest Perpetrator: A Family Member No One Wants to Treat* 43, 57 (Anne L. Horton et al., eds., 1990) (finding that 76.6 percent of child molesters believed that something could have been done prior to the sexual assault to prevent it).

[177] John Douglas, *Obsession: The FBI's Legendary Profiler Probes the Psyches of Killers, Rapists and Stalkers and Their Victims and Tells How to Fight Back* 107 (1998).

[178] Douglas, *supra* note 177, at 109.

[179] For a complete discussion, *see* Morse, *supra* note 18; *see also* Bruce J. Winick, "Sex Offender Law in the 1990s: A Therapeutic Jurisprudence Analysis," 4 *Psychol. Pub. Pol'y & L.* 505, 514 (1998). Winick states: "[W]e think it fair to hold people responsible for their own personalities . . . ." Winick at 514. He goes on to argue that

> Excusing people from responsibility because of their personality traits must be rejected for the same reason that arguments based on determinism or universal causation must be rejected: its acceptance "would require a complete restructuring of our sense of ourselves as responsible agents, our moral practices more generally, and, not least, our system of criminal justice."

Winick at 514 n.48 (quoting Morse, *supra* note 18, at 1594); Morse adds: "The law assumes that people who are characterologically thoughtless, careless, [etc.] can be expected to control themselves and should be held accountable if they violate the law." Morse, *supra* note 18, at 1602 (quoted in Winick, *supra*, at 514).

[180] Baumeister et al., *supra* note 28, at 232.

[181] Lamb, *supra* note 31, at 76.

[182] Ward & Hudson, *supra* note 141, at 97.

Chapter 2

Professional Standards for Civil Commitment Programs

by Janice K. Marques, Ph.D.

Constitutional and Treatment Issues 2-2
    Legal Context 2-3
    Clinical Context 2-4
Relevant Guidelines and Standards 2-5
    General Resources 2-5
    State Guidelines 2-5
    Professional Guidelines 2-5
Requirements of the *Turay* Injunction 2-6
The Professional Standards 2-7
    Staff Training and Supervision 2-8
        Properly Trained Staff and Clinical Supervision 2-8
        Staffing Structure and Roles 2-8
        Consistency in Treatment Planning 2-8
    Treatment Components and Measures of Progress 2-9
        Individual and Comprehensive Treatment Plans 2-9
        Components Provided in Institutional Programs 2-10
        Monitoring and Feedback 2-10
        Identifiable Phases and Conditional Release 2-10
    Treatment Environment 2-11
        Nonpunitive Treatment Environments 2-12
        Adequate Space 2-12
        Staff Behavior 2-12
        Consistently Enforced Policies 2-12
        Residents' Grievances 2-13
        Residents Who Refuse Treatment 2-13

---

   * The views expressed are those of the author and do not necessarily represent the policies of the California Department of Mental Health or the opinions of the U.S. District Court, Western District of Washington.

    Program Review and Oversight 2-13
        Internal Review Procedures 2-14
        External Oversight 2-14
Summary and Conclusions 2-15

CONSTITUTIONAL AND TREATMENT ISSUES

In the past decade, the resurrection of laws providing for the civil commitment of sexual offenders has required state agencies to develop new treatment programs for these individuals. Despite the fact that by the 1990s the field of sexual offender treatment had matured as a clinical specialty, the task of setting up these new programs was a difficult one for many reasons. The new commitment laws passed quickly, and many were "urgency" statutes that required programs to accept referrals before treatment approaches and regimens were developed and staff could be trained. The individuals entering the programs were understandably upset about being detained after serving their prison sentences. Many had no interest in treatment, were previous treatment failures, or had been advised by counsel not to participate in the program. Most treatment professionals had little or no experience working with such high-risk, treatment-resistant offenders. States had problems finding secure facilities that were designed for treatment rather than incarceration. There was also a pervasive sense of uncertainty around these new programs due to the fact that the constitutionality of the commitment laws was the subject of intense debate.

Given this context, it is not surprising that the new civil commitment programs, such as the State of Washington's Special Commitment Center (SCC), were open to criticism and were challenged in court. Not long after the program started in 1990, a number of SCC residents filed lawsuits in federal court, alleging that the conditions of confinement at the facility violated their civil rights. In one case, *Turay v. Seling*,[1] a resident of the SCC contended that his rights were violated by the program's managers in a number of ways, including their failure to provide him with adequate mental health treatment. Following a 1994 jury verdict adverse in part to the defendants, they were enjoined by U. S. District Court Judge William L. Dwyer to take certain steps to make constitutionally adequate mental health treatment available to residents.[2] In a subsequent court order, I was appointed as special master in the *Turay* case to provide expert assistance to the defendants in bringing the SCC treatment program into compliance with the injunction, and to provide reports to the court on the program's progress.

Unfortunately, at the time of my appointment there were no published standards that specifically defined adequate mental health treatment for sexual offenders under civil commitment. As a result, my assignment to assist the program was really twofold: to document the applicable professional standards and to help build a program that met these standards. In this chapter, I will describe the first of these tasks, the elucidation of the professional standards that apply to civil commitment programs such as the SCC. My description will begin with a brief overview of the legal and clinical foundations for this work, along with the relevant guidelines and standards I have consulted. Then I will present and discuss the specific professional standards that the SCC and similar programs should meet.

Legal Context

Although I was appointed as a sexual offender treatment expert rather than as a legal expert, understanding the constitutional requirement for treatment has helped guide my work as special master. Questions about what is required for adequate mental health treatment have been addressed in a number of previous federal court cases. In a recent ruling on the *Turay* case, the court summarized the key decisions as follows:

> The Fourteenth Amendment Due Process Clause of the United States Constitution requires state officials to provide civilly-committed persons, such as these plaintiffs, with access to mental health treatment that gives them a realistic opportunity to be cured or to improve the mental condition for which they were confined. *See Youngberg v. Romeo*, 457 U.S. 307, 319-22 (1982); *Ohlinger v. Watson*, 652 F.2d 775, 778 (9th Cir. 1980). This rule applies to sex offenders, and "[l]ack of funds, staff or facilities cannot justify the State's failure to provide [those confined] with that treatment necessary for rehabilitation." *Ohlinger v. Watson*, 652 F.2d at 778-79. The *Youngberg* constitutional standard "determines whether a particular decision has substantially met professionally accepted minimum standards." *Society for Good Will to Retarded Children, Inc. v. Cuomo*, 737 F.2d 1239, 1248 (2d Cir. 1984).
>
> Accordingly, these plaintiffs, and others involuntarily confined through civil proceedings, cannot simply be warehoused and put out of sight; they must be afforded adequate treatment. Although confined, they are not prisoners. They are entitled by law to "more considerate treatment and conditions of confinement than criminals whose conditions of confinement are designed to punish." *Youngberg*, 457 U.S. at 322. Recognizing these requirements, the Washington statute provides that "[a]ny person committed pursuant to this chapter has the right to adequate care and individualized treatment." RCW 71.09.080(2).
>
> As to the nature of the treatment, the State "enjoy[s] wide latitude in developing treatment regimens [for sex offenders]," *Kansas v. Hendricks*, 521 U.S. 346, 368 n.4 (1997), and "liability [on a claim of constitutional deprivation] may be imposed only when the decision by the professional is such a substantial departure from accepted professional judgment, practice, or standards as to demonstrate that the person responsible actually did not base the decision on such a judgment." *Youngberg*, 457 U.S. at 323. The *Hendricks* Court rejected a facial challenge to a Kansas statute modeled on Washington's, noting that by committing sex offenders "to an institution expressly designed to provide psychiatric care and treatment" the state "has doubtless satisfied its obligation to provide available treatment." 521 U.S. at 368 n.4.[3]

According to the courts, then, civil commitment programs are to provide adequate mental health treatment under conditions that are not designed to punish residents. Also, although states are authorized to design their own treatment programs, they are not to deviate substantially from accepted professional standards.

Clinical Context

By the mid-1990s, sexual offender treatment had become a recognized area of specialization among mental health professionals. Although most "sexual psychopath" laws had been repealed by then, many mental health and correctional agencies had gained considerable experience running institutional programs for sexual offenders, and there had been significant growth in the number of community-based programs that specialized in the assessment and treatment of this population.[4] Despite sparse federal funding for research in this area, there was a growing body of knowledge on both assessment and treatment of sexual offenders. Several edited volumes and special editions of scholarly journals had been published on this clinical specialty. The Association for the Treatment of Sexual Abusers (ATSA), an international professional organization established in the mid-1980s, was sponsoring both a quarterly journal and an annual conference on research and treatment with sexual offenders. The ATSA meetings regularly presented clinical innovations, program descriptions and outcome data from the newer cognitive-behavioral treatment programs in the United States and Canada. In the early 1990s, an ATSA committee took on the task of documenting the current professional standards in the field and published a practitioner's handbook.[5] This booklet, which provided general practice guidelines as well as specific recommendations about treatment targets and interventions, was perhaps the clearest evidence that there was a developing consensus regarding what programs should provide in the way of offense-specific treatment.

Despite the significant progress that had been made in establishing guidelines for clinicians who treat sexual offenders, the task of documenting the specific professional standards that apply to civil commitment programs was not a simple one. There were several reasons for this, such as the fact that these new programs were being implemented in a wide range of settings, including state hospitals, prison wings, and stand-alone facilities.[6] There was considerable variation in the treatment environments, the qualifications and organization of the staff, and the intensity of the treatment regimens. The oversight of the programs also varied. Some programs were subject to stringent state licensing regulations and national accreditation criteria, and others required virtually no external review.

Another difficulty arose from the fact that most of the current state-of-the-art programs had been developed for offenders in prison or in the community. Programs in these contexts were organized around an outpatient or day treatment framework, not the inpatient treatment model found in the mental health facilities that treat civilly committed patients. In the latter model, a broad range of treatment and ancillary services is delivered by a multidisciplinary team in the context of a twenty-four-hour treatment environment. Thus, although the new civil commitment programs were able to adopt many of the offense-specific treatment components that were used in other settings, there was still significant program development that needed to be done. This work was particularly challenging because of the heterogeneity of the resident population. The programs were admitting individuals who would have been screened out of many existing programs, such as offenders with special needs (e.g., major mental disorders and developmental disabilities), extensive criminal histories, or a strong opposition to treatment. As a result, there was a need for clinicians to expand and refine existing treatment protocols in order to effectively serve this diverse and often challenging group of individuals.

RELEVANT GUIDELINES AND STANDARDS

General Resources

A number of important resources were available to me as I worked on the documentation of current professional standards for treating sexual offenders under civil commitment. First, of course, there was the experience of myself and my colleagues who had developed, implemented, and evaluated institutional treatment programs for sexual offenders. In particular, the consultation provided by Drs. Craig Nelson and Anita Schlank regarding the operation of their inpatient programs was important in clarifying and confirming the relevant standards of practice.

Second, there were many written resources available, including treatment standards recognized by courts, various licensing and accreditation requirements developed for other mental health facilities, and position statements on civil commitment published by professional organizations. I reviewed, for example, the "standards governing care and treatment in psychiatric facilities" that were recognized in *Wyatt v. Stickney*.[7] A variety of standards used for the inspection of mental health facilities for licensing or accreditation purposes have also been relevant to this work. Although these documents did not specifically address the treatment of sexual offenders, they were informative about the parameters of adequate mental health treatment, including staffing and organization, treatment planning and records, patient advocacy, quality assurance, and program oversight.

State Guidelines

State agencies have published specific guidelines regarding the treatment of sexual deviance. For example, the Colorado Sex Offender Management Board[8] has developed an extensive set of standards and guidelines for the assessment, evaluation, treatment, and behavioral monitoring of adult sexual offenders. In Minnesota, the Department of Corrections established standards for the certification of sexual offender treatment programs in state-operated facilities.[9] Perhaps most importantly, that state also developed a separate set of regulations that govern the operation of their civil commitment program for sexual offenders.[10] These regulations include requirements for staff qualifications and training, treatment planning, program services, behavior management, and disciplinary measures.

Professional Guidelines

Following the *Kansas v. Hendricks*[11] decision, a number of professional groups distributed relevant position papers and task force reports. In 1999, the American Psychiatric Association[12] released a task force report on sexually dangerous offenders that is largely critical of the new civil commitment laws but that also stresses the need for appropriate diagnostic and treatment procedures. A 1997 position statement by the

National Association of State Mental Health Program Directors (NASMHPD) emphasizes the need for mental health agencies to determine which sexual offenders are to be committed and to ensure that dangerous sex offenders are not housed with mentally ill patients. NASMHPD followed this statement with a more extensive technical report that includes guidelines for treatment, security, and patient rights.[13]

Some recent ATSA publications have been highly relevant to the task of clarifying the current professional standards. ATSA updated and greatly expanded its guidelines for practitioners[14] and presented the new guidelines at its 1997 annual conference.[15] It has also released a position statement on civil commitment that includes specific recommendations in the areas of treatment environment, staffing, oversight, and treatment components, including community aftercare.[16]

Finally, significant program developments and ideas about best practices have been shared in a number of national meetings and conference sessions. Two ATSA panel presentations have focused on defining the essential elements of civil commitment programs[17] and on developing programs that work.[18] There have also been two "civil commitment summits," national meetings in which administrators and clinicians from various states describe their programs and procedures, share approaches to common problems, and discuss standards of care.

REQUIREMENTS OF THE *TURAY* INJUNCTION

In addition to the guidance provided by the many resources discussed above, my work was of course given direction by the injunction in the *Turay* case. The court's initial ruling[19] reviewed the facts of the case, including the specific program deficiencies that were identified during the trial and the jury's overall finding that the defendants (the SCC) had failed to provide the plaintiff with access to constitutionally adequate mental health treatment. The ruling further indicated that continued confinement without access to mental health treatment, as required by the U.S. Constitution, would result in irreparable harm to the plaintiff. As a result, the court ordered that the plaintiff was entitled to injunctive relief tailored to remedy this constitutional violation. The defendants were enjoined to do the following:

A. Adopt and implement a plan for initial and ongoing training and/or hiring of competent sex offender therapists at SCC.

B. Implement strategies to rectify the lack of trust and rapport between residents and treatment providers.

C. Implement a treatment program for residents which includes all therapy components recognized as necessary by prevailing professional standards in comparable programs where participation is coerced. As agreed to by defendants, this shall include the involvement of spouses and family members in the treatment of residents, and plans for encouraging the visitation and support of family members.

D. Develop and maintain individual treatment plans for residents that include objective benchmarks of improvement so as to document, measure, and guide an individual's progress in therapy.

E. Provide a psychologist or psychiatrist expert in the diagnosis and treatment of sex offenders to supervise the clinical work of treatment staff, including monitoring of the treatment plans of individual residents, and to consult with staff regarding specific issues or concerns about therapy which may arise.

In the six years since these instructions were issued, the court has regularly conducted hearings on injunctive compliance and has issued additional orders that address specific issues raised by the parties, myself, or other witnesses. Subsequent orders have also served to clarify the requirements of the injunction. In one of these,[20] the court emphasized the need for the SCC to ensure that proposed program improvements would be implemented, and added the following requirement:

F. Objective external oversight will be needed to guarantee that the essential program features operate in practice and not just on paper.

THE PROFESSIONAL STANDARDS

As I indicated earlier, my assignments as special master were to assist the SCC in achieving compliance with the injunction and to keep the court apprised of the program's progress. Both tasks required that I specify the objectives or standards the program needed to attain in the areas covered by the injunction. The balance of this chapter presents my description of the current professional standards that apply to civil commitment programs. These statements have served to guide the ongoing program development efforts at the SCC and to provide a structure for my periodic assessments of the extent to which the program was providing adequate mental health treatment.

In describing the standards, I was mindful of two conflicting needs: (1) the need to operationalize the elements of the injunction in order to provide clear guidance to the program and (2) the need to allow (as the courts have emphasized) the state to have wide latitude in developing its treatment regimens. As a result, I attempted to write statements that were specific enough to provide direction and feedback, but that did not address the details of the program's content or operations.

Although they have not been through a formal rule-making process, the standards listed here have been widely disseminated and discussed at several professional meetings, including two ATSA conferences and the first civil commitment summit meeting. A statement of these standards was also admitted into evidence in the *Turay* case, without dispute by any party, as a summary of applicable professional standards.[21]

In my periodic reports to the court, I have used the elements of the injunction to organize my assessment of the program's progress toward the goal of providing adequate mental health treatment. Because this framework has been useful to both the court and the parties, I have also organized the standards along the same lines.

The following sections discuss the professional standards that pertain to the four program areas addressed by the court:

- Staff training and supervision
- Treatment components and measures of progress
- Treatment environment

- Program review and oversight

Staff Training and Supervision

Staff training and supervision includes items A and E of the injunction, requiring the SCC to have competent staff and clinical supervision that is provided by qualified professionals. There are four specific standards in this program area:

- Program staff are adequately trained to provide residential care and treatment components.
- Clinical direction and supervision are consistently provided by qualified professionals.
- All staff understand the treatment model, its structure, and their roles.
- Treatment planning and clinical decisions are consistent across teams.

Properly Trained Staff and Clinical Supervision. Civil commitment programs must be staffed by a team of individuals who are adequately trained and supervised. Because the clients in these programs are diverse and often challenging, staff need both initial and continuing training, at all levels of care. Program managers should specify the competencies required for various staff classifications, identify core training requirements for each, and indicate how performance will be evaluated. In addition to formal training, new direct care staff need on-the-job mentoring and feedback sessions. Clinical staff, particularly those who have not worked with sexual offenders, also need direct feedback from experienced treatment providers on their delivery of treatment components. As the injunction indicates, all clinical staff need to have qualified professionals available to provide ongoing supervision and case consultation. Having a clinical leader who organizes and directs the treatment program is also important, in order to build a coherent program structure and a strong multidisciplinary team.

Staffing Structure and Roles. Civil commitment programs will vary in how staff roles are defined; for example, some will have residential care staff involved in formal treatment groups, and others will not. Because of such differences, the standards do not prescribe a particular staffing structure or set of roles for programs to use. They do, however, emphasize the need for each staff member to have a basic understanding of the program's mental health treatment model and the role he or she plays in the overall treatment effort. In most inpatient mental health programs, direct care staff on the unit are considered part of the treatment team. Their contributions include de-escalating incidents, observing and charting resident behaviors that occur outside of treatment activities, and participating in treatment planning and the assessments of residents' progress in treatment. Staff must therefore also understand the residents' behavioral patterns as well as their individual treatment plans and goals. Also, because clinical and direct care staff are in different but supporting roles, there is often a need for cross-training and teambuilding in order to ensure that teams work effectively together.

Consistency in Treatment Planning. The final standard in this area, consistency in treatment planning and decision-making, relates to the common practice of having the program staff organized into multidisciplinary treatment teams that have primary responsibility for a group of residents. As programs grow and the number of teams increase, some mechanism is needed to ensure that the program is being delivered consistently across teams. Although important clinical decisions—such as whether a resident is ready to move to the next phase of treatment or into the community—are made on a case-by-case basis, the decisions should be made using similar measures and criteria.

Treatment Components and Measures of Progress

Standards for treatment components and measures of progress include items C and D of the court's injunction, which required the SCC to have adequate treatment planning, a multimodal program, and measures of progress in therapy. Five standards describe what civil commitment programs need to have in this area:

- Treatment plans are individualized and comprehensive.
- The program offers the components that are typically provided in institutional programs.
- There is ongoing monitoring of services to ensure quality and consistency.
- Systematic measures of progress are used, and feedback is regularly provided to participants.
- The program has identifiable phases, including a community release program.

Individual and Comprehensive Treatment Plans. According to published professional standards,[22] adequate treatment begins with an evaluation of the client and the development of a comprehensive treatment plan. This is an industrywide standard, of course, but individualized treatment planning is even more important in civil commitment programs than in some other treatment settings (such as those that rigorously screen participants or offer only psychoeducational classes). The individuals entering civil commitment programs are a very diverse group. Nearly all have been diagnosed with paraphilic disorders, but they also manifest a broad range of other clinical syndromes, including major mental disorders, developmental disabilities, neurological impairments, and serious medical conditions. As a result, a one-size-fits-all approach to treatment planning and programming is wholly inappropriate. Strategies and interventions that work for one individual will simply not work for others.

To be individualized, treatment plans must assess the special needs of each resident and prescribe treatment interventions that are responsive to his life challenges and learning style. Psychiatric evaluation and psychological/neurological testing are often needed before the team can determine how a resident's treatment should proceed. For those who refuse to participate in treatment, plans should include strategies for overcoming obstacles and engaging them in the treatment process.

To be comprehensive, plans should include both short- and long-term treatment goals and should address not just sexual deviance but the resident's functioning in other life domains as well. These include health issues, substance abuse, family relationships, educational, vocational, and recreational needs, and resident strengths. Although such areas may be considered ancillary to the treatment of sexual deviance, you must consider factors that are predictive of the individual's success on release. For example, if a resident's offenses occurred when he was unemployed, isolated from family, depressed and using drugs, these elements need to be addressed in his treatment plan.

Components Provided in Institutional Programs. As the courts have indicated, states must provide civilly committed persons with access to treatment that gives them a realistic opportunity to be cured or to improve the mental condition for which they were confined.[23] For offenders with substantial histories of committing sexual crimes, the prevailing professional opinion is that an intensive, multimodal program is required to offer such an opportunity. Consistent with ATSA principles, most current programs are based on a cognitive-behavioral model, and include psychotherapy groups as well as other treatment components that address specific risk factors for sexual offending. Common treatment targets include cognitive distortions, deviant sexual interests, and deficits in the areas of empathy, intimacy, anger management, and social skills. Comprehensive programs also provide adequate psychiatric services, including the use of antiandrogen and psychotropic medications when indicated.

There is agreement that adequate treatment should include the development of individual relapse prevention plans and social support networks to ensure that treatment gains are maintained. The *Turay* injunction recognizes the importance of family support and involvement and requires the program to include spouses and family members in treatment efforts. A detailed review of the treatment components that are included in current civil commitment programs is provided by Lieb and Nelson.[24]

Monitoring and Feedback. Programs need mechanisms to document and monitor the services they deliver. This includes keeping records of treatment and other services provided, monitoring the quality and consistency of the services, and tracking resident participation in activities. Clinical supervisors should review treatment plans, manuals for treatment components, and other materials (tests and homework assignments) used in the program. Direct observation of the treatment components is also very important because staff need feedback from experienced clinicians regarding how they deliver the program's services.

Systematic record-keeping is necessary not just for program monitoring but also for tracking residents' progress in the program. Because they are comprehensive and in most cases require years to complete, civil commitment programs must ensure that feedback is provided to participants along the way. As Schlank[25] has emphasized, this requires programs to develop treatment goals that are objective and include observable behaviors. The development of particular goals and milestones provides for formal measures of progress that should be used to assess therapeutic progress on a regular basis. For example, if program services are provided according to a quarter or trimester schedule, teams can use the breaks between terms to compile treatment participation data and to organize and provide feedback to residents. Feedback should include an assessment of the resident's level of participation and his progress as determined by the program's formal measures and the observations of the multidisciplinary team. Each resident should understand where he is in the program and what is expected of him in order to advance in treatment.

Identifiable Phases and Conditional Release. Having identifiable phases in the program facilitates the measurement of treatment progress. While treatment plans and regimens need to be individualized, it is also important to identify common program themes and steps that participants will go through as they advance in treatment. For example, most civil commitment programs include an orientation and evaluation phase, several phases that emphasize skill development and application, and an advanced phase that focuses on preparing the resident to enter community treatment. Because each phase has specific goals, this structure helps treatment managers develop appropriate components and measures of progress. It also helps treatment teams organize and focus their efforts, and makes the therapeutic process more understandable and predictable to residents.

Although the number and content of phases will vary across programs, the treatment structure must include a phase in which qualified residents are conditionally released to a less restrictive setting. The need for institutional programs to provide community aftercare has long been recognized,[26] and the failure to include this element in a civil commitment program has been called a "fatal problem."[27] More recently in the *Turay* case, this treatment phase has been "confirmed by all experts on both sides as a vital part of the professional minimum standards."[28] Unfortunately, despite this consensus, programs have been slow to develop this aspect of treatment, and the goal of having a seamless transition to the community has proven to be an elusive one. Putting together a community release component involves more than simple contracting with a qualified outpatient provider to continue the individual's treatment plan. It requires arranging housing and employment, building family and social supports, ensuring that the offender is adequately supervised, and working on community notification and acceptance.

Despite the complexity of the task, a viable community release program must be in place for residents who reach their residential treatment goals. If a program is to succeed, it must be shown that release to a less restrictive setting is possible through treatment. This demonstration of the program's credibility is critical not only to the residents who are actively involved in treatment, but also to residents who are unsure about or refusing treatment, to residents' families and significant others, and to program staff. All of these individuals need to see a legitimate program in operation, one in which therapeutic progress is recognized and community reentry is possible.

Treatment Environment

Treatment environment issues are addressed in item B of the court's injunction, which requires the program to "implement strategies to rectify the lack of trust and rapport between residents and treatment providers." This deceptively simple statement has been the most difficult part of the injunction to define and measure, and developing specific work plans for making improvements has been a challenge. My early assessments of the program indicated that trust and rapport were really part of a broader issue involving the development of an environment that supported treatment. Work in this area has therefore included a number of strategies aimed at creating a positive and consistent treatment environment. Six standards describe what an adequate program should provide in this area:

- The program is housed in a treatment-oriented (not punitive) environment.
- Adequate space is provided for living, treatment, other activities, and for separation among resident groups.

- The behavior of all staff is therapeutic and professional.
- Program policies are consistently enforced.
- Residents are treated with respect, and have opportunities to have their grievances addressed.
- The program addresses the long-term care needs of those who are not engaged in treatment activities.

Nonpunitive Treatment Environments. Although professionals agree that programs should be provided in a treatment-oriented environment, the details of what this involves have not been agreed on. It is clear, however, that the essential issues are the characteristics of the physical plant, the attitudes and professionalism of the staff, and the program's policies and practices related to resident management.

As we know, civil commitment programs are housed in various settings, from converted prison units to licensed psychiatric hospitals. Although it is not impossible to operate a mental health program within the confines of a prison, this arrangement presents serious and persistent obstacles to creating the nonpunitive environment that civilly committed persons need. Detailed documentation of these problems can be found in my periodic reports to the court[29] and in a recent description of the Kansas program.[30] It is clearly advisable for programs to be housed in facilities designed for treatment and not for incarceration.

Adequate Space. In addition to being housed in a nonpunitive setting, civil commitment programs need adequate space for their residents and activities. This includes housing, treatment, education, and recreation areas that are sufficient for the program's resident population, activities, and staff. Because of the diversity of committed residents, the need arises to separate them and the living space should allow for the separation when necessary. At SCC, for example, residents in active treatment had to be separated from individuals who were actively harassing and intimidating them. A program may also need to house certain residents together for programmatic reasons (e.g., moving residents ready for community transition to a less supervised area) or because of safety concerns (e.g., separating particularly vulnerable individuals from predatory residents).

Staff Behavior. The behavior of all personnel should reflect the treatment mission of the program. Although direct care staff play an important role in maintaining security, their role is very different from that of a correctional officer. They have the most contact with the residents, interacting with them daily, and it is important that they treat residents in a professional, therapeutic, and respectful manner. Direct care staff are also usually part of the treatment team and help to assess residents' progress. Their attitudes and skills are critical in setting the tone of the program. They should be familiar with residents' behavioral patterns and be able to recognize and interrupt problems that are developing on the unit. Clinical staff should spend time on the unit to model therapeutic attitudes and interactions to help direct care staff develop the skills they need.

Consistently Enforced Policies. The development of clear and consistent policies that govern program operations is essential to creating and maintaining a treatment-oriented environment. Policies should reflect a therapeutic, not punitive, stance toward residents. Policies covering topics that directly affect residents—such as grievance procedures, rights and privileges, living unit rules, visiting and family involvement, resident abuse, and management of behavioral incidents—need to be clearly written and made available to residents. Staff training will help ensure that everyone understands the policies, and staff supervision will help ensure they are consistently enforced on all shifts. At the management level, programs need a system in place to track policy violations and determine whether any staff training or policy provisions should be revised.

Residents' Grievances. Program managers need to ensure that residents' complaints are heard and their feedback about the program's operation considered. Staff should make efforts to get resident input on new rules and procedures, and administration and resident representatives should have regular meetings to address common concerns and resident proposals. A resident advocate available to help residents with their complaints will help ensure that their rights are protected. Although program staff should attempt to work informally with residents to resolve individual complaints and problems as they occur, a formal grievance mechanism also needs to be in place. This should include clear procedures for residents to submit their grievances and for appropriate staff to give those grievances a timely review and response. Residents should also have the opportunity to appeal the initial grievance response in order to have their problem considered by management. The program should keep data on grievance activities to measure the effectiveness of the process and to identify program areas needing improvement.

Residents Who Refuse Treatment. The final standard in this area addresses the importance of having opportunities for all residents to engage in productive activities. Ideally, all will be actively engaged in treatment as well as participating in the program's educational, vocational, recreational, and social activities. Unfortunately, no program is currently achieving this ideal, and each has a proportion of its residents refusing to participate in treatment. Some such residents are resourceful and stay busy (e.g., writing and doing legal research), but others remaining idle, some for many years.

There is general agreement that programs need to provide structure and activities for these individuals and must not ignore or "warehouse" them. This does not mean that a complete program of alternative activities needs to be developed for treatment-resistant residents. It does mean that they should have treatment plans to address their individual needs, to describe possible therapeutic engagement strategies, and to identify goals such as those related to fitness and health, education, vocational skills, hobbies, or family and social relationships. This in turn requires the program to have sufficient staff and resources to provide educational, vocational, recreational, and family/social programs as well as resident job assignments. Having these residents actively engaged in some form of self-improvement and other constructive pursuits can significantly contribute to the maintenance of a positive and supportive treatment environment.

Program Review and Oversight

The program review and oversight area responds to the court's requirement that an oversight function should guarantee that the program's essential features operate in practice and not just on paper. If states are to provide adequate mental health services, they should have the same kinds of internal and external oversight mechanisms in their civil commitment programs that they have in their other mental health institutions. Two standards describe the review and oversight mechanisms that should be in place:

- The program has internal review procedures.
- The program has external oversight, through either a licensing agency or other entity.

Internal Review Procedures. There is considerable variation in how mental health programs monitor the adequacy and consistency of the services they deliver. Most, however, include these features:

- A quality assurance/improvement program (to ensure systematic, continuous review of the program's progress toward meeting its service goals);
- Resident advocacy services (to ensure the consideration of residents' input and the protection of their rights);
- A policy review function (to track policy compliance, to document exceptions, and to make necessary revisions);
- Procedures for the internal investigation of incidents (to give management the information needed to respond to serious allegations such as employee misconduct or resident abuse).

External Oversight. External oversight of mental health programs also varies and may include state licensing surveys, evaluations by national accreditation groups, and reviews by federal authorities (for programs receiving federal funds). When appropriate, civil commitment programs should have the same external oversight procedures as do other state mental health programs. For example, if a state licensing authority oversees the state's public mental health facilities, it should also oversee its civil commitment program. In most cases, the oversight structures should include:

- A governing body with direct authority over the program's administrator;
- Regular inspections of the program by outside professionals;
- An ombudsman to provide objective review of complaints, incidents, and policies; and
- The external investigation of serious incidents by an agency not affiliated with the program (such as a state police agency).

Because civil commitment programs are relatively new and provide services that are quite specialized, the inspections of care by outside professionals are a particularly important part of external oversight. These surveys should be conducted using a structured protocol that covers applicable state regulations as well as current professional standards. Ideally, each inspection team will include a clinician with expertise in the treatment of sexual offenders. The inspection report should identify specific deficiencies in the program, and program managers should be required to develop plans of correction to address these in a timely manner.

SUMMARY AND CONCLUSIONS

Although this generation of civil commitment programs is still relatively new, professionals in the field agree that a number of conditions must be met if people committed to residential treatment are to receive adequate mental health treatment. These essential conditions can be summarized as follows:

1. *The program must operate in a treatment-oriented, not punitive, environment.* The conditions in a state's civil commitment facility should be similar to those in its other secure mental health facilities, not its prisons. The program's organization, policies, rules, and operations should be clearly reflected in its treatment mission. Standard features of mental health programs should be in place, such as patient advocacy and mechanisms for ensuring the quality of care provided. The program should also be subject to the same kind of external oversight and review procedures as are the state's other mental health institutions.

2. *The program must be consistent with current professional standards for the treatment of sexual offenders.* This includes having a competent clinical team, individualized treatment plans, and a full range of treatment interventions as well as clearly defined phases of treatment and systematic measurement of residents' progress in the program.

3. *The program must demonstrate that release is possible through treatment.* To be successful, a civil commitment program needs to have a fully developed conditional release mechanism. Residents who reach their residential treatment goals and are ready for a less restrictive setting should be moved into the community for ongoing supervision and treatment.

Footnotes

[1] No. C91-664WD (unpub. op., 1997), originally Turay v. Weston, No. C91-664WD (unpub. op., W.D. Wash. 1994).

[2] Turay v. Weston, *supra* note 1, Order and Injunction, June 3, 1994.

[3] Findings of Fact, Conclusions of Law, and Order Re Motions Heard 4–5, April 18–21, 2000, Turay v. Seling, *supra* note 1, May 5, 2000.

[4] R.E. Freeman-Longo, S.L. Bird, W. Stevenson & J.A. Fiske, *Nationwide Survey of Treatment Programs and Models* (1995).

[5] *The ATSA Practitioner's Handbook* (S.H. Jensen, ed., Association for the Treatment of Sexual Abusers, 1993).

[6] *See* Lieb & Nelson, Chapter 5, this volume.

[7] 325 F. Supp. 781 (M.D. Ala. 1971), and subsequent orders in that case, 344 F. Supp. 373 (1972), *reprinted in* R.M. Levy & L.S. Rubenstein, *The Rights of People With Mental Disabilities: The Authoritative ACLU Guide to the Rights of People With Mental Illness and Mental Retardation* (1996).

[8] *Standards and Guidelines for the Assessment, Evaluation, Treatment, and Behavioral Monitoring of Adult Sex Offenders* (Colorado Department of Public Safety, 1996 and 1999 rev. ed.).

[9] Minn. R. ch. 2965 (1997).

[10] Minn. R. ch. 9515 (1995).

[11] 117 S. Ct. 2072 (1997).

[12] *Task Force on Sexually Dangerous Offenders* (American Psychiatric Association, 1999).

[13] *Issues Pertaining to the Development and Implementation of Programs for Persons Civilly Committed for Treatment Under Sexually Violent Predator Statutes* (NASMHPD Medical Directors Council, 1999).

[14] *Ethical Standards and Principles for the Management of Sexual Abusers* (ATSA, 1997).

[15] W.D. Murphy, J.K. Marques & S. Jensen, *ATSA's Revised Ethical Standards and Principles*, presented at ATSA's Sixteenth Annual Research and Treatment Conference in Arlington, Va., Oct. 1997.

[16] *Civil Commitment of Sexually Violent Offenders* (ATSA, 1997).

[17] J.K. Marques, J.V. Becker, G.A. Messer, C. Nelson & A. Schlank, *Treatment of Sexual Predators: Essential Elements of Successful Civil Commitment Programs*, presented at ATSA's Eighteenth Annual Research and Treatment Conference in Orlando, Fl., Sept. 24, 1999.

[18] J.K. Marques, J.V. Becker, C. Nelson & A. Schlank, *The Evolution of Civil Commitment Programs: New Ideas for Solving Common Problems and Developing Programs That Work*, presented at ATSA's Nineteenth Annual Research and Treatment Conference in San Diego, Ca., Nov. 3, 2000.

[19] *Supra* note 2.

[20] Turay v. Weston, *supra* note 2, Order on Plaintiff's Renewed Motion for Injunctive Relief and Contempt, and Defendants' Motion for Release From Injunction, Feb. 4, 1997.

[21] Findings of Fact, *supra* note 3.

[22] E.g., ATSA, *supra* note 14.

[23] *See* Youngberg v. Romeo, 457 U.S. 307 (1982).

[24] *See* Chapter 5, this volume.

[25] "Guidelines for the Development of New Programs," in A. Schlank & F. Cohen (Eds.), *The Sexual Predator: Law, Policy, Evaluation, and Treatment* (1999).

[26] F.H. Knopp, *Retraining Adult Sex Offenders: Methods and Models* (1984); J.K. Marques, *An Innovative Treatment Program for Sex Offenders: Report to the Legislature* (California Department of Mental Health, 1984).

[27] V.L. Quinsey, *Review of the Washington State Special Commitment Center Program for Sexually Violent Predators* (1992), *reprinted as* Appendix 1 in J.Q. La Fond, "Washington's Sexually Violent Predator Law: A Deliberate Misuse of the Therapeutic State for Social Control," 15 *U. Puget Sound L. Rev.* 655–708, at 706.

[28] Findings of Fact, *supra* note 3, at 12.

[29] *E.g.*, J.K. Marques, *Thirteenth Report of the Special Master*, Turay v. Seling, *supra* note 1, May 14, 1998; and *Sixteenth Report of the Special Master*, Turay v. Seling, Sept. 9, 1999.

[30] A.T. DesLauriers & J. Gardner, "The Sexual Predator Treatment Program of Kansas," in A. Schlank & F. Cohen (Eds.), *The Sexual Predator: Law, Policy, Evaluation, and Treatment* (1999).

Chapter 3

Admissibility of Expert Testimony in Sexually Violent Predator Proceedings

by John Petrila, J.D., L.L.M. and Randy K. Otto, Ph.D.*

Introduction	3-2
Evidentiary Requirements	3-3
The *Frye* Rule	3-3
The *Daubert* Rule	3-4
Federal Rules of Evidence	3-5
Evidentiary Challenges to Expert Clinical Testimony	3-5
Assessment Methods	3-6
Clinical Assessment	3-6
Anamnestic Assessment	3-6
Guided or Structured Clinical Assessment	3-6
Actuarial and Adjusted Actuarial Assessments	3-7
Arguments Against Adjusted Estimates	3-7
Perceived Reliability	3-8
Use in SVP Assessments	3-8
Statutory Requirements and Challenges to Expert Clinical Testimony	3-8
History of Sexual Offending	3-9
"Sexual Nature" of Nonsexual Offense	3-9
Expert's "Special Knowledge" Requirement	3-10
Presence of a Mental Disorder That Is Causally Related to Sex Offending	3-11
Lack of Control	3-13
Modified Lack of Control Standard	3-13
State's Burden of Proof	3-14

---

* Address correspondence regarding this chapter to the authors at 13301 Bruce B. Downs Blvd., Tampa, Florida, 33612; petrila@fmhi.usf.edu; otto@fmhi.usf.edu.

    Risk for Sexual Reoffending 3-14
        Issue of Expert's Ability to Assess Risk 3-14
        No Assessment Approach Considered Illegal 3-14
        Minnesota's Structured Approach 3-15
        Attacks on Expert Testimony 3-17
    Florida's Rejection of Actuarial Instruments 3-19
        Use of *Frye* Test to Determine Exclusion 3-19
        Scrutiny of "Scientific Principle" 3-20
    Getting Beyond the Appearances of Scientific Judgment 3-20
Summary and Conclusions 3-21

INTRODUCTION

In 1991, the Washington legislature passed the first of a new generation of sexual offender laws. While "sexual psychopath" laws of the 1930s and 1940s allowed for indeterminate civil commitment of sexual offenders as an alternative to criminal disposition,[1] newer laws provide for indeterminate civil commitment of sexual offenders, most typically subsequent to criminal disposition. In the past decade, approximately 20 states have passed "sexually violent predator" (SVP) statutes.[2]

The new SVP statutes have been challenged on a variety of grounds:

1. *Definition of "mental illness."* One argument is that the statutes define mental illness too broadly and employ definitions different from those included in traditional civil commitment laws. Persons subject to such laws argue that because the SVP laws have been characterized as civil commitment statutes, they should employ the more restrictive definitions of mental illness found in state commitment statutes.

2. *Lack of available treatment.* Another challenge focuses on the lack of available treatment, with critics of the SVP statutes arguing that the lack of good treatment in the facilities to which sex offenders are committed indicates that the state is more interested in detaining those subject to the law than in rehabilitating them.

3. *Future dangerousness predictions.* A third criticism of the SVP laws is that the statutes require a prediction of future dangerousness or reoffense risk that cannot be made with any accuracy.

4. *Constitutional violations.* A fourth argument is that these statutes violate constitutional guarantees against double jeopardy and ex post facto punishment.[3]

As we know, the U.S. Supreme Court ultimately considered the constitutionality of such statutes in *Kansas v. Hendricks*,[4] ruling in a 5-4 vote that Kansas's indeterminate commitment statute was constitutional. In its decision, the Court rejected arguments that the Kansas statute's use of the term "mental abnormality" rather than "mental illness" made the act exceed the authority of the legislature. The Kansas law defined "mental abnormality" as a congenital or acquired condition affecting the emotional or volitional capacity which predisposes the person to commit sexually violent offenses in a degree constituting such person a menace to the health and safety of others.[5]

The Court asserted that

[T]he term "mental illness" is devoid of any talismanic significance. Not only do "psychiatrists disagree widely and frequently on what constitutes mental illness," but the Court itself has used a variety of expressions to describe the mental condition of those properly subject to civil confinement."[6]

Given the Court's decision in *Hendricks*, the constitutional validity of SVP legislation appears assured. However, there are continuing challenges to the application of SVP laws in specific cases, a number of which focus on the basis for and validity of clinical testimony. There has also been continuing discussion in the courts regarding the reliability and validity of clinical testimony, and the various approaches examiners take to clinical assessment and the different assessment instruments they use. In this chapter, we describe and discuss clinical assessment approaches used in SVP evaluations and review legal challenges to expert opinions offered in the context of SVP hearings. We begin first with a brief discussion of the legal principles governing the admissibility of scientific testimony.

EVIDENTIARY REQUIREMENTS

The *Frye* Rule

Courts serve as the gatekeeper in determining whether expert testimony will be admitted into evidence, and they rely on a number of legal rules in making this determination. Historically, the most common rule has been the *Frye* rule. In *Frye v. United States*,[7] a federal court ruled that expert testimony based on a precursor of the polygraph was inadmissible in a criminal proceeding. The court observed that

[W]hile the courts will go a long way in admitting expert testimony deduced from a well-recognized scientific principle or discovery, the thing from which the deduction is made must be sufficiently established to have gained general acceptance in the particular field in which it belongs.[8]

The *Frye* rule, also known as the general acceptance test, directs that the courts will admit testimony that is accepted as scientifically grounded by the pertinent professional field. Interpretations based on the Minnesota Multiphasic Personality Inventory (MMPI-2), a structured measure of psychopathology and behavior that is a core assessment instrument, are one example of expert opinion that has passed the *Frye* test.

The *Frye* test has been criticized on a number of grounds.[9] Some critics offer that the test is too conservative, as it may bar acceptance of a new technique which has yet to be "generally accepted" by the relevant field or discipline. At the same time it has been criticized as too liberal, as a particular technique may gain "general acceptance" despite questionable scientific grounding. An example of the former problem is that testimony based on a series of well-validated measures designed to assess a defendant's comprehension of *Miranda* warnings[10] is excluded in some jurisdictions because some clinical psychologists and psychiatrists are not familiar with the measures. An example of the latter is that testimony based on invalidated or poorly validated assessment techniques (e.g., human figure drawings) is routinely admitted because the instruments are used by many psychologists and psychiatrists.

Finally, the *Frye* test has been criticized because of the difficulty both in defining "general acceptance" and ascertaining exactly when it occurs and in identifying the "particular field" to be considered when trying to determine general acceptance. For example, in a recent Florida SVP case that considered the admissibility of testimony regarding reoffense risk based on actuarial instruments,[11] a trial judge described as "without merit" the state's argument that the "relevant scientific community" when determining general acceptance was limited solely to those mental health professionals who conduct SVP evaluations. The court added that "absurd" conclusions could be reached if the state's argument was accepted, noting that in another context the court would not limit its inquiry solely to polygraph examiners when attempting to determine the general acceptance of the polygraph.

The *Daubert* Rule

Despite its critics and its limitations, the *Frye* rule continues to be used in many jurisdictions. However, in 1993, the U.S. Supreme Court reconsidered how the federal courts should go about determining admissibility of expert testimony based on scientific knowledge in the case *Daubert v. Merrell Dow Pharmaceuticals*.[12] The *Daubert* rule, stemming from the Court's opinion, has become the standard for admitting expert testimony in the federal courts and in a growing number of state jurisdictions. The Court held here that courts should consider four factors when deciding whether to admit scientifically based expert testimony:

- Testability or falsifiability using the scientific method;
- Whether error rates are known;
- Whether the matter at issue has been subjected to peer review and publication; and
- General acceptance in the relevant field (the core of the *Frye* standard).[13]

The *Daubert* rule, stemming from the Court's opinion, has become the standard for admitting expert testimony in the federal courts and in a growing number of state jurisdictions. Subsequent decisions[14] suggest that the rule also applies to testimony based on clinical expertise and experience, including testimony of mental health professionals.[15]

The *Daubert* case generally is read as focusing on the validity of scientific evidence, a standard that might lead to different results than *Frye* in some circumstances. For example, under *Daubert*, a newer but well-validated test might be admitted more readily than under *Frye* (see, for example, the discussion of the *Miranda* waiver instruments above). More importantly, the *Daubert* standard appears to give the court more discretion in deciding whether to admit some types of evidence. Testimony based on a procedure that might be generally accepted in a particular field or discipline may not pass the validity test at the heart of *Daubert*, but a new technique that is scientifically sound yet not "generally accepted" by the discipline may.

Federal Rules of Evidence

It is worth noting that the *Daubert* decision applied the Federal Rules of Evidence, which have also had a significant impact on the development of state evidentiary rules. The Federal Rules provide the foundation for determining admissibility in the federal system and in those states adopting *Daubert*. Federal Rule 401 provides that "relevant evidence" means evidence " having any tendency to make the existence of any fact that is of consequence to the determination of the action more probable or less probable than it would be without the evidence." This language ("having any tendency") creates a broad gate for admissibility of evidence in general.

Federal Rule 403, which provides that even relevant evidence "may be excluded if its probative value is substantially outweighed by the danger of unfair prejudice, confusion of the issues, or misleading the jury," allows the court to exclude testimony that while helpful to decision-makers, may inappropriately bias or confuse them.

Federal Rule 703 states that

> [I]f scientific, technical, or other specialized knowledge will assist the trier of fact to understand the evidence or to determine a fact in issue, a witness qualified as an expert by knowledge, skill, experience, training, or education may testify thereto in the form of an opinion or otherwise.

This rule establishes the basic criteria for introducing expert testimony. It identifies the minimal requirements regarding both the content of the expert testimony (it must address complicated issues that are beyond the understanding of the decision-maker) and the consideration of who is expert (the expert must have knowledge that the decision-maker does not, as a function of the expert's experience, education, training, or skill).

Federal Rule 704 directs that "testimony in the form of an opinion or inference otherwise inadmissible is not objectionable because it embraces an ultimate issue to be decided by the trier of fact . . . .." This rule permits the testifying experts to offer opinions on the legal issue at hand, a subject of much controversy within the law and psychology field.[16]

EVIDENTIARY CHALLENGES TO EXPERT CLINICAL TESTIMONY

In proceedings conducted under SVP laws, there have been a number of challenges, under both the *Frye* and *Daubert* standards, to the admissibility of testimony based on a variety of clinical assessment approaches. These challenges arise in large measure because in many cases, expert testimony offered by mental health professionals provides important evidence regarding the legal questions that must be decided under SVP statutes. Before discussing those legal challenges, it is useful to briefly discuss the different types of clinical assessment techniques that inform clinical opinion.

Mental health professionals who conduct SVP evaluations use a variety of assessment procedures and techniques including traditional clinical assessment, anamnestic assessment, structured or guided clinical assessment, actuarial assessment, and adjusted actuarial assessment.[17] These procedures and techniques have a variety of both strengths and weaknesses.

Assessment Methods

Clinical assessment, anamnestic assessment, and guided clinical assessment, described below, are traditional and well-accepted assessment approaches that mental health professionals use in their everyday practice. Testimony based on these assessment approaches is typically admitted in a variety of legal proceedings in which an individual's mental state is an issue, and such testimony is rarely challenged. Proceedings may involve criminal competence, criminal responsibility, sentencing, child custody, personal injury, guardianship, testamentary capacity, worker's compensation, or some similar issue. The existence of research identifying the limitations of these approaches generally, and their limitations in assessing risk for sexual reoffending specifically,[18] in combination with the existence of alternative evaluation methods specifically for sex offender assessment, has resulted in challenges to the validity of such recidivism risk assessment within the context of SVP statutes. As we will see, these challenges have been generally unsuccessful.

Clinical Assessment. Mental health professionals have historically used the clinical assessment approach. With this approach, the examiner gathers and processes test data, interview data, and historical information and then offers his or her opinions, impressions, and judgments about the examinee. This is a relatively unstructured approach by which examiners gather any information they consider relevant and use it to inform their clinical opinions. As a result, the assessment process and corresponding opinions may vary considerably among examiners. Although this likely lack of reliability in technique limits the validity of opinions formed on the basis of this assessment approach, the courts have historically admitted testimony based on this approach.

Anamnestic Assessment. Anamnestic assessment is a specific type of clinical assessment whereby the examiner attempts to identify risk factors through a detailed review of the examinee's history. Using information gathered via clinical interview, record review, and perhaps testing, the examiner focuses on themes or commonalities in the examinee's behaviors, which the examiner then uses to identify risk or protective factors. This approach is likely to suffer from the same kinds of limitations as general clinical assessment.

Guided or Structured Clinical Assessment. In a guided or structured clinical assessment, the examiner must still gather and process information gained during the course of a clinical evaluation, but in contrast to general clinical assessment, the data he or she seeks and considers is identified a priori as a function of empirically demonstrated relationships to the risk in question.[19] Although the examiner's clinical judgment is still necessary, the data on which the judgments are based have some empirically established predictive value. Judgments made using this structured approach should be more reliable across examiners and thus have the potential to be more valid than judgments based on unstructured clinical assessment. Judgments using this technique should also be more valid to the degree that the factors the examiner considers indeed have some relationship to the risk question at hand.

Actuarial and Adjusted Actuarial Assessments

In contrast to the various clinical assessment techniques described above, examiners using an actuarial assessment approach offer opinions, judgments, classifications, or predictions based on fixed and explicit rules.[20] Actuarial formulae can include general static factors that do not change (e.g., sex), historical static factors that cannot change (e.g., offense history, history of abuse), and dynamic or changeable factors (e.g., current problems with substance abuse, completion of a sex offender treatment program). Assuming that the formula items reliably lend themselves to scoring by examiners, then at the very least, an actuarial approach should provide more reliable clinical judgments than the considerably less structured clinical assessment approaches described above. However, the inter-rater reliability of such formulae cannot be assumed.[21] In the cases *In re Keinitz*[22] and *People v. Poe*,[23] experts calculated different actuarial values using the same clinical information.

Over the past six years, researchers have developed a number of actuarial instruments designed to identify an offender's risk for recidivating, for example: the Rapid Risk Assessment for Sexual Offense Recidivism, or RRASOR;[24] the Minnesota Sex Offender Screening Tool and Revised Screening Tool, or MnSOST and MnSOST-R;[25] the Sex Offender Risk Appraisal Guide, or SORAG;[26] and the Static-99.[27] Although there is considerable variability among the measures, all provide estimates of a sex offender's likelihood for reoffending within a specified period of time based on a variety of static and dynamic factors.

It is generally agreed that all of these instruments consist primarily of static (i.e., nonchanging) factors, meaning that scores that are obtained for offenders (and the associated risk estimates) are not likely to change much over time (e.g., after treatment, after a period of nonoffending, with age).

"Pure" actuarial decision-making—complete reliance on formulas to make decisions—is rarely if ever used in general clinical practice or in forensic practice. This is probably due in part to the fact that only a limited number of actuarial tests exist, each intended for use in only limited circumstances. In addition clinicians, including those who advocate the use of actuarial formulae, are often reluctant to accept the results of actuarial tests at face value without the opportunity to modify predictions after considering factors not accounted for by the actuarial formulae. This means that in practice, almost all clinicians who employ actuarial instruments use an "adjusted actuarial" approach. Hanson has described this as an approach in which the clinician "begins with an actuarial prediction, but expert evaluators can then adjust (or not) the actuarial prediction after considering potentially important factors that were not included in the actuarial measure."[28]

Arguments Against Adjusted Estimates. Proponents of the strict actuarial method argue against "adjustment" of actuarial estimates, noting that research has demonstrated that adjusted decisions are typically no more accurate and may be less accurate than those made by the actuarial equation alone.[29] Indeed, the logic of using a "clinically adjusted actuarial approach" seems a bit strained insofar as the examiner uses an actuarial procedure rather than a clinical assessment procedure because of the former's presumed superiority, only to then take the actuarial findings and "correct" them using assumedly inferior clinical judgment. In reality, the intrusion of clinical judgment into the actuarial decision-making process means that the process is, by definition, no longer actuarial.

Perceived Reliability. Although actuarial methods have the *potential* to produce more reliable and more valid decisions than those made using clinical methods,[30] there is in fact little evidence that actuarial judgments of risk for violent or sexual reoffending are more reliable or valid than other types of assessments for reoffending. One literature review does suggest that actuarial predictions of sexual violence are more accurate than predictions based on traditional or unstructured clinical assessments,[31] but this conclusion is based on a review of only sixteen studies, none of which directly compare actuarial and clinical decisions in the same sample. Also, the predictive validity estimates offered for some of the actuarial methods likely over-estimate their true predictive validity, as some of the instruments have not been cross-validated, which typically results in lower estimates of predictive validity. It is worth noting that actuarial methods appear to be only slightly (if at all) more accurate than decisions based on structured or guided clinical predictions.[32] Perhaps most important, there is no data on the validity of *adjusted* actuarial assessment of risk for sexual reoffending, the technique used by almost all professionals who employ actuarial tests in their assessments.[33]

Use in SVP Assessments. Reliance on actuarial instruments may be challenged for a number of reasons. First, as noted above, actuarial decision-making is rarely if ever used by mental health professionals in any other context. Clinicians' day-to-day decisions regarding diagnosis, treatment, or violence risk assessment are not based on actuarial tests or instruments. Actuarial assessment may be considered by some to be a novel assessment approach that is not generally accepted for purposes of mental health assessment. On the other hand, there is anecdotal evidence that these instruments are used on a regular basis by mental health professionals who conduct SVP evaluations.[34]

Use of actuarial instruments may also be challenged on the grounds that while showing some potential, the approach has not demonstrated adequate reliability and validity and fails to meet basic assessment standards set out in the *Standards for Educational and Psychological Testing*.[35] Campbell[36] and Otto, Borum, and Hart[37] argue that before actuarial instruments can be used in SVP evaluations, their reliability and validity must be demonstrated. Although the validity of some actuarial instruments has been demonstrated, considerable questions remain. Campbell and Otto et al. also argue against use of these instruments prior to peer review and without the provision of basic supporting documentation such as test manuals.

STATUTORY REQUIREMENTS AND CHALLENGES TO EXPERT CLINICAL TESTIMONY

Although there is some variability in the structure of SVP laws across states, most follow a similar format. All states require (1) a history of sexual offending, (2) the presence of a mental abnormality or mental disorder, and (3) an increased risk for sexual reoffending, as a function of the predicate or underlying mental disorder. Some statutes require a finding that the SVP has an inability to control his sexual offenses, and others require a finding of impaired control. Each of these elements may result in the production of and challenge to clinical testimony.

History of Sexual Offending

Under all SVP statutes, an individual who is subject to civil commitment must have some history of sexual offending, typically defined in terms of prior convictions or pleas for sexual offenses. Of the SVP statutory legal prongs, this is the least likely to involve expert testimony. Rather, satisfaction of this requirement is likely to hinge on the respondent's history of arrests and convictions.

Although a majority of states do not specify a minimum number of convictions necessary for eligibility,[38] some do, presumably in an attempt to limit the pool of potential committees. For example, California requires conviction for offenses against two or more victims.[39] A conviction or guilty plea for a sexual offense is not required in all states, however. In Florida, for example, persons found not guilty of sexual offenses by reason of insanity are subject to the law, as are juveniles who have been adjudicated delinquent in regard to sexual offenses.[40] Persons charged with or convicted of seemingly nonsexual offenses that are nonetheless considered to be "sexually motivated" can also be committed as SVPs.

"Sexual Nature" of Nonsexual Offense. While the majority of SVP commitments are likely to be pursued based on a conviction for or plea to a sexual offense of some type, it is conceivable that a mental health professional might offer "expert testimony" about whether a nonsexual offense was sexual in nature or sexually motivated. For example, in Florida, because nonsexual offenses can form the basis of an SVP commitment, a state attorney might seek to have a mental health professional offer an opinion that a seemingly nonsexual offense such as burglary or simple assault was actually sexually motivated.

At least one case has addressed the issue of expert testimony on the question of whether an offense was sexually motivated, and the two appellate courts hearing the case differed in their reasoning on the issue. In *State v. Watson*,[41] the examinee, after completing a long prison sentence after pleading guilty to a charge of false imprisonment, challenged a petition by the State of Wisconsin that sought to confine him under the state's SVP law on expiration of his prison term. The Wisconsin statute permitted confinement of persons who had been convicted of a sexually violent offense and had a mental disorder that made it substantially probable that the person would engage in acts of sexual violence. As defined by Wisconsin law, a "sexually violent offense" could be either a sexual crime or, as in *Watson*, a "sexually motivated" offense.

The court of appeals affirmed the trial court's dismissal of the state's petition against Watson on the ground that the state did not show probable cause that the offense was sexually motivated.[42] At the initial hearing in trial court, the state's only witness was a psychologist who diagnosed the defendant as suffering from a paraphilia and testified that Watson's false imprisonment of the victim was sexually motivated, a necessary criterion for the state to meet because false imprisonment itself is not a sexual offense. On cross-examination, the expert acknowledged that his opinion rested entirely on a statement the victim had made to a probation officer in a presentence investigation conducted in 1980—fourteen years prior to the hearing in which the psychologist testified. In the statement in question, the victim reported to the probation officer that the defendant had stated "Now you are going to suck me off, bitch." The psychologist testified that his conclusion that the act was sexually motivated was based solely on the alleged statement of the respondent. The state initially attempted to have the psychologist discuss the statement as a lay witness, not as an expert, but was prevented from admitting the statement because it was hearsay. So the prosecutor had the psychologist testify as an expert, thereby allowing for a hearsay exception since it formed the basis of his (expert) opinion. The trial court subsequently dismissed the state's petition, in large measure because the expert's opinion had been based on hearsay contained within a document that itself was hearsay.

Expert's "Special Knowledge" Requirement. The court of appeals[43] agreed that the petition should be dismissed but for somewhat different reasons. The appellate court questioned whether the psychologist's opinion should be afforded the weight given "expert" opinion, as an expert's opinion had to depend on "special knowledge or skill or experience . . . not within the ordinary experience of [hu]mankind." The court held that that standard could not be met on the issue of sexual motivation, because the opinion rested simply on a hearsay observation made by a layperson. In addition, the appellate court ruled that because the statement the psychologist relied on was hearsay, there was no ability to test the underlying reliability of the opinion.

However, the Wisconsin Supreme Court reversed the court of appeals, finding that the psychologist *could* testify as an expert in these circumstances and that the state had produced sufficient evidence to meet its probable cause burden.[44] The court ruled that

> [A]n expert ought to be able to draw reasonable inferences from facts, an expert ought to be able to show how a person's offense relates to the person's purported mental disorder, explaining both consistencies and inconsistencies, interpreting the person's statements and explanations . . . and offering an analysis of whether there is a consistent pattern of conduct in the person's experience which reveals sexual motivation and intent.[45]

The court also ruled that an expert could rely on hearsay in forming and providing his or her opinion.

Although the Wisconsin Supreme Court concluded that a psychologist could provide expert opinion on whether an offense was sexually motivated, it is less clear to us that such an opinion should be considered "expert." The psychologist in *Watson* admitted that he based his "expert opinion" on a single statement purportedly made by the examinee and relayed to a probation officer by the victim. He also acknowledged that he did not assume the statement to be true and that he did not reach an independent conclusion about its veracity. Given this, in combination with the explicit nature of the defendant's statement, it seems doubtful that the expert's interpretation of the statement and his associated opinion about the examinee's motivation was based on knowledge or experience not held by laypersons. In addition, there is little evidence that mental health professionals have a scientifically reliable and valid way of assessing motivation, either in general or with respect to sexual behavior.

At a minimum, the witness called to testify as an expert on issues of motivation should anticipate a challenge to "expert" status and, if qualified as an expert, make clear the limitations on testimony regarding whether an offense is sexually motivated. In addition, as in other forensic settings, experts should be cognizant of the fact that the parties, particularly the state, may attempt to use them as a vehicle for putting hearsay material before the court that might otherwise be inadmissible. Although under Federal Rule of Evidence 703 experts generally may rely on hearsay in formulating their opinions, the expert should be wary of being used primarily as a subterfuge for the admission of otherwise inadmissible testimony.

Presence of a Mental Disorder That Is Causally Related to Sex Offending

All SVP laws require the presence of a mental disorder or mental abnormality of some type, although the terminology and definitions employed vary across jurisdictions. A review of the various state statutes makes clear that the definition of mental disorder in SVP statutes is typically broader and more expansive than in similar types of statutes with predicate mental disorder requirements (e.g., general civil commitment, insanity). For purposes of commitment as an SVP, Florida law defines mental abnormality expansively as "a mental condition affecting a person's emotional or volitional capacity which predisposes the person to commit sexually violent offenses," and it specifically references personality disorders as a predicate condition.[46] In contrast, Florida's civil commitment law limits the predicate condition to mental illness, which it defines as "an impairment of the emotional processes that exercise conscious control of one's actions or of the ability to perceive or understand reality"; it specifically excludes "conditions manifested only by antisocial behavior or substance abuse impairment."[47]

Expert testimony is an integral aspect of this legal requirement and it may be challenged in a number of ways, as discussed below.

    1. *Formal diagnosis.* First, the defense may challenge the expert's formal diagnosis. Most experts will offer a diagnosis grounded in the latest version of the *Diagnostic and Statistical Manual of Mental Disorders* (DSM-IV).[48] Although defense attorneys may challenge the reliability[49] and validity of the diagnostic system in general,[50] such challenges are unlikely to be successful[51] given the courts' history of accepting DSM-based diagnoses in essentially all types of cases in which an individual's mental state is at issue and expert testimony is admitted (e.g., criminal competence, criminal responsibility, sentencing, child custody, personal injury, guardianship, testamentary capacity, worker's compensation).

    2. *Diagnoses outside the DSM.* Diagnoses that are not included within the DSM may be more vulnerable to challenge. Most forensic examiners will address the issue of psychopathy, given its relationship to general criminal offending and sexual offending,[52] and some examinees referred for commitment may receive a diagnosis of Personality Disorder Not Otherwise Specified—Psychopathy or be described as having psychopathic traits. Because psychopathy is not included in the main body of the DSM-IV or the appendix, challenges to this diagnosis and concept may be expected, but such challenges are unlikely to prove successful[53] given the research literature supporting such conceptualization[54] and the courts' general deference on diagnostic issues.

3. *Specific diagnoses.* In addition to challenges to the basic diagnostic system and diagnoses not included within the DSM, there may be challenges to specific diagnoses. Most often contested may be diagnoses related to the various sexual disorders—pedophilia and other paraphilias, sexual sadism, or sexual disorder not otherwise specified. Experts may anticipate considerable energy being focused on their conclusions about the examinee's deviant sexual interest, a DSM requirement for many of the sexual disorder diagnoses that are likely to form the basis of an SVP commitment.[55] In those cases where some type of sexual disorder diagnosis is offered, the examiner will often infer that the examinee does indeed harbor deviant sexual interests (as opposed to simply engaging in the sexual behavior for other reasons). Cases in which an examinee has previously admitted to deviant sexual interests or where plethysmograph data are available may provide exceptions to this general rule. Although this area of testimony is perhaps most vulnerable to attack and challenge given how conclusions about deviant sexual interest are arrived at in the majority of cases, it has received little attention in appellate cases.

4. *Connection of disorder to reoffense risk.* In addition to the above, challenges may be offered regarding the connection between the underlying mental disorder or diagnosis offered by the expert and the examinee's risk for sexual offending. In most states, presence of a mental disorder and risk for reoffending is not enough; there must be a causal relationship between the two. While the connection between sexual offending and paraphilias such as pedophilia is apparent and not particularly vulnerable to challenge, the connection between sexual offending and a variety of other diagnoses—such as substance abuse or dependence, antisocial personality disorder, or borderline personality disorder—is less clear.

5. *Diagnosis outside relevant statutory definition.* The expert may also be vulnerable to a challenge (or find his or her testimony judged unpersuasive) if the expert's opinion or diagnosis is not anchored in the relevant statutory definition or on judicial modification of the statutory definition. For example, in the case *In re Linehan*,[56] a defendant successfully challenged a commitment under Minnesota's SVP law on the ground that the diagnostic material provided by the state's experts did not meet the definition of a psychopathic condition *as modified by the Minnesota Supreme Court.* Although the state's experts both testified that Linehan met the statutory definition of a psychopathic personality, the Minnesota Supreme Court reversed Linehan's commitment in large part because the experts did not refer in their testimony to the definition that the U.S. Supreme Court had articulated several decades earlier in considering the constitutionality of Minnesota's first-generation SVP law. The Supreme Court had ruled that the law could only apply if a trial court found

1. A "habitual course of misconduct in sexual matters" and
2. "[A]n utter lack of power to control . . . sexual impulses" so that
3. [I]t is likely the person will "attack or otherwise inflict injury, loss, pain or other evil on the objects of [his] uncontrolled and uncontrollable desire."[57]

Because the experts' testimony had not been grounded in this judicial modification of the statutory definition, the experts did not provide the necessary proof for the "utter lack of . . . control" embedded in the judicial definition. Therefore, the Minnesota Supreme Court ruled that the trial court's order committing Linehan was based on inadequate evidence.

This decision reveals the importance of understanding the relationship between clinical diagnoses and *legal* definitions that incorporate diagnoses. As noted above, SVP laws do not rely wholly on a diagnosis as a trigger for commitment, nor, as the U.S. Supreme Court made clear in *Hendricks*, does a state law even have to rely on traditional notions of mental illness or diagnostic nomenclature. Therefore it is important that mental health professionals conducting such assessments and providing expert testimony understand the interplay between traditional diagnosis and the state law definitions that control judicial decision making in this context.

Lack of Control

A number of state SVP laws require a link between the person's mental disorder and a loss or lack of volitional control. For example, one of the two Minnesota laws requires an "utter lack of power to control" sexual impulses. Of course, the focus on volitional control and impairment is not limited to SVP laws; for example, the "irresistible impulse" prong of the insanity defense, which is used in approximately twenty jurisdictions,[58] requires an assessment of whether the defendant's actions were beyond his or her control or volition. The issue of volition is a difficult one for mental health professionals to address in a variety of spheres, in part because it is a legal as well as clinical issue and in part because even the best clinical efforts to make sense of it are problematic. In a position paper on the insanity defense, the American Psychiatric Association characterized the problem in this manner:

> The line between an irresistible impulse and an impulse not resisted is probably no sharper than that between twilight and dusk. . . . The concept of volition is the subject of some disagreement among psychiatrists. Many psychiatrists therefore believe that psychiatric testimony (particularly that of a conclusory nature) about volition is more likely to produce confusion for jurors than is psychiatric testimony relevant to a defendant's appreciation or understanding.[59]

The question of a lack of control or impaired control has been litigated primarily in Minnesota, undoubtedly because of a decision by the Minnesota Supreme Court that a finding of an "utter lack of control" was a necessary predicate to commitment. In a recent review of Minnesota cases, Held[60] reported that despite this requirement, Minnesota courts had upheld commitments even in situations in which the defendant had "groomed" his victims or otherwise planned his assaults. This appears to reflect judicial realism that a literal application of a standard of "utter lack of control" might effectively nullify the statute, given the difficulties in meeting such a standard.

Modified Lack of Control Standard. Other courts have rejected arguments that an SVP law that incorporates a volitional element must necessarily be read as creating an "irresistible impulse" standard. In *Kansas v. Hendricks*,[61] the Supreme Court held that for a person to be committed under the Kansas statute, the person's mental abnormality or personality disorder must make it "difficult, if not impossible, for the person to control his dangerous behavior."[62] A Washington respondent in an SVP proceeding argued that this language meant that Washington's statute, which is similar to the Kansas statute, must be interpreted as incorporating the irresistible impulse standard.[63] The reason the subject of the petition made this argument is that the Washington courts had previously rejected the irresistible impulse prong of the insanity defense. If the respondent in *Thorell* argued successfully that the SVP statute incorporated an irresistible impulse test, then his commitment under that statute could be invalidated because the Washington courts rejected that test in criminal law. However, the court of appeals rejected the claim as being without merit.

State's Burden of Proof. When a defendant claims an irresistible impulse as the basis for an insanity defense, he generally bears the burden of demonstrating that he suffered from an irresistible impulse. However, in an SVP hearing the state must demonstrate (at least under one of Minnesota's laws) that the defendant's conduct was virtually irresistible. Because a failure on the part of the state to meet its burden may result in freedom for an individual who has committed sexual offenses, courts may be more willing in assessing the state's case to read the record expansively to find that the defendant lacks enough control to meet the statutory criteria. Similarly, the courts may allow mental health professionals considerable leeway when offering testimony related to control and impulsivity.

Risk for Sexual Reoffending

The greatest focus of legal challenges to expert testimony in SVP hearings is on the issue of risk assessment, in terms not only of the examiner's conclusions, but of the tools he or she relied on in forming those opinions. Expert testimony regarding examinees' risk for reoffending is best understood when placed in historical context.

Issue of Expert's Ability to Assess Risk. The ability of mental health professionals to assess violence risk generally and to identify persons at increased risk for violent offending has received considerable attention from the courts.[64] This may be due in part to the extensive professional literature that has been critical of mental health professionals' abilities in this area, including that of Ennis & Litwack[65] and Ennis & Emery,[66] who offer the most stinging [and most biased] criticism. R. K. Otto provides a review of the history and context of this debate.[67]

Despite some agreement about the limited ability of mental health professionals to assess risk for violence, the courts have consistently allowed such testimony. For example, in *Barefoot v. Estelle*,[68] perhaps the most significant case regarding the ability of mental health professionals to assess violence risk, the U.S. Supreme Court acknowledged the limited abilities of such professionals in this arena yet ruled that their testimony was permissible, noting, "The suggestion that no psychiatrist's testimony may be presented with respect to a defendant's future dangerousness is somewhat like asking us to disinvent the wheel."[69] In this context, then, it should be expected that while the courts may scrutinize the ability of mental health professionals to assess risk for sexual violence and reoffending, the courts will ultimately permit such testimony, regardless of their perception that it is limited or problematic.

No Assessment Approach Considered Illegal. One issue the courts have been asked to resolve is whether examiners must use a specific approach. As might be expected, in some cases respondents have challenged clinical assessment techniques, while in others, they have challenged actuarial and adjusted actuarial techniques. The courts generally have been reluctant to exclude expert testimony based on any technique. In *State v. Kienitz*,[70] the subject of an SVP commitment petition claimed that an expert testifying that reoffending was "substantially probable" (the Wisconsin standard) must base his or her opinion on an actuarial method. The three expert witnesses who testified in the case—two for the state and one for the defense—all diagnosed Kienitz as a pedophile. The state's experts based their conclusions that the respondent met the statutory standard for future risk on a review of correctional, psychiatric, and institutional records, but they were unable to interview Kienitz because he refused to participate. One state witness also used the Violence Risk Appraisal Guide[71] (VRAG) and testified that the respondent obtained a score similar to individuals who had a general violence recidivism rate of 44 percent in a seven-year period and a 58 percent rate over ten years. The expert further testified that he integrated the VRAG findings with impressions formed based on a review of the clinical record, suggesting use of an "adjusted actuarial" approach.[72]

The defense expert concluded that Kienitz presented only a 50-50 chance of reoffending and argued that the opinions of the state's witnesses were compromised because there was no scientific way to integrate the various factors correlated with recidivism and that they relied on clinical judgment to do so. He further argued that studies showed that recidivism predictions based on clinical judgment were accurate no better than between 50 percent and 52 percent of the time. Based on his scoring on the VRAG, which he presented as the most accurate risk assessment tool available, the psychologist called by the defense concluded that the respondent presented a 35 percent probability for reoffending over seven years and 48 percent probability over ten years.

In upholding the trial court's order committing the respondent as an SVP, the court of appeals rejected the defendant's argument that a purely actuarial approach was legally required. The court cited with approval an earlier opinion on this case by the Wisconsin Supreme Court that there was a "lack of consensus in the behavioral sciences on various issues relating to sex offenders"[73] and noted that the defendant's argument "not only obliterates the distinction between the legal standard and behavioral science standards, but, in essence, requires adherence to one particular behavioral science methodology."[74] The Wisconsin Supreme Court later affirmed the court of appeals ruling.[75]

Minnesota's Structured Approach. The Minnesota Supreme Court also rejected an attempt to make an actuarial approach to risk assessment legally required. In *In re Linehan*,[76] the court in a previous case had already created a comparatively structured approach to risk assessment. It instructed the trial courts, in considering whether an individual subject to commitment under the state's SVP law was a serious danger to the public, to consider the following factors:[77]

- The person's relevant demographic characteristics (e.g., age, education, and the like)

- The person's history of violent behavior (paying particular attention to recency, severity, and frequency of violent acts)

- Base rate statistics for violent behavior among individuals of this person's background (e.g., data showing the rate at which rapists recidivate, the correlation between age and criminal sexual activity, and similar statistics)
- The sources of stress in the environment (cognitive and affective factors that indicate that the person may be predisposed to cope with stress in a violent or nonviolent manner)
- The similarity of the present or future context to those contexts in which the person has used violence in the past
- The person's record with respect to sex therapy programs

A dissenting *Linehan* opinion crystallized the debate that occurs regarding the use of actuarial formulae or instruments in such circumstances. The dissenting judge stated, "I am at a loss to understand what the base rate statistics for violent behavior among individuals of this person's background . . . can possibly contribute with respect to predicting the seriousness of the danger to the public posed by the release of a certain person." This judge added that it is the record of habitual offending of the person in question that provides a basis for the legal prediction of serious danger to the public, not the behavior of others. The judge concluded by arguing that

[N]ot only are the statistics concerning the violent behavior of others irrelevant, but it seems to me wrong to confine any person on the basis not of that person's own prior conduct but on the basis of statistical evidence regarding the behavior of other people."[78]

In a subsequent case, the court made clear that despite the debate just noted, there was "no statutory or precedential support for the argument that actuarial methods or base rates are the sole permissible basis for prediction."[79] A Minnesota court of appeals decision further demonstrates the courts' reluctance to question the approach underlying expert opinions and puts the significance of statistical methods in proving risk predictions in perspective, noting that

[E]ven if [the respondent] could demonstrate that the statistical methods employed in some of the testing mechanisms (e.g., the Sex Offender Screening Tool (sic) or the Hare checklist) were wholly invalid and unreliable, that would not necessarily be determinative because the test results are only one part of all the evidence the court is to consider.[80]

In one Ohio SVP case the state did not present testimony from an expert, but relied largely on the testimony of a probation officer. A court of appeals rejected the respondent's argument that a sexual predator commitment *had* to rest on expert testimony.[81] The court then turned to the testimony of the defendant's two experts. These experts had based their testimony, in part, on results of the revised Hare Psychopathy Checklist and the MMPI-2 and had testified that mental health professionals could not predict the likelihood of future sexually oriented offenses "to any degree of scientific certainty." The court, in language suggestive of the U.S. Supreme Court in *Barefoot*, ruled that despite the experts' reservations about predicting future dangerousness, "[T]he legislature has nonetheless charged trial courts with the responsibility for doing so." The court then upheld the commitment, relying on the brutality of the defendant's offense (which had occurred twenty years earlier) as well as the defense expert's testimony that he had identified behavioral characteristics "arguably suggestive" of future sexual offending.

This case illustrates one potential pitfall for even the most conscientious of experts. Here, an apparent attempt by the defendant's experts to explain their reservations about predicting dangerousness were swept aside. Sections of the experts' testimony regarding the individual, which were drawn from the MMPI-2 and the PCL-R results, were then used to buttress the state's claim that the state's burden in fact had been met.

Attacks on Expert Testimony. Attorneys may also seek to bar testimony based on one or more actuarial assessment instruments on the ground that they fail to meet the requirements of the *Frye* test (Is the technique generally accepted within the pertinent field?) or the *Daubert* test (Is the technique of proven validity?). The questioning of an expert presented below illustrates an approach taken in a *Frye* jurisdiction in which the attorney sought to exclude opinions based on certain instruments, including the SORAG, the RRASOR, and the VRAG. These questions are taken from a transcript excerpted in a memorandum of law filed with the defense's *Frye* motion to exclude evidence. This motion resulted in a ruling excluding these instruments (*State v. Klein*,[82] discussed in more detail below):

> Q. So if we don't know how many of these individuals are going to recidivate within five years, we cannot say whether any particular individual who scores two on the RRASOR is going to recidivate within five years, or at all, from that data, right?
>
> A. Yes, sir. You're doing the right thing. You're pointing out that this instrument alone should not be solely relied upon to make that kind of decision.
>
> Q. To summarize then, do you have an opinion within a reasonable degree of scientific certainty as to whether any of these instruments, the RRASOR, the MnSOST, the MnSOST-R, the VRAG, the SORAG, the PCL-R, the PCL:SV, the MCMI-III, the MMPI-2, or the SVR-20, whether any of those instruments can predict within a reasonable degree of scientific certainty future sexual violence?
>
> A. . . . My opinion is that none of them have been demonstrated to do, with a significant enough degree, scientifically to have confidence that they are able to . . . I do not feel that any of these tests can predict with a sufficient degree of accuracy that they should be in any way depended upon.
>
> Q. Other than the narrow community of people who do evaluations of alleged violent sexual predators for the state, other than that small sub-group of people, is there any other scientific community or academic community or community of practitioners where these actuarial instruments are generally accepted for the prediction of future sexual violence?
>
> A. The answer is none that I know of. . . .
>
> Q. . . . If we take a number of screening tools, none of which has strong predictive validity, and we add them together, then what do we have?

A. Just a conclusion based on a lot of bad data.

This line of attack seeks to establish that the various instruments in question do not have widespread acceptance beyond the "sub-group" of evaluators who use them, and it focuses on the fact that the instruments cannot predict *individual* recidivism. This gets to a central argument in the debate over prediction versus risk assessment based on probabilities. Most would probably concede that probabilistic estimates are the best one can do in these circumstances, but SVP statutes focus on the individual (though usually asking probabilistic questions, such as whether the defendant is "more likely than not" or is "highly likely" to reoffend). It may be difficult in practice to integrate emerging professional standards, which emphasize probabilistic assessments, with statutory standards, which may emphasize individual predictions.

One court, deciding a *Frye* challenge to the SORAG and the RRASOR, ruled that these instruments were simply "refinements on the widely accepted VRAG, and that they utilized the same methodology."[83] Therefore, in the court's view, the *Frye* test was not relevant since the instruments relied on were neither new nor novel. Although the defense did not contest the experts' use of the VRAG, noting that it was widely accepted, had been "cross-validated," and was "found effective" in repeated studies, it challenged the experts' reliance on the RRASOR and SORAG and claimed that they failed to meet the requirements of *Frye*. The court (and state) seized on these concessions to side-step the *Frye* question on the grounds that the instruments were "refinements on the widely accepted VRAG . . . and they utilized the same methodology."[84]

The assessment instruments that have emerged in recent years provide, to varying degrees, at least a patina of scientific credibility to risk assessments. However, in purely legal terms, it appears that an approach that combines actuarial instruments with some form of clinical judgment provides a foundation for expert opinion that courts are reluctant to disturb. For example, in *People v. Poe*,[85] both state experts testified that the respondent's chance of reoffending over the next ten years, based on his RRASOR score, was less than 50 percent. The respondent argued that given this fact, it was not "likely" that he would reoffend and the state had not met its burden of proof. The court rejected this argument, noting:

> [I]t is unnecessary to engage in a debate about what minimum percent risk using this scale would support the conclusion that it is likely that person will reoffend, because all the experts who testified . . . *agreed that the numerical results of this scale should not be used in isolation when assessing the likelihood of reoffending.*"[86]

In *State v. Kienitz*,[87] discussed earlier, Wisconsin's state expert adopted an adjusted actuarial approach whereby he administered the VRAG and then integrated the score with "clinical information." This approach led the expert to adjust upward the respondent's risk for reoffending by "at least" 10 percent from the VRAG estimate. The defense expert relied solely on actuarial instruments and adopted a strict actuarial approach. Although the trial court found the defense expert's testimony to be more credible, it ruled that the evidence in general supported a finding that respondent met the SVP criteria.

In another Wisconsin case, *In re Wilson*,[88] the court of appeals characterized the defendant's score on the RRASOR as "highly predictive of future sexual offenses." In its conclusion that there was a high risk of reoffending, the court also noted the defendant's substance abuse, failure at treatment, and refusal of subsequent sex offender treatment. In *Kienitz*, a respondent argued that the trial court had inappropriately "double counted" factors associated with reoffending because it relied on the defendant's VRAG score (which includes both items that assess the examinee's history of arrests and correctional supervision failures) and then went on to cite independently the respondent's history of offenses and supervision failures and to conclude that the respondent was at even higher risk for reoffending than the VRAG estimates might suggest. The Wisconsin Supreme Court ruled that it was for the trier of fact to determine which evidence is credible and how much weight to afford it. Therefore, the issue the respondent raised went to matters within the trial court's discretion, and in the state supreme court's view there was "more than sufficient" evidence to prove beyond a reasonable doubt that the defendant was much more likely than not to reoffend.[89]

The VRAG and SORAG have also been challenged, unsuccessfully, as providing predictions of sexual violence that are "barely better than chance" and "just about the same as flipping coins."[90] The revised Hare Psychopathy Checklist,[91] a nonactuarial instrument for which there is good reliability and validity data in terms of increased risk for violent and nonviolent offending,[92] has also been challenged on the grounds that it has not been normed using African-American populations. This challenge, in a death penalty case, was also rejected by the courts.[93]

Florida's Rejection of Actuarial Instruments

Two cases in Florida go against the courts' general reluctance to bar expert testimony, regardless of its basis. In *State v. Klein*,[94] subsequent to an involved *Frye* hearing, the trial court granted the respondent's motion to exclude expert testimony based on results of the RRASOR, MnSOST and MnSOST-R. The trial judge ruled that "the test instruments do not possess the scientific reliability required under *Frye*, nor has the general acceptance of the test instruments been established in the relevant scientific community."

Use of *Frye* Test to Determine Exclusion. In a more sweeping opinion—*In re Valdez*[95]—a three judge panel ruled that the RRASOR, the MnSOST-R, the VRAG, the PCL-R, the SVR-20 and the Static 99 could not be admitted in hearings under Florida's sexual offender statute, nor could any testimony regarding or relying upon them be admitted. The court, applying the *Frye* test, considered use of these instruments a "new or novel scientific principle." Accordingly, it first determined whether the instruments or testimony based on them would assist the trier of fact. The court ruled that it would not because the instruments did not predict specific acts or offenses enumerated in the Florida sexual offender statute. The court then turned to the heart of the case, whether testimony based on these instruments was "based on a scientific principle or discovery that is sufficiently established to have gained general acceptance in the particular field to which it belongs." The court noted that it was difficult to ascertain precisely what the scientific principle at issue was: the court observed that the instruments themselves were not a scientific principle, nor was the use of the instruments a scientific principle. The court rejected the state's arguments that actuarial instruments were used elsewhere—for example, to screen for the risk of heart attack or suicide; the court noted that there was a difference between screening and prediction.

Scrutiny of "Scientific Principle." The court concluded that the scientific principle being advanced was that future criminal acts could be scientifically predicted; that such a prediction could be made solely on the basis of selected items of biographical and historical information about the individual; that a scoring system could be devised capturing relevant information; and that the scoring scheme could be applied "to any individual, anywhere, at any time, and it will . . . yield a prediction (of that individual's future criminal acts) which has some quantifiable degree of accuracy with respect to that individual." The court said that this proferred "scientific principle" was not generally accepted, citing testimony by an expert for the defendant that the American Psychiatric Association had concluded that long-term predictions of risk could not be reliably made. The court also rejected the State's argument that the relevant "field" for inquiry on the issue of general acceptance was the approximately 150 psychologists performing sex offender evaluations. The court said that such a small sample did not constitute "general acceptance," the heart of the *Frye* test.

Both Florida opinions are recent, and one can anticipate appeal of one if not both cases. The cases are the first to broadly reject the use of actuarial instruments in sex offender hearings and are worth noting for that reason.

Getting Beyond the Appearance of Scientific Judgment

Florida's questioning of the appearance of scientific scrutiny aside, the majority of court opinions to date suggest that appellate courts are generally unwilling to exclude opinions based on any of a variety of assessment techniques, and that they instead prefer to rely on the judgment of trial courts in deciding whether evidence is credible and should be admitted. It seems that the courts will allow examiners considerable leeway in determining how to go about conducting assessments. In general, the courts seem reluctant to apply the relevant rules (i.e., *Frye*, *Daubert*) with any force. Rather, they appear content to characterize concerns about the reliability and validity of assessment techniques as going to the weight of the *evidence*—a matter for the discretion of the trial court. Although some courts have struggled to understand the science on which the instruments are based, even if a court questions the reliability of a particular instrument in a particular case, the tendency is to find evidence "in the overall record" sufficient to prove that a defendant meets SVP criteria. This suggests that an expert who relies on both actuarial instruments and "clinical judgment" as bases for his or her opinion will be best equipped to withstand a legal challenge.

This does *not* suggest that such an approach is the most valid, but only that the courts seem most impressed by a mixture of evidence. We believe that the courts should more rigorously question the underlying bases for the conclusions of examiners in cases like this. As noted above, nothing is known about the validity of judgments that use a combination of actuarial and clinical data (i.e., judgments based on the "adjusted actuarial" approach), and there is no basis to claim that one's opinions based on an adjusted actuarial approach are as valid as judgments based on an actuarial approach. Yet examiners routinely use such an approach to elevate the probability that an individual will reoffend beyond 50 percent even when tests such as the RRASOR yield scores as low as a 24.8 percent chance for reoffending over five years and a 36.9 percent chance over ten years.[96] There is no question that public safety concerns in these cases are paramount. However, the jaundiced observer might offer that the net effect of judicial decision making in this arena is that the appearance of scientific credibility is most important.

SUMMARY AND CONCLUSIONS

Since the most recent wave of legislation allowing for the indeterminate civil commitment of "sexually violent predators" is less than ten years old, attorneys, mental health professionals, and others can expect that issues related to assessment of persons subject to SVP statutes will continue to be the subject of litigation. Essentially all aspects of the assessment process and resultant expert opinion are likely to be challenged at some point in various courts throughout the states; the number of challenges is likely to be greatest immediately after new legislation is passed, with a decrease in challenges over time as the state courts wrestle with and resolve issues of admissibility of expert testimony.

Given the stakes involved and the controversial nature of this legislation, mental health professionals who conduct SVP evaluations should expect attorneys (for both the defense and the state) litigating these issues to be better prepared and more knowledgeable about assessment techniques and diagnostic issues in this area than they are in other mental health litigation (such as standard civil commitment, criminal competence, or criminal responsibility proceedings). Most appellate court decisions to date suggest that courts will defer to individual clinical judgments of examiners and be reluctant to exclude testimony, ruling instead that concerns over assessment techniques go to the credibility and weight of the evidence—matters committed to the discretion of the trial judge. For this reason, examiners testifying in SVP proceedings must be explicit about the limitations of the techniques they rely on and clear about the differences between predicting individual risk and assessing probabilities of future risk. While it is important for experts to be explicit about these matters in any forensic setting, it may be particularly important in SVP hearings because of the great reluctance of courts to find for the respondent. In other words, sloppy clinical technique may be forgiven more easily in this context, which means that mental health professionals must be extraordinarily clear not only about their opinions, but about their bases for those opinions and any limitations on their testimony.

Footnotes

[1] *See* S.J. Brakel & B.A. Weiner, *The Mentally Disabled and the Law* (3d ed.) (Washington, D.C.: American Bar Association); E.S. Janus, "Sexual Predator Commitment Laws: Lessons for Law and the Behavioral Sciences," *Behavioral Sciences and the Law* 18, 5–21.

[2] L. Fitch, "Sex Offender Commitment in the United States," 9 *J. Forensic Psychiatry* 237–240.

[3] *See* In re Blodgett, 518 N.W. 2d 609 (Minn. 1994); In re Young, 857 P.2d 989 (Wash. 1993). *See also* Alan Held, "The Civil Commitment of Sexual Predators—Experience Under Minnesota's Law," in *The Sexual Predator: Law, Policy, Evaluation, and Treatment* (A. Schlank & F. Cohen, eds., 1999).

[4] 521 U.S. 346 (1997).

[5] Kan. Stat. Ann. § 559-29a02(b) (1994).

⁶ Hendricks, *supra* note 4, at 359.

⁷ 293 F. 1013 (D.C. Cir. 1923).

⁸ Frye, *supra* note 7, at 1014.

⁹ D.L. Faigman, D.H. Kaye, M.J. Saks & J. Sanders, *Modern Scientific Evidence: The Law and Science of Expert Testimony* (1997).

¹⁰ *See* T. Grisso, *Manual for Understanding and Appreciation of Miranda Rights Tests* (1998) and *Juveniles' Waivers of Miranda Rights: Legal and Psychological Competence* (1981).

¹¹ State v. Klein, No. 05-1999-CF-08148 (18th Cir. Brevard Cty. Fla. 2000).

¹² 509 U.S. 579 (1993).

¹³ D.L. Faigman et al., *supra* note 9, at 17–19.

¹⁴ *E.g.*, Kumho Tire Co. v. Carmichael, 526 U.S. 137 (1999).

¹⁵ *See also* D.L. Faigman, "The Evidentiary Status of Social Science Under Daubert: Is It 'Scientific,' 'Technical' or 'Other' Knowledge?", 1 *Psychol. Pub. Pol. & L.* 960 (1995); D. Shuman, *Psychiatric and Psychological Evidence* (1994 & Supp. 1997).

¹⁶ *See* C. Slobogin, "The Ultimate Issue Issue," 7 *Behav. Sci. & L.* 259–266; G.B. Melton, J. Petrila, N. Poythress & C. Slobogin, *Psychological Evaluations for the Courts: A Handbook for Attorneys and Mental Health Professionals* (2d ed. 1997); S. Morse, "Law and Mental Health Professionals: The Limits of Expertise," 9 *Prof. Psychol.* 389–399.

¹⁷ *See* R.K. Otto, "Assessing and Managing Outpatient Violence Risk in Outpatient Settings," 5 *J. Clin. Psychol.* 1239–1262 (2000); R.K. Hanson, "What Do We Know About Sex Offender Risk Assessment?", 4 *Psychol., Pub. Pol. & L.* 50–72.

¹⁸ *See* R.K. Hanson, *The Development of a Brief Actuarial Risk Scale for Sexual Offense Recidivism* (Ottawa: Department of the Solicitor General of Canada, User Report No. 1997-04, 1997); R. Dawes, D. Faust & P. Meehl, "Clinical Versus Actuarial Judgment," 243 *Science* 1668–1674; W. Grove & P. Meehl, Comparative Efficiency of Informal (Subjective, Impressionistic) and Formal (Mechanical, Algorithmic) Prediction Procedures: The Clinical-Statistical Controversy," 2 *Psychol. Pub. Pol. & L.* 293–323; W.M. Grove, D.H. Zald, B.S. Lebow, B.E. Snitz & C. Nelson, "Clinical Versus Mechanical Prediction: A Meta-Analysis, 12 *Psychol. Assessment* 19–30; P. Meehl, *Clinical Versus Statistical Prediction: A Theoretical Analysis and a Review of the Literature* (1996).

¹⁹ For examples of such approaches, *see* D.P. Boer, S.D. Hart, P.R. Kropp & C.D. Webster, *Manual for the Sexual Violence Risk-20: Professional Guidelines for Assessment of Risk of Sexual Violence* (Burnaby, British Columbia: Mental Health Law and Policy Institute, Simon Fraser University, 1997); C.D. Webster, K.S. Douglas, D. Eaves & S.D. Hart, *Manual for the HCR-20: Assessing Risk for Violence* (version 2) (Burnaby, British Columbia: Mental Health Law & Policy Institute, Simon Fraser University, 1997); and P.R. Kropp, S.D. Hart, C.D. Webster & D. Eaves, *Manual for the Spousal Assault Risk Assessment Guide* (2d ed.) (Vancouver: British Columbia Institute Against Family Violence, 1995).

²⁰ *See* P. Meehl, *supra* note 18.

²¹ This is further discussed in R.K. Otto, R. Borum & S. Hart, *Professional Issues Concerning the Use of Actuarial Instruments in Sexually Violent Predator Evaluations* (2000) (unpublished manuscript submitted for publication).

²² 585 N.W.2d 609 (Wis. App. 1999).

²³ 74 Cal. App. 4th 826 (Cal. Ct. App.1999).

²⁴ *See* R.K. Hanson, *supra* notes 17, 18.

²⁵ *See* D.L. Epperson, J.D. Kaul & D. Hesselton, *Final Report on the Development of the Minnesota Sex Offender Screening Tool—Revised* (1998), Paper presented at the 15th annual research and treatment

convention of the Association for the Treatment of Sexual Abusers, Vancouver, British Columbia; *see also* S. Huot, "The Referral Process," in *The Sexual Predator: Law, Policy, Evaluation, and Treatment* (A. Schlank & F. Cohen eds., 1999).

[26] *See* V.L. Quinsey, G.T. Harris, M.E. Rice & A.C. Cormier, *Violent Offenders: Appraising and Managing Risk* (American Psychological Association, 1998).

[27] R.K. Hanson & D. Thornton, "Improving Risk Assessments for Sex Offenders: A Comparison of Three Actuarial Scales," 24 *Law & Hum. Behav.* 119–136.

[28] R.K. Hanson, *supra* note 17, at 53.

[29] V.L. Quinsey et al., *supra* note 26; E. Janus & P. Meehl, "Assessing the Legal Standard for Predictions of Dangerousness in Sex Offender Commitment Proceedings," 3 *Psychol. Pub. Pol. & L.* 33–64.

[30] *See, e.g.,* R. Borum, R.K. Otto & S. Golding, "Improving Clinical Judgment and Decision Making in Forensic Evaluation," 21 *J. Psychiatry & L.* 35–76; R. Dawes et al., *supra* note 18; H. Garb, *Studying the Clinician: Judgment Research and Psychological Assessment* (American Psychological Association, 1988); H. Garb, "Toward a Second Generation of Statistical Prediction Rules in Psychodiagnosis and Personality Assessment," 10 *Computers in Human Behavior* 377–394; W. Grove & P. Meehl, *supra* note 18; W. Grove et al., *supra* note 18; D. Mossman, "Assessing Predictions of Violence: Being Accurate About Accuracy," 62 *J. Consulting & Clinical Psychol.* 783–792; P. Meehl, "Psychology and the Criminal Law," 5 *U. Richmond L. Rev.* 1–30; R.K. Otto & J. Butcher, "Computer-Assisted Psychological Assessment in Child Custody Evaluations," 29 *Fam. L.Q.* 79–96.

[31] R.K. Hanson & M.T. Bussierre, "Predicting Relapse: A Meta-Analysis of Sexual Offender Recidivism Studies," 66 *J. Consulting & Clinical Psychol.* 348–362.

[32] R.K. Hanson & M.T. Bussierre, *supra* note 31; *see also* R. Dempster, *Prediction of Sexually Violent Recidivism: A Comparison of Risk Assessment Instruments* (unpublished master's thesis, Simon Fraser University, Burnaby, British Columbia, 1998).

[33] *See* Otto, Borum & Hart, *supra* note 21.

[34] The use of such instruments is required by some state agencies that administer SVP evaluation programs, but there are no specific data regarding their acceptance or use by mental health professionals. Whether general acceptance as set out by *Frye* should hinge on how many mental health professionals in the field use them is questionable, given mental health professionals' history of using invalid measures and techniques.

[35] American Education Research Association, American Psychological Association, National Council on Measurement in Education (1999).

[36] T.W. Campbell, "Sexual Predator Evaluations and Phrenology: Considering Issues of Evidentiary Reliability," 18 *Behav. Sci. & L.* 111–130.

[37] *Supra* note 21.

[38] A. Held, "The Civil Commitment of Sexual Predators—Experience Under Minnesota's Law," in *The Sexual Predator: Law Policy, Evaluation, and Treatment* (A. Schlank & F. Cohen, eds., 1999).

[39] Cal. Welf. & Inst. Code § 6600(a) (West 2000).

[40] Fla. Stat. Ann. §§ 394.912(2)(b), 394.912(2)(c) (West Supp. 2000).

[41] 573 N.W.2d 899 (Wis. App. 1997); 595 N.W.2d 403 (Wis. 1999).

[42] Watson, *supra* note 41, 573 N.W.2d 899.

[43] Id.

[44] Watson, *supra* note 41, 595 N.W.2d 403.

[45] Watson, *supra* note 41, 595 N.W.2d at 413–414.

[46] Fla. Stat. Ann. §§ 394.912(5), 394.912(10) (West. Supp. 2000).

[47] Fla. Stat. Ann. § 394.455(18) (West 1998).

[48] American Psychiatric Association (Washington, D.C.: American Psychiatric Press, 1994).

[49] Historically, challenges to the diagnostic system have typically alleged that psychiatric diagnoses are so unreliable as to render them invalid. *See, e.g.,* J. Ziskin (Ed.), *Coping With Psychiatric and Psychological Testimony* (Los Angeles: Law & Psychology Press, 1995). The argument was that a diagnostic system so poor that two different mental health professionals had difficulty agreeing about the diagnosis was invalid. And indeed, there was considerable research indicating that diagnoses based on the first two iterations of the DSM were highly unreliable. Reliability of psychiatric diagnosis was reported to be much higher, however, with the shift in diagnostic procedures embodied in DSM-III, DSM-III-R, and DSM-IV. This led proponents of psychiatric diagnoses to argue that criticism leveled at the earlier diagnostic systems was unwarranted, as diagnostic reliability has been proven. A point apparently lost by many, however, is that the acceptable rates of diagnostic reliability were obtained using structured clinical interviews—an approach used by few practicing clinicians. Additionally, inter-rater reliability was not high for all diagnoses, and some diagnoses (e.g., personality disorders) continued to show low rates of reliability. Thus, while some experts may testify that the problem of the unreliability of psychiatric diagnoses was addressed by the advent of the DSM-III and its later versions, this may not actually be the case, particularly when a diagnosis is based on an unstructured interview or assessment.

[50] *See* R. Reisner, C. Slobogin & A. Rai, *Law and the Mental Health Systems: Civil and Criminal Aspects* 417–419 (3d ed., 1999).

[51] *See*, e.g., State v. Green, 984 P.2d 1024 (1999); In re Walker, 731 N.E.2d 994 (Ill. App. Ct. 2000).

[52] *See* R.D. Hare, *Manual for the Hare Psychopathy Checklist—Revised* (Multi-Health Systems, 1991).

[53] *See, e.g.,* United States v. Barnette, 211 F.3d 803 (4th Cir. 2000).

[54] *See* R.D. Hare, *supra* note 52; R.D. Hare, "Psychopaths and Their Nature: Implications for the Mental Health and Criminal Justice Systems," in T. Millon, E. Simonson, M. Birket-Smith & R. Davis (Eds.), *Psychopathy: Antisocial, Criminal, and Violent Behavior* 188–212 (1998); *see generally* T. Millon et al., *Psychopathy*.

[55] *See, e.g.,* People v. Dacayana, 91 Cal. Rptr. 2d 121 (1999).

[56] 518 N.W.2d 609 (Minn. 1994).

[57] Pearson v. Probate Court of Ramsey County, 307 U.S. 270, 274 (194), *aff'g* 287 N.W.2d 297 (Minn. 1939).

[58] Melton et al., *supra* note 16, at 200.

[59] American Psychiatric Association, *Statement on the Insanity Defense* 12 (1982).

[60] *Supra* note 3.

[61] *Supra* note 4.

[62] Hendricks, *supra* note 4, at 358.

[63] In re Thorell, No. 42237-5-1 (unpub. op.,Wash. Ct. App. 2000).

[64] *See*, e.g., Barefoot v. Estelle, 463 U.S. 880 (1983).

[65] B. Ennis & T. Litwack, "Flipping Coins in the Courtroom: Psychiatry and the Presumption of Expertise," 62 *Cal L. Rev.* 693–723.

[66] B. Ennis & R. Emory, *The Rights of Mental Patients* (1978).

[67] R.K. Otto, "On the Ability of Mental Health Professionals to 'Predict Dangerousness': A Commentary on Interpretations of the 'Dangerousness' Literature," 18 *L. & Psychol. Rev.* 43–68.

[68] *Supra* note 64.

[69] Barefoot v. Estelle, *supra* note 64, at 896.

[70] *Supra* note 22.

[71] V.L. Quinsey, G.T. Harris, M.E. Rice & C.A. Cormier, *Violent Offenders: Appraising and Managing Risk* (American Psychological Association, 1998).

[72] It is interesting to note, of course, that both the defense and one of the state experts used the VRAG, an instrument used to identify people at risk for engaging in general acts of violence, including sexual violence, to derive estimates of Keinitz's risk for *sexual* offending. Apparently based on his review of the respondent's clinical record, the psychologist called by the state who had used the VRAG indicated that he had increased the VRAG estimate of the respondent's risk for reoffending by at least 10 percent. How he came up with this number is anybody's guess.

[73] State v. Kienitz, *supra* note 22.

[74] Id.

[75] Kienitz, *supra* note 22.

[76] 518 N.W.2d 609 (Minn. 1994).

[77] In re Linehan, *supra* note 76, at 614.

[78] In re Linehan, *supra* note 76, at 616.

[79] In re Linehan, 557 N.W.2d 171, 189 (Minn. 1996).

[80] In re Shaw, No. C3-96-2131, 1997 Minn. App. LEXIS 544 at *2 (Minn. Ct. App. 1997).

[81] State v. Lauderdale, No. 17036, 1998 Ohio App. LEXIS 6383 at *4 (Ohio Ct. App. 1998).

[82] *Supra* note 11, at 620.

[83] In re Thorell, *supra* note 63.

[84] In re Thorell, *supra* note 63, at 15.

[85] *Supra* note 23.

[86] Poe, *supra* note 23, at 831 (emphasis added).

[87] *Supra* note 22.

[88] No. 99-0052, 2000 Wis. App. LEXIS 116, at *2 (Wis. App. 2000).

[89] State v. Kienitz, *supra* note 22, at 721.

[90] In re Dean, No.17320-8-III, 2000 Wash. App. LEXIS 811, at *811 (Wash. App. 2000).

[91] *Supra* note 52.

[92] R.D. Hare, "Psychopaths and Their Nature," *supra* note 54.

[93] United States v. Barnette, *supra* note 53.

[94] *Supra* note 11.

[95] No. 99-000045C1 (unpub. op. Pinellas Cty., 6th Cir., Aug. 21, 2000). The three judge panel heard claims regarding these instruments in 14 cases consolidated for this argument. The first of these cases in the opinion was *In re Valdez*, hence its use here.

[96] *See, e.g.,* People v. Poe, *supra* note 23.

Chapter 4

In the Wake of *Hendricks*—States Seem "Committed" to SVP Programs

by Ken Kozlowski, J.D., M.L.S.

The Broad Reach of *Hendricks* 4-2
United States Supreme Court 4-3
Circuit and District Courts 4-5
    First Circuit 4-5
    Second and Third Circuits 4-5
    Fourth Circuit 4-6
    Fifth Circuit 4-7
    Sixth and Seventh Circuits 4-7
    Eighth Circuit 4-7
    Ninth Circuit 4-8
    Tenth, Eleventh, and D.C. Circuits 4-9
State Court Decisions 4-9
    Alabama 4-9
    Arizona 4-10
    California 4-10
    Illinois 4-11
    Indiana 4-11
    Kansas 4-12
    Massachusetts 4-13
    Michigan 4-14
    Minnesota 4-14
    Missouri 4-15
    New Jersey 4-15
    Washington 4-16
    Wisconsin 4-17
    Other States 4-18
        Colorado 4-18
        Connecticut 4-18
        District of Columbia 4-18

>   Florida 4-18
>   Kentucky 4-18
>   Maine 4-18
>   Montana 4-18
>   Nebraska 4-18
>   New York 4-19
>   North Dakota 4-19
>   Ohio 4-19
>   Oregon 4-19
>   Pennsylvania 4-19
>   South Dakota 4-19
>   Texas 4-19
>   Vermont 4-19
>   Virginia 4-19
> Conclusion 4-19

THE BROAD REACH OF *HENDRICKS*

In 1997, the U.S. Supreme Court decided in *Kansas v. Hendricks*[1] that the civil commitment following a prison sentence of offenders classified as "sexually violent predators" (SVPs) does not violate the Constitution's prohibition of double jeopardy[2] or its ban on ex post facto[3] lawmaking. The Court held that Hendricks's involuntary confinement following his release from prison does not amount to a second prosecution and punishment because of the civil nature of the Kansas Sexually Violent Predator Act,[4] and that his ex post facto claim was flawed because this clause pertains exclusively to penal statutes. The Court found that the act had no retroactive effect because it did not criminalize conduct that was legal before its enactment. Nor did it deprive Hendricks of any defense available to him at the time of his crimes.

Over three years have passed since the *Hendricks* decision; sexual predator laws have since been passed in at least seventeen other states,[5] and many courts have used *Hendricks* to justify civil commitments of SVPs. The purpose of this chapter is to examine how the courts have been handling civil commitment cases; we will also look at the unintended effect of *Hendricks* on the constitutionality of sex offender registration and notification laws (Megan's Laws). *Hendricks* allows courts to rebut the double jeopardy and ex post facto arguments of the registration cases that were starting to clog the courts' dockets. *Hendricks* has also been used to characterize the nature of the federal government's detention of individuals waiting to be deported. Throughout the United States, a number of cases have dissected, and continue to dissect, the definitions within the various SVP laws and the legislative intent thereof.

The American legal system has been, to say the least, very busy with these issues. Searches of the online legal research systems Lexis and Westlaw show that about 260 separate cases have cited *Hendricks* as some type of authority. In addition, over 200 law journal articles have been written on some aspect of sexual predator laws, with a smaller subset of that amount dealing with the civil commitment of SVPs. *Hendricks* touches all aspects of the sexual predator statute. There are cases that deal with questions such as:

- Is the statute punitive in nature?

- Are the conditions within a commitment facility any different from those encountered in a facility that houses those convicted of a crime?

- What is meant when a statute describes the "dangerousness" of an individual?

- Are offenders entitled to certain constitutional safeguards even though the commitment hearing is classified as civil in nature?

This chapter concentrates on cases that have criticized or distinguished *Hendricks* in some way as well as decisions that have discussed *Hendricks* in a favorable light; cases that merely cite *Hendricks* are not covered. We will start with the U.S. Supreme Court, follow with the federal circuits and districts,[6] and finish with state courts, citing applicable state legislation where it is important to the discussion. States not covered within this chapter do not have any case law citing *Hendricks* for any reason. (See Table 4.1 for a list of recent articles discussing the legal issues raised by *Hendricks* and related cases and laws.)

UNITED STATES SUPREME COURT

The U.S. Supreme Court dealt recently with the issue of unlawful confinement in *Seling v. Young*,[7] in which the Court acknowledged that both the State of Washington and the Ninth Circuit considered Washington's sexual predator commitment law to be civil rather than punitive in nature. Thus confinement in Washington's Special Commitment Center could not be deemed punitive "as applied" to a single individual in violation of the double jeopardy and ex post facto clauses and provide cause for release. The Court reviewed Young's allegations and termed some of them serious, but considered only how the allegations could be evaluated as presented in a double jeopardy and ex post facto challenge under the assumption that the statute was civil. An as-applied analysis would therefore never conclusively resolve whether a particular scheme was punitive.

Young pointed out that the Court had considered conditions of confinement in the past in evaluating the validity of confinement schemes in *Hendricks*, but the Court noted that the question *Hendricks* presented was whether the Kansas act at issue was punitive and that that act was patterned after the Washington act. Permitting Young's as-applied challenge would allow an "end run" around the Washington Supreme Court's decision that the act was civil. The Court found that sexually violent predators who are committed have a remedy for the alleged conditions and treatment regime at the Commitment Center. It is up to the Washington courts to determine whether the Center is operating in accordance with state law. The facts of this case are further discussed in the section on the Ninth Circuit, which heard the case as *Young v. Weston*.

The only other mention of *Hendricks* is found in Justice Kennedy's dissent in the partial birth abortion decision from the 1999–2000 term.[8] Disappointed that the majority had overturned the Nebraska law that criminalized partial birth abortions, Justice Kennedy stated that there was substantial authority for allowing the state to

Table 4.1
Selected Articles on Legal Issues

Billbrey, R. (1999, Nov./Dec.). Civil commitment of sexually violent predators: A misguided attempt to solve a serious problem. *Journal of the Missouri Bar, 55,* 321–329.

Cook, J. H. (1999). Civil commitment of sex offenders: South Carolina's Sexually Violent Predator Act. *South Carolina Law Review, 50,* 543–563.

Falk, A. J. (1999). Sex offenders, mental illness and criminal responsibility: The constitutional boundaries of civil commitment after *Kansas v. Hendricks. American Journal of Law and Medicine, 25,* 117–147.

Hornby, R. L. (2000). New Jersey Sexually Violent Predator Act: Civil commitment of the sexually abnormal. *Seton Hall Legislative Journal, 24,* 473–508.

Janus, E. S. (2000). Sex offender commitments in Minnesota: A descriptive study of second generation commitments. *Behavioral Sciences and the Law, 18,* 343–374.

Kesler, R. A. (1999). Running in circles: Defining mental illness and dangerousness in the wake of *Kansas v. Hendricks. Wayne Law Review, 44,* 1871–1898.

King, C. A. (1999). Fighting the devil we don't know: *Kansas v. Hendricks*, a case study exploring the civilization of criminal punishment and its effectiveness in preventing child sexual abuse. *William & Mary Law Review, 40,* 1427–1469.

La Fond, J. Q. (2000). The future of involuntary civil commitment in the U.S.A. after *Kansas v. Hendricks. Behavioral Sciences & the Law, 18,* 153–167.

Pearman, B. C. (1998). *Kansas v. Hendricks*: The Supreme Court's endorsement of sexually violent predator statutes unnecessarily expands state civil commitment power. *North Carolina Law Review, 76,* 1973–2015.

Ramsey, C. B. (1999). California's Sexually Violent Predator Act: The role of psychiatrists, courts, and medical determinations in confining sex offenders. *Hastings Constitutional Law Quarterly, 26,* 469–504.

Slobogin, C. (1999). A prevention model of juvenile justice: The promise of *Kansas v. Hendricks* for children. *1999 Wisconsin Law Review,* 185–226.

---

take sides in a medical debate even when fundamental liberty interests are at stake, and even when leading members of the profession disagree with the conclusions drawn by the legislature. He looked to *Hendricks* to support his argument that legislatures should be afforded the "widest latitude" when there is a disagreement among medical professionals.[9] The disagreement in *Hendricks* revolved around psychiatric professionals not being in complete harmony in classifying pedophilia as a "mental illness." The Kansas statute based commitment on "mental abnormality."

The Kansas legislature was given "wide latitude" in adopting its SVP law. The Nebraska legislature was not afforded the same consideration concerning partial birth abortions. Given the current makeup of the Court, "wide latitude" is probably going to be prevalent in future Supreme Court decisions.

CIRCUIT AND DISTRICT COURTS

First Circuit

The Court of Appeals for the First Circuit has mentioned *Hendricks* in passing only. Peter Filippi was declared incompetent to stand charges on racketeering and was civilly committed for a period not to exceed four months.[10] Filippi tried to make the argument that *Hendricks* changed the landscape of civil commitment laws by requiring "dangerousness" as well as "mental illness" but the court disagreed, stating that *Hendricks* did not hold that dangerousness was always a condition of commitment.

The district courts of the First Circuit decided a few cases that touch on issues present in *Hendricks*. *Hermanowski v. Farquarson*[11] concerns a case of federal detention pending deportation. The District of Rhode Island held that the detention should protect the community from exposure to further criminal acts by an alien who has been convicted of an aggravated felony. In this case, Hermanowski was a petty thief. The court cited *Hendricks* for the proposition that the determination that an individual is a danger to the community is, by itself, an insufficient basis for detaining that individual indefinitely. The court also stated, again looking to *Hendricks*, that the Supreme Court is hesitant to sanction civil detention based on a finding of dangerousness alone, without a finding that the detainee is dangerous and unable to control himself.[12]

In *Roe v. Farwell*,[13] the District of Massachusetts relied on *Hendricks* in holding that a state law requirement of sex offender registration was closely analogous to the civil commitment of a sexually dangerous person, in that both sanctions attempt "to grapple with the problem of managing repeat sexual offenders" and of recidivism. The court found Roe's claims of double jeopardy and ex post facto application of laws to be without merit.

Massachusetts passed a bill in September 1999 reauthorizing the indefinite civil commitment of "sexually dangerous persons."[14] Most assuredly there will be more cases arising out of this legislative event.

Second and Third Circuits

The Second Circuit also looked to *Hendricks* in dealing with a challenge to its version of Megan's Law.[15] In *Doe v. Pataki*,[16] three plaintiffs attacked the sex offender registration law on ex post facto grounds; the court's decision hinged on whether the requirements constituted punishment. In finding no ex post facto violation, the court borrowed the Supreme Court's analysis in *Hendricks* to determine that the New York legislature meant to establish a civil proceeding. The court then held that it would reject legislative intent only where a party challenging the statute provides "the clearest proof" that "the statutory scheme [is] so punitive either in purpose or effect as to negate [the state's] intention" to deem it "civil."[17] Because of *Hendricks*, the Second Circuit was able to dispose of *Doe v. Pataki* as well as a Connecticut case dealing with a similar notification law.[18]

Nothing of great substance has reached the district courts throughout the Second Circuit, although one case deals with the recommitment of an insanity acquitee.[19] The Southern District of New York cited *Hendricks* for the proposition that "previous instances of violent behavior are an important indicator of future violent tendencies."[20]

The Third Circuit offers nothing in the way of guidance on civil commitment of SVPs. Three cases that deal with the punishment aspect of sex offender registration were all decided based on *Hendricks*'s holding that civil commitment, as analogized with the requirements of registration, is not punitive in nature.[21]

Fourth Circuit

The Fourth Circuit offers a twist on civil commitment. In 1970, John Walsh was given a seventy-two-year sentence after pleading guilty to rape and kidnapping. Under Maryland law at that time, he was examined at a state psychiatric treatment facility and was adjudged eligible to remain there. His sentence was suspended and he was civilly committed to the institution. A change in the law in 1977 did away with the suspension of sentences because there was criticism that some inmates were being held at the facility long after their original sentences had expired. In 1990, Walsh was no longer eligible to remain at the institution. The court holding jurisdiction over Walsh could have released him, ordered probation, or sent him back to the Department of Corrections to serve the remainder of his sentence. The court chose the latter. Walsh appealed, saying that according to *Hendricks*, his civil commitment to the psychiatric facility was not a form of punishment. Therefore, he argued, the reimposition of his criminal sentence necessarily increased his punishment. In *Walsh v. Corcoran*,[22] the Fourth Circuit, properly amused by the argument, stated that the fact that Walsh was given credit for time served during the civil commitment did not increase his punishment irrespective of the nature of his confinement at the psychiatric facility.

One Fourth Circuit district court case deals with civil commitment, although not of a sexual predator.[23] David Henley entered the federal correctional system after pleading guilty to bank robbery in 1990. In 1996, he began a term of supervised release. Within a day of his release he overdosed on amphetamines, and after a few such episodes he was diagnosed as suffering from several substance abuse disorders in early remission, borderline personality disorder, and antisocial personality features. He was assigned to a long-term care program, but absconded. Because of his psychiatric diagnosis, the court recommended that Henley be released to the custody of either the attorney general, authorities from his state of domicile, or a suitable treatment facility. The court held that Henley should be held until his mental condition was such that his release, or his conditional release, would not create a substantial risk of bodily injury to another person or serious damage to property of another. The court ultimately held, with deference to *Hendricks*, that it did not appear that the involuntary commitment of an individual with a personality disorder linked to future dangerousness was unconstitutional.

As we can see from the cases thus far, not many contain the same fact situation as *Hendricks*. However, *Hendricks* is being used to justify many state actions that may have been overturned without the 1997 decision being on the books.

Fifth Circuit

The Fifth Circuit Court of Appeals published no decision speaking to civil commitment of sexual predators. One case, *Zadvydas v. Underdown*,[24] deals with the detention of a person being deported from the United States. The court decided that the detention was lawful while Zadvydas was considered either a danger to the community or a flight risk, as long as good faith efforts to effectuate deportation continued and reasonable parole and periodic review procedures were in place.

Only one district court case in the Fifth Circuit discusses sex offender commitment, with respect to a sex offender notification law.[25] The pattern here follows all of the others discussed thus far.

Sixth and Seventh Circuits

The Sixth Circuit's cupboard is bare with respect to civil commitment decisions. The appeals court decided one case concerning sex offender registration,[26] and a Michigan district court decided another on the same subject.[27]

Nor are any relevant cases found in the Seventh Circuit. A few decisions used *Hendricks* to support ex post facto arguments, but the fact patterns differed too much from civil commitment issues to offer any help to this analysis.

Eighth Circuit

In light of *Hendricks*, the Eighth Circuit remanded the case *Young v. Weston*[28] to the district court. Because Young was transferred to a federal facility in the state of Washington, the Ninth Circuit ultimately handled the case, so it will be discussed in the next section.

One district court case with a very complicated background also appears within the Circuit. In *Ayers v. Doth*,[29] petitioner Doth presented a facial constitutional challenge to the Minnesota Sexually Dangerous Persons (SDP) Act.[30] Doth was committed concurrently under the SDP law and Minnesota's Psychopathic Personality Commitment (PP) Act.[31] After *Hendricks* was decided, Doth filed a writ of habeas corpus saying he should be released because the SDP law does not require proof that he suffers from a "mental disorder" or that he "lacks the ability to control his impulses." Under the PP law, however, a person can be committed if there is clear and convincing evidence he has displayed an utter lack of power to control his sexual impulses. The court found that the record reflected that Doth had shown the requisite "utter lack of power to control" his sexual impulses. Thus, even though Minnesota's SDP Act may contain some constitutional infirmities, Doth had neither suffered, nor was threatened with, an actual injury that was traceable to the constitutional flaw and that was likely to be redressed by the issuance of the habeas corpus writ.

The fate of Minnesota's SDP law seems to have been decided by the 1997 *Linehan v. Minnesota*[32] case. In light of *Hendricks*, Linehan was bounced back to the state, and in 1999, the Minnesota Supreme Court again affirmed the law.[33] Linehan's fate was sealed when the U.S. Supreme Court denied his writ of certiorari.[34]

Ninth Circuit

The Ninth Circuit has seen plenty of action in the civil commitment arena. The first case we will look at, *Page v. Torrey*,[35] sets the tone for the question of whether civil commitment is in fact punishment. Page attempted to file various actions under the Prison Litigation Reform Act (PLRA) while he was civilly committed under California's Sexually Violent Predators Act.[36] The court ruled that Page was not a "prisoner" under the PLRA.

Next up is a challenge to Washington's civil commitment statute.[37] In *Donaghe v. Seling*,[38] Donaghe petitioned for a writ of habeas corpus alleging that his commitment violates the Constitution's double jeopardy clause. The court held that the writ be denied because Donaghe failed to present the "clearest proof" that the statutory scheme under which he was detained was punitive in purpose and effect. His allegation challenging the statute as applied also failed.

In *Young v. Weston*,[39] the Ninth Circuit stated that while the Washington statute has survived scrutiny in the past, Young, if his alleged facts are proved, will establish the punitive nature of his confinement and would be entitled to relief. Among the facts alleged by Young are:

- He has been subject to conditions more restrictive than those placed either on true civil commitment detainees or even those placed on state prisoners.

- The Special Commitment Center is located wholly within the perimeter of a larger Department of Corrections facility and relies on the Department of Corrections for a host of essential services, including library services, medical care, food, and security.

- The conditions of confinement at the Special Commitment Center are not compatible with the Washington statute's treatment purposes.

The Ninth Circuit found that the Washington state courts did not afford Young a full and fair hearing concerning the conditions of confinement in the Special Commitment Center. The trial court refused to allow Young to present factual evidence at trial on either the actual conditions of confinement or the quality of treatment, either in a challenge to the law or before the jury. The Washington Supreme Court also did not afford Young a fair hearing. The U.S. Supreme Court heard this case as *Seling v. Young*[40] in October 2000 (see discussion in Supreme Court section above) and maintained both the constitutionality and civil nature of the Washington statute. Young failed in his double jeopardy and ex post facto claims.

In 1992, the state of Hawaii passed a commitment act authorizing the creation of the Sex Offender Treatment Program (SOTP).[41] The act allows prison authorities to label certain prisoners as sex offenders and compels their participation in the SOTP. The label "sex offender," however, brings certain consequences: an inmate loses eligibility for furlough or favorable housing and must complete the SOTP as a precondition to parole eligibility. In *Neal v. Shimoda*,[42] inmates attacked the act as being violative of the ex post facto clause. The inmates argued that the SOTP applied retrospectively, that they were being labeled as sex offenders for acts that they were accused of committing prior to 1992, and that these consequences demonstrated that the SOTP, taken as a whole, disadvantaged them. The court stated that before the *Hendricks* decision the claims had substantial merit, but that with the application of *Hendricks* to the SOTP, summary judgment for the defendants on the inmates' ex post facto claim was proper.

The state of Washington continues to have problems with its standard of care in civil commitment centers. In the case *Turay v. Weston*,[43] Turay filed suit against the state's Special Commitment Center in which he lost all claims but one, that he was not provided adequate mental health treatment. The court issued an injunction in 1994 requiring the state to take all reasonable steps within its power to provide committed individuals with constitutionally adequate mental health treatment. The court subsequently held the defendants in contempt for failing to comply with the injunction and ordered them to pay into the court's registry $50 per day per resident until the injunction's requirements were complete or substantially complete.

The case moved in and out of the courts with the state attempting to dissolve the injunction and the plaintiffs moving for additional sanctions. The latest decision concerning the matter was handed down in *Turay v. Seling*.[44] The court found that the state had failed to make constitutionally adequate mental health treatment available to the Special Commitment Center residents and had departed so substantially from professional minimum standards as to demonstrate that its decisions and practices were not based on professional judgment. Even though *Hendricks* stated that the state enjoys wide latitude in developing treatment regimens, the Ninth Circuit could find no merit to Washington's treatment plans. The court enumerated a number of items that still needed to be taken care of before the injunction could be terminated, and it set out a stringent schedule of when and how the state would report on progress to a special master. (See Marques, Chapter 2 this volume, on the requirements of the *Turay* injunction.)

Tenth, Eleventh, and D.C. Circuits

The Tenth Circuit has decided no cases of relevance to the civil commitment of sexually violent predators. One district court case, *Femedeer v. Haun*,[45] used *Hendricks* to determine the constitutionality of Utah's sex offender notification act in the context of an ex post facto challenge.

No cases within the Eleventh and the District of Columbia Circuits shed any additional light on how *Hendricks* is being used to blunt arguments concerning double jeopardy and the ex post facto clause. Next we will take a look at state court decisions.

STATE COURT DECISIONS

Alabama

One notable Alabama case uses the *Hendricks* scheme of looking toward legislative intent to determine whether the ex post facto clause could be invoked to strike down a community notification law. In *State v. C.M.*,[46] the state held that the its Community Notification Act[47] was unconstitutional as applied to juveniles. The court looked at the legislative intent not only of the notification act, but also of the Juvenile Justice Act.[48] The court saw the intent of the latter act as to keep the identities of juveniles from public disclosure because the purpose of this act is not to punish, but to rehabilitate. The court went on to state that applying the provisions of the Community Notification Act to juveniles would totally abolish long-standing Alabama precedent by directly contradicting the stated goal of the Juvenile Justice Act, which is to return a juvenile to his or her home as quickly as possible. This case was probably rightly decided, but with more and more juveniles committing adult-like sex offenses, the future may be different.

Arizona

A rather lengthy (thirty pages) Arizona Court of Appeals decision used *Hendricks* as a blueprint to thwart a challenge to Arizona's Sexually Violent Persons Act.[49] In *Martin v. Reinstein*,[50] the appellate court, and the trial court before it, closely analyzed *Hendricks* and saw many analogies to the case presently before them. The courts examined Arizona's act and found that the Arizona legislature includes, and requires, far more treatment than does the Kansas legislature. The Arizona act mandates that a person found to be an SVP "shall receive care, supervision, or treatment"[51] and be housed "in the state hospital or a licensed behavioral health or mental health inpatient treatment facility," not in a jail or prison.[52] In addition:

- Those responsible for treating SVPs are required to keep detailed records of the treatment.[53]
- The state had hired an expert to set up Arizona's treatment program.
- Arizona's act provides for alternatives less restrictive than full custodial detention.

The appellate court held that Arizona's SVP Act satisfies any of the *Hendricks* dissent's concerns regarding treatment and placements. The court found the act to be civil in nature and not violative of the rights to be free from ex post facto laws or double jeopardy. The court had to look at a number of different issues within this case: equal protection, due process, free speech, vagueness, and overbreadth. Each and every one was decided against the petitioners.

California

On January 2, 1996, the district attorney for Santa Clara County filed a petition seeking to commit Christopher Hubbart under California's Sexually Violent Predators Act.[54] Hubbart was in the custody of the Department of Corrections and scheduled to be discharged from parole on January 25, 1996. The declaration averred that Hubbart qualified as an SVP because he had sustained convictions for sexually violent offenses against at least two victims. Hubbart objected to his coming commitment on due process, double jeopardy, and ex post facto principles. The California Supreme Court, in *Hubbart v. Superior Court*,[55] found no merit in Hubbarts' claims. Two experts submitted reports concluding that Hubbart suffered from a diagnosable mental disorder. The experts agreed that the risk of reoffense in Hubbart's case was "high" and that Hubbart was likely to commit more sexually violent crimes if released into the community. Relevant factors included the number and frequency of violent sexual assaults Hubbart committed during his brief periods of freedom, his lack of insight into the seriousness of his problem and lack of means of to control precipitating stress, and his inability to empathize with his victims.[56] The court held that Hubbart had not demonstrated that California's SVP law imposed punishment or implicated ex post facto concerns. For those who are fans of legal opinions, there is very good commentary within this opinion on the aspects of dangerousness and treatment.[57]

California courts have been busy with civil commitment and sex offender registration litigation. At least twenty-seven appellate cases have cited *Hendricks* since the decision was released in 1997.

One additional California case, *People v. Superior Court of Fresno County*,[58] deals with a dismissal of a petition to *extend* a civil commitment. The SVP-resident who initiated the action offered only one medical evaluation, and the trial court mistakenly thought that the SVP Act required at least two and dismissed the petition and ordered him released. The resident then proceeded to get reclassified as an SVP, but the trial court still refused to recommit him. He appealed, and the higher court held that one evaluation was enough and that the trial court should have held a probable cause to determine whether the SVP's status had changed. The trial court order was vacated and they were instructed to hold the probable cause hearing.

Illinois

Illinois has both an SVP Commitment Act[59] and an Illinois Supreme Court case to testify to its constitutionality. In the case *In re Samuelson*,[60] David Samuelson was about to be released. The state called on the Illinois Supreme Court to overturn a trial-level decision in favor of Samuelson that invalidated the state's sexual offense commitment statute. The state filed a petition attempting to declare Samuelson an SVP, a prelude to civil commitment under the statute, and the state supreme court reversed the lower court's decision. The court held in favor of the state, following *Hendricks* right down the line. The usual suspects— double jeopardy and ex post facto—entered into the opinion. Two very recent Illinois appellate cases[61] have been decided on pretty much the same fact pattern as *Samuelson*. In both cases, Illinois' SVP law has been upheld against all constitutional challenges.

Indiana

In *Spencer v. O'Connor*,[62] an Indiana Court of Appeals articulated the *Hendricks* decision as providing an "intent-effects" test for determining whether a law was constitutional under the double jeopardy and ex post facto clauses. The intent is legislative intent, and the effects come into play when the scheme provided by the law is so punitive in nature as to negate the intent. This is the first case to put a label on the analysis used by the *Hendricks* court. *Spencer* is a sex offender registration case that, of course, survived judicial scrutiny. The court held that the notification provision does not inflict punishment and that no constitutional relief is available to the plaintiff. Two other Indiana cases[63] cite *Hendricks*, but they have nothing to do with sex offenders. *Hendricks* was used to solve problems concerning whether a penalty was civil or criminal.

Kansas

Kansas is the home state of the *Hendricks* decision. The first case we will look at is *In re Crane*.[64] Crane appealed his commitment as an SVP, alleging that the state had to prove he was unable to control his dangerous behavior. The lower court held that the state need only prove the existence of a mental disorder that makes a sex offender likely to reoffend. To come to a decision, the Kansas Supreme Court decided to look directly at the requirements of the state's SVP Act. The court held that Kansas's statutory scheme for commitment of SVPs does not expressly prohibit confinement where there is not a finding of uncontrollable dangerousness; it stated that a "fair reading" of the Act gives the opposite impression.

Under the Kansas Act, a "sexually violent predator" is defined as

> any person who has been convicted of or charged with a sexually violent offense and who suffers from a mental abnormality or personality disorder which makes the person likely to engage in repeat acts of sexual violence.[65]

"Mental abnormality" is defined as a

> condition affecting the emotional or volitional capacity which predisposes the person to commit sexually violent offenses in a degree constituting such person a menace to the health and safety of others.[66]

The phrase "likely to engage in repeat acts of sexual violence"

> means the person's propensity to commit acts of sexual violence is of such a degree as to pose a menace to the health and safety of others.[67]

The court's take was that the Kansas legislature specified that a person subject to commitment, in addition to having some history of a sexual offense or offenses, must be likely to engage in future dangerous sexual behavior on account of a mental condition. The mental condition could effect volitional capacity or emotional capacity. Volitional capacity concerns the exercise of the will; while the act does not clearly define emotional capacity, the state identified it as an alternative faculty that could be affected by the mental condition. The court reasoned that because volitional capacity involves the exercise of the will, emotional capacity must involve something other than the exercise of the will. The court looked again at *Hendricks* and came to the conclusion that commitment under the act was unconstitutional without a finding that the defendant cannot control his dangerous behavior, despite the intent of the Kansas SVP Act. Justice Thomas, speaking for the majority in *Hendricks*, stated that to be constitutional, a civil commitment must limit involuntary confinement to those "who suffer from a volitional impairment rendering them dangerous beyond their control."[68] Crane, however, suffers from a "personality disorder" that does not concern itself with volitional control. The jury in Crane's trial was not instructed to make a finding as to Crane's inability to control his behavior; the Kansas Supreme Court decided that such a finding *is* required. The court found error in the failure to so instruct the jury, reversed Crane's SVP commitment, and remanded for a new trial.

Another Kansas Supreme Court case with excellent analysis of *Hendricks* is *In re Care & Treatment of Hay*.[69] *Hay* raises numerous issues concerning the constitutionality of the SVP Act, including:

- The Act is criminal in nature;
- The Act violates the prohibition against double jeopardy;
- The Act violates the prohibition on ex post facto laws;
- The Act violates substantive due process;
- The Act violates procedural due process;
- The Act violates guarantees of equal protection;
- The Act is overly broad and vague;
- The filing of the petition under the Act violates a 1993 plea agreement between the State and Hay; and
- A commitment pursuant to the Act constitutes cruel and unusual punishment.

The court held that *Hendricks* directly disposed of the first four of *Hay*'s contentions. The court also held that although the remaining issues *Hay* raised were not directly ruled on by the U.S. Supreme Court in *Hendricks*, each was without sufficient justification to require or allow the court to strike down the Act on the basis of unconstitutionality.

The last Kansas case considered here has to do with language within the statute that directs the state to hold a commitment trial within sixty days of the probable cause hearing.[70] In the case *In re Brown*,[71] Brown attacked the validity of a commitment trial (in which he was designated an SVP) that was held 600 days after his probable cause hearing. The appeals court agreed with Brown, holding that the use of the term "shall" indicates the legislature mandated that the commitment trial be held within sixty days after the probable cause hearing. Brown also alleged that his rights to a speedy trial were violated. That allegation was dismissed because of the civil nature of the proceeding. The court ultimately held that the lower court disregarded the clear, mandated language of the statute relating to time limitations. The appeals court was left with "no choice" but to conclude that it was an error to deny Brown's motion to dismiss.

So now we have some decisions that, notwithstanding the constitutionality of *Hendricks*, are being decided in the favor of sex offenders.

Massachusetts

The Massachusetts legislature reauthorized the indefinite civil commitment of sexually dangerous persons in September 1999.[72] Chapter 123A had been unused for the previous nine years.[73] The cases challenging this law have yet to make it to the appellate courts. An anomaly has been occurring in Massachusetts, however. It seems juries have been releasing petitioners who have challenged their confinement under the old law at nearly twice the rate that the judges have been.[74] It is almost certain that the Massachusetts law will be challenged, but if *Hendricks* remains the law of the land, the challenges should fail.

Michigan

Michigan has only one case citing *Hendricks*, and it surprisingly stems from a law that was repealed in 1966, the Criminal Sexual Psychopath Act (CSPA).[75] However, the release provisions under the CSPA remained in effect due for those already committed pursuant to Michigan Administrative Order No. 1969-4. The case *People v. Williams*[76] initiated a challenge to the CSPA. Williams had been convicted of one murder, adjudged a sexual psychopath, and committed indefinitely to a state hospital. After being released he was convicted of another murder, but his conviction was reversed on appeal. Instead of releasing Williams, the court ordered his return to the Department of Mental Health for confinement and examination to test his supposed recovery. Williams filed a discharge petition, was denied, and appealed.

The appeals court compared the CSPA to Kansas's sexual predator law as applied in *Hendricks* and found that even though the CSPA no longer existed in its original form, it did survive constitutional scrutiny. The problem with this case, as with *In re Crane*, the Kansas case discussed eariler that was overturned, is that there was no finding of a lack of volitional control. Williams was diagnosed with an antisocial personality disorder with a probability of reoffending. The opinion did not discuss volitional control as is required by *Hendricks*. Williams's later appeal to the Michigan Supreme Court was denied.

Minnesota

In 1999, the Minnesota Supreme Court decided a case remanded to them due to the *Hendricks* decision, *In re Linehan*,[77] finding Minnesota's Sexually Dangerous Person (SDP) Act[78] to be constitutional. Linehan had been civilly committed under a previous state law, the Psychopathic Personality (PP) Commitment Act.[79] This act required that for a person to be committed, he or she must evidence an "utter lack of power to control" sexual impulses. The current SDP law, passed in 1994, makes it necessary to prove that the person has *an inability* to control the sexual impulses.

The Minnesota Supreme Court analyzed *Hendricks* and found that it served to limit involuntary civil confinement to those who suffer from a volitional impairment rendering them dangerous beyond their control. The court quoted some language from *Hendricks* concerning volitional control. It found that the Kansas SVP Act

> requires a finding of future dangerousness, and then links that finding to the existence of a "mental abnormality" or "personality disorder" that *makes it difficult*, if not impossible, for the person to control his dangerous behavior (emphasis added).[80]

The Minnesota court took that language, coupled it with the "utter lack of control" language from the old PP Act, and decided that even though a lack of volitional control had to be evidenced it did not have to be a total lack of control, just an "adequate" lack of control. The court found that Linehan's difficulty with volitional control satisfies the *Hendricks* test for constitutionality.

A blistering dissent accused the majority of selectively reading *Hendricks*. The dissent felt that Linehan's civil commitment should be based on a finding of a "volitional impairment rendering him dangerous beyond his control."[81]

Minnesota has more than a few cases on the books that attempt to deal with the issue of volitional control. The standard now under the SDP is "adequate," not "utter," lack of control. In a decision released subsequent to *Linehan*, a Minnesota appeals court held that the *Linehan* decision had settled the apparent conflict between *Hendricks* and the SDP Act. The U.S. Supreme Court also denied certiorari to Linehan,[82] so the matter seems settled in Minnesota.

Missouri

An interesting case in Missouri has held that under Missouri's Sexually Violent Predator Act,[83] the Attorney General may not appeal a finding that a person *is not* a sexual predator. In *In re Salcedo*,[84] the court found that the statute did not contain any provision allowing the Attorney General to appeal such an adverse finding. In Missouri, a probate court judge determines whether there is probable cause for a finding of SVP status. The sex offender has avenues of appeal available to combat an SVP designation, while the state does not. The court held that if the Missouri legislature had intended the Attorney General to have the power to appeal, it would have included it in the statute.

New Jersey

New Jersey's Sexually Violent Predator Act[85] is also a civil commitment act. A recent decision, *In re S.L.*,[86] asks whether an individual subject to the SVP law who is presently either incarcerated or a resident in a state psychiatric facility and on conditional extension pending placement (CEPP) status is entitled to a fourteen-day notice before temporary commitment to the state's SVP facility. CEPP status refers to a resident who is otherwise entitled to be discharged but who cannot be discharged immediately because appropriate placement is unavailable. The person therefore remains confined pending further order of the court; he is considered "incapable of competently exercising" his right to be discharged because of his diminished capacity to survive in the outside world.[87] The state argued that such a long notice may cause an individual to escape or become agitated at the prospect of further confinement. The court concluded that providing the notice outweighed any concerns of the state, but held that seven days would be sufficient.

Another case, *In re D.M.*,[88] deals with the offering of testimony at a commitment hearing. The judge who decided to commit under New Jersey's sexual predator law did not allow the individual to offer testimony at his hearing. The court held that the lower court's refusal to permit D.M. to present witnesses contravened the most elementary requirements of procedural due process. In addition, the judge did not articulate his reasons for commitment, and the doctor who examined D.M. had concluded that D.M.'s condition did not meet the requisite statutory commitment criteria. Procedural safeguards are still very important in a civil commitment hearing where liberty interests are at stake.

Washington

Washington has had some action on the civil commitment front, some of which has been chronicled in the Ninth Circuit Court of Appeals section above. It seems the state has been having trouble with its commitment facilities and has had to deal with many challenges to its SVP law because of the sometimes punitive nature of the commitments.

One such case is *In re Turay*.[89] Turay attempted to attack Washington's commitment statute[90] based on the conditions at the Special Commitment Center, characterizing them as punitive and violative of the prohibition against double jeopardy. The Washington Supreme Court alluded to the *Turay* case developments in federal court and held that whether conditions of confinement at the SCC meet constitutional standards is irrelevant in its opinion, because Turay's remedy for those unconstitutional conditions was not a release from confinement. Turay's remedy was, according to the court, an injunction action and/or an award of damages—Turay had already received both of those via his federal litigation. Accordingly, he had an adequate remedy that would guarantee that the conditions at the SCC would meet or exceed constitutional standards.[91]

Another case, *In re Petersen*,[92] concerns whether a committed sex offender has the right to an appeal of an annual show cause hearing or must file a motion for discretionary review. The Washington Supreme Court held that an appeal is subject to discretionary review and that no right to have an appeal heard exists.[93] Petersen also tried to argue that the Washington statute does not provide for an indefinite term of commitment, but requires the determination beyond a reasonable doubt that he is an SVP for his confinement to continue. Petersen pointed to what was said in *Hendricks* about the Kansas statute, which is substantially similar to the Washington law:

> [C]ommitment under the Act is only potentially indefinite. The maximum amount of time an individual can be incapacitated pursuant to a single judicial proceeding is one year. sec. 59-29a08. If Kansas seeks to continue the detention beyond that year, a court must once again determine beyond a reasonable doubt that the detainee satisfies the same standards as required for the initial confinement.[94]

The Washington Supreme Court disputed the *Hendricks* Court's contention about the Kansas statute by stating that the "Supreme Court is simply wrong about this."[95] The Washington court read both statutes and found no requirement of an annual hearing with a "beyond reasonable doubt" requirement. In fact, the Kansas statute *does* contain a "beyond a reasonable doubt" standard within its language and has since its enactment in 1994. Concerning the standard of proof that must be established during the annual review hearings, the statute reads:

> The burden of proof at the hearing shall be upon the state to prove beyond a reasonable doubt that the committed person's mental abnormality or personality disorder remains such that the person is not safe to be placed in transitional release and if transitionally released is likely to engage in acts of sexual violence.[96]

The court upheld the trial court's judgment that Petersen had not established probable cause to believe his condition had changed. Despite the court's misreading of the Kansas statute, the standard of proof at a hearing was irrelevant because Peterson failed to establish the probable cause to hold one. The court also stated that he had failed to demonstrate that his yearly evaluation was invalid either because the evaluator did not examine him personally or because he was denied the presence of counsel at the examination.

An appeals court case from 1999, *In re Gallegos*,[97] held that a sex offender did not have the right to have his attorney help with answering questions on a psychological exam that would determine whether he was a sexual predator. The court stated that the attorney could observe, but to have the attorney assist would tend to undermine the validity of the test. Gallegos also challenged the validity of the statute, but his arguments were found to lack merit due to the *Hendricks* decision's holding that the commitment of an SVP was a civil proceeding and that involuntary confinement pursuant to the act was not punitive.

The courts of appeal of Washington have decided a few other cases concerning civil commitments of SVPs, but the decisions have all fallen in line behind *Hendricks*.[98]

Wisconsin

The State of Wisconsin has a statute dealing with the commitments of sexually violent persons. Most state court decisions have revolved around the definition of "substantially probable" as found under subsection 7 of Wisc. Code 980.01:

> (7) "Sexually violent person" means a person who has been convicted of a sexually violent offense, has been adjudicated delinquent for a sexually violent offense, or has been found not guilty of or not responsible for a sexually violent offense by reason of insanity or mental disease, defect or illness, and who is dangerous because he or she suffers from a mental disorder that makes it *substantially probable* that the person will engage in acts of sexual violence (emphasis added).[99]

In *State v. Douglas*,[100] Douglas claimed that Chapter 980 was unconstitutionally applied to him because both of the State's experts at trial used an improper definition of the "substantial probability" standard. He asserted that both experts defined substantial probability as "more likely than not" and the term should have been defined as "extremely likely." The trial court's instructions to the jury did not define substantial probability. Before the briefs were filed in Douglas' appeal, the same appellate court deciding this case decided that the term meant "considerably more likely to occur than not to occur." The court, looking closely at the trial court record, found that the defense introduced the definition that Douglas now claimed was improper. The defense elicited the "more likely than not" standard from an expert witness during cross-examination where, in response to defense counsel's inquiry as to the term's meaning, the witness testified: "substantial probability means more likely than not, and the higher it goes beyond more likely than not, the more substantial." Defense counsel then used the "more likely than not" expression in his closing argument to the jury. The court held that Douglas could not select one course of action in the trial court and then, on appeal, allege error precipitated by that course of action.

In *State v. Shaw*,[101] Shaw protested that the trial court had erred by instructing the jury that "substantially probable" meant "more likely than not." The appellate court reversed and remanded back to the trial court for a determination using the "considerably more likely to occur than not to occur" standard as used in *Douglas*. After Shaw again lost in the lower court, the Wisconsin Supreme Court denied review of his case.[102]

Wisconsin also has a case that touches on the aspect of indefinite confinement. In *State v. Lowery*,[103] Lowery argued that the Wisconsin statute subjected him to a lifetime of confinement. The Wisconsin court, borrowing from *Hendricks*, stated that under its statute—as in the Kansas statute—the maximum amount of time an individual can be incapacitated pursuant to a single judicial proceeding is one year.[104]

One Wisconsin case touches on the right to remain silent. In *State v. Zanelli*,[105] Zanelli refused to participate in his formal evaluation prior to the filing of a commitment petition. His refusal to participate was testified to at trial by the doctor who conducted the evaluation, as well as being alluded to by the prosecutor during closing argument. Ordinarily, the right to remain silent would only be available in a criminal trial. However, provisions within the Wisconsin statute effectively incorporate into sexual predator proceedings the constitutional rights of those accused of a crime.[106] The appellate court reversed the judgment of commitment and ordered a new trial.

Other States

Colorado. Colorado courts, although having several cases that have cited *Hendricks*, have not been involved with the civil commitment of sexually violent predators.

Connecticut. Connecticut has had no cases citing *Hendricks* as yet.

District of Columbia. The District of Columbia has a Sexual Psychopath Act[107] on its books, but the act does not deal with post-release commitments.

Florida. Florida does have a law dealing with the involuntary civil commitment of sexually violent predators,[108] but there is no case law as yet.

Kentucky. Two cases in Kentucky cite *Hendricks*, but civil commitment is not part of the equation in either. In both cases,[109] Kentucky's Sex Offender Registration Act[110] was found to be constitutional.

Maine. Maine has had no cases on either civil commitment or sex offender registration.

Montana. Montana jurisprudence contains no cases concerning a civil commitment following a release from incarceration. One case cites *Hendricks*, but it concerns a release from a state hospital after an acquittal by reason of mental disease or defect.[111] The court attempted to determine whether the offender still suffered from a "mental illness."

Nebraska. No relevant cases have been decided in Nebraska.

New York. New York has no state court cases dealing with civil commitments of sexual predators.

North Dakota. One North Dakota case appears, *Grosinger v. M.D.*,[112] in which the plaintiff attacked his classification as a sexually dangerous individual under North Dakota law.[113] The North Dakota Supreme Court dismissed Grosinger's double jeopardy and ex post facto claims using *Hendricks* as a blueprint.

Ohio. Ohio has a phenomenal total of sixty-one cases citing *Hendricks*. Unfortunately, they shed no light on civil commitments, as the state does not have a sexual predator commitment statute. Ohio does have a sex offender registration law that has been challenged time and time again,[114] sometimes successfully. The Ohio Supreme Court's most recent decision on the subject, *State v. Williams*,[115] should shut the door on too many more of the challenges; after reviewing other states' registration laws and the Ohio law's own legislative history, it determined that although Ohio's registration law had an impact on the lives of sex offenders, the law addresses legitimate governmental interests.

Oregon. No cases from Oregon cite the *Hendricks* decision. It seems that in the Pacific Northwest, Washington gets most of the attention with its civil commitment statute.

Pennsylvania. No cases are found in the Keystone State that deal with civil commitments, although numerous cases have used *Hendricks* to knock down double jeopardy and ex post facto arguments.[116]

South Dakota. Similar to Pennsylvania, South Dakota has no law on involuntary civil commitments, but it has some case law on sex offender registration.[117]

Texas. Texas has a law dealing with civil commitments of sex offenders[118] but has no appellate case law challenging the statute.

Vermont. Vermont does not have an SVP commitment act, but one case cites *Hendricks* in the course of a discussion on "dangerousness." The Vermont court stated, in citing *Hendricks*, that the Supreme Court has "never required State legislatures to adopt any particular nomenclature in drafting civil commitment statutes."[119]

Virginia. There is no case law as yet from Virginia on civil commitments. Virginia does have a sexual predator commitment statute, but it will not be effective until July 1, 2001.[120]

CONCLUSION

The *Hendricks* decision was obviously a watershed event for SVP civil commitment laws in the United States. The laws now seem almost impervious to challenges by the offenders. However, some challenges based on procedural aspects sometimes succeed. Those challenges do not have any overall effect on the constitutionality of the laws themselves. The states, and in particular Washington, have to strive to preserve the civil nature of the commitment facilities where the offenders are held.

The other consequence of *Hendricks* has been chronicled within the case summaries above—namely, the assistance it has given courts and prosecutors in establishing the constitutionality of their sex offender registration and notification laws.

There may be further challenges to the civil commitment laws. If the states follow the guidelines established by the *Hendricks* decision, most, if not all of them, should be unsuccessful.

Footnotes

[1] 521 U.S. 346 (1997).

[2] U.S. Const. amend. V ("... nor shall any person be subject for the same offense to be twice put in jeopardy of life or limb.").

[3] U.S. Const. art. I, § 9, cl.3 ("No Bill of Attainder or ex post facto Law shall be passed ...") and art. I, § 10, cl.1 ("No State shall ... pass any bill of attainder, ex post facto law ...."). *Black's Law Dictionary*, 7th ed., defines a Bill of Attainder as a "special legislative act prescribing capital punishment, without a trial, for a person guilty of a high offense such as treason or a felony." *Black's* defines an ex post facto law as one that "applies retroactively ... by criminalizing an action that was legal when it was committed."

[4] Kan. Stat. Ann. § 59-29a01 et seq. (1994).

[5] Arizona, California, Florida, Illinois, Iowa, Kansas, Kentucky, Maine, Minnesota, Missouri, New Jersey, North Dakota, South Carolina, Texax, Virginia (effective July 1, 2001), Washington, and Wisconsin.

[6] There are thirteen judicial circuits in the U.S. federal court system. The First through Eleventh and the District of Columbia Circuits take care of all civil and criminal litigation, while the Federal Circuit handles patent matters. All fifty states, the District of Columbia, Puerto Rico, and the Virgin Islands are represented within district courts established by federal law. For instance, the Sixth Circuit comprises Michigan, Ohio, Kentucky, and Tennessee. All of these states have a number of district courts that are apportioned by size and population. If one appeals a decision from one of the district courts, it would be handled by the Sixth Circuit Court of Appeals located in Cincinnati, Ohio. All of the other districts and circuits are similarly set up.

[7] 121 S. Ct. 727, 730 (2001).

[8] Stenberg v. Carhart, 120 S. Ct. 2597, 2630 (2000).

[9] Hendricks, *supra* note 1, at 360 & n.3.

[10] United States v. Filippi, 211 F.3d 649 (2000).

[11] 39 F. Supp. 2d 148 (D.R.I. 1999).

[12] Hendricks, *supra* note 1, at 358.

[13] 999 F. Supp. 174 (1998).

[14] Mass. Gen. Laws ch. 123A (1999).

[15] New York's Sex Offender Registration Act, N.Y. Correct. Law §§ 168–168v.

[16] 120 F.3d 1263 (1997).

[17] Doe, *supra* note 16, 1274.

[18] Roe v. Office of Adult Probation, 125 F.3d 47 (1997).

[19] Francis S. v. Stone, 995 F. Supp. 368 (S.D.N.Y. 1998).

[20] Francis S., *supra* note 19, at 388.

[21] *See* Casalvera v. Comm'r, 998 F. Supp. 411 (D. Del. 1998); Alan A. v. Verniero, 970 F. Supp. 1153 (D.N.J. 1997); E.B. v. Verniero, 119 F.3d 1077 (3d Cir. 1997).

[22] U.S. App. LEXIS 5459, at *18 (4th Cir. 2000).

[23] United States v. Henley, 8 F. Supp.2d 503 (E.D.N.C. 1998).

[24] 185 F.3d 279 (1999).

[25] Lee v. Louisiana, 1998 U.S. Dist. LEXIS 12843 (E.D. La. 1998).

[26] Cutshall v. Sundquist, 193 F.3d 466 (6th Cir. 1999).

[27] Lanni v. Engler, 994 F.Supp. 849 (E.D. Mich 1998).

[28] 122 F.3d 38 (8th Cir. 1997).

[29] 58 F. Supp.2d 1028 (D. Minn. 1999).

[30] Minn. Stat. §§ 253B.02(18b), 253B.185 (2000).

[31] Minn. Stat. § 253.02(18b) (2000).

[32] 552 U.S. 1011 (1997).

[33] In re Linehan, 594 N.W.2d 867 (Minn. 1999).

[34] Linehan v. Minnesota, 120 S. Ct. 587 (1999).

[35] 201 F.3d 1136 (9th Cir. 2000).

[36] Cal. Welf. & Inst. Code §§ 6600-6609.3.

[37] Wash. Rev. Code §71.09.

[38] No. 98-36272, 1999 U.S. App. LEXIS 23181, at *3 (9th Cir. 1999).

[39] 192 F.3d 870 (9th Cir. 1999).

[40] *Supra* note 7, 121 S. Ct. at 737 (2001).

[41] Haw. Sess. Laws 304-05 (Act 164).

[42] 131 F.3d 818 (9th Cir. 1997).

[43] No. C91-664WD (unpub. op., W.D. Wash. 1994), later known as Turay v. Seling, No. C91-664WD (unpub. op. W.D. Wash. 1997).

[44] 108 F. Supp. 2d 1148 (W.D. Wash. 2000).

[45] 35 F. Supp. 2d 852 (D. Utah 1999).

[46] 746 So. 2d 410 (Ala. Crim. App. 1999).

[47] Ala. Code § 15-20-20 et seq. (2000).

[48] Ala. Code 12-15-1.1 et seq. (2000).

[49] Ariz. Rev. Stat. §§ 36-3701 et seq. (2000).

[50] 195 Ariz. 293, 987 P.2d 779 (Ariz. Ct. App. 1999).

[51] Ariz. Rev. Stat. §§ 36-3707(B), 36-3712(B) (2000).

[52] Ariz. Rev. Stat. § 36-3707(B) (2000).

[53] Ariz. Rev. Stat. § 36-3712(B) (2000).

[54] *See supra* note 36.

[55] 19 Cal. 4th 1138, 969 P.2d 584 (1999).

[56] Hubbart, *supra* note 55, 19 Cal. 4th at 150, 969 P.2d at 592.

[57] Hubbart, *supra* note 55, 969 P.2d at 599.

[58] 80 Cal. App. 4th 820 (Cal. Dist. Ct. App. 2000).

[59] 725 Ill. Comp. Stat. 207/1 et seq. (West 2000).

[60] 189 Ill. 2d 548, 727 N.E.2d 228 (2000).

[61] People v. Varner, 248 Ill. Dec. 518, 734 N.E.2d 226 (Ill. App. 2000); Winterhalter v. People, 730 N.E.2d 1158 (Ill. App. Ct. 2000).

[62] 707 N.E.2d 1039 (Ind. Ct. App. 1999).

[63] *See* State v. Hurst, 688 N.E.2d 402 (Ind. 1997); Freidline v. Civil S. Bend, 733 N.E.2d 490 (Ind. App. 2000).

[64] 7 P.3d 285 (Kan. 2000).

[65] Kan. Stat. Ann. 59-29a02(a) (1999).

[66] Kan. Stat. Ann. § 59-29a02(b) (1999).

[67] Kan. Stat. Ann. § 59-29a02(c) (1999).

[68] *Hendricks, supra* note 1, at 358.

[69] 263 Kan. 822, 953 P.2d 666 (1998).

[70] Kan. Stat. Ann. § 59-29a06 (1999).

[71] Kan. App. 2d 117, 978 P.2d 300 (1999).

[72] Mass. Gen. Laws ch.123A, 1999 Mass. Acts 74.

[73] *See* Lisa Kavanaugh, "Massachusetts's Sexually Dangerous Persons Legislation: Can Juries Make a Bad Law Better?", 35 *Harv. C.R.-C.L. L.* 509 (2000).

[74] Kavanaugh, *supra* note 73, at 510 n.9.

[75] Mich. Comp. Laws § 780.501 et seq. (1968).

[76] 454 Mich. 851, 560 N.W.2d 629 (1997).

[77] 594 N.W.2d 867 (Minn. 1999).

[78] Minn. Stat. §253B.02(18c) (2000).

[79] Minn. Stat. §§ 526.09, 526.10 (1992).

[80] *Hendricks, supra* note 1, at 358.

[81] In re Linehan, *supra* note 33, at 882.

[82] Linehan v. Minnesota, *supra* note 34.

[83] Mo. Rev. Stat. §§ 632.480–632.513 (2000).

[84] No. 22998, 2000 Mo. App. LEXIS 731 (Mo. Ct. App. 2000).

[85] N.J. Stat. Ann. §§ 30:4-27.24–30:4-27.38 (West 2000).

[86] 94 N.J. 128, 462 A.2d 1252 (1983).

[87] S. L., *supra* note 86, 94 N.J. at 139.

[88] In re D.M., 313 N.J. Super. 449, 712 A.2d 1277 (1998).

[89] 139 Wash. 2d 379, 986 P.2d 790 (1999).

[90] Wash. Rev. Code § 71.09 (2000).

[91] Turay, *supra* note 89, 139 Wash. 2d at 420.

[92] 138 Wash. 2d 70, 980 P.2d 1204 (1999).

[93] *See* Wash. R. App. P. 2.3(b).

[94] *Hendricks, supra* note 1, at 364.

[95] In re Petersen, *supra* note 92, 138 Wash. 2d at 79.

[96] Kan. Stat. Ann. § 59-29a08(b) (1999).

[97] 95 Wash. App. 1055 (1999).

[98] *See* In re Nicholas, 95 Wash. App. 1043 (1999); In re Brooks, 94 Wash. App. 716 (1999), In re Gaff, 90 Wash. App. 834 (1998); In re Clewley, 89 Wash. App. 1045 (1998).

[99] Wisc. Code § 980.01 et seq. (1999).

[100] 229 Wis. 2d 250; 599 N.W.2d 665 (Wis. Ct. App. 1999).

[101] 226 Wis. 2d 160, 594 N.W.2d 419 (Wis. Ct. App. 1999).

[102] State v. Shaw, 233 Wis. 2d 84, 609 N.W.2d 473 (Wis. 2000).

[103] 226 Wis. 2d 561, 596 N.W.2d 501 (Wis. Ct. App. 1999).

[104] *See* Wis. Code § 980.07 (1999); Kan. Stat. Ann. § 59-29a08(b) (1999).

[105] Wis. 2d 358, 569 N.W.2d 301 (Wis. Ct. App. 1997).

[106] *See* Wis. Code § 980.03(2)(b) (A "person who is subject of the petition has the right to remain silent . . ."); Wis. Code § 980.05(1m) ("At the trial to determine whether the person who is the subject of a petition under s. 980.02 is a sexually violent person, all rules of evidence in criminal actions apply. All constitutional rights available to a defendant in a criminal proceeding are available to the person.").

[107] D.C. Code Ann. §§ 22-3503–22-3511 (1999).

[108] Fla. Stat. Ann. §§ 394.910 et seq. (West 2000).

[109] Hall v. Commonwealth, No.1999-CA-000518-MR, 2000 Ky. App. LEXIS 72 (Ky. Ct. App. 2000); Hyatt v. Commonwealth, No. 1999-CA-000703-MR, 2000 Ky. App. LEXIS 71 (Ky. Ct. App. 2000).

[110] Ky. Rev. Stat. Ann. § 17.500 (2000).

[111] State v. Woods, 285 Mont. 46, 945 P.2d 918 (1997).

[112] 1999 N.D. 160, 598 N.W.2d 799 (1999).

[113] N.D. Cent. Code ch. 25-03.3 (1999).

[114] Ohio Rev. Code ch. 2950 (2000).

[115] 88 Ohio St. 3d 513, 728 N.E.2d 342 (2000).

[116] *See, e.g.,* Commonwealth v. Gaffney, 557 Pa. 327, 733 A.2d 616 (1999).

[117] Meinders v. Weber, 2000 S.D. 2, 604 N.W.2d 248 (2000).

[118] Tex. Health & Safety Code §§ 841.001 et seq. (2000).

[119] *Hendricks, supra* note 1, at 359.

[120] Va. Code Ann. § 37.1–70.1 (Michie 2000).

Part 2

Clinical Issues

Several years ago, the role of clinicians in the debate about civil commitment was to address whether mental health diagnoses were being inappropriately used and to predict whether the adoption of SVP laws would negatively affect the treatment of the seriously mentally ill. Given that SVP statutes have appeared to withstand the constitutional challenges, clinicians have now become more involved in ensuring the quality of treatment offered to individuals who are civilly committed. Part 2 discusses various aspects of quality treatment programs.

In Chapter 5, Roxanne Lieb and Craig Nelson provide an overview of the progress in various states toward establishing viable treatment programs for those civilly committed as sexual offenders. The authors offer a helpful comparison of the individual approaches to this problem. Civil commitment is not just an American experience, of course. In Chapter 6, David Thornton describes its adoption by the United Kingdom. He outlines the similarities and differences between the United States and the United Kingdom and addresses how the latter is attempting to broaden the reach of these statutes.

In Chapter 7, Rick Harry speaks from the experience of having handled the administrative concerns of the longest-standing civil commitment program for sexual offenders. He discusses issues such as program location, program jurisdiction, and the numerous staffing concerns that are unavoidable in such programs.

John Bergman has conducted intensive dramatherapy sessions in sexual offender programs throughout several countries and has identified specific concerns that emerge when working with SVP programs. He shares his observations and recommendations in Chapter 8. In Chapter 9, Joanne Fairfield describes the importance of working with the nonoffending partners and other family members of sex offenders. Her three-part model appears particularly well adapted to the treatment needs of the civil commitment population.

Initially, programs were mainly concerned with providing adequate in-patient groups, but during the past few years the focus has turned more toward the release of the first detainees under the SVP laws. In Chapter 10, Anita Schlank and Pam Bidelman discuss the various dilemmas treatment providers face when planning for a program's first releases back to the community. A detailed description of one program's plan for gradual reintegration is presented.

In Chapter 11, Harry Hoberman updates his chapter from volume one of this series by noting relevant changes to psychological assessment techniques used in the commitment trials of sexual predators. This chapter is essential reading for any professional called upon to provide expert testimony in sex offender cases.

Chapter 5

Treatment Programs for Sexually Violent Predators—A Review of States

by Roxanne Lieb, M.P.A. & Craig Nelson, Ph.D.*

Introduction	5-2
Treatment Standards	5-3
Population Characteristics	5-3
Previous Treatment	5-4
Multiple Diagnoses; Personality Disorders	5-5
Program Settings	5-6
Secure Psychiatric Hospital	5-6
Mental Health Facility Within a Prison	5-6
Free-Standing Secure Facility	5-8
Staffing	5-9
Staff Levels and Patterns	5-9
Psychiatric Hospitals	5-9
Free-Standing Facility	5-9
Prison-Based Program	5-11
Training and Expertise	5-11
Cohesion of Treatment Team	5-11
Cost of Staffing	5-11
Treatment Programming	5-12
Cognitive-Behavioral Approaches	5-12
Medications	5-13
Behavior Therapy	5-13
Assessment	5-14
Treatment Planning	5-15
Program Phases	5-15

---

* The views expressed here are those of the authors and they do not necessarily reflect the policies of the California Department of Mental Health or the Washington Institute for Public Policy.

  Ancillary Treatment Programming 5-15
  Special Populations 5-15
Residential Management Issues 5-16
  Resistance to Treatment 5-16
  Harassment of Staff 5-17
  Strategies to Minimize Difficulties 5-17
  Resident Advocacy 5-18
State Provisions for Least Restrictive Alternative 5-18
  Transition to Outpatient Setting 5-19
  Community Notification Issues 5-20
  Types of LRA Facilities 5-20
Summary 5-21

INTRODUCTION

  While much of the recent attention to the civil commitment of sex offenders concerns the constitutionality of the commitment statutes, there has been relatively little focus on the treatment programs developed to implement these new laws. With its 1997 *Kansas v. Hendricks* decision (117 S. Ct. 2072 (1997)), the U.S. Supreme Court found constitutional the involuntary commitment of sexually violent predators (SVPs) following the completion of their prison terms. The Court majority held that the state has an obligation to provide care and treatment, but also that the constitutionality of the Kansas SVP commitment law does not rest on having a treatment program with demonstrated effectiveness in curing sex offenders. In a concurring opinion on the case, however, Justice Kennedy cautioned that if "treatment provisions were adopted as a sham or mere pretext, there would have been an indication of the forbidden purpose to punish." Justice Breyer's dissenting opinion expressed concern that Hendricks was provided treatment only after his release date from prison, and the inadequacy of that treatment suggested that it was punitive. Thus it does appear that the Supreme Court suggests that while treatment may be an "ancillary goal" of the civil commitment of sex offenders, an adequate program may be necessary to uphold the statute.

  Several lower federal court decisions have emphasized the importance of treatment in state SVP programs. In the *Turay v. Weston* (No. C91-664WD (unpub. op., W.D. Wash. Feb. 4, 1997)) Order and Injunction (Order and Injunction), the district court ruled that the state of Washington was not providing constitutionally required treatment in its SVP program and appointed a Special Master to oversee efforts to bring the program into compliance (see Marques, Chapter 2, this volume). In a related case, the U.S. Court of Appeals for the Ninth Circuit determined that "actual conditions of confinement may divest a facially valid statute of its 'civil' label . . ." (*Young v. Weston*, 192 F.3d 870 (9th Cir. 1999)). At the time of this writing, this matter is under review by the U.S. Supreme Court. Clearly, the courts have a strong interest in the law's constitutionality as it is applied in individual states. Both the treatment program and the residents' conditions of confinement will influence the overall validity of state statutes.

  In this chapter, we will describe states' efforts to develop and provide adequate treatment to committed SVPs, including treatment standards, population characteristics, siting and staffing of programs, treatment and assessment approaches, resident management issues, and least restrictive alternatives.

TREATMENT STANDARDS

Like many mental health laws, most statutes are relatively silent about the specific types of treatment that should be offered to SVPs (Brakel & Cavanaugh, 2000). As of yet, standards to which treatment programs for SVPs can be held accountable continue to evolve. Marques thoroughly reviews the development of such standards in Chapter 2 of this volume. In addition, the Association for the Treatment of Sexual Abusers (ATSA, 1998) has prepared a position paper, and the National Association of State Mental Health Program Directors (NASMHPD, 1999) has provided a technical report on the treatment of SVPs. White it is beyond the scope of this chapter to review all of these recommended standards, we can state the general guidelines that apply when developing an SVP treatment program. Such a program should:

- Clearly operate in a treatment-oriented, not a punitive, environment;
- Provide services consistent with current professional standards for sex offender treatment;
- Present the possibility of conditional release through treatment; and
- Contain oversight mechanisms and grievance procedures to ensure that the program's operations and decision-making are open to external review.

POPULATION CHARACTERISTICS

To determine the appropriate treatment and programming needs for an SVP population, it is first necessary to gain an understanding of the basic characteristics of this group. At the time of this writing, sixteen states have enacted SVP statutes that authorize civil commitment following criminal conditions; to date, this has resulted in the commitment of 885 people. Some other states have sexual predator laws governing sentencing or registration and notification that is not related to civil commitment. The Texas statute requires outpatient treatment for SVPs, which differentiates its commitment law from those of other states. Virginia has passed an SVP statute that becomes effective in July 2001. In addition, about 830 sex offenders are detained in SVP facilities while awaiting trials, and close to forty have been conditionally released. Conditional release typically occurs following treatment, but in some states, courts can order an SVP directly to a less restrictive alternative. One state, California, estimates that of all adult sex offenders released from prison, less than 2 percent have been subject to commitment as SVPs (California Legislative Analysts Office, 1999). Table 5.1 presents these numbers in detail.

Like most sex offenders, the vast majority of SVPs are male, although Washington, Minnesota, and California have all committed a female. In a 1999 survey of SVP programs in six states (California, Illinois, Iowa, Minnesota, South Carolina, and Washington), Hennessy (1999) found the average SVP was slightly over forty-one years old, with a range from eighteen to seventy-three years of age.

Table 5.1
Detained, Committed, and Conditionally Released SVPs by State, June 2000

State	Detained SVPs	Committed SVPs	Conditional Released	Total
Arizona	71	30	17*	118
California	140	242	1	383
Florida	172	12	0	184
Illinois	61	52	4	117
Iowa	12	12	0	24
Kansas	25	40	1**	66
Massachusetts	32	0	0	32
Minnesota	8	158	1	167
Missouri	25	5	0	30
New Jersey	71	20	1 deported	92
North Dakota	1	7	0	8
South Carolina	85	22	0	107
Washington	63	55	5	123
Wisconsin	63	230	5	306
Total	829	885	35	1,757

*On least restrictive alternative.
** Five additional persons were on conditional release but have been returned to prison because of violations.

Wisconsin has committed a ninety-five-year old man (Maller, 2000). This older population is not surprising given the significant criminal history that is required for SVP commitment in most states. Because of this comparatively older population, SVP programs must plan for more extensive and expensive medical care than typically provided in most correctional and mental health facilities.

Further analysis of the Hennessy (1999) survey indicated that of 268 SVPs, 38 percent were identified as rapists, 53 percent as child molesters, and 9 percent as both child molesters and rapists. This data is somewhat skewed, however, because over one-half of the sample represents California, which has a much higher percentage of child molesters. The reported population of the remaining five states was almost evenly distributed between child molesters and rapists.

Data from California, with the largest SVP program in the country, indicate that 30 percent of this population had victimized males exclusively, 56 percent females, and 10 percent both genders (victim identification was not readily available on the remaining 4 percent of the population). The relatively large number of SVPs with male victims is likely influenced by the state's use of actuarial prediction tools that heavily weight male victims as a risk factor for sexual reoffending (Hanson, 1997; Hanson & Bussiere, 1998; Hanson & Thornton, 1999).

Previous Treatment

Many of those committed as SVPs have previously received treatment. It is estimated that approximately one-third of those in California and over one-half of those

Table 5.2
SVP Diagnoses (Individuals can have more than one.)

Diagnosis	Percentage
Personality disorder	67%
Pedophilia	53%
Other paraphilias	48%
Mood disorder	16%
Thought disorder	5%
Other diagnoses	22%

in Minnesota (Janus, 2000) have had previous inpatient treatment experiences. For the Minnesota population, 96 percent of those with prior treatment experience had either quit in an early phase of treatment or had been terminated by staff due to poor compliance. Despite this previous treatment experience, they have either reoffended or failed to reduce their risks sufficiently to be released to the community. This suggests that traditional approaches may be inadequate in addressing the treatment needs of this high-risk population.

Multiple Diagnoses; Personality Disorders

Table 5.2 reports the diagnostic profiles of 342 SVPs in the survey treatment programs (Hennessy, 1999). Of course, many SVPs carry multiple diagnoses. The large number of detected paraphilias is to be expected given that state commitment laws typically require some type of mental disorder or abnormality combined with sexual dangerousness. Typically, a nexus must be found between this diagnosis and risk for sexual reoffense.

Turning to California, the data show that 134 SVPs agreed to phallometric assessments to determine their sexual arousal profiles. Approximately 60 percent exhibited a "deviant" profile (defined as clinically significant levels of arousal to stimuli depicting children or aggression toward women), 12 percent emitted nondeviant profiles, and the remaining 28 percent were classified as nonresponders. This information points to the necessity of including interventions that are specifically designed to impact these deviant urges and behavior.

The number of identified personality disorders, usually antisocial personality disorder, is also noteworthy. A pervasive pattern of disregard for and violation of the rights of others characterize this diagnosis (APA, 1994). Psychopathy is viewed by many experts as an extreme version of this disorder (Cleckley, 1982; Hare et al., 1991). In the California program, for instance, 143 of the SVP patients have been administered the Psychopathy Checklist—Revised (PCL-R) (Hare, 1991). About 28 percent of the population tested were in the clinically significant range (scores >30) for psychopathy. It is expected that there would be a high representation of psychopaths in the SVP population. As with having male victims, psychopathy is recognized as a significant risk factor for recidivism (Harris et al., 1991; Hemphill et al., 1998; Quinsey et al., 1995). The relatively large proportion of psychopaths in the treatment population has a significant impact on the operation of the program; their manipulative tendencies with both staff and other residents can pose serious management problems. In addition, the literature suggests relatively poor treatment motivation and outcomes with this population (e.g., Ogloff et al., 1990; Seto & Barbaree, 1999).

The survey indicated a substantial number of SVPs with clinically diagnosable mood and thought disorders. Thus, a significant proportion of the population also requires traditional mental health treatment services, such as psychotropic medications, in addition to offense-specific sex offender treatment.

PROGRAM SETTINGS

Table 5.3 compares state statutes according to the responsible state agency and type of setting designated in the statute to provide care and treatment of civilly committed sex offenders. With the exception of Massachusetts, the states have selected a human services rather than correctional agency to preside over operations. This choice helps to distinguish an SVP commitment from the punishment purpose associated with the corrections purview. At least two states (Florida and Illinois) have contracted with a private firm to provide treatment services to this population.

States have generally selected one of three types of facilities to house and treat SVPs— secure psychiatric hospitals, mental health facilities within prisons, and freestanding secure facilities. The advantages and disadvantages of each type of facility are summarized below.

Secure Psychiatric Hospital

Some states, such as California and Arizona, use a secure state psychiatric hospital setting for their programs. Where a program is housed within an existing psychiatric hospital or is administered through a common organization, SVP staff can take advantage of existing staff expertise in regard to setting up and operating a mental health treatment program. The SVP staff may also have access to medical care, external oversight in the form of licensing and accreditation agencies, availability of educational and vocational services, and access to services for residents who may suffer from a major mental illness or a developmental disability.

A disadvantage of this type of setting is that the physical plant and operating procedures may not be adequate for a high-functioning and criminally sophisticated population. The staff may not have expertise in treating the personality disorders or paraphilias of SVPs. Also, the licensing and accreditation standards for these facilities typically emphasize the needs of a clientele exhibiting classic symptoms of psychosis or organic brain dysfunction, diagnoses that are rare within an SVP population.

Mental Health Facility Within a Prison

States such as Washington and Kansas have placed their programs within the confines of correctional facilities. The programs are typically run by treatment staff who

Table 5.3
State SVP Programs

State	Responsible Agency	Setting
Arizona	Health Services	Hospital
California	Mental Health	Hospital
Florida	Children and Family Services	Free-standing secure facility
Illinois	Human Services	Free-standing secure facility
Iowa	Human Services	Forensic mental health facility within Corrections
Kansas	Social and Rehabilitative Services	Forensic mental health facility within Corrections
Massachusetts	Department of Corrections	Correctional facility
Minnesota	Human Services	Free-standing secure facility & hospital
Missouri	Mental Health	Authorized to contract with Corrections
New Jersey	Human Services	Secure facility operated by Corrections
North Dakota	Human Services	Hospital
South Carolina	Mental Health	Secure facility
Virginia*	Mental Health, Retardation and Substance Abuse Services	Mental health facility within the perimeter of a correctional facility
Washington	Social and Health Services	Mental health facility within a correctional facility
Wisconsin	Social Services	Free-standing secure facility

* Law scheduled for implementation in 2001.

report to a human services agency, with perimeter security and auxiliary services (e.g., food, visiting policies, laundry) provided by the correctional agency (see

DesLauriers's and Gardner's discussion of the Kansas treatment program in volume 1 of this book). The security of prison walls is reassuring to both the public and elected officials, but the difficulties of these "arranged marriages" can be quite profound. Even when representatives of the two agencies actively strive toward cooperation, the differences in agency missions make conflict inevitable. Consider the following questions:

- Are SVPs, like prisoners, subject to strip searches after each visitation with family and friends? Are their phone calls monitored?
- If there is a disturbance in the SVP program, which staff responds? If it appears that seclusion is needed, where is the SVP resident taken? Which agency controls decisions regarding seclusion and isolation?
- Can SVPs use the prison recreation yard, the dining area, the law library, the hobby shop? If so, must they be segregated from prisoners?
- If an SVP resident attempts to escape, do correctional officers use weapons?

The federal court injunction in Washington State (Order and Injunction) offers extensive documentation of the conflicts inherent in running a treatment-oriented facility inside a prison. The Special Master's reports in this case detail the layers of decisions necessary to operate a facility inside prison walls.

Free-Standing Secure Facility

A third option, such as the Minnesota Sex Offender Treatment Program (Schlank et al., 1999), is a free-standing secure treatment facility. Such institutions can be specifically designed and licensed for the SVP population. This option provides physical and operational security, avoids contact between the SVP population and either psychiatric patients or offenders, and provides a specialized treatment atmosphere for sex offenders. The program managers can establish treatment protocols and operating procedures that make the most sense for a sex offender population (e.g., rules regarding possession of pornography, Internet use, and visitation by children).

The clear disadvantage of this option is cost—Minnesota has spent $16.75 million constructing the 100-bed facility at Moose Lake (Schlank et al., 1999). Washington has budgeted $14 million for Phase One of a free-standing facility planned for McNeil Island; forty-eight beds are scheduled to be available in 2002. The final price tag of the 402-bed facility, scheduled for completion in 2006, is estimated at $81 million (Ziegler, 2000). At present, California is locating a site for a secure treatment facility for up to 1,500 SVPs. This new facility is expected to cost as much as $300 million to construct and to employ as many as 2,000 people (*Bakersfield Californian*, 1998). Any state planning such a facility must anticipate some opposition from neighboring communities. Despite the economic advantages of new jobs, communities under consideration to house these facilities express the fear that their area and its residents will see increased crime and carry a stigma (Rainey & Turene, 2000).

STAFFING

The effectiveness of any mental health treatment program depends largely on the quantity, quality, expertise, and motivation of its staff. To deliver a quality treatment program, the state (or a contractor) must recruit and retain sufficient qualified clinical staff (see Harry, Chapter 7, this volume). The remote locations of many SVP programs, in combination with a population that is difficult to treat, resistive, and often litigious, only complicates these staffing challenges.

Staffing considerations must first ensure a sufficient number of employees to provide a safe and secure environment. Staff levels must be adequate so that violence among residents is prevented or can be quickly contained. In addition, staff need to vigorously monitor the environment for potential contraband (particularly weapons, drugs, or deviant pornography) and provide sufficient vigilance to prevent escapes. To promote a positive therapeutic milieu, staff must interact with the residents, observe and monitor their behaviors, and intervene before problematic situations develop. The consequences of allowing a weak, disinterested staff to run a program for sexually dangerous persons has been revealed at several points in history, most recently in England (Quinsey, 1999).

Staff Levels and Patterns

The Hennessy survey (1999) found that the six SVP programs studied relied on multi-disciplinary professional teams to plan and deliver treatment. The staffing patterns and professional credentials required by any program depend to some degree on the program's location and its physical capacities. Programs in psychiatric hospitals, prison settings, and free-standing SVP facilities all have different staff patterns.

Psychiatric Hospitals. Programs located in traditional psychiatric hospitals usually require all staff to be licensed and credentialed. In addition, psychiatric hospitals are likely to provide a larger number of medical staff (physicians, psychiatrists, and registered nurses) than programs placed in free-standing secure facilities or prison environments.

For example, in the psychiatric hospital where the California program is located, the budgeted staffing ratios provide for 1.5 physicians and psychiatrist, 4.2 doctoral level clinical psychologists, 6.2 master's level trained social workers, 3.7 bachelor's level trained rehabilitation therapists, 1.5 teachers, and 85.5 nursing staff for every 100 SVPs. Direct care is provided through nursing staff who include registered nurses and licensed psychiatric technicians. Psychiatric technicians must complete a full-time, one-year community college curriculum and are licensed by the state. Minimum unit coverage is typically one nursing staff for every eight SVPs on the day and evening shift and one staff for every sixteen SVPs on the night shift. These ratios may be increased based on patient need, and a psychiatrist and a nonpsychiatric physician is on duty within the facility twenty-four hours per day.

Free-Standing Facility. The free-standing facility in Minnesota has six social workers, six behavior analysts, six psychologists, six recreation therapists, and six recre-

Table 5.4
Staffing Ratios Per 100 SVPs at Three Different Types of Facilities

Staff	Minnesota Sex Offender Program—Free-Standing Secure Facility	California's Sex Offender Commitment Program—Psychiatric Hospital	Washington's Special Commitment Center—Within Correctional Facility
Physician/Psychiatrist	1	1.5	0.5 Psychiatrist Prison physician on call
Psychologist	4	5.2	5.1
Social worker	4	6.2	1.6
Forensic therapists	N/A	N/A	16
Behavior analysts	4	N/A	N/A
Rehabilitation therapist	4 Recreation therapists 4 Recreation program assistants	3.7	2
Education	3	1.5	Contract services
Direct care staff	54.0 Residential security counselors 8.0 RNs	85.5 RNs and licensed psychiatric technicians	56.9 Residential rehabilitation counselors
Unit staffing ratios	1:8—Days & evenings 1:16—Nights	1:8—Days & evenings 1:16—Nights	1:8—Days & evenings 1:15—Nights

ation program assistants assigned to its 150-bed facility. Minimum unit coverage is approximately one direct care staff for every eight SVPs on each living unit on the day and evening shifts and one for every twelve SVPs during the night shift. Residential security counselors staff the units; the minimum qualifications for this position are a high school education and satisfactory completion of a written exam. The treatment team also includes three teachers, eight professional nurses (providing twenty-four-hour coverage), a full-time physician, and a part-time psychiatrist (Schlank et al., 1999). Round-the-clock physician or psychiatrist coverage is not required in this setting, as psychiatric needs are few and registered nurses can assess the need for possible transfer to a hospital for medical emergencies.

Prison-Based Program. For the 120 residents in Washington's prison-based program, the state employs seventy-five residential rehabilitation counselors and supervisors who provide direct care supervision on the living units. As in the free-standing treatment facility, these staff have a minimum of a high school education with specialized training and orientation provided through the treatment program. In addition, six psychologists, two master's level social workers, two recreation therapists, and twenty forensic therapists (Ziegler, 2000) provide treatment activities. Table 5.4 summarizes this information.

These figures are not provided to encourage direct comparisons between programs, nor are they meant to dictate adequate staffing levels. Instead, they are presented as examples of staffing available at some typical treatment programs. State law or court orders can also significantly influence staffing levels. Some programs provide extensive forensic evaluation and testimony to the courts for annual placement hearings; clearly, such obligations influence staffing requirements for psychiatrists or psychologists.

Training and Expertise

The number of employees is only one element in determining staff adequacy. Training and expertise are also of paramount importance. At present, academic education within university systems does not provide trainees the specialized knowledge and experiences to treat sex offenders, even for the those with the most advanced degrees (ATSA, 1997). Therefore, SVP programs must be prepared to provide the specialty training of many of their own staff in sex offender treatment.

This training must go beyond a general orientation to the SVP population or the program's major treatment components. New hires need rigorous specialty training and supervision from experienced clinical staff, supplemented by access to on-site colloquia and training seminars by external experts. Support in the form of release time, conference fees, and travel expenses is essential so staff can attend conferences that focus on sex offender topics and acquire the requisite competence to treat the population.

Cohesion of Treatment Team. Staff cohesion is an important element of a successful inpatient treatment program. All clinical staff members of the program, from the unit staff to the most highly trained clinicians, must work collaboratively, sharing information and participating in the development and execution of each SVP's treatment plan. The potential for inappropriate boundary violations with the population is extremely high. This potential is diminished when you maintain an inclusive treatment team approach that includes all staff and presents clearly defined roles and open lines of communication.

Because of the unique challenges of this population, staff often find the work difficult. They must establish professional boundaries with residents, maintain consistent limits, and sustain enthusiasm for the work. The staff must believe that the treatment has value and that those they treat, if cooperative and motivated, will benefit from the program and increase the opportunity for community release. These ingredients are key to the development of a therapeutic alliance with the residents.

Cost of Staffing. For any mental health treatment program, staffing is the primary cost driver. Based on personal communication with various SVP treatment program clinical directors, the typical costs of care and treatment for the SVP population ranges from $90,000 to $120,000 per year. These figures exclude the costs associated with (1) identifying dangerous sex offenders about to be released from prison, (2) court expenses for trials, and (3) related litigation brought by SVPs against their programs.

TREATMENT PROGRAMMING

What treatment activities should occur within an SVP program? As a starting point, we will examine those therapy components viewed as essential in sex offender treatment programs.

Cognitive-Behavioral Approaches

Most experts believe that cognitive-behavioral interventions offer the most effective treatment approaches for sex offenders (Marshall & Barbaree, 1990; Marshall et al., 1991). Meta-analyses of treatment outcome studies with sex offenders have found biological and cognitive-behavioral treatment approaches to be the most effective in reducing recidivism (Alexander, 1999; Hall, 1995). Thus, these are components that should be incorporated into any legitimate SVP treatment program.

Cognitive-behavioral approaches such as relapse prevention (Laws, 1989; Pithers et al., 1983) have gained popularity in recent years. A 1994 national survey of sex offender treatment programs found that a majority of programs used this specific approach (Freeman-Longo et al., 1995). The relapse prevention framework has been extended for specific application to SVPs (Marques et al., 2000). Hennessy's 1999 survey of major SVP programs found that all of the programs were primarily cognitive-behavioral in their orientation, and five out six relied extensively on relapse prevention.

Cognitive-behavior therapy and relapse prevention are primarily oriented toward changing risk factors related to sexual offending. The model does not aim to "cure," but rather to help individuals learn strategies for effective self-control of deviant sexual impulses and behavior. The concept of control involves the offender's active participation in the behavior change process and stresses realization that continued abstinence from offending requires constant vigilance and effort. This approach allows that sex offenses are neither simple nor isolated events, that rape and child molestation are complex behaviors with multiple determinants ranging from broad lifestyle factors and cognitive distortions to deviant sexual arousal patterns and more circumscribed skill deficits.

Under this paradigm, the major treatment task is to identify the specific risks for reoffense and to plan and practice coping strategies to reduce these risks. Risk management strategies may include correcting distorted thinking, learning control of deviant sexual urges, learning to empathize with the victim, improving interpersonal relationships skills, handling negative emotional states such as boredom or anger, using medications effectively, eliminating substance abuse, and identifying and avoiding high-risk situations (Nelson et al., 1988). Hennessy (1999) reports that some of the specific treatment foci and techniques the SVP treatment programs have identified as effective include:

- Sex education
- Sexual assault cycles
- Behavior offense chains
- Cognitive distortions and thinking errors
- Victim empathy
- Interpersonal relationships and family relationships
- Communication skills
- Positive, prosocial sexuality
- Substance abuse

Medications

Some medications, especially antiandrogens, have proven to be effective tools in the treatment and management of sexual offending (Bradford, 1990; Prentky, 1997). Antiandrogens reduce testosterone levels and the sexual drive in males. Although they do not alter the triggers for an individual's sexual arousal, they do seem to reduce the intensity and frequency of sexual urges, making control and management more feasible.

Selective serotonin reuptake inhibitors (SSRIs) are used in the management and treatment of sex offenders (Federoff, 1993). These commonly used antidepressants have also been found to interrupt obsessive-compulsive behavior and to lower libidinal drive.

All six SVP programs surveyed by Henessy (1999) report the use of medications in their programs. The survey shows that about 7.5 percent of residents had medications prescribed for sex offense-specific behaviors. The percentage is higher for SVPs actively involved in offense-specific treatment, with 13 percent of these individuals being administered either an antiandrogen or an SSRI as part of the management and treatment strategy for their deviant sexual behavior.

While medications may play an active role in the treatment of some SVPs, it is important not to see this form of treatment as a panacea or "cure" for the sexual disorders that afflict these individuals. Instead, they are one component of a comprehensive, multimodal treatment approach.

Behavior Therapy

Behavior therapy involves modifying deviant sexual arousal patterns through reconditioning and learning principles. For many sex offenders, especially those with the lengthy history of illicit sexual behavior found among SVPs, deviant sexual arousal is a significant risk factor for reoffending. That is, many child molesters may have little or no sexual interest toward adults while having a strong preference toward children. Similarly, rapists may actually prefer forced sex to mutually consenting sex with an adult partner.

Typically, behavior therapy involves repeated pairing of aversive stimuli, such as unpleasant odors or distressing thoughts, to the deviant sexual fantasies, with the eventual goal that deviant stimuli will no longer evoke sexual arousal. Similarly, behavioral techniques can be directed to enhance sexual arousal to appropriate stimuli such as mutually consenting sex with an adult partner. Generally, these treatment techniques are included only as a component of a more comprehensive treatment program. Specific behavioral techniques include covert sensitization, odor aversion, masturbatory satiation, and verbal satiation.

While behavioral reconditioning techniques have demonstrated an ability to modify these deviant sexual arousal patterns in the treatment setting, these effects may not always generalize into other environments. They may be short-lived unless regular booster sessions are included as part of the treatment regimen (Quinsey & Earls, 1990). Five of the six programs surveyed report the availability of some type of behavior therapy, usually covert sensitization (Hennessy, 1999).

Assessment

As in any mental health treatment program, thorough and comprehensive evaluation is necessary to identify appropriate targets of treatment and to effectively plan individualized treatment. While common psychological instruments like the Minnesota Multiphasic Personality Inventory (MMPI-2), Millon Clinical Multiaxial Inventory (MCMI-3), or projective testing may have utility in identifying comorbid psychological conditions that need to be addressed in treatment, they have limited value in helping therapists identify sex offender-specific problems and deficits (Murphy & Peters, 1992; Schlank, 1995). Instead, a variety of sex offender-specific tests and instruments have been developed to identify specific treatment targets for sex offenders. Five of the six SVP treatment programs in Hennessy's study (1999) report that they have incorporated specific batteries of commonly used sex offender assessment instruments, including the Multiphasic Sex Inventory (Nichols & Molinder, 1984), a variety of measures of cognitive distortions (Abel et al., 1984; Bumby, 1996; Burt, 1980), and structured procedures for assessing psychosexual history (Paitich et al., 1977).

In determining an appropriate assessment battery, paper-and-pencil tests can be particularly problematic. These instruments typically lack validity indicators and are composed of face valid items that are subject to demand characteristics. As a group, sex offenders have the motivation and ability to manipulate the results of these tests to present themselves in the most favorable light. Their motivations are powerful, as freedom may be tied to an absence of deviance.

Many SVP programs use phallometric assessment to gain a more objective measure of sexual deviance and interests. These instruments assess physiological arousal to a variety of sexual stimuli and themes, and they help counter any manipulated results derived from less valid instruments. While phallometric evaluations can be manipulated, they still offer a more objective measure of sexual deviance and interests. In addition, they provide information that can be particularly targeted to treatment through the use of behavioral reconditioning or medications. Hennessy (1999) reports that four out of the six programs surveyed rely on phallometric assessments. Polygraph examinations also help determine the veracity of the sexual history and can monitor high-risk behavior and fantasies in both the treatment and management of sex offenders (Hagler, 1995; O'Connell, 2000). Three of the six treatment programs employed polygraphs in their standard assessment procedures.

Relevant assessment is critical to the treatment planning process. A consistent, reliable, and valid assessment provides the foundation for the treatment planning process. A good assessment should be able to measure factors tied to the treatment program's theoretical orientation as well as identify targets for intervention. It should also contain potential measures of change and of treatment progress.

Treatment Planning

Most modern standards for mental health treatment programs require regularly updated written treatment plans, and SVP treatment programs should be no exception. Hennessy (1999) reports that all of the programs he surveyed conduct treatment planning meetings on at least a triannual or quarterly basis. These planning sessions produce written plans that are tailored to an individual SVP. They describe his current functioning and identify his progress or lack of progress to date, and they indicate relevant future treatment activities and interventions.

The heart of the treatment planning process lies in being able to identify a clear set of achievable goals and the specific steps towards their achievement.

Program Phases

In its policy statement related to SVP laws, ATSA (1998) recommends that programs be structured with identifiable phases so that committed residents can gauge their progress in treatment. All six programs from the Hennessy (1999) study are organized into such distinct treatment phases. This structure provides clear feedback to residents on their treatment progress and should indicate clear goals for treatment advancement. While state residential programs vary from four phases (Minnesota) to as many as seven (Washington), the precise number of phases is unimportant as long as they include objective, reliable indices that direct treatment and mark progress in ways that are meaningful to both the SVPs and the staff treating them.

Ancillary Treatment Programming

Whether or not SVPs actively pursue sex offender-specific treatment, many may benefit from other treatment components that are typical in mental health programs. Substance abuse treatment, in particular, may play an important adjunctive treatment role (see Plum, this volume). In the Minnesota program, over half of the SVPs were diagnosed with substance abuse dependency disorders (Janus, 2000). Educational, vocational, substance abuse, and therapeutic recreation program opportunities should be readily available and integrated into the SVP programs.

Special Populations

While the criminal histories of those committed under SVP statutes are often similar in terms of frequency patterns, their clinical problems are not necesarily similar.

SVPs who are intellectually limited and developmentally disabled need special programming that goes beyond simply "dumbing down" the material (Haaven & Coleman, 2000). Housing these individuals with higher-functioning SVPs may invite predatory behavior, and alternative living arrangements should be considered.

While relatively few SVPs are female, several women have been committed under these statutes. Women sex offenders will likely differ in their psychological dynamics and require variations in treatment approach from their male counterparts (Eldridge & Saradjian, 2000; Schwartz & Cellini, 1995). Typically, SVP programs are exclusively male; females are usually housed and treated in separate units or facilities.

About 10 percent of the SVP population committed thus far suffer from a major mental illness such as a thought, mood, or organic brain disorder. To the extent possible, these illnesses must be stabilized and brought into remission before you can reasonably expect that sex offender-specific treatment can have an impact (Knopp, 1984). Programs housed within existing psychiatric facilities have the distinct advantage of access to resources to provide appropriate treatment. Other types of facilities need to arrange solutions to provide appropriate care and treatment. Minnesota, for example, with its free-standing facility, has opted to transfer its mentally ill SVPs to a secure psychiatric center for appropriate care and treatment.

While there are definite strengths to a structured and consistent treatment program approach, no SVP treatment program should be restricted to a rigid and unyielding treatment regimen. SVPs present a varied and diverse set of problems to be encountered. Program designers must account for this and allow for individualization based on varied needs.

RESIDENTIAL MANAGEMENT ISSUES

Resistance to Treatment

Although SVP residential treatment programs share features with general mental health facilities and with other types of sex offender programs, certain aspects are clearly unique. It is a recognized fact that many sex offender treatment programs encounter significant resistance to treatment among their population. It is also true that most programs rely on at least a minimal amount of motivation and cooperation. Some programs are voluntary, while others have dire consequences—such as revocation of community probation or a negative parole recommendation—for failure to attend or participate. Sex offender programs frequently have an option to terminate treatment for those who fail to minimally cooperate, fail to show adequate treatment progress, or present the greatest risk for reoffending. None of these options can be relied on in SVP programs.

SVPs represent a coerced population that do not volunteer for and often do not desire treatment. For instance, less than one-third of the SVPs in California are participating in that state's treatment program. While the percentage of SVPs who actively participate in treatment may increase as programs mature (Janus, 2000), significant numbers are likely to continue to opt out of the sex offender-specific treatment opportunities made available to them. They often see themselves as "victims" of the system or as political prisoners, and their energies may be devoted to mounting legal challenges rather than the treatment of the psychological conditions that have resulted in their confinement. To further compound these factors, a high proportion of psychopathic and character-disordered individuals are caught up by the SVP commitment net. Moreover, many programs have a large number of pre-committed individuals. Many of these offenders, on advice from their attorneys, refuse to actively participate in treatment activities lest they reveal details about their thinking or urges that could be used against them in their future commitment proceedings.

Harassment of Staff

It is not unusual for some members of the SVP population to attempt active sabotage against treatment activities or the therapy environment. They may intentionally disrupt treatment groups, turning their backs on group leaders, verbally abusing staff or making sexual comments to them, and threatening to sue or file complaints against the professional licenses of those assigned to their cases. SVPs who express a desire to be active in the treatment process may be pressured, physically threatened, and in other ways intimidated by those who resist treatment.

Many SVPs can be quite cunning, and the institutional staff members are at risk to be manipulated by these offenders. This manipulation may take the form of attempting to seduce vulnerable staff members in order to gain some form of advantage, attempting to smuggle contraband (e.g., drugs) into the institution, or to effect an escape.

Strategies to Minimize Difficulties

A variety of strategies have been pursued to address these residential management issues. For example, some programs attempt to separate those individuals actively participating in treatment from those who refuse treatment so as not to contaminate a fledgling therapeutic milieu. Other programs separate committed from pre-commitment residents. In this way, the negative effects of those who decline and actively discourage program participation can be minimized on those who become actively engaged in the treatment process.

In its Sex Offender Commitment Program, California has attempted to design treatment activities that are sensitive to the legal situation of its pre-commitment SVPs. Initial treatment activities are largely educational and didactic in nature, which allows SVPs to gain important information about the commitment statute, the treatment model, typical cognitive distortions used by sex offenders, and typical effects on victims of sexual abuse. The pre-committed SVPs are not required to actively participate in the group discussion but are expected to attend. As long as their behavior is not disruptive, they are eligible for institutional levels that allow them freedom of movement within the confines of the security compound. In this way, the treatment focus of the program is maintained without resorting to the warehousing of treatment-resistant individuals.

An additional strategy for management is the vigorous criminal prosecution of SVPs who commit offenses (such as assault or possession of drugs) while in the treatment program. In some states, SVPs may also be serving parole time while in the program. In these cases, parole revocation procedures can be instituted that return the SVP to prison for serious rule infractions.

Some programs have established incentives for program compliance or treatment advancement. For example, the Minnesota Sex Offender Program increases the hours residents may work and earn money in jobs provided through the institution as the residents progress to higher phases of treatment (Schlank et al.,1999). To encourage program and institutional rule compliance in Kansas, that state's Sexual Predator Treatment Program established a point system whereby residents can exchange points for special privileges such as spending their own money on outside fast-food purchases (DesLauriers & Gardner, 1999). The most viable incentive, of course, is that cooperation and treatment motivation will result in eventual community release. Without such incentives, programs will labor to contrive ways to garner cooperation with treatment.

Resident Advocacy

An essential element to SVP management is to have a viable resident rights, advocacy, or ombudsman program. The purpose of such programs is to ensure that residents' rights are maintained and to provide them a way to address and satisfactorily resolve SVP grievances. To provide legitimacy to the SVP program, the program structure and its staff must be nonpunitive, professional, and willing to withstand justifiable constructive criticism so that an atmosphere of respect and trust can be maintained.

STATE PROVISIONS FOR LEAST RESTRICTIVE ALTERNATIVE

Several states have laws that provide for a least restrictive alternative (LRA) to secure confinement. Most commonly, these statutes provide for conditional release following treatment, when the person's dangerousness is considered diminished. In Arizona and Virginia, the courts can order persons into a less restrictive setting at the beginning of the commitment. Table 5.5 summarizes the LRA provisions for seven states. The Texas statute provides only for outpatient treatment of persons identified as SVPs, so its entire program might be categorized as an LRA. A multidisciplinary team reviews offenders serving sentences for sex offenses who may be repeat sexually violent offenders. Those assessed to meet the statutory definition are subject to the legal procedures commonly found in states with SVP laws.

After trial, however, the Texas court commits persons found to meet the statutory SVP definition to outpatient treatment and supervision coordinated by a case manager. The court sets monitoring and supervision conditions and the case is transferred to a district court where the person resides. A state Council on Sex Offender Treatment is responsible for implementing the statute. At the time of this writing, the Texas law was under appeal; thus, it is premature to consider this state's experience with this approach.

In the other states, attention on the conditional release end of the law is relatively recent. During the first years after the implementation of SVP statutes, state policy leaders and executive agencies concentrated on the "front end" aspects of the law—identifying individuals who met the statutory criteria, assessing dangerousness, creating treatment programs, and developing policies and procedures for program opera-

Table 5.5
States With Less Restrictive Alternatives

State	Less Restrictive Alternatives (LRA)
Arizona	Court can order conditional release to an LRA at any point.
California	With court approval, resident can be placed in a forensic conditional release program in the community.
Illinois	Petition for conditional release can be filed when six months have elapsed since initial commitment or subsequent petition for release.
New Jersey	Court can order conditional discharge with community reintegration plan recommended by treatment team.
Minnesota	Resident can file petition for provisional discharge when six months have elapsed since initial commitment or subsequent petition for release.
Virginia	Conditional release possible if resident does not require inpatient hospitalization but does need outpatient treatment and conditional release does not present undue public safety risk.
Washington	Conditional release after commitment possible; annual reviews are necessary.

tions. For many states, these steps have been accomplished, and the focus now is on creating a transition from the treatment program to the community. Here again, the states and their programs face challenges.

Transition to Outpatient Setting

A viable program should strive to create a seamless transition from residency to the outpatient setting. This implies consistency in treatment orientation and the open exchange of information between the two settings. Community therapists should become involved early in the residential treatment process. They should take an active role in preparing each resident for the step into community treatment and supervision, helping to identify and address potential community risks in treatment before a resident is released. If an SVP begins to show signs of heightened risk or treatment "backsliding," procedures need to be in place that allow revocation to residential treatment. In Minnesota, a transitional unit is provided in St. Peter for SVPs preparing for community reentry. This transitional unit is closely tied clinically to the main residential treatment facility, and it provides a stepwise release and adjustment for the offender's community reintegration.

Community Notification Issues

From the SVP's vantage, leaving the facility and regaining liberty should ideally occur as quickly as possible and involve as few restrictions as possible. From the public's vantage, however, someone committed and treated under the onerous label "sexually violent predator" warrants continuous close supervision, no matter how successful clinicians believe his treatment was. Great strides have been made in recent years to create reliable and valid risk prediction tools, but most rely heavily or exclusively on unchangeable (static) historical factors to predict recidivism. No commonly accepted instrument exists that suggests when a high-risk individual has sufficiently benefited from treatment and can be safely released to the community. Short of finding that an SVP has become so physically debilitated as to be unable to commit a sex crime, there are no absolute ways to conditionally release someone and guarantee the results. Therefore, a careful supervision and monitoring plan must be built into any LRA placement. A containment approach that includes a community safety philosophy, multidisciplinary collaboration, and specific management tools such as polygraphs and substance abuse testing has been proposed with high-risk sex offenders (English, 1998; Cumming & McGrath, 2000) and should be considered with SVPs.

Community notification of released high-risk sex offenders has drawn, and will continue to draw, attention to the transition of SVPs from secure residential care into LRA placements. Treatment programs and the SVPs themselves must be prepared to weather the public reaction. This includes detailing not only the SVP's offense history, but also his progress in treatment, the indices used to determine his readiness for community placement, and the measures that will be taken to monitor his behavior and provide surveillance.

Types of LRA Facilities

With the exception of Arizona with its separate facility on-site, states have generally relied on individualized arrangements for SVPs on conditional release. In Washington, for example, two individuals live at home and are monitored with electronic equipment and local law enforcement and corrections' personnel, two are housed in a group home operated by a private operator, and one lives in a specialized institution in another state. The group home arrangements cost the state approximately $100,000 per resident per year; this covers housing, treatment, supervision, and electronic monitoring. The offenders who reside at home cost it about $12,000 a year for monitoring equipment and prescribed medication (Legal costs are not included in these estimates; for one person, those costs were $80,000 for one year.). Washington is currently examining options for a group facility for program graduates; at the time of this writing, three residents are close to completing their treatment phases (Duran, 2000).

The federal court reviewing Washington's program has paid significant attention to the state's plans for resident transition to the community. The *Turay* injunction response includes numerous action plans to ensure that "effective structures are in place to facilitate community transition" (Marques, 2000). The challenges posed by this injunction are quite significant. When local politicians and community residents learned that a soon-to-be closed juvenile facility was under consideration for Special Commitment Center releases, their reaction was swift and negative (Haley, 2000). For private operators, the risks and liability associated with this population cause much concern. Nevertheless, the state will need to find placements for those who complete the institutional program.

Wisconsin faced significant hurdles in finding a placement for one individual. Ordered by the court in 1977 to release a convicted child molester from its SVP program (*In re Shawn D. Schulpius*, unpublished opinion), the state pursued a series of options with halfway houses that were unsuccessful. Local officials threatened to yank one facility's conditional use permit when it became known they were considering accepting this individual (Doege, 1999). One halfway house that did accept an SVP came under public scrutiny when officials learned he had obtained a prescription for Viagra (Associated Press, 1999).

SUMMARY

When sexually violent predator laws were first enacted in the early 1990s, the primary hurdles appeared to be constitutional. With the Supreme Court's decision in 1997, the statutes' challenges shifted to the operational ground—how do states that enact an SVP law create a viable treatment program? What happens day to day that can lessen the risks posed by dangerous sex offenders, preparing them and their communities for an eventual release?

With this relatively new commitment, clear treatment standards have yet to emerge, and the treatment programs designed to implement these laws remain in their infancy. It is clear, however, that these programs must include the essential components of any comprehensive treatment regimen for sex offenders. While staffing patterns and location may vary across settings, the program providers must be competent and trained professionals who are committed to the success of the program. The programs must provide wide-ranging mental health services for a diverse population and present a realistic opportunity for community release. Many have criticized the sex offender civil commitment statutes as little more than a poorly veiled disguise to keep dangerous sex offenders incarcerated indefinitely. Now that these statutes are in place, the challenge is to ensure viable treatment is established to support the laws that will protect the public, while also serving the SVPs who are subject to commitment.

References

Abel, G. G., Becker, J. V. & Cunningham-Rathner, J. C. (1984). Complications, consent and cognitions in sex between children and adults. *International Journal of Law and Psychiatry, 7,* 89–103.

Alexander, M. A. (1999). Sexual offender treatment efficacy revisited. *Sexual Abuse: A Journal of Research and Treatment, 11,* 101–116.

American Psychiatric Association. (1994). *Diagnostic and statistical manual of mental disorders* (4th ed.). Washington, DC: American Psychiatric Press.

Associated Press. (Dec. 17, 1999). Sex predator accused of getting Viagra prescription while at halfway house. *Milwaukee Journal Sentinel*, available online at http://www.onwis.com/wi/121799.

Association for the Treatment of Sexual Abusers (ATSA). (1997). *Ethical standards and principles for the management of sexual abusers.* Beaverton, OR: Author.

Association for the Treatment of Sexual Abusers (ATSA). (1998). *Civil commitment of sexually violent offenders*. Position paper adopted Nov. 6, 1998.

Bakersfield Californian. (Dec. 10, 1998). Tehachapi proposed as site for new state mental hospital.

Bradford, J. M. W. (1990). The antiandrogen and hormonal treatment of sex offenders. In W. L. Mashall, D. R. Laws & H. E. Barbaree (Eds.), *Handbook of sexual assault: Issues, theories, and treatment of the offender*. New York: Plenum.

Brakel, S. J. & Cavanaugh, J. L. (2000). Of psychopaths and pendulums: Legal and psychiatric treatment of sex offenders in the United States. *New Mexico Law Review, 30*, 69–94.

Bumby, K. M. (1996). Assessing the cognitive distortions of child molesters and rapists: Development and validation of the MOLEST and RAPE scales. *Sexual Abuse: A Journal of Research and Treatment, 8*, 37–54.

Burt, M. (1980). Cultural myths and supports for rape. *Journal of Personality and Social Psychology, 38*, 217–230.

California Legislative Analyst's Office. (1999). A "containment" strategy for adult sex offenders on parole. *Cross-Cutting Issues: Judiciary and Criminal Justice*. Sacramento: Author.

Cleckley, H. (1982). *The mask of sanity* (4th ed.). St. Louis, MO: Mosby.

Cumming, G. F. & McGrath, R. J. (2000). External supervision: How can it increase the effectiveness of relapse prevention? In D. R. Laws, S. M. Hudson, & T. Ward (Eds.), *Remaking relapse prevention with sex offenders: A sourcebook*. Newbury Park, CA: Sage.

DesLauriers, A. T. & Gardner, J. (1999). The sexual predator treatment program of Kansas. In A. Schlank & F. Cohen (Eds.), *The sexual predator: Law, policy, evaluation, and treatment*. Kingston, NJ: Civic Research Institute.

Doege, D. (Dec. 31, 1999). Most predators find a place, attorney argues. *Milwaukee Journal Sentinel*, available online at: http://www.jsonlive.com/news/metro.

Duran, S. (Apr. 22, 2000).Three sexual predators may soon be freed. *The News Tribune*, available online at: http://www.search.tribunet.com/archive.

Eldridge, H. & Saradjian, J. (2000). Replacing the function of abusive behaviors for the offender: Remaking relapse prevention in working with women who sexually abuse children. In D. R. Laws, S. M. Hudson & T. Ward (Eds.), *Remaking relapse prevention with sex offenders*. Newbury Park, CA: Sage.

English, K. (1998). The containment approach: An aggressive strategy for the community management of adult sex offenders. *Psychology, Public Policy, and Law, 4*, 218–235.

Federoff, J. P. (1993). Serotonergic drug treatment of deviant sexual interests. *Annals of Sex Research, 6*, 105–121.

Freeman-Longo, R. E., Bird, S., Stevenson, W. & Fiske, J. A. (1995). *1994 nationwide survey of treatment programs & models serving abuse-reactive children and adolescent & adult sex offenders*. Brandon, VT: Safer Society Press.

Haaven, J. L. & Coleman, E. M. (2000).Treatment of the developmentally disabled sex offender. In D. R. Laws, S. M. Hudson & T. Ward (Eds.), *Remaking relapse prevention with sex offenders: A sourcebook*. Newbury Park, CA: Sage.

Hagler, H. H. (1995). Polygraph as a measure of progress in the assessment, treatment and surveillance of sex offenders. *Sexual Addiction and Compulsivity, 2*, 98–111.

Haley, J. (Apr. 26, 2000). Sex predators won't be housed at Indian Ridge. *The Everett Herald*, available online at http://www.heraldnet.com/Stories/oo/4/26/12546925.htm.

Hall, G. C. N. (1995). Sexual offender recidivism: A meta-analysis of recent treatment studies. *Journal of Consulting and Clinical Psychology, 63*, 802–809.

Hanson, R. K. (1997). *The development of a brief actuarial risk scale for sexual offense recidivism*. (User Report No. 97-04). Ottawa, Canada: Department of the Solicitor General of Canada.

Hanson R. K. & Bussiere, M. T. (1998). Predicting relapse: A meta-analysis of sexual offender recidivism studies. *Journal of Consulting and Clinical Psychology, 66*, 348–362.

Hanson, R. K. & Thornton, D. (1999). *Static 99: Improving actuarial risk assessments for sex offenders*. (User Report No. 99-02). Ottawa, Canada: Department of the Solicitor General of Canada.

Hare, R. D. (1991). *The Hare Psychopathy Checklist—Revised Manual.* Toronto: Multi-Health Systems.

Hare, R. D., Hart, S. D. & Harpur, T. J. (1991). Psychopathy and DSM-IV criteria for antisocial personality disorder. *Journal of Abnormal Psychology, 100*, 391–398.

Harris, G. T., Rice, M. E. & Cormier, C.A. (1991). Psychopathy and violent recidivism. Law and Human Behavior, 15, 625–631.

Hemphill, J. F., Hare, R. D. & Wong, S. (1998). Psychopathy and recidivism: A review. *Legal and Criminological Psychology, 3*, 139–170.

Hennessy, M. T. (1999). A survey of the nation's sexual predator treatment programs. Doctoral dissertation, University of Denver.

Janus, E. S. (2000). An empirical study of Minnesota's sex offender commitment program. *Sex Offender Law Report, 1*, 49–63.

Kansas v. Hendricks, 117 S. Ct. 2072 (1997).

Knopp, F. H. (1984). *Retraining adult sex offenders: Methods and models.* Brandon, VT: Safer Society Press.

Laws, D. R. (Ed.). (1989). *Relapse prevention with sex offenders.* New York: Guilford Press.

Maller, P. (Feb. 1, 2000). Even at 95, molester is a threat, jury told. *Milwaukee Journal Sentinel*, available online at: http://www.onwis.com/news/state/jan00/oldpred01013100.asp.

Marques, J. K. (2000). Seventeenth report of the special master, *Turay v. Seling*, No. C91-664WD (unpub. op. W.D. Wash. 2000).

Marques, J. K., Nelson, C., Alarcon, J. M. & Day, D. M. (2000). Preventing relapse in sex offenders: What we learned from SOTEP's experimental treatment program. In D. R. Laws, S. M. Hudson & T. Ward (Eds.), *Remaking relapse prevention with sex offenders.* Thousand Oaks, CA: Sage.

Marsh, V. (1998). Sexually violent predators may soon prey on Virginia's public hospitals. *Network Newsletter.* Virginia Alliance for the Mentally Ill, available online at: http://www.216.156.111.229/articles/svp_crisis/svp-06-17-98.htm.

Marshall, W. L. & Barbaree, H. E. (1990). Outcome of comprehensive cognitive-behavioral treatment programs. In W. L. Marshall, D. R. Laws & H. E. Barbaree (Eds.), *Handbook of sexual assault: Issues, theories and treatment of the offender.* New York: Plenum.

Marshall, W. L., Jones, R., Ward, T., Johnston, P. & Barbaree, H. E. (1991). Treatment outcome with sex offenders. *Clinical Psychology Review, 11*, 465–485.

Murphy, W. D. & Peters, J. M. (1992). Profiling child sexual abusers: Psychological considerations. *Criminal Justice and Behavior, 19*, 24–37.

National Association of State Mental Health Program Directors (NASMHPD). (1999). *Third technical report by the Medical Directors Council.* Alexandria, VA: Author. Available online at: http://www.nasmhpd.org/svpfinal.htm.

Nelson, C., Miner, M., Marques, J., Russell, K. & Achterkirchen, J. (1988). Relapse prevention: A cognitive behavioral model for treatment of the rapist and child molester. *Journal of Social Work and Human Sexuality, 7*, 125–143.

Nichols, H. R. & Molinder, I. (1984). *Multiphasic sex inventory manual: A test to assess psychosexual characteristics of the sexual offender.* Tacoma, WA: Nichols & Molinder.

O'Connell, M. A. (2000). Polygraphy: Assessment and community monitoring. In D. R. Laws, S. M. Hudson & T. Ward (Eds.), *Remaking relapse prevention with sex offenders: A sourcebook.* Newbury Park, CA: Sage.

Ogloff, J. R. P., Wong, S. & Greenwood, A. (1990). Treating criminal psychopaths in a therapeutic community program. *Behavioral Sciences and the Law, 8*, 181–190.

Order and Injunction, Turay v. Weston, later known as *Turay v. Seling*, No. C91-664WD (unpub. op. W.D. Wash. 1997).

Paitich, D., R., Langevin, R. Freeman, R., Mann, I. & Handy, L. (1977). The Clarke SHQ: A clinical sex history for males. *Archives of Sexual Behavior, 6*, 421–436.

Pithers, W. D., Marques, J. K., Gibat, C. C. & Marlatt, G. A. (1983). Relapse prevention with sexually aggressive persons: A self-control model of treatment and maintenance of change. In J. G. Greer & I. R. Stuart (Eds.), *The sexual aggressor: Current perspectives on treatment.* New York: Van Nostrand Reinhold.

Prentky, R. A. (1997). Arousal reduction in sexual offenders: A review of antiandrogen interventions. *Sexual Abuse: A Journal of Research and Treatment, 9,* 335–347.

Quinsey, V. L. (1999). Comment on Fallon, P., et al. Report of the committee on inquiry into the personality disorder unit, Ashworth Special Hospital, vol. 1. *The Journal of Forensic Psychiatry, 10,* 631–644.

Quinsey, V. L. & Earls, C. M. (1990). The modification of sexual preferences. In W. L. Marshall, D. R. Laws & H. E. Barbaree (Eds.), *Handbook of sexual assault: Issues, theories, and treatment of the offender.* New York: Plenum.

Quinsey, V. L., Rice, M. E. & Harris, G. T. (1995). Actuarial prediction of sexual recidivism. *Journal of Interpersonal Violence, 10,* 85–105.

Rainey, J., & Turene, V. D. (June 1, 2000). Poor areas pin hopes on facility for sex offenders. *Los Angeles Times.*

Schlank, A. (1995). The utility of the MMPI and MSI for identifying a sexual offender typology. *Sexual Abuse: A Journal of Research and Treatment, 7,* 185–194.

Schlank, A., Harry, R. & Farnsworth, M. (1999). The Minnesota sex offender program. In A. Schlank & F. Cohen (Eds.), The sexual predator: Law, policy, evaluation, and treatment. Kingston, NJ: Civic Research Institute.

Schwartz, B. K. & Cellini, H. R. (1995). Female sex offenders. In B. K. Schwartz & H. R. Cellini (Eds.), The sex offender: Corrections, treatment, and legal practice. Kingston, NJ: Civic Research Institute.

Seto, M. C. & Barbaree, H. E. (1999). Psychopathy, treatment behavior, and sex offender recidivism. *Journal of Interpersonal Violence, 14,* 1235–1248.

Turay v. Weston, No. C91-664WD (unpub. op.W.D. Wash. June 3, 1994).

Young v. Weston, 192 F.3d 870 (9th Cir. 1999).

Ziegler, A. (2000). Personal communication with author. Executive Assistant at Washington State Special Commitment Center.

Chapter 6

Civil Commitment of Dangerous, Personality-Disordered Offenders— Developing a Model

by David Thornton, Ph.D.

Introduction 6-1
The Concept of Dangerous Severe Personality Disorder 6-2
Risk Assessment Methodologies Relevant to DSPD 6-3
    Actuarial Instruments 6-3
    Case Formulations 6-3
    Structured Clinical Judgment 6-4
Assessing Personality Disorder for DSPD 6-4
Assessing the Link to Risk 6-5
A Possible Process 6-5
    1. Actuarial Classification Based on Widely Available Data to
       Serve as a Screen for High-Risk Offenders 6-5
    2. Specialist Instrument-Based Risk Classification 6-7
    3. Preliminary Assessment of Personality Disorder and
       Its Link to Risk 6-8
    4. First Tribunal Hearing 6-8
    5. Residential Assessment 6-9
    6. Second Tribunal Hearing 6-9
    7. Release 6-9
        Prior Record/Current Behavior Scales 6-10
        Psychometric Tests 6-10
Reflections 6-11

INTRODUCTION

In July 1999, the British government issued a consultation paper examining options for the management of a group of people conceptualized as exhibiting "dangerous severe personality disorder" (DSPD). One of these options was for a system of civil commitment similar in many respects to that operating for high-risk sex offenders in many parts of the United States of America.

This proposal is highly controversial. A common objection is that it involves a misuse of mental health legislation to achieve a criminal justice purpose (preventative detention). Advocates of the proposal argue that it could combine better protection of the public with better treatment services for a damaged and disadvantaged group that is normally offered little effective treatment.

At this writing, no final decision has been made as to whether this kind of civil commitment will be introduced in Britain or the form that it will take if it is implemented. As a preliminary to making this decision, a great deal of preparatory work has been commissioned. This includes formulating standards and models for the processes that would be involved, and developing and testing assessment and therapeutic tools on which any such system would depend.

This chapter describes a model that evolved as part of this preparatory process, along with some thinking and internal research that has been involved in its development.

THE CONCEPT OF DANGEROUS SEVERE PERSONALITY DISORDER

DSPD refers to persons:

1. Who present a substantial risk of committing an offense likely to cause serious harm to a person;

2. Who show a general disorder of personality;

3. And in whom the risk presented appears to be functionally linked to the personality disorder.

Some trade-off between risk and harm can be envisaged as well. The difficulty here of course is that harm is a consequence of an offense rather than a feature of the offense itself (except in some special cases like murder). Thus, there is no perfect correlation between offender behavior and harm. Indeed sometimes the difference between murder and assault is the efficiency of medical services, not the behavior of the offender. Nevertheless, offending behavior can be identified as "dangerous" to the extent that it has the potential for leading to serious psychological and/or physical harm of a kind from which it is not easy or quick to recover.

In evaluating particular activities, it will be relevant to consider the various kinds of serious harm to which the activities might potentially lead, and both the extremity of the harms concerned and the likelihood that the activity would actually lead to these harms if repeated. The level of risk regarded as pertinent should depend on the severity of the harm that is possible. Thus, the general rule might be that DSPD criteria were met if the person is assessed as "more likely than not" to commit an offense that could be expected to lead to serious psychological and/or physical harm. But this threshold might appropriately be lower if the harm envisaged were more profound—for example, sadistic rape, the abduction and torture of children, or the death of a victim.

RISK ASSESSMENT METHODOLOGIES RELEVANT TO DSPD

There are two commonly used approaches to risk assessment: (1) statistically derived, "actuarial" risk assessment instruments and (2) individual case formulation. Each approach has its strengths and weaknesses. Neither alone would be sufficient to demonstrate that DSPD criteria were met. Accordingly, they need to be combined in a structured way that employs their strengths while minimizing their weaknesses.

Actuarial Instruments

"Actuarial" risk assessment instruments are based on statistical research that examines the performance of large samples of offenders and identifies factors that are statistically associated with the outcome of interest (here, offenses liable to cause serious harm). Statistical procedures are then used to estimate an equation for predicting the outcome of interest from these risk factors. A clear-cut example of this approach is the Offender Group Reconviction Scale developed in England by Copas and Marshall (1998). The original version of this scale was based on 14,000 offenders discharged from prison or sentenced to probation in 1990, and it predicts reconviction for any offense. The revised version, produced by Taylor (1999), was based on 30,000 similar offenders from 1995 cohorts, and it enables prediction of both reconviction for any offense and reconviction for sexual or other violent offenses. Similar methods, though generally on much smaller samples, have been used to establish predictors for violence in North American populations (e.g., Quinsey et al., 1998). The essential feature of this approach is that the individual is characterized in terms of the typical performance of the risk classification group to which he or she has been assigned.

This approach has been remarkably successful as a method of producing groups with typically different performances, and it is reliably more successful in prediction than ordinary clinical judgment. This method can be routinely applied on a large scale; it is essentially objective in character; and the quality of different prediction instruments can be straightforwardly determined by research.

The method does, however, have two limitations. First, to date it has only been possible to develop good models of this kind for relatively broad classes of behavior (i.e., all violence) rather than violence causing serious harm. Second, it has no mechanism for establishing a link between personality disorder and risk.

Case Formulations

The case formulation approach seeks to develop a theoretical model of the behavior of the individual being assessed. Ideally, it involves the bringing together of a number of different potential lines of explanation to create a holistic picture of the individual. Case formulations are evaluated not through statistical research, but by comparing the relative plausibility of alternative formulations in relation to the facts about an individual (e.g., facts about his environment, behavior patterns, performance on specialist tests, and the like).

For people unfamiliar with the case formulation approach it may sound rather like ordinary, unstructured clinical judgment, something known not to work well. It does differ from unstructured clinical judgment in a number of important respects, however. First, case formulations are systematically challenged and tested with new data in a way that does not always happen when individual clinical judgments are made. Second, done properly, case formulations are produced through the dynamic interaction and evolving consensus of a multidisciplinary team that is able to deploy a range of expertise.

It is not known whether case formulation can classify groups of individuals as accurately as statistically based risk assessment instruments. Case formulation is certainly much more expensive and cumbersome to apply. It is, on the other hand, the only method that can make predictions about individual cases considering them as individuals, that can make judgments about the form of future offending (how harmful is it likely to be), and that can determine whether risk is linked to personality disorder.

Case formulation is most likely to yield misleading results when the base rate for the target behavior (offenses causing serious harm) is very low. The approach implicitly assumes that the group being evaluated contains a substantial proportion that will engage in the target behavior (unless there is some effective intervention).

Structured Clinical Judgment

An interesting integration of the statistical and the case formulation approaches, sometimes described as structured clinical judgment, entails constraining case formulations to using factors that statistical research has shown to be generally associated with the kind of offending being considered. Tools like the Historical Clinical Risk Management (HCR-20) (Webster et al., 1997) and the Sexual Violence Rating Scale (SVR-20) (Boer et al., 1997) can be used to facilitate this kind of integration. It is notable that assessments made in this structured but nonactuarial way have been shown to be as accurate as actuarial scales while yielding information that is more clinically useful (Douglas et al., 1999).

The proposed model for DSPD assessment described below combines both these notions.

ASSESSING PERSONALITY DISORDER FOR DSPD

It is proposed that for DSPD assessment, "personality disorder" (PD) could be defined as any enduring pattern of relating and behaving that deviates markedly from the cultural norm, is expressed in a range of contexts, is resistant to change, and causes harm to the self or others.

This definition is broadly consistent with the way PD is defined in the tenth edition of the World Health Organization's *International Classification of Diseases* (ICD-10) (1992) and in the fourth edition of the *Diagnostic and Statistical Manual of Mental Disorders* (DSM-IV) (American Psychiatric Association, 1994). It differs from the general criteria for PD given in these systems only in that it emphasizes observable expressions of PD (relating/behaving) over inferred (harder to observe) features (thinking/internal experience). A broad definition of PD is thought to be preferable to the use of specific diagnoses given the lower reliability of existing PD categories and the frequency of multiple diagnoses.

ASSESSING THE LINK TO RISK

Determining that personality disorder is linked to risk would be based on case formulation. Specifically, a link would be diagnosed if the case formulation implies that features of the personality disorder contribute in a substantial way to risk assessed by the individual. To determine this, the assessor would need to identify at least two documented instances of criminal behavior that either had, or might have, led to serious harm. They would then seek to determine whether in either of these instances something that could reasonably be seen as an expression of personality disorder had contributed to the behavior.

Alternatively, it could be determined that personality disorder was linked to risk if the presence of the personality disorder made it substantially more difficult for ordinary therapeutic or criminal justice processes to reduce the risk. Such a judgment would depend on an analysis of the range of treatments plausibly available through alternative criminal justice or health dispositions.

A POSSIBLE PROCESS

A possible way of implementing these concepts for the purpose of DSPD assessment might work in the manner described below.

1. Actuarial Classification Based on Widely Available Data to Serve as a Screen for High-Risk Offenders

In the first step, actuarial risk classification instruments would be used to identify a group whose probability of being reconvicted for sexual or violent offenses is at least 50 percent. The actuarial instrument used would need to be easy to score on the basis of routinely available data. The intention would be that this system would operate automatically and on a very large scale, certainly being applied to anyone coming in contact with the criminal justice system. It is likely that this phase will be an automatic, computer-run operation.

Underlying this are large databases that hold records of all conviction and sentencing events in England and Wales. A system for capturing more extensive data on social and personal risk factors is now also being developed and is due shortly to be implemented. The Offender Assessment System, known as OASys (Clark, 2000), will provide a comprehensive national database for all offenders given probation or prison sentences. The sheer volume of data in these systems makes the development of actuarial classification systems relatively straightforward.

An objection to this proposal would be that existing actuarial predictors only use variables that depend on complex and time-consuming assessment procedures. Clearly, instruments like the Violence Risk Appraisal Guide (VRAG) (Quinsey et al., 1998) could not be administered on the scale envisaged here. Simple but effective actuarial classification is possible, however. Table 6.1 shows the violence classification scheme used in a recently developed risk classification instrument known as Risk Matrix (RM) 2000 (Thornton, 2000).

Table 6.1
Violence Predictor in Risk Matrix 2000

Risk Matrix 2000/Violence	
1. Age at Commencement of Risk	Points
Under 18	4
18–24	3
25–34	2
35–44	1
Older	0
2. Violent Appearances	Points
0	0
1	1
2, 3	2
4+	3
3. Any Burglaries?	
No	0
Yes	2

Total Points	Category
0, 1	I
2, 3	II
4, 5	III
6+	IV

Table 6.2 shows the rates of violent reconviction associated with these risk categories for a cross-validation sample of imprisoned sex offenders followed for at least sixteen years after release. Violence was defined quite narrowly here. The only convictions counted were those in which the formal legal charge implied a causing of physical harm (in England, charges like murder, manslaughter, wounding, assault). Sexual assaults were not included unless they gave rise to a separate violence conviction. The full RM2000 process has a separate predictor for sexual offenses. Further cross-validation of this scale on other samples has shown similar levels of predictiveness, with a receiver operating characteristic (ROC) area under the curve (AUC) of at least 0.75 in different samples. (See Hoberman's discussion of the statistical aspects of prediction in Chapter 11, this volume, for a detailed explanation of the ROC area under the curve.)

No doubt it will be possible to improve on these results. Nontheless, even this simple scale is sufficiently effective that a meaningfully large group of offenders who present at least a 50 percent risk of reconviction for violence can be defined.

Table 6.2
Violence Rates Among Sex Offenders by RM2000/Violence Category

Category	Percentage Reconvicted for Violence
I	5% of 151
II	19% of 130
III	41% of 96
IV	63% of 46

2. Specialist Instrument-Based Risk Classification

Routine screening on a massive scale will inevitably produce significant numbers of erroneous assessments. There will be clerical errors in recording data, and staff making the more complex judgments required for OASys variables will vary in how well trained they are for the task. Additionally, the kinds of variables used in Step 1 will necessarily be limited, as they have to be easy to obtain and record. And data collected at this level will be designed to discriminate across the whole range of risk levels, not specifically to discriminate high-risk offenders.

Step 2 would use a limited group of highly trained assessors who would both check that OASys variables had been correctly assessed and would apply a range of more sophisticated assessment instruments chosen on the basis of their ability to discriminate among individuals already assessed as high risk. The HCR-20 and the VRAG are well-known examples of instruments with this potential. The principle would be that this assessment should include at least three risk assessment instruments of this kind. Selection of instruments should be based on currently available research. Since research continues to develop rapidly, the selection of instruments should be expected to change as new findings become available. It is suggested that an annual review of relevant research should be commissioned to produce guidance for assessors. A certification process supported by a training program for assessors should also be developed. It is suggested that training and certification should be university based and available (for an appropriate fee) to independent assessors as well as to those who might be employed as part of the DSPD assessment system.

As part of this process, the assessor would seek to interview the offender. This would contribute information that can be used in the risk assessment. The risk assessment scales can, however, be scored from file information, so the overall procedure could still operate if the offender declined to cooperate.

Use of multiple scales will inevitably lead to some cases having an uneven profile across different scales—appearing high risk on some but not on others. In such instances, the assessor would consider the particulars of the case and propose an interpretation that makes sense of the discrepancy. Judgments about level of risk would follow from the interpretation. There is no doubt that this creates some additional complication, but it must be remembered that this is an issue that cannot be avoided because it will be raised by independent assessors employed by lawyers working for the offender.

A potential way forward here is to use multivariate analysis to decompose prediction scales into a number of underlying dimensions. Uneven profiles across different scales can then usually be understood on the basis of the particular scales differing in how they assign weight to particular dimensions. In the long run, it should be possible to develop statistical data on the predictive significance of particular combinations of the underlying dimensions to aid in the interpretation of uneven profiles across particular prediction scales.

This second step would screen out a number of individuals who, despite their initial OASys classification, no longer met the "more likely than not" criterion. Cases eliminated would be those who had been incorrectly scored on OASys variables and those who ceased to meet the criterion when a broader range of instruments was applied. Thus, only those who clearly and robustly met the actuarial criteria would be passed on to the next phase of DSPD assessment.

3. Preliminary Assessment of Personality Disorder and Its Link to Risk

Offenders whose risk level was confirmed at Step 2 would also be assessed to see whether they appeared to meet the criteria for personality disorder. In addition, a preliminary case formulation would be developed to determine whether (1) their risk was functionally linked to the identified personality disorder or (2) the presence of the personality disorder would make it substantially harder for interventions routinely available within the health service or the criminal justice system to reduce risk (i.e., the link criteria).

There is an issue here as to who should carry out this preliminary case formulation. It is suggested that the best approach might be for this to fall to a team from one of the residential assessment units (see Step 5). This would have the advantage of making for greater continuity with that assessment.

Where the risk assessment and the preliminary case formulation suggested that DSPD criteria were met, a referral would be made to a Tribunal capable of making DSPD orders. The alternative outcome would be a report indicating DSPD criteria were not presently met, possible with referral to other services where this seemed appropriate.

4. First Tribunal Hearing

In this step, the assessors would receive the reports from Steps 1, 2, and 3 and also consider any independent expert evidence offered, and then determine whether the evidence for DSPD criteria being met was sufficiently strong to justify referral for a residential assessment.

While it would be possible for the tribunal to consist of an ordinary court, there are some disadvantages to this—notably, that neither the judge nor the jury would have substantial experience in hearing these complex cases. A better procedure might be modeled on the English Discretionary Lifer Panel (the body that, in English law, can order the release of prisoners given indeterminate sentences for offenses other than murder). Discretionary lifer panels are defined in law, always chaired by a judge, and must include a psychiatrist and an independent member with relevant experience (normally a retired chief probation officer, an academic criminologist, or like professional) and drawn from the parole board. Having a relatively small group from which a DSPD tribunal would be composed would allow this group to rapidly gain experience in the relevant kind of cases, while also making it possible to ensure that group members received training in the issues relevant to these kinds of decisions.

5. Residential Assessment

This step would take place in dedicated, secure residential units. The process would essentially be one of case formulation by multidisciplinary teams supported by more extensive social-developmental investigation, behavioral observation, and specialist testing (e.g. neuro-cognitive assessment).

This process would be intended to produce a definitive case formulation from which recommendations would be derived as to whether DSPD criteria were met. The case formulators would also be expected to offer advice on the treatment and risk management of the individual within the DSPD system. This would include indicating the kind of progress the individual should be expected to make before his risk was deemed low enough for movement to lower security conditions; it would also include indicating the issues that might be particularly critical for future risk management in lesser security and, where appropriate, in the community.

An essential feature of residential assessment is that it should not be tightly time limited. Three months would be a reasonable initial assessment period, but the team should be able to apply for and obtain further periods if the team members can reasonably maintain that they are unable to form an evaluation. This might be the case where, for example, the offender has not cooperated sufficiently with the assessment process, or where the team is seeking additional information that they expect will be available within a reasonable period of time.

6. Second Tribunal Hearing

In this step, the assessors would consider recommendations from the residential assessment, evidence available at the earlier tribunal hearing, and independent expert evidence. They would either make a DSPD order or conclude that DSPD criteria were not met.

7. Release

Although there are challenges involved in properly identifying offenders who meet DSPD criteria, a much greater challenge for any such system is how these offenders can eventually be released. The rhetoric used to justify committing such dangerous individuals in the first place makes it particularly hard to justify maintaining to the public that they have somehow become safe to release. It would be all to easy then for DSPD containment to become a form of preventative detention implemented under the disguise of a mental health facade, with patients being detained forever in "treatment institutions." Such a result would defeat one of the public policy goals of the proposed DSPD system—better services for personality-disordered patients. It would also lead to what would become a significant drain on public finances and would probably eventually be determined to be unlawful under European human rights laws.

To avoid this outcome, we need both effective treatment methods to lower risk and effective assessment methods to determine whether a particular individual's risk has been effectively lowered. There is now considerable evidence that appropriately designed and implemented treatment programs can lower risk (McGuire, 1995). The chief difficulty is with assessment. Most risk assessment instruments use only static variables and so cannot determine when risk has declined. To address this difficulty, a number of new studies have been run and their results are summarized below.

Prior Record/Current Behavior Scales. Clark (1994) has developed a system for correctional officers to systematically record facets of prison inmates' current behavior. The relation of these scales to subsequent violent behavior was investigated in two samples—one of sex offenders and the other of violent offenders (defined in terms of their index offense). Cases were classified into thirds, on a behavioral continuum defined in terms of Clark's Belligerence and Impulsiveness dimensions. Similar results were obtained in both samples, so they are combined here. Logistic regression analysis showed that both static risk classification and behavioral ratings made significant independent contributions to current behavior. This pattern is summarized in Table 6.3, where "bad behavior" refers to the top third of the continuum in terms of this composite dimension and "bad record" refers to categories III and IV from the Risk Matrix 2000 classification. The outcome shows the rates of violent reconviction over a variable follow-up period that averaged two to three years.

The striking feature of these results is that only when an actuarial classification indicating higher risk is combined with impulsive and belligerent behavior in prison is a meaningful rate of violent reoffense observed. A high-risk static classification combined with good current behavior was followed by a very low rate of reoffense, a rate essentially similar to that of those with good prior records. This kind of result encourages the view that a sustained absence of belligerent or impulsive behavior in a secure setting would indicate lower risk than would be expected on the basis of an actuarial classification based on static variables.

Psychometric Tests. In a second study we looked at the significance of psychometric test results for subsequent conviction. A test battery containing the Gough Socialization Scale (Gough, 1960) and a locally created measure of attitude to offense (assessing the extent to which the prisoner "took responsibility" for his offending) was administered before and after prisoners completed a Cognitive Skills program. Scores on both these scales were correlated (negatively) with reconviction, but logistic regression analysis indicated that when both pre- and post-treatment scores were entered into the regression equation, only post-treatment performance was predictive. Further, the two scales combined in a useful way. In Table 6.4, Offense Attitude refers to a score on the Cognitive Skills scale, and General Attitude refers to a score on the Gough scale. "Poor" in both cases indicates a score below the sample mean.

These results indicate that whatever attitudes they started with, those offenders who by the end of treatment have both a generally responsible attitude and have taken responsibility for their offenses have a drastically reduced rate of reoffending.

Table 6.3
Future Violence by Prior Record and Current Behavior

Static Risk Category and Current Behavior	Rate of Violent Reconviction
Good record & good behavior	2% of 48
Good record & bad behavior	9% of 11
Bad record & good behavior	3% of 31
Bad record & bad behavior	27% of 30

Table 6.4
Future Violence by Test Batteries

Offense Attitude	General Attitude	Two-Year Reconviction Rate
Poor	Poor	60%
Poor	Good	50%
Good	Poor	53%
Good	Good	27%

Taken together, these results suggest that assessments made during or after treatment can indicate a level of risk much lower than that expected solely on the basis of actuarial assessment and, thus, that there can be a meaningful and evidence-based way of justifying release for those initially identified as high-risk on an actuarial basis.

REFLECTIONS

No doubt the tools and research results reported here will be improved and built upon before any DSPD system is implemented in Britain. Nevertheless, even at this stage they are sufficient to suggest that such a system is potentially viable both in initial identification of appropriately dangerous offenders and in providing meaningful criteria for their release.

An interesting feature of the way the civil commitment concept is being developed in Britain is the care currently being taken to develop appropriate systems and tools before legislation is passed. With this thoughtful planning, it is to be hoped that the British system will avoid some of the difficulties that are apparent in other jurisdictions, which have been far quicker to pass related legislation.

References

American Psychiatric Association. (1994). *Diagnostic and statistical manual of mental disorders* (4th ed.). Washington, DC: American Psychiatric Press.

Boer, D. P., Hart, S. D., Kropp, P. R. & Webster, C. D. (1997). *Manual for the sexual violence risk-20: Professional guidelines for assessment of risk of sexual violence*. Burnaby, British Columbia: Mental Health Law and Policy Institute, Simon Fraser University.

Clark, D. (1994). Evaluation of behavioural changes after intervention. *Inside Psychology: The Journal of Prison Service Psychology, 2*, 2–43.

Clark, D. (2000). *Offender Assessment System*. Unpublished paper, to be submitted for publication.

Copas, J. B. & Marshall, P. (1998). The offender group reconviction scale. *Journal of the Royal Statistical Society, 47*, 159–171, Series C.

Douglas, K. S., Cox, D. N. & Webster, C. D. (1999). Violence risk assessment: Science and practice. *Legal and Criminological Psychology, 4*, 149–184.

Gough, G. H. (1960). Theory and measurement of socialization. *Journal of Consulting Psychology, 24*, 23–30.

Home Office & Department of Health (1999). *Managing dangerous people with severe personality disorder*. Available from Department of Health, P.O. Box 777, London, SE1 6XH, England.

International Classification of Diseases (10th ed.) (1992). Geneva, Switzerland: World Health Organization.

McGuire, J. (Ed.) (1995). *What works: Reducing re-offending*. New York: John Wiley & Sons.

Quinsey, V. L., Harris, G. T., Rice, M. E. & Cormier, C. A. (1998). *Violent offenders: Appraising and managing risk*. Washington, DC: American Psychological Association Press.

Taylor, R. (1999). *Predicting reconvictions for sexual and violent offenses using the revised offender group reconviction scale*. Research Findings 104. Home Office Research, Development and Statistics Directorate. Available from Information and Publications Group, Room 201, Home Office, Queen Anne's Gate, London, SW1H 9AT, England.

Thornton, D. (2000). *Static and dynamic components of risk*. Paper presented to Her Majesty's Prison Service Treatment Managers Conference, December 2000. Harrogate, England.

Webster, C. D., Douglas, K. S., Eaves, D. & Hart, S. D. (1997). *Manual for the HCR-20: Assessing risk for violence* (version 2). Burnaby, British Columbia: Mental Health Law and Policy Institute, Simon Fraser University.

Chapter 7
Civil Commitment Programs—Administrative Concerns

by Rick Harry, C.O.O., M.S.O.P.

Introduction 7-1
Program Location—Urban or Rural? 7-2
    Site Requirements 7-2
    Medical Issues 7-3
    Recruitment 7-3
    Resident Services 7-3
    Contact With Local Government 7-4
Staffing Levels 7-4
    Security and Treatment Requirements 7-4
    Direct Care Staff 7-5
    Professional Care Staff 7-5
    Administrative Staff 7-5
Staff Recruitment and Training 7-6
    Direct Care and Support Staff 7-6
    Professional Staff 7-7
    New Employee/Refresher Training 7-7
    Boundary Issues 7-9
Program Jurisdiction 7-10
    The MSOP Experience 7-10
    Dual Jurisdiction Issues 7-10
Summary and Directions for the Future 7-11

INTRODUCTION

This chapter highlights the important administrative considerations that go into establishing a civil commitment program for sexual offenders. One aspect of program operations that has been firmly driven home over the past several years is that there clearly is an *indistinct* line between clinical and administrative operations with respect to many issues encountered day to day. The ability of clinicians and administrators to function as a true team, in a cooperative effort to operate the program, is a major strength. Therefore, an initial goal is to have an administrator who has an appreciation for, if not experience in, clinical issues and a clinical director who has the ability to recognize the limitations occasionally presented by either administrative bureaucracy or regulatory agencies. A compatible working relationship between the lead administrative and clinical staff is a major component of program success.

In this chapter information is presented relative to selecting a site for the program, determining staffing levels, providing initial and continuing staff training and development, budgetary issues, who should have jurisdiction over the program, and some potential problem areas in the day-to-day operation of a relatively large civil commitment program.

PROGRAM LOCATION—URBAN OR RURAL?

Site Requirements

Once a state makes the decision to fund a program in concert with statutory language that allows for the civil commitment of sexual offenders, picking the best site to house the program is often the first hurdle to be overcome. A program located in a rural area may seem at first to have the better chance of displeasing as few people as possible. However, locating a program in a rather isolated rural area presents many difficulties. While most communities will not complain about the potential impact of employees' salaries on their local economy, they will have serious concerns and anxieties about the potential impact of the housed offenders on community safety. They will worry about the potential for residents of the program to be outside of the secure perimeter of the facility. With the possible exception of taking residents under supervision to occasional medical appointments in the local area, a community may be adamant that the men should not have access to the facility's grounds, even under supervision, due to the perceived safety risk to the general population should a resident elope.

A program located in a small community that is unwilling to accept the residential transition aspect of treatment might force a state to use a different type of site for transition purposes. It is imperative for rather obvious reasons to allow residents a gradual assumption of increased privileges over a significant period of time. This is vital in a successful transition program. But it may simply be impossible to implement this aspect of your program at your inpatient treatment site if you are in a small community that will not accept it.

Therefore, a prime consideration in determining physical location is whether you will be able to provide the full array of treatment services, including transition, at the site. If not, you will have to develop alternate plans for their provision. The alternate plans may often be less than convenient, but that does not necessarily mean the provision of the services is less effective at another site.

Optimally, a program would be sited in a location that allowed for resident transition, provided a full array of specialized medical services, and had readily available resources for the required work force.

Medical Issues

Administrators of civil commitment programs have noted that the average age of their residents tends to be somewhat higher than the average age of sex offenders in other treatment programs, and that a number of their residents have significant medical concerns that require ongoing monitoring and treatment. Having physician services available onsite decreases the necessity to transport men to routine medical appointments. Depending on your program's size, you may need either a full- or a part-time family practice physician (Family practitioners provide well-rounded services at reasonable cost; internists tend to drive up costs.). Residents with special medical needs that cannot always be met at the facility will need to be transported to area clinics and hospitals. Without physician services at the facility, a significant amount of time and staff resources will be consumed in transporting residents to medical care providers.

To provide a professional level of services on a twenty-four-hour per day basis, consider employing a sufficient number of registered nurses to ensure that there is always a nurse in the facility. Use of the registered nurse position allows for a professional assessment relative to the need for services at any time. For example, without a nurse in the facility during the night shift, it might be necessary to transport a resident complaining of chest pains to an emergency room for assessment rather than performing it at the facility. Since some residents may report a somatic complaint with the hope of a free ambulance ride and a welcome change or scenery, even for a short period of time, the ability to provide most assessments at the treatment site is the preferred arrangement.

Recruitment

Under the staff recruitment and training section of this chapter, information is presented about staff qualifications for the provision of necessary security and treatment services. Locating a program in an essentially rural area at some distance from a major metropolitan city will present recruitment problems. In a small community or rural area, the program may be a major employer from the perspective of both numbers and pay ranges and benefit packages. You may find it relatively easy to recruit individuals for the direct care staff (often called Security Counselors), but recruiting a professional staff with advanced degrees may be a challenge. When choosing a physical location, first explore the size and range of the pool from which your potential staff may be hired.

Resident Services

A program located in a small community may also experience difficulty arranging for some necessary community services. It may be difficult to find a dentist, barber, optometrist or similar provider who is willing to either come to the facility to provide services or have the men brought to him or her. There are at least two issues at work here. First, there simply are fewer professionals and service providers in or near a small city or rural area. Couple the scarcity of vendors with the relatively high demand for the same services from local citizens, and acknowledge some reluctance from many vendors to put sex offenders in contact with nonoffenders (e.g., in a waiting room). Other vendors may be uninterested outright in providing any amount of service. This may force program administrators to become very innovative in securing professional services. Contacts with professional schools and offering advanced students a rather unique clinical opportunity has been effective for some programs.

Contact With Local Government

Considering the issues mentioned above, it seems that a location relatively near a larger city is a desirable site for a myriad of reasons. Wherever a civil commitment program for sex offenders is located, it is imperative for the program's administrators to establish and maintain clear communication with local governmental officials. Often local citizens react when they hear rumors about a pending transitional facility for sex offenders. A discussion first with local leaders is an effective way to avert problems caused by misinformation and public distortions. Your top program administrator or clinician might even regularly attend the local city council meetings to answer questions and present a general status report on the program's activities. This kind of initiative helps prevent misinformation circulating in the community.

STAFFING LEVELS

Security and Treatment Requirements

To effectively operate a treatment program for civilly committed sex offenders, you must employ a wide variety of staff, for both security and treatment purposes. All committed residents have been determined to present a safety risk to the general population. Therefore, you should make a policy decision to offer the program in a secure setting at any site being operated as part of the program, with the exception of your transition services very near the end of the treatment process. Transition arrangements still address the public safety factor, of course, with safeguards built into the transition and provisional discharge plans, but the actual physical setting during much of the latter portion of transition does not necessarily provide physical security measures. By the time a resident is in transition, the need for physical security is diminished or the resident should not be in transition. Accountability is provided by monitoring, visiting, checking residents' logs, and the like.

Starting with the premise, then, that treatment is offered in a secure setting, your consideration of the types and numbers of staff you require must address both the security and treatment requirements. The treatment process is complex, and staff must be expected to interact with residents in an appropriate manner throughout each day. Therefore, staff at all levels must be knowledgeable about treatment-related information and must know what is happening with each resident on a day-to-day basis. The intent is for all staff in the facility to be able to observe and document resident behavior, whether the behavior is appropriate or inappropriate.

All staff are also expected to confront inappropriate actions through the residents' participation in team meetings in which staff can discuss the behavior with the resident and, possibly, issue consequences for the behavior. Consequences for inappropriate behavior typically include a restriction on activities or behavior along a defined continuum from more (e.g., full privileges) to less allowable privileges for a period of time.

Direct Care Staff

To accomplish such stated intentions, the residential treatment units must be staffed sufficiently to perform all tasks. This means there are usually more direct line staff assigned to a shift than would be necessary were their primary job restricted only to security. For efficient use of available staff, many programs house residents in twenty-five-bed units. Each twenty-five-bed residential unit may be staffed with three or four direct care providers on the first and second shifts of the day with one or two for the night shift. Of course, in addition to the unit staff there are always staff in the facility who do not work directly on the units who may be called on in emergency situations.

Often, direct care staff who do not work directly on units are assigned duties more classically security related in nature. They may staff a Control Center as well as provide "rover" services, transports, and the like. In some programs staff may be rotated from residential to security, but in others they may function in only one area or the other, usually where the security functions require special training. Where staff are covered by a collective bargaining agreement, they may have the opportunity to bid for another position when vacancies occur. In some of the newer facilities security is controlled by a very sophisticated touch screen computer system. Operators must use the computer system to open doors, operate intercoms, monitor video cameras, and isolate alarms when necessary. This training commitment precludes rotating staff into security who would not use their skills often enough to maintain a proficient level of performance.

Periodically review and evaluate your direct care staffing patterns for their appropriateness with regard to both security and treatment-related needs. This evaluation is important because it helps you monitor the overall operating cost of the program as the number of resident commitments fluctuates (usually by increasing).

Professional Care Staff

The other large staff component involves individuals who provide a professional/clinical service to the residents. Each residential unit may typically be assigned additional staff such as a psychologist, social worker, behavior therapist, recreational therapist, and a recreational program assistant. One residential supervisor may oversee the function of two or more units. Staff not assigned to specific units would obviously include a clinical director, an assistant clinical director, registered nurses, teachers, a rehabilitation counselor, and work therapy staff.

Administrative Staff

A facility can function with a minimum of administrative and ancillary staff, although having an administrative staff person in the facility as an Officer of the Day (OD) on a twenty-four-hour per day basis is recommended. Having an OD designated in charge at all times provides a way to address the myriad of problems that seem to occur at any time.

STAFF RECRUITMENT AND TRAINING

Generally, programs do not seem to be located in areas having a large mass of potential employees with relevant experience in providing sex offender specific therapies, or, for that matter, in operating secure treatment facilities. The task of recruiting staff and providing them with adequate initial and continuing training requires constant attention.

Direct Care and Support Staff

A program should specify the minimum educational and/or experience levels required for various staff categories. Direct care staff—referred to in some programs as treatment support staff—have a minimum educational qualification of either a high school diploma or a general education degree (GED). Depending on the program, qualifying individuals desiring employment may have to:

- Pass a written examination;
- Survive a pre-employment interview;
- Have a physical health examination by a practitioner of their choice;
- Test negative for tuberculosis;
- Pass a physical assessment process that measures the individual's ability to perform the essential physical requirements of the position; and
- Pass a criminal background check.

The recruitment of ancillary staff for housekeeping, food services, maintenance, and similar work is usually not an issue with applicants readily available.

Since these are truly "treatment" programs, it is not unusual to find that a number of applicants have previously worked in various capacities at programs for mentally ill, chemically dependent or developmentally disabled people. This can initially present some problems because the prior nature of the applicants' relationship to those residents was primarily that of a caretaker. While the applicants have had experience working with vulnerable adult populations, they may still require a significant adjustment to relate appropriately to the often manipulative nature of the sex offender, who requires a much more professional approach. The "personal touch" presented by some staff accustomed to "caring" for non-sexual offending residential populations is certainly problematic. Employees from other state programs may also claim open positions in your sex offender program, bypassing the interview process and then finding that they cannot make an adequate adjustment to this population. In many states collective bargaining agreements do allow for such "claimers," who may come from lay-off lists. The challenge is to adequately retrain these staff members to function appropriately in their new setting. Program directors may also encounter problems with a few staff members who do not maintain appropriate boundaries (This is addressed in more detail later in the chapter.).

Some staff hired into direct care positions may perceive their jobs as requiring an added emphasis on the security component and spend less attention on the therapeutic, counseling, or role modeling aspects of the job. They may see their work more from a custody perspective and experience difficulty interacting properly with the residents. Their personal emotional reactions to many of the offenses committed by the residents may make it difficult for them to interact in an appropriate, respectful manner.

These tendencies—to perform tasks in either too caretaking or too custodial a manner—both present problems for effective program management. It is necessary, to the extent possible, to assess these tendencies in applicants during the interviewing and hiring process. This effort will never prove to be completely successful, however, and it is incumbent upon the program to provide all staff with training in appropriate behavior when interacting with residents.

We noted earlier that in a well-run program, all facility staff are generally involved in one fashion or another with treatment. Simply put, this means it is necessary, for example, that a housekeeper not only knows how to clean terrazzo, but also knows the proper way to interact with residents encountered or being supervised during the course of a work shift. The various do's and don'ts of treatment must be presented to all staff and their skill levels must be evaluated and upgraded as necessary on a continuing basis.

Professional Staff

Due to the tendency for these programs to be located in rural areas, it is often difficult to recruit professional staff with ideal backgrounds. Even therapists with outpatient sex offender treatment experience may be unfamiliar with both the severity of the multiple paraphilias and the extremely close teamwork required in residential settings working with severely personality-disordered individuals.

Staff who have previously worked in residential juvenile offender programs, residential chemical dependency treatment programs, or partial hospitalization programs for those with borderline personality disorder often make the easiest adjustment to this population. This appears to be due to their experience with setting firm, consistent limits and their ability to easily identify the frequent attempts on the part of residents to manipulate and split staff. To attract quality staff, provide as much financial support as you possibly can for continued training. Bring in internationally recognized experts for in-house training and pay tuition costs for sex offender-specific training conferences. If possible, affiliate your program with a local university's faculty to provide more attractive recruitment potential.

New Employee/Refresher Training

The initial basic training package presented to all staff must be comprehensive, with much of the basic training accomplished before staff have any contact with residents and perhaps even before they enter your facility's secure perimeter. Training should encompass the following, at a minimum:

- Presentations on the program's clinical treatment program philosophy and design

- Interpersonal relations
- Maintaining boundaries
- Functioning as a team member
- Introduction to human sexuality
- Behavior management policies and practices
- Patient care training
- Therapeutic intervention
- Critical incident debriefing
- Infection control
- Stress management
- Patients' rights
- First aid
- Cardiopulmonary resuscitation
- Sexual harassment
- Affirmative action
- Regulatory requirements
- Facility security practices
- Personality disorders
- Food handling
- Data practices and confidentiality
- Medical record documentation and charting practices
- Emergency procedures
- Negotiation techniques
- Employee right to know
- Safety program
- Appreciation of diversity

A staff personal defense course should be designed to teach skills necessary to reduce stressful situations in order to prevent a physical intervention. Optimally, an intervention course will train employees to use verbal techniques as their primary resource. Staff should acquire skills in verbal negotiation. However, should negotiation fail, staff must have available the necessary physical skills to contain a resident and prevent physical assault to other residents or to staff. This personal defense training should have a mandatory annual refresher. Depending on your program and regulatory requirements, many of the other initially required classes should also have annual refreshers.

Program directors must be prepared to allow significant amounts of time for staff training, both for security and treatment-related topics and for maintaining healthy working relationships among staff. It may be beneficial to bring in consultant trainers to work with staff on team building and, at times, to conduct team mediation sessions for particularly dysfunctional situations.

Boundary Issues

The initial new employee training in maintaining proper boundaries between staff and residents and in functioning as a member of an interdisciplinary team must be followed by continuing training in both areas. With regard to proper boundaries, you may quickly discover that some staff are highly vulnerable to resident manipulation. This is a common discovery. Some residents are very adept at discerning areas of staff vulnerability and then attempting to use this knowledge to their own benefit. Make your staff highly aware of this resident tendency and encourage them to monitor both their own behavior and that of their co-workers. Frequent refresher training in boundary issues is beneficial. Occasionally a staff person may become involved in a nontherapeutic relationship with a resident. To reduce the incidence of this, clinicians and administrators must closely monitor and assess staff behavior in this very critical and potentially serious area.

As with boundaries, not all staff have the ability to function appropriately as a member of an interdisciplinary team. Some staff clearly do not have an intrinsic understanding of basic team concepts, thus necessitating ongoing dialogue with them about team-related issues. Some individuals may seem to be under the impression that since many decisions are made by a "team," not only does everyone have equal say in the outcome, but their opinion will always prevail. Such staff members tend to be highly critical of decisions made by consensus and of team members who do not agree with their personal point of view. This criticism can be very divisive and have an adverse impact on the ability of staff to work together. At times, a staff person may disagree with an otherwise consensual decision of the team, which will rarely represent a problem unless the staff person handles the disagreement inappropriately. An example of the latter is that the staff person may tell the resident about the disagreement, which can cause staff splitting and the creation of a "good staff versus bad staff" situation. A disagreement may also result in friction among staff in the work place, creating issues the supervisor must not ignore.

After some initial experiences with dysfunctional team members, you will quickly acknowledged that the "sheep dip" method of team building is insufficient. Healthy teams require constant maintenance and attention. Staff must be comfortable in voicing their opinions without fear of ridicule from peers, but they also must be willing to concede that they will not "get their way" all the time.

In issuing consequences for resident behavior, quick and consistent staff action is essential. Without healthy teams in constant communication regarding actions taken by residents and consequences issued by staff, the resident population has the ability to focus their energies on the inconsistencies of staff behavior rather than their own actions.

PROGRAM JURISDICTION

The MSOP Experience

Over the past five years, representatives from several states have visited the Minnesota Sex Offender Program (MSOP) facility in Moose Lake, Minnesota in an effort to learn how, and perhaps why, the Minnesota program functions. One of the most commonly asked questions from those visitors involves why the program falls under the jurisdiction of the Department of Human Services (DHS) for both security and treatment without any involvement of the Minnesota Department of Corrections (DOC). Many states that have or are considering civil commitment laws intend to have their DOC provide the security, or custody, services and their equivalent of the DHS provide the clinical treatment services. Note, however, that states with this arrangement often report continuing difficulties with maintaining a good working relationship between the two agencies.

In Minnesota, the civil commitment statute—also known as the "Minnesota Commitment and Treatment Act"—calls for a person civilly committed as either a sexual psychopathic personality or a sexually dangerous person to be treated in a secure treatment facility under the administrative direction of the Commissioner of Human Services. The statute further defines a "secure treatment facility" as either the Minnesota Security Hospital or the Minnesota Sexual Psychopathic Personality Treatment Center (MSPPTC), which the Minnnesota legislature conceptually created in its 1992 legislative session. The facility was designed and built purposefully to provide a secure treatment environment for the MSOP. The possibility for a dual DOC/DHS role in operating the program was never given serious consideration. The great majority of civilly committed individuals admitted to the MSOP have fulfilled their criminal sentences by the time of their commitment, and the state was aware that continued confinement in a correctional facility could result in additional court challenges to its commitment statute.

Dual Jurisdiction Issues

Civilly committed individuals for whom the correctional system has no jurisdictional authority are most appropriately treated in a facility operated solely by a state's DHS or equivalent. When residents are housed in a facility operated by a correctional authority, it is more difficult to present a comprehensive treatment environment even when the entire treatment staff are under DHS direction. This difficulty is clearly not due to any concerted effort on the part of DOC staff to make life difficult.

The rules covering inmate behavior in a prison setting are quite different from those governing mental health programs for individuals under civil commitment who have had their civil rights restored. Depending on program licensure, in some states residents are covered by some type of Bill of Rights for Health Care Facilities. Such rights may include the possession of personal property, privacy in all types of communication, advocacy services, and other services. The implementation of these rights may be difficult in a secure treatment setting. For example, staff may have to examine with the resident present all incoming mail in order to prevent the introduction of contraband. Often these bills of rights were initially drafted for use in other healthcare settings such as nursing homes, not secure facilities. Many such rights would be difficult to meet in a correctional setting. While it is certainly possible for two agencies to cooperatively operate treatment programs for civilly committed sex offenders, when correctional sentences are no longer applicable it appears easier for a single, noncorrectional entity to have overall responsibility for program management.

Irrespective of program location, it is highly recommended that the program be allocated a separate operation appropriation to avoid the perception that resources meant for other disability populations are being used for sex offenders. Program directors should request their funding agencies to seek a program-specific allocation to avoid any criticism that they are taking funding away from other disabled populations.

Civil commitment program directors should be prepared to adequately explain their cost of care figures, as they will be significantly higher than sex offender treatment costs in correctional facilities. Generally, correctional facilities do not staff their living units with as many direct care personnel as do the civil commitment programs. The latter require some additional staffing to effectively provide the twenty-four-hour per day treatment focus. Comparisons will inevitably be made between the cost of care per day, per resident in a DOC facility compared to a Human Services facility.

SUMMARY AND DIRECTIONS FOR THE FUTURE

Civil commitment programs present a number of challenges to administrators, legislators, treatment providers, and communities. It is often difficult to obtain both local and state support for a program designed for a dangerous, treatment-resistant population, and it is equally challenging to recruit and retain quality staff. Program planners must know how to predict potential problems and especially to learn from the mistakes made in earlier and other existing programs.

Civil commitment program directors may also wish to look at admission predictions for several years in the future and determine any actions currently required to avoid unsustainable growth in their population. One state, Minnesota, is recognizing the need to find a way to decrease the amount of time offenders spend in the civil commitment program in order to keep the program at a manageable size.

At the present time, the Minnesota DOC and DHS are working cooperatively in an effort to design a treatment continuum for individuals either civilly committed at the time of the criminal sentencing or identified as potential candidates for civil commitment while they still have correctional time remaining to be served. It is believed that efforts to engage these individuals in a treatment program while in prison may help provide a seamless transition into the civil commitment program and result in shorter stays in the DHS facility. Furthermore, some DOC inmates may make adequate gains while in treatment in the prison environment and thus obviate the need to continue with treatment in the DHS facility.

Cooperative efforts such as these are necessary in order to prevent steadily increasing admission rates to the civil commitment programs. Staff from both departments in Minnesota are optimistic about the potential of their efforts.

Chapter 8

Using Drama Therapy to Uncover Genuineness and Deception in Civilly Committed Sexual Offenders

by John Bergman, M.A., R.D.T., M.T./B.C.T.

The Therapist's Lodestone	8-2
A Lifetime of Secrecy and Deception	8-3
Deception and Attachment	8-3
The Implicit "Dangerous World" Theory of Mind	8-4
Discordant Lying and Agents of Change	8-4
Experiential Therapies	8-5
The Action Forum for Struggle	8-6
Design of Drama Therapy Sessions	8-7
Classic Presentations of the Nongenuine Self: Butting Into the Offender's Map	8-8
The Overly Intellectualized Client	8-8
The Detached and Passive Client	8-8
The Overly Compliant Client	8-8
The Indignant, Outraged, Rigid, and Morally Righteous Client	8-9
The Reality of Play	8-10
Modified Confrontation	8-10
The Adult Rapist	8-11
The Sense of Genuineness	8-12
Elements of a Successful Drama Therapy Session	8-12
Remaking Meaning	8-14

THE THERAPIST'S LODESTONE

An untreated civilly committed sexual offender is a clear and likely threat to someone in the free world. He already has either so many victims and/or a combination of antisocial beliefs, sexual dangerousness, and distorted theories about sexuality that in actuarial terms alone he poses a huge danger to society. For the therapists working with such a client, the task of helping him to change is far more onerous than in the usual prison offender program.

Genuine change is the therapist's lodestone. In civil commitment, a demonstration of the ability to make a genuine change of behavior is the only avenue of release. In almost any other incarcerated setting, the client will eventually get out whether or not he changes. In civil commitment settings, this is mostly untrue. The client must change. He must adjust his disordered arousal; he must show his empathy for others; he must demonstrate his understanding and ability to incorporate the didactic material in the psychoeducational groups; he must demonstrate improved anger management skills and communication skills. He must also contribute to the group, adjust to criticism, break the convict code and criticize others, and demonstrate a commitment to having healthier relationships, even with the very staff who represent, to him, the essence of containment. Change is huge, especially if he has lived as a criminal or according to well-entrenched antisocial beliefs.

Accordingly, treatment providers in civil commitment programs go to great lengths to ensure that their assessments of client progress in treatment are based on methods that are as objective as possible. However, despite those efforts, most measures still involve some degree of subjectivity, requiring treatment providers to rely, at least in part, on their sense of the client's genuineness or deception as true markers for whether the client should or should not progress through the institutional hoops to freedom. It is a hard task. The dedicated antisocial offender, for example, can sometimes present a composed compliance, a certain charming manner that can nearly pass as change. The possible combination of a client's learned and well-practiced deceptive behavior, intense shame over his deviancy or his own still suppressed experience of being assaulted, and the powerful incentive to deceive in order to get one's freedom all can make it very difficult to judge a client's genuineness in treatment, especially where the "genuine" behavior moves him along in the system.

It is this writer's contention that many parts of a treatment session in a civil commitment facility involve moment-to-moment assessment of a client's genuine or deceitful presentation of self. Therapists do this automatically, often without realizing what an intrinsic force of habit this is, using every skill that they have to deduce client honesty—hence, the extraordinary value of experiential therapies in the field of civil commitment. Experiential therapies, especially drama therapy, are a critical component for therapists trying to determine whether a client is merely acknowledging change or has truly incorporated change into his practical reality. Experiential therapies, with their changeable and unpredictable emphasis on the here and now rather than the remembered past, push offenders beyond their zones of comfort and past their carefully created postures of reason, exposing the deceptive defense.

This chapter examines how the drama therapist focuses on the deceptive self, or schema, stripping away the deceptive mask and encouraging the genuine self even though the stakes are as high as they are for the civilly committed offender.

A LIFETIME OF SECRECY AND DECEPTION

Deception and Attachment

Most sexually offending clients have spent some part of their lives hiding their behaviors, fascinations, affect, moods, and thoughts from teachers, parents, siblings, partners, the police, and anyone who might either regiment or control or put a stop to their sexual activities. In many cases, the client has been forced at an early age to suppress his own traumatic experiences at the hands of others and is distrustful, dissociative, or fearful of any experience that might reawaken his memories. Thus, he works hard at maintaining a protective and hypervigilant approach to the world. Many early, unsafe attachment experiences have shattered any potential to trust or even to engage with others (Solomon & George, 1999). Thompson has recently written:

> Early experiences of sensitive or insensitive care contribute to the growth of broader representations concerning a caregiver's accessibility and responsiveness, as well as to beliefs about one's deservingness of care. Such expectations not only enable immediate forecasts of the sensitivity of the caregiver's responsiveness, but also guide future relational choices and expectations, self appraisal, and behavior towards others. (Thompson, 1999, p. 267)

In other words, where the child experiences the world as unsafe, as a place where crying out meets not love but violence, where care is inconsistent and nurturance grudging, then the basic message of therapy—trusting the validity of the authority of group work and the decency of the therapist as both a channel for communication and for embedding change—may well be destroyed. When one learns early that the world will surely not honor its promises to be good, supportive, or decent, it sends an intense global message of meaning to the client.

> Individuals with insecure working models (of attachment) may, because of the distrust or uncertainty engendered by their relational expectations, anticipate less support from others, and may actually deter the kind of supportive care from which they would benefit. In fact, when their partners respond negatively to their distrust or hostility, it confirms their expectations concerning the unreliability of others' acceptance, and their views of themselves as unworthy of such care. (Thompson, 1999, p. 267)

This potent combination of secrecy, shame, terror, and distorted perceptions of the world's motives do not disappear easily, if at all. Nor does the essential decency and goodness of the therapist seem to guarantee change. In fact, the goodness of the therapist can intimidate the client further into making deceptive linkages with the therapist for fear of being rejected. Most people in therapy want the approval of their therapist and may subsume many behaviors and even beliefs in order to get that affective support.

It is not merely the conscious deception that affects therapists, but the old, unconscious deception and resistance that is so hard to change. It is not surprising that the norm in civil commitment includes phallometric assessment or Abel screening, polygraph assessments, testing and grading, and intense scrutiny. It is as if their distrust creates our distrust.

The Implicit "Dangerous World" Theory of Mind

The clients' ancient experiences with the world, their failed or insecure attachments, seem to create "cognitive distortions that are generated by maladaptive implicit theories concerning the nature of victims, the offender and the world . . ." (Ward &Keenan, 1999, p. 835). Ward & Kennan suggest that people actively create these maladaptive implicit theories.

> Individuals learn that the mind interprets situations and that people may represent the same event differently. The mind actively construes and interprets information, rather than passively copying events in the world. Therefore, people do not have direct access to reality, but rather construct the world mentally. It is this construction that guides their actions and interpretations of others' actions. (Ward & Keenan, 1999, p. 824)

According to Ward & Keenan, it appears as if the maps of meaning for sexual offenders are narrow, circumscribed, and with dangerous dimensions of meaning. The authors suggest that one of the implicit theories that underlie pedophiles' constructs of meaning is based on the core belief that the world is dangerous and, therefore, fearful: "The world is a dangerous place and other people are likely to behave in an abusive and rejecting manner to promote their own interests" (Ward &Keenan, 1999, p. 829).

This implicit theory of the world, in the writer's experience with offenders, leads to hiding and protecting the private self at all costs from discovery, and it severely circumscribes active new participation in the world. This "map of meaning" supports a minimalist way of life that leads to rigidity and passive reactivity. The map of meaning is, of course, a metaphoric road map of experiences, reasoning, and private analyses that people unconsciously and automatically use to create the meaning of their experiences.

Civilly committed sex offenders show a rigid adherence to the beliefs, attitudes, and internal stories that contribute to their maps of meaning and their specific automatic reactions to their perceptions. This rigidity and these implicit theories of the world support sexual violence on a habitual and long-term basis. Ward & Keenan suggest that the implicit dangerous world theory can lead directly to the mental support of revenge and punishment, or to a subset map in which only children are dependable and that only they can honestly provide the love that the men believe they must have.

When offenders fail to change any of their sexual actions, beliefs, implicit theories or maps of meaning it may, in fact, be a natural adherence to a conscious or unconscious portrait of self. Certainly this portrait is guarded with great ferocity. Therefore, the "map" may feel more "genuine" to the client and change will feel at best very uncomfortable, if not downright threatening.

DISCORDANT LYING AND AGENTS OF CHANGE

When a client declares that he will not and does not want to change, this insistence constitutes a rejection of "genuineness" as we (treatment staff, program standards, legal mandates) define it. It is our implicit theories versus his. To be genuine necessarily includes the willingness to accept a critique of our behaviors, beliefs, and mental constructs of meaning in order to make valid efforts to change. This writer is stretching the context of genuineness here to accommodate the idea that when offenders challenge their own implicit theories, they alter their stance and map concerning interpersonal relationships in such a way that they can more readily attach and bond. This more secure attachment is part of the mechanism of changing to a more genuine and healthy expression of thought and feeling.

Whether the client who openly says he will not change rises to the level of deception is another matter. Nominally, deception is a proactive stance—the client is totally aware of what he is doing. Deception can also be beyond the reach of cognitive awareness; his defiance or sense of resistance protects him from experiencing that vulnerable sensation of possibly being wrong and automatically closes down all egodystonic information paths.

More traditionally, deception in therapy refers to the attempt to mask what you believe for the sake of getting acceptance by treatment staff and therefore closer to freedom. This writer's experience suggests that in a commitment setting, lies create the greatest form of discord in the therapist, followed closely by violence. If one watches therapists at work with clients, or discusses with them after a session what they actually did, it is a remarkable process. In essence, the therapist makes hundreds of decisions every minute (whether about group mood, attitudes expressed in the face, body, vocal tone, glances, eye contact, and so forth). The therapist adjusts, rephrases, decides on whether to use a metaphor, changes tempo as he or she experiences resistance, support, and the presence of discords that signify lying.

Could it be that very physical systems interpret the lie as being dangerous in the commitment system? That is, the discordance of the lie says that we may have lost connection with the client and that (1) the therapy is temporarily disrupted; (2) the client is absent; and (3) the client is masking in order to protect himself or set up an attack. Do we deeply sense the failed attachment style, or is it the difference in genuineness and the discordant connection with our own implied theories that is so jarring? There is no doubt, in this writer's experience, that in the civil commitment field it is the lying, the lack of genuineness, that sets therapists on edge.

When there is a convergence of feelings, beliefs, and meaning with the therapist's instinctive therapeutic sense of what is genuine, then there is congruence between therapist and client.

Genuineness takes effort, commitment, energy, close attention to all details, close attention to one's actual interior sensations of self, time, support, and moderated confrontation. Without this effort, genuineness cannot be easily arrived at for the civilly committed offender. All of this scrutiny has to also include real opportunities for the client to try out new behavioral responses to his perceptions of meaning and to incorporate new active pictures of self using different affective intensities—in other words, to alter his "maps of meaning."

EXPERIENTIAL THERAPIES

Experiential therapies, including drama therapy, music, dance, and art therapy, have a complex relationship in the current treatment hierarchies in the United States. On the one hand, Freeman-Longo (1995) notes that over 9 percent of treatment providers to sex offenders claim to use aspects of drama therapy, a figure that would be much higher if providers were asked whether they used role play in their work. On the other hand, any experiential therapist will tell you of the anxiety that many institutions have over the use of any modalities that might be affectively "hot" or outside the currently sanctioned modality, that of cognitive behavioral therapy. For instance, one past author in the field (Pithers, 1995) wrote a very uninformed article about dramatherapy in which he failed to quote or mention any of the rich works on dramatherapy and psychodrama. Among other faults, the article simply fails to mention such remarkable theoreticians and practitioners as Blatner (1991, 1997, 1999), Blatner and Blatner (1997), Bannister (1997), Landy (1993, 1994) and others. This is not untypical of knee-jerk, negative responses to experiential work.

Experiential therapies in the treatment of sexual offenders in the United States have not received a great deal of support as compared to New Zealand, Australia, or even Great Britain. In these countries role reversals, role taking, sculpting, and the whole panoply of drama therapy techniques have been incorporated in many different programs. The adult sex offender program in the State of Victoria, which actively uses drama therapy, recently had its entire program reviewed by Professor Steven Hudson (2000).

A therapist's hesitancy to use experiential therapies is, in this writer's opinion, even more problematic in the area of the successful treatment of sexually offending clients, in particular clients who have been civilly committed. As a practicing drama therapist who has worked with civilly committed offenders in two institutions for quite a few years, this writer is mindful of the concerns of therapists in those institutions who prioritize for me the work they want done with the offenders. It is clear that their highest priority is really the evolution and determination of genuineness and health in the client.

The Action Forum for Struggle

Drama therapy disrupts discourse, even the usual discourse of regular therapy. Drama therapy can mutate events and change form. A role play can begin in a sixteenth century bar, become a weather report, and finish in a gibberish argument between an ant and a crow. The integrity of drama therapy depends not on logical discourse, but merely on the logic of its own moments. Its great strength is its emphasis on change, being "in the moment," high energy and dedicated engagement, spontaneity, playing for fun, and playing anew. It releases the client from daily logic but seeks the client's real responses to his perceptions of the world. It is a great threat to the poseur, the coaster, the sociopath who would get by with minimal engagement in change. He can only experience drama therapy as unexpected and dangerous. But this is what is totally necessary for the civilly committed offender.

According to Sherry Stephenson (1993), the original meaning of the Greek word for drama is "drao," which means "struggle." Drama therapy is an action forum for struggle. It is a forum where the client's private self can emerge, get used to being watched, and become consciously aware of others. It makes private knowledge public, and so threatens the integrity of implicit theories. Drama therapy mimics and creates the people and situations that the clients must learn to interact with publicly and genuinely.

Drama therapy's dynamism intensely challenges the deceptiveness of the client. It works so quickly because it is experienced in the moment and because its form and meanings are instantly mutable. It uses lateral thinking strategies in metaphor, story form, or "as if" form. This helps offenders incorporate meanings that challenge their own secret meanings—their old maps of meaning. This also means that the therapist has a new tool for assessing genuineness, the offender's simple use of lateral strategies in a group session.

In this writer's experience as a drama therapist working with sexual offenders, when these clients begin to become genuine, there are significant differences in interaction and behavior in group. Palpably, they begin to engage in healthy thinking, take time to sift through possibilities, especially in answering questions, engage strongly in the event of therapy, and overtly avoid "we-they" battles. In drama therapy terms, they can do the following: play weak roles against their previous type without protest or shame, clearly describe and enact role reversals, create alternative roles as well as unguided roles for themselves, use time "on stage" effectively, and clearly distinguish between self and created or imagined others. This leads to the ability to switch affect with some degree of finesse.

Design of Drama Therapy Sessions

In designing drama therapy sessions for civilly committed offenders, exercises and role work are chosen that will detect and extend therapeutic change. Typically, after many meetings with therapists to discuss the work they want, the following areas are most commonly recommended:

- Creating situations in which the clients experientially confront their distorted maps of meaning, whether as core beliefs or implicit theories of the world
- Testing the depth and strength of change for which a client presents himself as being ready
- Assisting clients in achieving some degree of affective authenticity
- Testing a client for the use of identified or learned internal self-controls in a pre-identified, high-risk situation
- Testing the client for genuineness where his group compliance is suspect

While the above list is in some ways similar to what might be found in any facility (and from many therapists), there are critical differences between the civil commitment arena and a state-run correctional facility. Staff members in a civil commitment facility are really working with issues of urgency, affective integrity, honesty, endurance, and therapeutic will—some of the main components of genuineness. In a correctional program, clients know that if they want to fight treatment to the bitter end they will eventually win and return to the free world. The sexual offender who will return to the free world has no reason to invest in change other than his own will or the new meaning he may give to the world. The civilly committed offender is another case altogether. Engaging in therapy, unless he overturns the legal restriction, is his only option to making it to the free world. This puts extraordinary pressure on the client to present a sustained image of compliance.

Drama therapy is an intense "drao" for the offender. While state-based clients may escape to freedom, civilly committed clients are trapped by time. The drao of sustaining an image will ultimately be challenged by the drao of being in the here and now, and that is the challenge implicit in the fabric of drama therapy.

CLASSIC PRESENTATIONS OF THE NONGENUINE SELF: BUTTING INTO THE OFFENDER'S MAP

The deceptive client usually attempts to minimize and deny but also presents as calm, peaceful, capable, jolly, and boyishly adjusted. Deceptive clients use a variety of strategies easily observed through the drama therapy tool. The depictions that follow indicate both the great range of deception and how the therapy tool works. The examples show how drama therapy helps facility staff to see clearly the offender's deception.

The Overly Intellectualized Client

In affective exercises this client will spend a lot of time questioning the exercise, often trying to subtly change the instructions into something that he would rather do. This client is anxious and very quickly jumps out of a role in a role play, which he has often only glancingly assumed. Thus, if the dramatherapist were to set a basic master/servant exercise in which the client is asked to take on the role of the servant, this client begins first by questioning what and who the role really is, gradually changing the servant from the lesser role to the dominant role of the master.

Part of the "sign" of genuineness may well be the ability to assume and maintain uncomfortable roles (i.e., not being the focal character, being the focal character, playing a subsidiary role comfortably).

The Detached and Passive Client

Drama therapy work with detached, passive clients is an exercise in minimalism. Let's take a simple, kinetically intense exercise such as imagining walking on a tightrope suspended between two skyscrapers. This is an exercise that can create intense body sensations, fear of falling, fear of heights, and so on. In some clients there will be an experience of excitement, fun, and even associations such as being in a circus. With the detached client there is often no creation even of the rope, or they walk casually as if there is no rope there, and tend to finish the exercise very quickly. There is neither risk nor engagement. During the processing period these types of clients give short, limited answers to the exercise experience, with no reference to any imagery. Their map of meaning does not carry references that will sustain meaning with this exercise, and thus they experience a limited laterality of thinking. They may act as if they did the exercise, while their kinetic and imagetic language betrays the deception.

The Overly Compliant Client

This very recognizable type of client acts initially in a very supportive way to the instructions of drama therapy exercises. Staff are often suspicious of these clients because they seem to have minimally established assertiveness skills and frequently shifting presentations of self. Though they are voluble, they are not strong. In a role play of a landlord demanding rent that is in arrears, the offender who plays the tenant who resists the compliant landlord-client invariably wins. In process work, the client is likely to argue that the situation was set up to make it impossible to collect the rent and that he could not throw the tenant out. His reasoning is likely to be very murky. In some extreme cases we have the experience of watching such a client replay the scene and at the climactic moment appear to dissociate. He cannot take on these roles. When the affective intensity is too high and there is too much perceived experiential aggressivity, he dissociates to avoid being there, in the line of fire.

If this client has, by some chance, reached a place where he is considered to be genuinely working, he will surely fail if the improvisation is a potentially pedophilic situation. If, for instance, the dramatherapist takes a young male doll, activates it by initiating eye contact between this client and the doll, and then in a child's voice, holding the doll, asks the client to "get me an ice cream, please," then in most cases the client will lose his perspective, focus too intensely on the doll, and perhaps even approach the doll-child with an imaginary ice cream.

The Indignant, Outraged, Rigid, and Morally Righteous Client

This type of client is often a classic portrait of deception and not at all uncommon in civil commitment facilities. This client finds drama therapy highly challenging and despite his protests to the contrary, shuts down any exercise, sculpts, role plays, or psychodramas. Rigid clients appear incapable of tolerating even the slightest egodystonic affect unless it is anger. They are suspicious of new ideas and tend to see drama therapy as emotionally assaultive. They signal, at first, that they are willing to give everything a try. In other words they signal that they are genuine and open. But even a very simple drama therapy exercise such as a series of walks, with each one different due to environmental changes, is enough for these clients to intensely question the work, distort it, and then insist that it is not the work they need. They may go on to say that this is "for children" and that they "did not come here to play," which is closer to the truth then they may really understand. The fear can gradually escalate and intensify their resistance.

These men's rigidity often originates from being the brunt of intensely righteous, affectively dangerous, and controlling parents. Their parents were often distant and affectively unattached, sometimes military parents. Play was considered unimportant or even "childish."

It is still remarkable even after twenty years to see how threatening the simple act of play can really be. The client who presents with a slightly quizzical air, apparently in charge of himself, even "confused" as to why he is in treatment, falls apart when asked to play. The self he presents is a deception, a creation for the moment of therapy. Doing a basic transformative exercise such as transforming an imaginary ball of mud into an object (a rope, a motorbike, a dentist's chair) can make these rigid controllers furious, embarrassed, even dramatically ashamed of their anxiety and imagined play incompetence.

The Reality of Play

Play is a remarkable antidote to the deceptive self. Play is characterized by free-form actions unrelated directly to the environment. These actions have to be "made up" or metaphoric (i.e., analogic). They might not exist in any environment that is known on the earth—that is, they are completely imaginary. Effective play has been seen to completely engross the player. It is affective and challenging, and it intensifies people's sense of self-efficacy and promotes broader and stronger interpersonal skill bases. Play is, for most people, a nonthreatening but vital addition to the arsenal of transformation and enrichment of life.

For civilly committed offenders it is threatening, sometimes a source of impotent shame. It is this very quality, though, that allows us to see whether the client has gradually moved from his limited cognitive scope to a broader and more affectively accepting interior stance. The act of play connotes the ability to scan internally for the thoughts that resist play and steer the player to the past shaming events. It also signifies the ability to accept new dimensions of meaning to things, people and places, to see some elasticity in the dimension and use of objects, and to do tasks very rapidly without needing to heed the incessant cry for validation before shame. Play challenges the fear of failure, the fear of looking stupid, of losing, of being shamed. The masking of these fears can lead to deception. The release of the masking can lead to genuineness. Play vitally challenges implicit theories and core beliefs such as entitlement and the notion that events are not controllable (Ward & Keenan, 1999). Play allows the client the chance to experiment with connecting with people in unguarded ways, and it provides a first line antidote to the anomie of facility life. Play is a vital component of change for the functioning drama therapist in a civil institution.

Modified Confrontation

Most honest therapists can point to ten to twenty clients who have successfully deceived them, whether in treatment or in the hoops leading to freedom. It is not always the overtly criminal or sociopathic client with a potent disregard for speaking or using the truth who gets by us. It can be the soft spoken, apparently fragile, paranoiac presenting offender. In one session, such a client quietly turned back the thrust of the sessions so that he could get this writer to deal only with his new and wondrous sense of how he felt so much less afraid. He carefully transferred my focus to his new and gentle connection with his cat and his attendant feelings. All of this was presented in a soft, almost tremulous voice. The subtext appeared to be, "I am hurt but I am really changing." Fortunately, another staff member broke the sticky illusion, reminding the client that another victim of his alleging sexual abuse had just come to light not a few moments before group (as he well knew). Most days this writer would have had his "deception alarm" ringing loudly, if only from the tremulous voice, the consistent, unwavering focus away from real treatment issues. Interestingly, even after the other staff members' comments, the client maintained a very dramatic look of shock—how could you?—and astonishment at being confronted. He barely realized that this intensified staff's knowledge of how much more deception he really practices, how private and rigid his map of meaning really is.

As an aside, I wish to state some support for the use of modified, connected confrontation. Over the last few years, the pendulum in sexual offender treatment has swung far from confrontation. Many therapists, especially in public, are quick to claim that the only effective, ethical way to work is to create warm, positive therapeutic alliances and that even a little confrontation is too much!

How one wishes it were so. Incarcerated clients, especially those who have committed many crimes, not just sexual crimes, and who show neither respect nor empathy for others, do not come willingly into therapy. Many clients are intensely invested in maintaining their secrets, not for fear of more criminal charges but because they genuinely like their life styles and dislike ours. These men will split staff, cause contention, and use intimidation or legal hairsplitting to resist any treatment overtures. Constantly moving the therapy goalposts, bending the idea of rehabilitation to suit their own needs, these clients have to learn clearly and quickly what the limits in our world really are. Warm connections are a crucial bridge across which the therapist and client must eventually meet, but the client must also experience our implacable adherence to doing the right thing, to the probity of our programs, to holding honest discourse. Directly confronting a lie is not an immoral act. Genuineness needs to exist in a culture of connection and intense truthfulness. The civilly committed client is in a bind—there simply is nowhere for him to hide anymore. Deception signifies the need to continue on in treatment. Endless deception means endless commitment. Only genuineness will begin to turn the key.

The Adult Rapist

Drama therapy is a multifaceted tool. It is kinetic, lateral, metaphoric; it uses multiple cognitive skills and is affectively intense and infinitely elastic. Through its use, the drama therapy practitioner can make a determination of deception quite quickly. For instance, take the adult rapist, who is angry, self-involved, highly defended and whose bravado initially helps him in appearing successful in drama therapy. Especially if he is in a group of more passive men, the adult rapist appears on the surface to easily pass one of the drama therapy tests—role variation. These men act with a veneer of confidence, voice their opinions and even offer to take some roles in the drama therapy work when the opportunity is given.

On the other hand, once some of the work begins these men quickly become self-conscious, protective, afraid to give up control, and on occasion they storm out of sessions. Even with the simplest of warmup exercises, if the exercises are simply physical and noncompetitive, these clients show their discomfort. In other words, in a simple verbal setting these adult rapists present as genuine, but in drama therapy their deceptiveness may well show through their discomfort.

For instance, here is a typical opening exercise. The clients mill around the drama therapist and then with a short, seven-second count, may have to touch two walls, a door, underneath a chair, a nose, and so on. The aggressive adult rapist will hang back, scan the others, and may even take this moment to leave. On his map of meaning, these moments have the potential to be humiliating. People are to be feared, and only revenge will make it safe. If he is narcissistic enough, he will convert this moment into an attack on him. Intriguingly, his abrupt exit is mirrored in the brevity of any of the roles he does take in later role plays. Adult rapists in the landlord/tenant situation have sometimes completely abbreviated the scene, shortening their sentences, ending any conflict in the situation. Genuineness includes genuine change and means for the client real changes in their self-confidence. If this type of self-confidence is translated into drama therapy terms, then it means the ability to improvise richly and capably in many roles outside of the accustomed role of controlling self. The adult rapist would be judged by time and role flexibility.

Drama therapy pierces deception by creating abnormal circumstances for the deceptive practices and straining the meaning-maker to adapt. Each of the above "types" of client responds almost predictably. The drama therapy exercises strain the rigidity of their implicit theories of world and create only predictable answers for the attachment danger. In other words, clients respond to drama therapy improvisations almost as if they were struggling to create meaning for their original assault. It is this that shows the real inability to achieve genuineness.

THE SENSE OF GENUINENESS

Elements of a Successful Drama Therapy Session

There are five aspects to a drama therapy session:

- Kinetic interactivity leading to free metaphoric play and action;
- Language action in play leading to role work;
- Gradual intensity in open role conflict, in which the client gradually extends the conflict issues to include self versus aspects of his global problems (This is where aspects of core beliefs such as "the child [and all children] wanted it" might be challenged.);
- Guided affective experiences outlined by the client, usually focusing on potent introjects from past traumatic experiences or more contemporary violent interaction (This work connects to some attachment issues.); and
- Interactive processing.

Generally, each segment of a session has a set of hurdles for the client; for example, the affective experience may revolve around a victim empathy exercise, perhaps within a play-based modality. The client then would have to control his resistance to play as well as to maintain his empathic skill during the problem. The client is tested, in other words, on:

1. His ability to blend his will to the will of the therapist through the dictates of the experiential event. He may also need to blend his will to the perceived needs of an imaginary figure, for instance his victim and the victim's imagined presence in the therapy room.

2. His skill at choosing actions during the experiential work that are congruent with the drama therapy problem and are affectively syntonic, whether the experience is simulated, play based, or derived from original experiences.

3. His fluidity with concepts derived or learned from psychoeducational programs in the facility and converted dynamically and appropriately to the needs of the experiential event.

4. His ability to strongly and affectively represent roles outside his usual repertoire. He need not be comfortable with the role—for example, presenting a dangerous or violent character.

5. His ability to move from one modality of drama therapy to another—for example, being able to go from role work in a play modality to a psychodramatic investigation of a troublesome relationship, perhaps with addiction, to making an empathic relationship with another client in role. This role fluidity is characteristic of quite successful people in the free world.

Again, any aspects of this work might be used with a variety of sexual offenders. These are all critical tests for the civilly committed sex offender. They test not only his skills and ability to acquire information, but also his real ability to incorporate what he is doing in treatment with behavior that simulates external world pressures. This is paramount where society's future safety is one of the spoken or unspoken criteria for the client's movement through the commitment system.

A successful drama therapy session is one in which the client reaches and exhibits genuineness. In a classic session, the client is first taken through physical warm-up exercises leading to kinetic associations in play mode and then to lateral language association. The client warms up his associative cognitive skills and shows his willingness to participate openly. This means that he is already effectively challenging his older belief systems about this work.

At this point, he is still working with other members of the group on the floor. But generally I will contract him to do some high-risk role plays, most significantly with men from the group who have histories of antisocial behavior such as theft and assault. The client will play the role of a weaker man or a woman and will be instructed to give special focus to the skills of negotiating, placating, agreeing, sympathizing, and giving up to a stronger man or woman. These role plays begin to test not only efficacy and comprehension, but specifically the realm of genuineness. The client is now ready to go on to harder work.

The client is asked to focus on someone to whom he still harbors resentment—for instance, a violent parent. That parent is then imagined to be in a chair in the center of the room. The client must first affectively begin an "unfinished business" conversation with this imagined figure. The client is encouraged to access as much of the feelings as he really has. When he reaches a natural conclusion he then role reverses, becoming the "reviled" figure. He may then continue role reversing. We watch for where he might freeze, signs of dehumanizing, and any resistance to the work.

Then the client is asked to put another chair on the floor, in which he is to imagine the same figure, except this is the "good" parent. He goes through the same process. We look for a number of signs here, especially if the client has been in treatment for any length of time. The signs are:

- Not becoming resistant;

- Not falling into dissociative states;
- Being able to take a reasonable amount of time to think, prepare, and act;
- Being able to switch comfortably from talking at the imagined figure to talking to the therapist and back again. This is a critical skill that we have in the free world, the ability to divide our attention again and again and to give intense attention to anything on which we choose to focus;
- Giving a fairly clear picture of both sides of a person who is "dangerous" to the client without becoming fixated on either the goodness or the badness. This is an enormously crucial exercise, as it is evidence of at least two changes—first, the possibility of forgiveness and therefore a change in attachment issues, and second, a change in his implicit "dangerous world" theories (i.e., sensing the possibility that not all people are dangerous and that it is possible that people are more shades of grey than all black);
- Accessing nontherapeutic language during this work. This is so important. Given that we visit many sites, one of our most common experiences is to listen to clients sound exactly like their therapists, and to have lost, changed, or given away all their native language. When the client is really accessing his interior picture/memory of an event, he sounds as he talks in nontherapy situations. This is a critical sign of genuineness and very hard to achieve;
- A fast and determined pacing to the story/act/action that moves from subject to subject and sometimes returns back to the original issue again;
- Relaxed eye contact and appropriate physical mirroring of the role states;
- Crossing the line to work with the therapist and not making any we/they statements;
- No "grooming" of the therapist; and
- Processing the work realistically (i.e., not seeing the work as meaning that treatment is finished).

In one case, the client demonstrated all of the above and was acknowledged by all the therapists to be finally working very effectively at change. In these cases the determination of genuineness is bolstered by the effective ability to handle complex demands in the experiential arena.

Remaking Meaning

The potency of the experiential demands forces clients either to block and resist or, if they are really working, to try to change. In cases of deception, the work is often to focus on the areas of resistance, to personify them, and to allow the client to confront them (e.g., in an empty chair) as a precursor to empathy work. Coming face to face with one's defenses in the affective tension of a drama therapy session can give the client a new "venue " for expression. Which is to say that the client, instead of responding only through his automatic map of meaning, can instead constructively use the drama therapy session as a surrogate meaning maker. This is one of the tenets of good therapy—that the session is a safe place for seeing what is possible. The client experiences the therapist as a new attachment surrogate, and in doing this starts the process of rewriting the meaning of his world. Drama therapy drives part of the process by creating experiences in which this process of meaning making can become highly charged. It is the presence of this act of remaking meaning that is the final real evidence of genuineness. And in a civil commitment setting, where the stakes are so high, drama therapy is one of the critical components of the test for genuine change and genuineness.

References

Bannister, A. (1997). *The healing drama: Psychodrama and dramatherapy with abused children.* London: Free Association Books. (New York: N.Y.U. Press).

Blatner, A. (1997). *Acting-in: Practical applications of psychodramatic methods* (3d ed.). London: Free Association Books.

Blatner, A. & Blatner, A. (1997). *The art of play: Helping adults reclaim imagination & spontaneity.* Philadelphia: Brunner/Mazel-Taylor & Francis.

Blatner, A. (1991). Role dynamics: An integrative psychology. *The Journal of Group Psychotherapy, Psychodrama & Sociometry, 44*, 33–40.

Blatner, A. (1999). Psychodrama. In D. J. Wiener (Ed.), *Beyond Talk Therapy: Action Approaches in Treatment.* Washington, DC: Heldref, www.heldref.org (subscription included in membership in ASGPP, 301 North Harrison St., Ste 508, Princeton, NJ 08540).

Freeman-Longo, R. E., Bird, S., Stevenson, W. F. & Fiske, J. A. (1995). *1994 nationwide survey of treatment programs and models serving abuse-reactive children and adolescent and adult sex offenders.* Brandon, VT: Safer Society Press.

Landy, Robert J. (1994). *Drama therapy: Concepts and practices* (2d ed). Springfield, IL: Charles C. Thomas.

Landy, Robert J. (1993). *Persona and performance: The meaning of role in drama, therapy, and everyday life.* New York: Guilford Press.

Pithers, W. D. (1997). Maintaining treatment integrity with sexual abusers. *Criminal justice and Behavior, 24*, 34–51.

Solomon, J. & George, Carol (1999). The measurement of attachment security in infancy and childhood. In J. Cassidy & P. Shaver (Eds.), *Handbook of attachment.* New York: Guilford Press.

Stephenson, S. (1993). Use of drama. In K. N. Dwivedi (Ed.), *Group work with children and adolescents.* London: Jessica Kingsley.

Thompson, R. (1999). Early attachment and later development. In J. Cassidy & P. Shaver (Eds.), *Handbook of attachment.* New York: Guilford Press.

Ward, T. & Keenan, T. (1999, Aug.). Child molesters' implicit theories. *Journal of Interpersonal Violence, 14*, 821–838.

Chapter 9

Working With Nonoffending Partners

by Joanne Fairfield, C.Q.S.W.

Why Work With Nonoffending Partners? 9-2
Impact on Partner of Discovery of the Abuse 9-3
    As an Individual 9-4
    On Relationship With Offender 9-4
    On Relationship With Victim 9-5
    On Relationship With Victim's Siblings 9-6
    On Relationship With Friends and Community 9-6
    Financial Concerns 9-6
    Support Services 9-7
The Integrated Treatment Model 9-7
    Program Philosophy 9-7
    When Is This Treatment Approach Appropriate? 9-7
    Framework and Goals 9-8
    Why Use a Cognitive-Behavioral Treatment Model? 9-8
        Modeling 9-10
        Respondent Conditioning 9-10
        Instrumental Conditioning 9-11
    A Gradual Process 9-11
Assessment of Nonoffending Partners 9-11
Group Work for Nonoffending Partners 9-15
    Group Work, Part A 9-16
        Address the Impact of Offending 9-16
        Increase Understanding of Victim Dynamics 9-16
        Increase Understanding of Offender Dynamics 9-16
        Provide an Alternative Model/Framework 9-18
    Group Work, Part B 9-19
        Learn to Identify and Challenge Cognitive Distortions 9-19
        Learn to Identify and Resist Grooming Strategies 9-19

> Introduce the Relapse Prevention Model and
> > Learn to Identify Cues 9-21
> > Develop Partner and Victim Alert Lists 9-22
> > Develop a Support Network 9-22
> Group Work, Part C1 9-22
Dyadic Work 9-22
> Assessing Readiness for Joint Work 9-23
> Joint Work, Part C2 9-23
> > Communication and Information 9-23
> > Practice Skills 9-24
> > Addressing Unresolved Issues 9-24
Therapist's Role 9-24
Summary 9-25

WHY WORK WITH NONOFFENDING PARTNERS?

Professionals involved in the treatment of the sex offender traditionally have relied on a combination of self-report by sex offenders, therapists' clinical judgment, and actuarial analyses of risk to make informed decisions. Of course, sex offenders have strong incentives to misrepresent both their progress in treatment and their offending, and clinical judgment is difficult to validate empirically. The integration of the parole and therapist professional network has helped us acquire another layer of information by which the offender's behavioral and therapeutic compliance can be examined more effectively. But we often overlook yet another valuable source of information—namely, the observations and experience of the nonoffending partners and other members of the offender's family. The information that the nonoffending partner can offer can significantly enhance the assessment and treatment of offenders, particularly in relation to the development and maintenance of the offender's relapse prevention plan.

When decisions about family separation and reunification are being made, and when the development of a support network for the offender is at issue, the process brings the nonoffending partner into a focal position. This chapter will present a multi-component intervention model for working with members of the offender's support network, which combines an understanding of both victim and offender dynamics. While this chapter's focus is the nonoffending partner, the treatment model is also applicable to working with other support persons in the sexual offender's proposed support network. These include people whom the offender has identified as potential support people, such as parents, siblings, or other significant people involved with them. Indeed, including people who have a diverse range of relationships and who are therefore in touch with various aspects of the offender's life leads to a far more effective support network. Clearly, whatever the nature of their relationship with the offender, members of the support network will benefit from a well-informed understanding of the offender's problems and treatment. The program provides nonoffending partners and others in the support network with the tools to effectively support themselves and the offenders in treatment and beyond.

For ease of discussion, we refer to the nonoffending partner as "she" and to the sexual offender as "he," as most partners are women and most offenders are men. Parental responses have been shown to be significant factors in moderating negative outcomes for children and young people who have been sexually abused. The premise for this text is that the sex offender's partner's response and understanding can be a significant factor in enhancing sex offender treatment. Sex offenders are not always reliable reporters of their behavior, which makes the external support network an invaluable adjunct to therapy. A well-informed support network can assist the offender's therapist and the supervising parole officer by providing feedback about how the offender is doing currently and by providing retrospective information that will help with developing an effective relapse prevention plan (Marshall et al., 1990). Clearly, the offender's partner is a key member of this support network. The better her understanding of offender dynamics, victim dynamics, and the relapse prevention model, the more effective a support person she will be for the sex offender. In both intrafamilial and extrafamilial abuse, the nonoffending partner can be an important external barrier to reoffending, whether or not the victim(s) is in the home.

Nonoffending partners are often very reluctant to engage in therapy. Partners who are parents of the victim will usually seek therapy for the child but view a recommendation of therapy for themselves as a sign that someone believes that they are at fault and their acceptance of therapy as an indication that they agree. When partners learn that their spouse has committed a sexual offense, their first reaction is often one of shock or denial. Thousands of questions run through their heads and a huge range of emotions (anger, hurt, betrayal, guilt, shame, mistrust) swamp them. In addition, they often experience changes in financial status and loss of support from family, friends, and the community. Where their child is the victim, they are also trying to address the child's needs, and those of any siblings.

Many partners break off the relationship with the offender; others deny the abuse took place; while still others actively side with the offender and blame the victim. No one of these types is easy to engage in treatment, but all can benefit from support and information. In addition, they all have valuable information about the offender's behaviors, attitudes, and beliefs, which will enhance the offender's treatment and increase the effectiveness of the child protection plan.

IMPACT ON PARTNER OF DISCOVERY OF THE ABUSE

The impact of sexual abuse on victims is well documented (Browne & Finkelhor, 1986). The symptoms exhibited by victims vary widely. Some seem to suffer minimal effects, while others suffer severe and sometimes long-lasting effects. Problems can include emotional difficulties such as sadness, anxiety, anger and shame; behavioral problems such as withdrawal and aggression (Courtois, 1988; Sgroi, 1982); and the development of cognitive distortions that lead to self-blame and distrust of others. In addition, victims often exhibit related somatic symptoms that can include headaches, sleep disturbance, and eating disorders (van der Kolk, 1988).

Nonoffending partners are frequently referred to by professionals as secondary victims. When one reviews the impact of the sex offender's behavior on their lives, their relationships, and their emotional responses, nonoffending partners appear to be affected in many ways that the primary victim is and to struggle with some similar issues.

Indeed, there is considerable evidence that in the case of child sexual abuse, nonoffending partners suffer significant levels of distress following a child's disclosure of abuse (Deblinger et al., 1993). This distress may not only impair their ability to be supportive of the child, but may also impair their ability to appropriately challenge and confront the offender, thereby limiting their effectiveness as a support person for the offender.

The partner feels the impact of the offender's behavior on a number of different levels. She feels the impact first on herself; and then on her relationship with the offender; in the case of intrafamilial abuse, on her relationships with the victim and his or her siblings; and on her relationships with others in the community. In addition, she must cope with numerous changes and practical issues.

As an Individual

Aside from the impact of the offending on the nonoffending partner as a parent and a partner (described below), she is greatly affected as an individual. Nonoffending partners experience a wide range of emotional responses, such as anger, hurt, betrayal, disbelief, guilt, shame, and depression. For some the depression is so intense that they suffer from suicidal thoughts or even attempt suicide. Their fear of loss is understandably significant, and it is reinforced by their sense of isolation. They often report a loss of trust in their own judgment and at times an overwhelming sense of failure. This is reflected in the generally negative and pessimistic view of the future that nonoffending partners often demonstrate.

Along with their loss of trust in their own judgment, they describe a loss of faith in others, not just in the offender. Indeed, it is not uncommon for nonoffending partners to retain some sense of faith in the offender while suffering a significant loss in their own self-image. This may be in part at least a reflection of the past and ongoing grooming and manipulation strategies that the offender has employed in his relationship with the nonoffending partner. In addition, many partners question their sexual attractiveness, report a loss of interest in sex, and express confusion about their own sexuality. A significant number also have to deal with their own history of abuse. They may experience intrusive memories or thoughts of their own abuse, or the abuse of the victim. A number of nonoffending partners also report sleep and appetite disturbance, increased generalized anxiety, problems with concentration, and irritability.

On Relationship With Offender

Following the discovery of the sexual offending, nonoffending partners are faced with incredibly difficult choices and decisions. Over and over they describe themselves as being caught in the middle and having to make impossible choices. Should they believe the victim or the offender? Should they try to hold onto the relationship or end it? There is tremendous confusion and conflict. Considering their relationship with the offender, they will often ask themselves many questions, such as, How could someone who has so many positive qualities do this? How could this have happened without my knowing? I thought he loved me—what's wrong with me? Why me/us? Why my child/my partner? These questions reflect the guilt, blame, and confusion they feel; their mistrust in themselves as partners; and their ambivalence or loss of trust in the relationship. Alongside this there is often an acute sense of betrayal, which is one of the hardest issues for nonoffending partners to address. They are often angry with the offender but may find it difficult to express, as they have conflicted loyalties.

Another block to addressing these issues is the anger and hurt that nonoffending partners may feel in relation to professionals. They may perceive themselves to be punished by the system along with the offender, which adds to their sense of blame and powerlessness. As the secrecy unfolds and the grooming and manipulation by the offender becomes clearer, partners initially suffer from a loss of faith in their own judgment. They struggle with feeling a fool for being "conned" by the offender. This can result in a loss of trust in their partner, in men, or in people in general. The impact this can have on their relationship with the partner or future partners must be addressed in treatment.

On Relationship With Victim

Immediately following the disclosure of the sexual abuse, the nonoffending partner is faced with the decision of whether to believe the victim. Disbelief and denial is very common at this stage. Given the nature of the information she is faced with and the associated pain, denial is not such a surprising first response. Often when people are faced with unbearable bad news such as the sudden death or serious illness of a loved one, denial is a common initial response. The losses and potential losses that both the nonoffending partner and the victim face following disclosure of sexual offense are many—loss of trust in self and others, loss of sense of control over one's life, loss of support, and loss of relationships, to name but a few. The nonoffending partner's fears for the future of her child are reflected in questions such as, Will he or she be permanently damaged? Become a homosexual? Become an offender? At a time when the child needs the nonoffending parent the most, she is reeling and struggling to cope with her own responses, which commonly include a sense of guilt or blame for the abuse. There is also usually a strong sense of failure as a parent. Many of those who were abused as children report that they "promised myself it would never happen to my child."

While struggling to cope with such feelings, the nonoffending partner must also cope with and understand the impact of the abuse on the child. This includes coping with the child's anger, which is often directed at her. Nonoffending partners are likely to be experiencing their own anger also. They may be angry at the victim for not telling sooner or at themselves for not helping the victim to tell sooner. They may be angry at themselves for not recognizing or preventing the abuse. It is clear that the feelings of fear, anxiety, pain, anger, and sadness experienced by the victim are also experienced by the nonoffending partner. The situation is compounded when the nonoffending partner has a personal history of abuse. Old issues such as self-blame, shame, and diminished self-worth become evident. Like the victim, the nonoffending partner has worked hard in the past to avoid thinking, talking about, or remembering her abuse. As a result, old coping strategies of denial, numbing, and avoidance surface along with the memories. This may be reflected in her response to the victim. Her response may be one of drawing closer or of ambivalence, jealousy, or scapegoating. These responses can be understood in part as a reflection of the general pattern of the parent-child relationship. Recognize, however, that the parent-child relationship has been shaped in part by the offender's grooming and manipulation of both the nonoffending partner and the victim.

On Relationship With Victim's Siblings

One of the first concerns of a nonoffending partner in cases of intrafamilial abuse is the fear of having the children removed by child protection services. The partner is coping with incredible conflicts and tensions, one possibly being balancing the siblings' desire for the offending parent to remain in the home against the need to protect the victim from further abuse. These tensions are often intensified by sibling rivalries between the victim and siblings, which again may well have been set up by the offender or exacerbated by his grooming strategies.

In addition, many unspoken fears haunt nonoffending partners, such as whether the siblings have also been sexually abused and feelings within of having possibly "failed" them as well. Other questions facing nonoffending partners include, What did the siblings know about the sexual abuse? What should they know now? How will the information affect them? They must face these questions while they are trying to cope with the siblings' own disparate responses to the situation.

On Relationship With Friends and Community

Where the offending is known of in the community, nonoffending partners often report that they are the object of curiosity, derision, and/or gossip. They frequently feel blamed and ostracized by their community and report that their children have been teased or insulted. Many report that they have lost close friends and have experienced rejection by their own family and the offender's family at a time when they need the support most. Where they have close friends who have remained supportive, partners often report that they find it hard to talk to them about the abuse for fear they will be blamed for it or lose what little support they have.

Problems also arise when the offending is not public knowledge. The partner wonders what to say, what cover story to use, who she can share her worries and concerns with, and how much to share. Whether the offending is public knowledge or not, the partner's loneliness and isolation is intense.

Financial Concerns

One of the first practical issues that nonoffending partners often have to address is the likely loss of finances at a time when they have additional costs to bear. Additional costs can include the cost of therapy for the victim or the offender, the cost of a second residence when an offender is required to move out, or the cost of a change in residence for the nonoffending partner and her family. At the same time, the partner is also expected to manage a complex and demanding schedule. This often means balancing work and children's school schedules, along with the demands of the legal process and therapy appointments, all at a time when she is at her lowest point emotionally. Where there is intrafamilial abuse, she must also try to meet the often conflicting emotional needs of the victim and siblings.

Support Services

Given the importance of the nonoffending partner's role in the recovery of the victim and her potential importance in the treatment of the offender, it is surprising that there are so few support services available for nonoffending partners. While there has been some development in this area for nonoffending parents of abused children, there is a dearth of services for partners of offenders. Whether seen as nonoffending parents or as partners, neither receives a lot of support. Rather, the usual practice is for professionals to place further demands on them. Nonoffending partners have more often than not been portrayed in the literature as collusive and indirectly, if not directly, responsible for the abuse of their children.

In *Treating Child Sex Offenders and Victims: A Practical Guide*, Anna Salter (1988, pp. 35–39) provides an excellent overview of the ways in which professionals have blamed victims and the nonoffending partners for sexual abuse. Although most nonoffending partners clearly do not fit the stereotypes, they have often encountered reflections of these harsh attitudes in their dealings with professionals, as well as with their extended family and community. As we have seen, nonoffending partners are often struggling to cope with their own responses as well as the responses of those around them. In addition, they have little or no information about sexual offending. The aim of therapy, therefore, is to provide them with the support, information, and skills they need.

THE INTEGRATED TREATMENT MODEL

Program Philosophy

The philosophies and beliefs behind sexual offender treatment programs need to be articulated and shared both within and across agencies, as close interagency work is essential in this field. If this is not done, we will have a poorly coordinated, incoherent response to sexual offending, and treatment will be less effective as a result. The basic beliefs that underpin the integrated model are as follows: First, sexual offending is a multidimensional problem that affects individuals, families, and communities. As such, individuals, families, and communities can benefit from education regarding the nature of sexual offending and its prevention. Second, sexual offending is viewed as a treatable problem. Third, sexual abuse is a process that occurs within relationships, not an isolated act, and treatment should reflect this. Finally, real prevention can become a reality through effective sex offender treatment, with the help of better-informed individuals, families, and communities.

When Is This Treatment Approach Appropriate?

The integrated treatment model initially grew and developed within a program for victims and their families. The model has been used primarily with cases of child sexual abuse, but also across a wide range of cases and settings. The majority of nonoffending partners and parents who have participated in the program are women. Male nonoffending partners seem more difficult to engage. The men who have participated have reported that they found the experience beneficial, but the engagement of men remains an area in need of further development. As stated earlier, this chapter focuses on work with nonoffending partners, the spouses and lovers of offenders in treatment; however, this approach can be, and has been, used with the parents and siblings of offenders as well as other support persons. It has been used where the offender is an adolescent and where he is an adult. It has been used in cases of both intrafamilial and extrafamilial abuse. It has been used where the nonoffending partner plans to reunite with the offender and where she plans to separate from and divorce him. It has been used in both inpatient and outpatient treatment settings. It has been used within victim and family programs and as part of sex offender programs.

Framework and Goals

The Integrated Model (see Figure 9.1) provides a framework for addressing the needs of each member of the family and suggests a sequence for undertaking each stage of the work. The model involves a combination of individual, group, dyadic, and family therapy and has three phases: referral, assessment, and treatment. As the figure shows, after the referral phase the model can be described in terms of four components: (1) the initial assessment, (2) group work, (3) dyadic work with the offender (and where relevant with the victim), and (4) family work. The second, third, and fourth components are described under "Treatment Options" in the treatment phase. All of these options involve both group work—with victims, nonoffending partners, and adult survivors, and dyadic work—with victims and siblings, victims and nonoffending partners, and offenders and partners.

What follows is an overview of the treatment program and a description of each of the nonoffending partner components. This treatment model is a structured, coherent, and practical approach within which therapists explain concepts, teach new skills, and provide opportunities for participants to practice their skills. Much of the early and intermediate phases of the work with the nonoffending partner is undertaken separately from the offender. The program is structured in this way to allow the partner to address her own emotional needs and fears without worrying about the impact on the offender. She is also able, with the support of the group and therapists, to explore key issues such as grooming and to practice the skills she will need to develop in order to become an effective support person.

The overall goal of the program is to provide nonoffending partners with the tools they need to effectively challenge and support the offender, while meeting the needs of their children and taking care of themselves. The approach does not require a lock-step application. It requires regular assessment of the potential strengths and vulnerabilities of the nonoffending partner (and others) and allows for flexibility in the amount of focus on any particular issue. It requires close collaboration between professionals. In turn, the model is designed to offer essential support and information to nonoffending partners and to be integrated with both offender and victim treatment.

Why Use a Cognitive-Behavioral Treatment Model?

The cognitive-behavioral treatment model can provide the theoretical framework for understanding the impact of offending and the development of interventions. One

Figure 9.1
Integrated Treatment Model for Nonoffending Partners

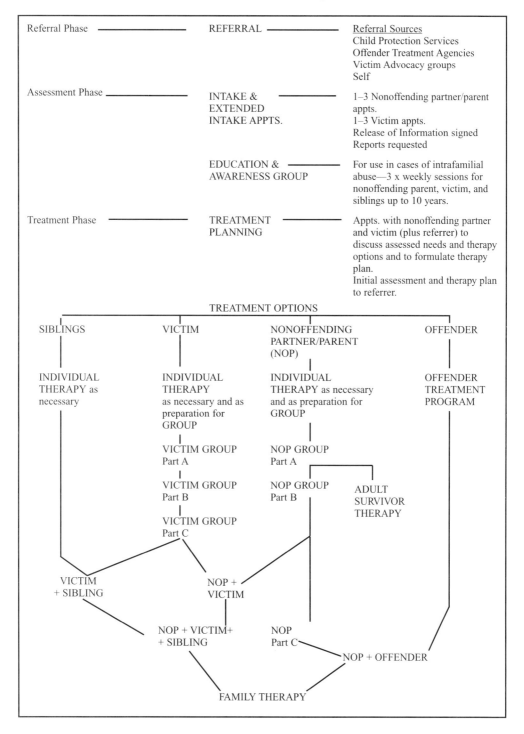

advantage of this treatment model is that it can be readily understood by families and professionals alike. Most important, the cognitive-behavioral treatment model is the core theoretical model for most established sex offender treatment programs. It also draws on therapeutic strategies that have already been proven successful in other victim programs (Deblinger & Heft, 1996), and it allows for the integration of the nonoffending partner's treatment with both the victim's therapy and the offender's treatment.

Cognitive-behavioral intervention seems particularly suited to addressing many of the needs and concerns of nonoffending partners for a number of reasons. It provides a combination of cognitive strategies, behavioral procedures, and emotional processing techniques that allow for tremendous flexibility when addressing the multiplicity of nonoffending partners' needs and the demands placed on them. The rationale and strategies for implementing the interventions are made explicit to clients, and this is particularly important to nonoffending partners, whose experiences have left them feeling that they have little or no control over their lives and who frequently report that they feel left out of the information loop. Cognitive-behavioral treatment requires the therapist and the client to work collaboratively, and this collaboration encourages feelings of empowerment and a greater sense of control and self-respect in the nonoffending partner. Finally, this treatment model offers the partners the skills they need to provide more effective support to the offender in treatment. They can also use some of these same skills to address their own issues.

The cognitive-behavioral model integrates learning theory, particularly the influence of conditioning, contingencies, and models in the environment, with the impact of cognitive factors. The model can be used to explain the symptoms and responses we see in nonoffending partners.

Modeling. Modeling is an example of a simple learning process that can explain the development of both positive and negative behaviors. Children who have been sexually abused sometimes imitate the offender's behaviors. Perhaps of greater concern is that sexually abused children also often mirror the offender's dysfunctional attitudes regarding the abuse, relationships, and sexuality. Offenders share their distortions in many ways. For example, by using the term "we"—as in "we shouldn't be doing this"—the offender implies that the child is the co-author of the assault and is therefore equally to blame.

The offender models these dysfunctional beliefs and attitudes through his grooming of the child and those around him. As one offender said when asked for his definition of grooming, "Grooming is getting them to think what I think, so that I can do what I want." Thus, through the grooming process the offender's cognitive distortions about who is responsible for the abuse, how harmful the abuse is, and what causes the abuse may be passed on to the victim. Likewise, the offender's cognitive distortions may be passed on to the nonoffending partner through the grooming process. This may explain why some family members appear to be the "mouthpieces" of the offender.

Respondent Conditioning. In respondent conditioning, when neutral stimuli are paired with stimuli that provoke unconditioned negative emotion, the neutral stimuli alone begin to elicit that same negative emotion. For example, one offender grooming strategy is to pick a fight and become aggressive and threatening towards the partner in order to have "permission" to storm out of the house. If the offender chooses to engage in this behavior toward his partner at most meals, then the previously neutral stimuli of eating a meal may now be paired with the unconditional fear-evoking stimulus of the offender's aggression. As a result of that learned association between eating a meal and aggression, the partner may learn to fear eating meals.

Instrumental Conditioning. Instrumental conditioning begins when negative emotional responses lead to the avoidance of previously neutral stimuli. The avoidance behavior is negatively reinforced each time, as there is a reduction in the negative emotion, which in turn increases the likelihood that the avoidance behavior will be used again. In the case of the example above, each time the partner successfully avoids eating a meal at home, she experiences a reinforcing reduction in fear and anxiety, which in turn increases the likelihood of future attempts to avoid eating meals.

A wider range of previously neutral stimuli may become paired with the fear evoking stimuli through the processes of generalization and higher order conditioning. For example, the partner may initially have feared only meals at home with the offender. Through generalization and higher order conditioning, she may learn to fear eating meals in general, across different settings. This can become increasingly debilitating as the number of stimuli that elicit the response grows. These conditioning principles provide a framework for understanding the development of symptoms in nonoffending partners and victims alike. Nonoffending partners and victims experience the same negative emotions of fear, anger, pain, anxiety, and sadness. The victims experience these feelings during and after the abuse. The nonoffending partners report experiencing such feelings during and after the disclosure and investigation. Like the victims, the partners work hard to avoid the negative emotions associated with the abuse. They avoid thinking of, talking about, or remembering the abuse; in addition, they use many of the mechanisms that victims use, such as avoidance, denial, and numbing, to cope with the disclosure and investigation. These avoidance strategies further strengthen the inappropriate associations made between psychological distress and reminders of the abuse and investigation. Continued avoidance prevents nonoffending partners from effectively processing and understanding the offending, leaving them with misperceptions and cognitive distortions related to the abuse and the offender.

A Gradual Process

Continued avoidance makes it hard to engage the nonoffending partner in therapy. The treatment approach therefore needs to be one of gradual exposure, with time to process information and new insights. As we mentioned earlier, the integrated treatment model allows for gradual exposure and intervention. Interventions are directed towards helping the nonoffending partner become more comfortable addressing abuse-related thoughts and memories and thus breaking the connection between negative feelings and addressing the offender's behavior. The program also allows the therapist to challenge cognitive distortions by providing the partner with information about offending and with alternative frameworks for understanding her own experience.

ASSESSMENT OF NONOFFENDING PARTNERS

To maximize the effectiveness of therapy, it is important to establish a collaborative partnership with the nonoffending partner. As already indicated, this can be difficult, as the partners come with many fears of being judged and of how their involvement will impact them and their families. Nevertheless, it is important to establish a relationship that includes acceptance and collaboration to ensure consistent attendance, to engage the nonoffending partner in the therapeutic process, and to access her knowledge. Nonoffending partners often have more information than either they or we realize. When they believe that their contributions are really valued and needed, and their emotional responses are acknowledged and validated, then they are much more likely to participate actively in the therapeutic process.

Clearly, the initial assessment phase is the first opportunity to establish this relationship. When conducting the initial assessment, the therapist should progress from the least to the most threatening material. The aims of the assessment are to evaluate the nonoffending partner's:

- Overall functioning;
- Understanding of sexual abuse in general;
- Understanding of the sex offender's offending history;
- Level of dependence on the sex offender;
- Quality of relationship with the offender; and
- Quality of relationship with the victim or potential victim, if they reside in the nonoffending partner's home.

The therapist is then able to assess the nonoffending partner's current ability to protect herself and her family.

Colboum-Faller (1988) provides an excellent outline of a nonoffending parent assessment. She suggests that the following areas be addressed in the initial assessment:

(a) current living situation; (b) level of education and employment history; (c) family background; (d) social supports; (e) relationship(s) with partner(s) including the alleged perpetrator; (f) children and relationship with children; (g) substance use, mental illness, and illegal activity; (h) sexual history; and (i) the sexual abuse. (p. 226)

An abbreviated version of Colboum-Faller's initial assessment guide appears in Table 9.1.

When addressing sexual abuse in the context of a nonoffending partner assessment, the therapist should pay particular attention to what the partner knows about the offenses and how much she knows of the offender's sexual offending history. In addition, it is important to find out how she found out about the offenses and offending history. It is not unusual for the offender to have been the primary source of information prior to the assessment, so the nonoffending partner is likely to have a minimized and somewhat distorted account. Questions to address in this area are:

- What do you understand the allegations or offenses to be?
- Who do you think is to blame?

Text continues on page 9-15

Table 9.1
Initial Assessment of Nonoffending Partner (based on Colboum-Faller (1988) outline)

Current Living Situation

1. Who is living in the nonoffending partner's household? How is the household supported financially?
2. Has the nonoffending partner's living situation changed since the disclosure?

Education and Employment History

3. How far did the nonoffending partner progress in education? What problems, if any, were there, and why?
4. Is the nonoffending partner's work history commensurate with her abilities and commitments?

Family Background

5. Complete a genogram.
6. Identify family alliances in the nonoffending partner's immediate and extended family. What is the nature of her relationship with each parent?
7. What discipline style and techniques were used by the nonoffending partner's parents? Any separations from family? If so, why and when?

Social Supports

8. What is the quality of the nonoffending partner's current relationships with her family of origin?
9. What is the quality of the nonoffending partner's relationships with the offender's family?
10. What is the quality of the nonoffending partner's relationship with friends, neighbors, or colleagues?
11. How does the nonoffending partner view her relationships with the various professionals?
12. Who does the nonoffending partner believe knows about the offending, who has she told, and what was the response of others?
13. Who can the nonoffending partner turn to in a crisis, when she has financial difficulties, or when she has problems with her children? Has this changed since the disclosure?

Relationships with Partners—Past and Present
The following issues should be explored in relation to each partner:

14. When and how did they meet?
15. How long before they became sexually involved?
16. What is (was) the division of labor or roles in the relationship? Have these changed over time?
17. What is the nonoffending partner's view of the quality of the relationship—both positive and negative aspects?
18. What is her view of the quality of the sexual relationship?
19. How would the nonoffending partner describe her partner's relationship(s) with the child(ren)?
20. What is the nonoffending partner's view or understanding of her partner's work history, use of alcohol or drugs, or criminal activities (past and present)?
21. Why did past relationships end?

Table 9.1 is continued on next page.

Table 9.1
Initial Assessment (cont'd)

Relationships with Children

The following issues should be explored in relation to each child:

22. Was the pregnancy planned?
23. What was the family's situation at the time of the pregnancy and birth?
24. What significant events are there in the child's history, including medical history?
25. How would the nonoffending partner describe the child? What does she like and dislike about him or her?
26. How is the child doing in school socially and academically?
27. What are the child's likes and dislikes?
28. How does the child get along with siblings, peers, the offender, and other family members?
29. How is the child disciplined and by whom?

History of Substance Abuse/Misuse

30. Does either the nonoffending partner or the offender have a history of substance abuse or misuse?
31. Does the nonoffending partner or offender have any history of criminal or illegal activity with respect to substance abuse or misuse? What type of history?
32. Has the nonoffending partner or offender ever received treatment for the abuse or misuse of drugs?

Mental Health History

33. What is the nonoffending partner's mental health history?
34. Has the nonoffending partner ever been hospitalized, received counseling, or been prescribed medications for mental health problems? When and how often?
35. Is the nonoffending partner experiencing sleep, appetite, or mood disturbances?
36. What is the nonoffending partner's perception and understanding of the offender's mental health history? Has he ever received treatment? When and how often?

Criminal History Regarding Drug Abuse

37. Does the nonoffending partner have any criminal history with respect to substance abuse or misuse?
38. Has she ever been involved in any other criminal or illegal activity? If so, how did she become involved? What were the consequences?

Sexual History

39. What is the nonoffending partner's premarital and extramarital sexual history, with her partner and with others?
40. What is the nonoffending partner's history of marital sexual relations?
41. Does the nonoffending partner have any history of childhood sexual relations?

Knowledge of Sexual Abuse/Sexual Offending History

42. How did the nonoffending partner find out about the offenses?
43. What was her response when she first learned of the offenses?
44. What does she understand the allegations and offenses to be?
45. Who does she think is to blame?
46. If disbelieving of the allegations, what explanation does she give for the allegations being made?
47. What does she perceive the consequences for the offenses will be?
48. Does she know of any other allegations against the offender?

Text continues from page 9-12

- What do you see as the consequences for the offenses?
- Do you know of any other allegations made against the offender?

Because the nonoffending partner is likely to have been groomed and manipulated by the offender, the therapist should not be alarmed by a partner's seemingly uncooperative or inappropriate reactions at the time of disclosure and during the initial assessment phase. Offenders frequently report how they groom and manipulate their partners, victims, and the relationship between partner and victim. The assessment should therefore be conducted in light of the nonoffending partner's position of being on the receiving end of offender behavior that is planned, calculated, and deliberate. This is not to negate the partner's entire relationship with the offender, which may have some genuine, positive qualities; but you must put those qualities in context. Therefore, when reviewing the assessment, the therapist should be alert to what indications there are of targeting and grooming.

It is worth reminding ourselves that while the information gathered in the course of the assessment is valuable, it should not be viewed as static, but as part of a process that the nonoffending partner is engaged in—a process of receiving and assimilating difficult and disturbing information. It is common for a nonoffending partner initially to have difficulty accepting the sexual abuse. However, as she is given more information and, more important, as she assimilates it, her position usually changes. The initial assessment is one of the therapist's first opportunities to begin to introduce some alternative perspectives through both the structure and process of the assessment. It should include an evaluation of the nonoffending partner's capacity to use new information in a positive way.

Many of the treatment issues identified in working with victims of sexual assault are also treatment issues for nonoffending partners. The issues include a fear of loss, a lack of trust in self or others, impaired self-image, a sense of failure, depression, denial, damaged relationships, anger, and isolation. In addition, many nonoffending partners have a history of being abused as a child or as an adult. In some cases there may also be concerns about eating disorders, suicidal ideation or gestures, and chemical dependency.

GROUP WORK FOR NONOFFENDING PARTNERS

The integrated treatment model has been successful in both individual and group formats, but group work is the preferred modality for working with nonoffending partners, who often suffer from a sense of isolation following disclosure of the offending. Some offenders also use grooming strategies that lead to their partners' isolation. Group work directly addresses their isolation; it gives nonoffending partners the opportunity to begin to develop an alternative support system. The participants can provide more support to each other than an individual therapist can. In addition, many nonoffending partners report that the group is one of the few places in which they can talk about the impact of the sex offender's behavior.

Throughout the program, the therapist seeks to explore and validate the nonoffending partner's emotional response. The therapist also educates, confronts, supports, and encourages her as she first come to terms with, and then learns to understand, the nature of her partner's offending and the treatment he is undertaking. One of the goals is to help the nonoffending partner move out of denial and into healing. Another is to give her the information and skills she needs to become a more effective support person for the offender treatment process, which in turn is effective support for the sex offender. The change process that she is engaged in is not that dissimilar from that of the offender (see Figure 9.2).

The structured group work approach that is briefly described below allows for the incorporation of the wide range of issues and concerns that work with a nonoffending partner presents.

Group Work, Part A

The aims and objectives of Part A group work are to address the impact of the offending, to increase the nonoffending partner's understanding of victim dynamics; to increase her understanding of offender dynamics; and to provide her with an alternative model or framework for dealing with her situation.

Address the Impact of Offending. The initial focus is on providing the nonoffending partners with the skills and understanding for coping with the emotional distress generated by the knowledge that their partner has offended. Nonoffending partners are encouraged to share their thoughts and feelings with the group and to talk about the impact the offending and its discovery has had on them as parents, partners, and individuals. Having explored what coping strategies they have used in the past, they are asked to identify a number of adaptive coping strategies for managing the stress. They are then asked to report on their use of these strategies at the beginning of each session. A common feature in group is the use of the "emotional temperature chart" as shown in Figure 9.3, which allows for the expression and validation of ambivalent feelings (James & Nasjleti, 1983, pp. 114–115).

Increase Understanding of Victim Dynamics. The therapist opens the discussion by sharing information with the group about the prevalence of sexual assault, the spectrum of sexually abusive behaviors, and the range of symptomatology suffered by victims. The impact of the abuse on the victim is discussed in terms of the victim's perception of (1) the relationship between the offender and the victim, (2) the relationship between the offender and the nonoffending partner/parent, (3) the duration of the abuse, (4) the frequency of the abuse, and (5) the nature of the abuse (e.g., the degree of violence in an assault). Discussion follows using case examples, remembering to reinforce that the five factors identified above are reviewed from the victim's perspective. The group members then use this framework to explore examples from their own experiences.

Increase Understanding of Offender Dynamics. The therapist presents Finkelhor's (1984, pp. 54–61) four preconditions for offending to the group as a model for beginning to understand sexual offending (see Figure 9.4). Particular attention is paid to preconditions 3 (overcoming external inhibitors) and 4 (overcoming the victim's resistance), as an introduction to grooming. Victims' blocks to telling/talking about the offending and the nonoffending partners'/parents' blocks to hearing/listening are

**Figure 9.2
The Change Process**

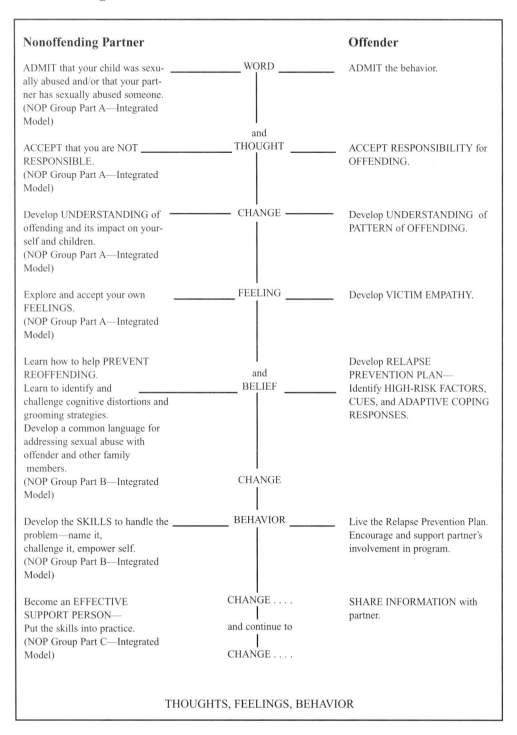

Nonoffending Partner		Offender
ADMIT that your child was sexually abused and/or that your partner has sexually abused someone. (NOP Group Part A—Integrated Model)	WORD	ADMIT the behavior.
	and	
ACCEPT that you are NOT RESPONSIBLE. (NOP Group Part A—Integrated Model)	THOUGHT	ACCEPT RESPONSIBILITY for OFFENDING.
Develop UNDERSTANDING of offending and its impact on yourself and children. (NOP Group Part A—Integrated Model)	CHANGE	Develop UNDERSTANDING of PATTERN of OFFENDING.
Explore and accept your own FEELINGS. (NOP Group Part A—Integrated Model)	FEELING	Develop VICTIM EMPATHY.
Learn how to help PREVENT REOFFENDING. Learn to identify and challenge cognitive distortions and grooming strategies. Develop a common language for addressing sexual abuse with offender and other family members. (NOP Group Part B—Integrated Model)	and BELIEF CHANGE	Develop RELAPSE PREVENTION PLAN— Identify HIGH-RISK FACTORS, CUES, and ADAPTIVE COPING RESPONSES.
Develop the SKILLS to handle the problem—name it, challenge it, empower self. (NOP Group Part B—Integrated Model)	BEHAVIOR	Live the Relapse Prevention Plan. Encourage and support partner's involvement in program.
Become an EFFECTIVE SUPPORT PERSON— Put the skills into practice. (NOP Group Part C—Integrated Model)	CHANGE . . . . and continue to CHANGE	SHARE INFORMATION with partner.

THOUGHTS, FEELINGS, BEHAVIOR

Figure 9.3
Emotional Temperature Chart (James & Nasjleti, 1983)

Group or individual charts can be used. They allow for a range of feelings in the group and in an individual. Group members are asked what is the most positive and most negative feeling that they have had in relation to the offender, the victim and themselves.

The Offender

I hate him, I wish we'd never met.   I love him so much.

1   2   3   4   5   6   7

The Victim

I wish they were dead.   I care about them so much.

1   2   3   4   5   6   7

Myself (nonoffending partner)

I wish I were dead.   I'm great.

1   2   3   4   5   6   7

Figure 9.4
Finkelhor's Four Preconditions

---

1. Has the motivation to sexually abuse.
2. Overcomes internal inhibitors.
3. Overcomes external inhibitors.
4. Overcomes the victim's resistance.

---

explored in the light of this information. Role plays have been used to explore these issues in more detail (see also Bergman, Chapter 8, this volume, on role play and dramatherapy). For example, the group members are each asked to write a short play about how they would "like" to have found out about the abuse. They are asked to include their understanding of blocks to listening and telling, and key things that they wish they had heard and that they would like to have been able to say. The members direct their own plays in group, using other group members to play the parts. The process of writing the play and then directing it helps them to identify and work through salient issues for them.

Provide an Alternative Model/Framework. In group, participants explore the interrelationship between thoughts, feelings, and behaviors. The therapist initially provides non-abuse related examples for illustration, such as: Someone on a diet is feeling a little "low" and depressed one day. She thinks if she has a bar of chocolate she will feel better but remembers she is on a diet. She still wants the chocolate, so she comes up with many justifications concerning why, just this once, it will do no harm. She might think, "I'll exercise more tomorrow," or "I've been very good—I deserve it." Her thoughts lead to her decision to have the chocolate, which in turn leads her to feel more depressed because she has let herself down and has not met her goal. The therapist then asks the participants to apply the model to their thoughts and feelings about the offending and then introduces a five-stage framework for exploring the cognitive, affective, and behavioral impact of the offender's behavior (see Figure 9.5). This framework and Finkelhor's four preconditions are frequently referred to as the therapy progresses.

Group Work, Part B

The aims and objectives of Part B group work are for the participants to learn to identify and challenge cognitive distortions, to learn to identify and resist grooming strategies, to learn about the relapse prevention model and how to identify "cues," to develop partner (and victim) "alert lists," and to develop a support network.

Learn to Identify and Challenge Cognitive Distortions. In this part, Finkelhor's four preconditions are reviewed and related to components of sex offender treatment. The group then focuses on precondition 2 (overcomes internal inhibitors) and the function of cognitive distortions in offending (Marshall et al., 1990; Laws, 1989). The participants learn how these distortions can cause the offender to deny, justify, minimize, and excuse the behavior and even to project blame on others. Having discussed some common everyday examples of cognitive distortions that the general population uses (e.g., "everyone else speeds," "just this once"), the nonoffending partners are given a list of cognitive distortions that sex offenders frequently use. They are asked to identify the distortions by type (e.g., "victim stance," "superoptismism") and then to identify the distortions they believe their offending partner has used. The therapist then discusses with them the importance of challenging and replacing cognitive distortions, using some of the same common everyday examples used earlier. The participants practice finding effective challenges and possible replacements to the cognitive distortions that their offending partner may have used, which they identified earlier. Throughout, the nonoffending partners are encouraged to identify any cognitive distortions of their own, particularly those they may share with the offender, and to practice challenging each other in group.

Learn to Identify and Resist Grooming Strategies. Offenders report that they groom and manipulate their victims and those around them. The function of this manipulation is not only to make it possible to offend, but also to make it as unlikely as possible to get caught. It is evident that the grooming and manipulation not only goes on before, during, and after the assault, but that it continues after the investigation and professionals often become targets as well. With this in mind, it is essential that nonoffending partners are able to identify grooming strategies and learn how they may be resisted.

The group first reviews Finkelhor's four preconditions, with the focus on precondition 3 (overcomes external inhibitors), and the therapist then introduces the concept

Figure 9.5
Five-Stage Framework for Group Members

As an introductory exercise, the group members identify on a scale of 1 to 10 their sense of control and then their self-esteem at each of the stages, including where they imagine or hope their sense of control and self-esteem will be when they are at Stage 5.

Group members then use the simple framework below to begin to map their thoughts, feelings, and behaviors at each of the five stages. The framework can also be used to map the nonoffending partner's perception of the victim's and the offender's thoughts, feelings, and behaviors.

	Thoughts	Feelings	Behaviors
Stage 1 Pre-Disclosure			
Stage 2 Investigation			
Stage 3 Assessment/ Legal process			
Stage 4 Healing/"Surviving"			
Stage 5 Moving on/ "Thriving"			

of grooming. The participants are given a list of common grooming strategies used by sex offenders and are again asked to identify which ones they believe their offending partners used in the past or use currently in relation to themselves or others. The group members are then asked to rate how effective they believe each of the strategies is and why. At this stage, the participants help each other to begin to identify ways of resisting grooming.

Introduce the Relapse Prevention Model and Learn to Identify Cues. The therapist introduces the nonoffending partners to the concept of a cycle or pattern of offending behaviors. The basic cycle outlined by Bays & Freeman-Longo (1989) includes a pretend normal phase, a build-up phase, an acting-out phase, and a justification phase (see Figure 9.6). The nonoffending partners are asked, based on their own experiences, to identify as much as they can of the cognitive, affective, and behavioral components of each phase of their offending partner's cycle. At this stage, most of the information the participants have is in relation to the build-up and justification phases. The partners then repeat this same exercise in relation to themselves. This process helps them to build up an increasingly detailed picture of the offender's cycle and the parallel cycle that they are engaged in. The relapse prevention model (Marlatt, 1985) is then introduced. With the information from the previous exercises, the nonoffending partners are able to begin to identify the offender's high-risk factors and cues. In

Figure 9.6
The Basic Cycle of Offending

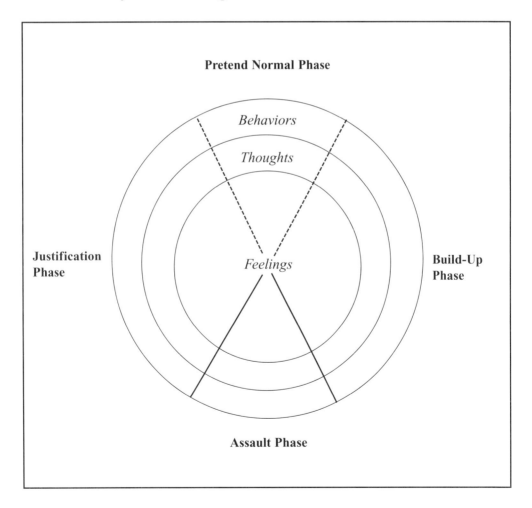

addition, as they review their own responses to the offender's behaviors, they are able to identify their own cues.

Develop Partner and Victim Alert Lists. Nonoffending partners are encouraged to be aware of and to value their own cues as possible signals that there may be a problem. By reviewing grooming strategies, their own cues, and the sex offender's cues, the partners begin to develop a valuable personal alert list. The list might include not only the offender's behavioral, interpersonal cues in his relapse prevention plan, but also the partner's emotional and cognitive responses that have been identified in the treatment process.

Develop a Support Network. An important component of self-care for nonoffending partners is the development of a support network for themselves independent of the sex offender's support network. This network should ideally be a mix of family, friends, and professionals. It often includes some of their peers from group.

Group Work, Part C1

The aims and objectives of this stage of the work are as follows:

- *Information*—The focus of this stage of group work is to prepare the participant and her offending partner for their joint sessions, as outlined in Part C2 of the integrated model. Over the course of the group, the therapist gradually shares the sex offenders' offense histories, their progress in treatment, and their relapse prevention plans. This can be done in group or one-on-one. In a group, this offers the opportunity for feedback from the other group members, support for the nonoffending partners as they absorb the information, and support from the group in identifying any cognitive distortions the partner may use to minimize the offender's behavior.

- *Preparation*—The nonoffending partners need to prepare for their upcoming joint sessions. Preparation includes helping them identify and discuss any anxieties or concerns they may have about this difficult work. Discussing their worries allows for their concerns to be addressed directly and thus reduces their anxiety. Role plays with feedback from other group members can be very useful at this stage. They can help the nonoffending partner practice skills she has learned and identify the questions and issues she wishes to address with her offending partner.

- *Support*—The group continues to serve as an important source of support for the nonoffending partner as she approaches the joint work with the offender. Where possible it can be useful to continue the group in tandem with the joint sessions, so that support can be sustained. This is particularly important where the nonoffending partner has a meager or fragile support network.

DYADIC WORK

Dyadic work refers here to "couple work," the work the nonoffending partner and the offender undertake together. This work should also be undertaken jointly by the nonoffending partner's therapist and the offender's therapist. It is important that the offender's therapist be directly involved in this work, as he or she is in a strong position to challenge any distortions or manipulations that the offender may use in the course of the sessions. Therapists should consider a group work format for this component of the treatment also. The potential benefits of the group setting at this point are continued support for the nonoffending partners and a wide range of feedback. In addition, as the offenders provide appropriate challenges and confrontations to each other, they model this essential skill for their nonoffending partners. One note of caution, however—the therapist must consider the risk that the group arena will allow offenders to form an inappropriate network.

Assessing Readiness for Joint Work

Determining when to initiate joint nonoffending partner and sex offender sessions depends on the assessment of both parties. It is crucial that the nonoffending partner be ready both emotionally and in terms of her skills level. The nonoffending partner should have progressed to where she can:

- Discuss her partner's offending with relatively little distress;
- Describe his offending in a way that is free of cognitive distortions;
- Identify and challenge his cognitive distortions using the skills she acquired in treatment;
- Identify the ways the offender has manipulated and groomed her; and
- Show an understanding of the relapse prevention model.

The therapist should emphasize that the joint sessions will provide an opportunity for the nonoffending partner and her partner to become closer as they discuss his offending, and that the sessions allow them to become accustomed to discussing difficult issues so that they can continue the therapeutic work on their own.

In cases of intrafamilial sexual abuse, the joint work involving the nonoffending partner/parent and the victim must be completed before joint sessions with the nonoffending partner and the offender (see Integrated Model, Figure 9.1).

Joint Work, Part C2

The aims and objectives of part C2 joint work between the nonoffending partner and the offender are to provide opportunities for open exchange of information and communication, for the nonoffending partner to practice the skills she learned in parts A and B of the treatment process, and for addressing unresolved issues.

Communication and Information. The joint sessions provide an opportunity for the nonoffending partner and the offender to communicate openly about his offending and to clarify any points of confusion or misunderstanding. It is not unusual for the offender to have shared a minimized and distorted offense history with his partner in the past. This stage provides for more honest sharing of his offense history and of his relapse prevention plan, as he identifies the grooming and manipulation strategies that he has used.

The offender is usually anxious about sharing this information. He is often concerned that his partner may reject him or will not understand. The offender's preparation for these sessions should include a discussion of not only what information the nonoffending partner needs, but also how to share it with her. He should be encouraged to share this information at a pace that allows his partner to ask questions, offer feedback, and absorb the information.

Practice Skills. A second important function of the joint sessions is that they provide an opportunity for the nonoffending partner to practice the skills which she has acquired in parts A and B. Initially the therapist provides support and models assertive communication with the offender, challenging thinking errors and distortions. As the sessions progress, the nonoffending partner's confidence in her skills grows, and the therapist's active supporting role decreases as the partner becomes more active in the sessions.

Addressing Unresolved Issues. The joint sessions are also an opportunity for the couple to begin to address unresolved issues. These can include concerns about past problems in their relationship, parenting, relationships with extended family, their sexual relationship, as well as more mundane and practical matters.

THERAPIST'S ROLE

The therapist has many roles over the course of his or her work with a nonoffending partner. The therapist advocates on behalf of the client, helping her to navigate and negotiate her way through unfamiliar systems and to work effectively with other agencies. The therapist is also an important role model in terms of communication skills and positive coping behaviors. The nonoffending partner can become an effective support person when she is able to discuss the sexual offending calmly. It is therefore important that the therapist models calm, matter-of-fact discussions of offending and sexuality.

This process begins at the assessment phase, when the therapist addresses the abuse directly in a calm, straightforward manner and provides opportunities for the nonoffending partner to discuss any concerns she may have. The therapist continues to demonstrate this style of communication as the therapy progresses. For example, the therapist may model more effective means of coping with emotions such as anger. Role plays can also be used here to provide opportunities to model effective communication in other areas. Humor can also be helpful in encouraging further communication and providing needed levity.

A key role for therapists who work with nonoffending partners is that of educator—a large component of the work is providing information. Therapists provide information about sexual abuse, offender dynamics, the impact of victimization, and offender treatment. They also teach nonoffending partners specific skills such as identifying and challenging cognitive distortions, recognizing the grooming and manipulation strategies and how deal with them, and the significance of high-risk factors and their cues.

Providing this information leads to significant changes in a nonoffending partner's cognitions, behaviors, and emotional responses. The therapist can employ a number of strategies to accomplish this. First, he or she should make an assessment of the nonoffending partner's baseline knowledge and understanding in order to tailor the approach to her individual needs. Second, the therapist should endeavor to create an environment where it is safe for the participant to take risks. This can be done by simultaneously demonstrating predictability and flexibility, by planning and preparing adequately for each session, and by designing interventions and tasks that will set her up for success. Third, by providing information and skills that have a direct application to the participant's real life experiences, the therapist can engage and encourage her active participation in the learning process. Finally, the group work approach facilitates a supportive, collaborative, and active interchange among all of the participants while at the same time allowing each to proceed at her own pace. This in turn encourages group participants to look to each other for solutions, rather than just to the therapist.

SUMMARY

This chapter presents a structured yet flexible treatment approach that addresses the diverse needs of the nonoffending partners and other support persons and the work required with them in the context of their relationships with other family members and their offending partners. The key elements of this approach are working in partnership with the nonoffending partner and providing her with the skills she needs to become an effective support person for the offender. The nature and timing of the nonoffending partner's involvement may vary. For example, for some it may be appropriate to become involved at the beginning of the offender's treatment. In other cases, either the offender or his partner may have too much anxiety about proceeding together right away and may defer becoming involved until later on or at a more gradual pace. It is not possible to address all the variations that may be made in this treatment model. Therapists need to be cognizant of the effect that different settings have as well as cultural differences and needs. The group work is structured in phases to allow for differences and for nonoffending partners to proceed at their own pace.

The integrated treatment model requires a strong commitment on the part of the nonoffending partner. She must be motivated to participate in sometimes-difficult exercises and to absorb challenging information. Taking a judgmental or confrontational stance at an early stage in treatment tends to be counterproductive. Nonoffending partners who are prematurely confronted about their minimization or denial of the allegations frequently respond by becoming more entrenched in their position. In practice such a stand usually proves to be unnecessary, as the thoughts and feelings of nonoffending partners often change as they develop a greater understanding of sexual offending and victim dynamics. It is not enough that we give nonoffending partners the information; we need to give them time, space, and the necessary support to assimilate that information and make it their own. For nonoffending partners to provide effective support for sex offenders in treatment, they need to recover and heal also.

References

Bays, L. & Freeman-Longo, R. (1989). *Why did I do it again? Understanding my cycle of problem behaviors: A guided workbook for clients in treatment.* Brandon, VT: Safer Society Press.

Browne, A. & Finkelhor, D. (1986). *A sourcebook on child sexual abuse.* London: Sage.

Colboum-Faller, K. (1988). *Child sexual abuse: An interdisciplinary manual for diagnosis, case management and treatment.* London: Macmillan.

Courtois, C. (1988). *Healing the incest wound: Adult survivors in therapy.* New York: W.W. Norton & Co.

Deblinger, E., Hathaway, C., Lippman, J. & Steer, R. (1993). "Psychosocial characteristics and correlates of symptom distress in non-offending mothers of sexually abused children." *Journal of Interpersonal Violence, 8,* 155–168.

Deblinger, E. & Heft, A. H. (1996). *Treating sexually abused children and their nonoffending parents: A cognitive behavioral approach.* London: Sage.

Finkelhor, D. (1984). *Child sexual abuse: New theory and research.* London: Macmillan.

James, B. & Nasjleti, M. (1983). *Treating sexually abused children and their families.* Palo Alto, CA: Consulting Psychologists Press.

Laws, D. R. (Ed.) (1989). *Relapse prevention with sex offenders.* London: Guilford Press.

Marlatt, G. A. (1985). Relapse prevention. New York: Guilford Press.

Marshall, W. L., Laws, D. R. & Barbaree, H. E. (1990). *Handbook of sexual assault: Issues, theories, and treatment of the offender.* New York: Plenum.

Salter, A. (1988). *Treating child sex offenders and victims: A practical guide.* London: Sage.

Sgroi, S. (1982). *Handbook of clinical intervention in child sexual abuse.* Lexington, MA: Lexington Books.

van der Kolk, B. (1988). "The trauma spectrum: The interaction of biological and social events in the genesis of the trauma response," *Journal of Traumatic Stress, 1,* 273–290.

Chapter 10

Transition—Challenges for the Offender and the Community

by Anita Schlank, Ph.D., L.P. and
Pam Bidelman, M.S.W., L.I.C.S.W.

The Need for Gradual, Controlled Transition 10-1
    Internal Risk Factors 10-2
    External Risk Factors 10-2
    Housing Issues 10-3
Aftercare Issues 10-3
Stakeholders 10-4
    Victim and Victim Advocates 10-4
    Policy-Makers 10-5
    County Government 10-5
    The Media 10-6
    The Sex Offender 10-6
    The Treatment Program 10-7
Transition and Technology 10-7
Ethical Issues 10-8
Summary 10-9

THE NEED FOR GRADUAL, CONTROLLED TRANSITION

In an effort to uphold the constitutionality of civil commitment statutes while they were under attack in the courts, prosecutors exerted much energy into pointing out that the population these laws targeted was the so-called "worst of the worst" of sex offenders in prison, and that they thereby required the special attention. This type of labeling seemed very effective to help pass and uphold the legislation; however, it is these same labels that make it very difficult to arrange for a successful transition of the civilly committed sexual offender back into the community. Treatment providers may run into significant obstacles when attempting to arrange for various placements of these individuals. Questions arise concerning liability, ethics, and methods for balancing the potentially conflicting interests of the various stakeholders.

Because offenders referred for civil commitment tend to have the most extensive offense histories, are more likely to have complex diagnostic pictures, and tend to have a history of being the most treatment-resistant, their progress through the civil commitment program is often extremely slow. In addition, many have also been referred after completing very lengthy prison sentences, creating a population likely to have been removed from society for many years, some possibly since adolescence. Leaving a familiar residential treatment setting can be difficult for some even after only a period of months. Those confined for a long period of time may find that the world has changed considerably since they were first incarcerated, and that adjustment is very difficult. Even those who verbalize a high motivation to return to the community are likely to experience some ambivalence and may fear that they might not be able to succeed. As one treatment provider notes, " for some, particularly those who have been lonely and alienated most of their lives, the attachments formed in treatment may be the closest and most genuine relationships they have ever realized" (Steele, 1995, p. 19-4).

Internal Risk Factors

A gradual transition period is very important to allow treatment providers to make sure that residents use the tools they have learned in treatment while they demonstrate responsibility through the use of gradually increased privileges. Offenders in sex offender treatment learn to identify the specific patterns of thoughts, emotions, and behavior that are correlated with the "build-up phase" prior to commission of their sex offenses (see Fairfield, Chapter 9, this volume). Those patterns tend to be repetitive, rigid, narrow, and ineffective relative to a responsible, offense-free life. Offenders can learn to recognize the "cues" of their internal risk factors (thoughts, emotions, behaviors, and physical sensations that suggest an internal high-risk factor might be activated). They then learn adaptive coping strategies, or thoughts and behaviors that will assist in the interruption of the chain of events leading to reoffense. Transition provides an opportunity for practicing those adaptive coping interventions in real-life situations, while still closely supervised. For example, an offender who has limited support from a family or friendship group, and who identifies loneliness as an internal risk factor, will use his transition process to increase his tolerance for feeling lonely, find appropriate sources of social support, and provide an accurate appraisal of his emotional state.

External Risk Factors

Another element of the treatment experience is identifying external risk factors in the environment that historically have been significant aspects of the chain of events leading to sex offenses. For instance, a sex offender who has a history of walking through neighborhoods at night in order to locate women living alone to target for victimization needs to consider carefully the time of day and location for any future walks. Other opportunities for encountering external high-risk factors can include establishments serving alcohol, "nontherapeutic" talk from co-workers, locations providing unexpected contact with children, and interactions with women other than staff members. Familiarity with the offender's internal and external risk factors and constructive coping responses is critical for the supervising staff in the transition process.

A gradual, closely supervised transition experience affords the offender valuable opportunities to practice new coping skills, an expanded repertoire of social behaviors and experiences, and increased confidence in exercising healthier problem-solving strategies. No amount of observation in a secure treatment setting can substitute for witnessing the offender deal with exposure to real-life internal and external high-risk factors. As one therapist notes, "conducting treatment exclusively in a secure, controlled institutional setting is like teaching someone to swim in a bathtub" (Steele, 1995, p. 19-2).

Housing Issues

Sex offenders referred for civil commitment usually have offense histories that for community notification purposes are likely to be considered to present the highest risk for reoffending, at least prior to participation in the treatment program. Successful completion of a lengthy, comprehensive treatment program, along with a period of gradual transition, is expected to lead to the lowering of risk level from "high" to "moderate"; however, even a moderate risk level can lead to rather extensive community notification. Therefore, access to housing can be extremely difficult for this population.

It may be preferable for offenders ending a lengthy period of incarceration to be referred for a halfway house type of placement, but the high profile nature of their cases may interfere with such a placement. And since they likely have no Department of Corrections time left to serve, that fact could be used to disqualify them from services contracted by Corrections. Other types of housing choices are already limited simply by the offender's background. For example, he may be restricted from locations near playgrounds, elementary schools, or apartments that are very close to bars. While pursuing the remaining choices, he may face fear on the part of landlords and neighbors that prevents access to many locations.

Often, the most successful arrangement is for the civil commitment program to arrange for its own "halfway house" or group home arrangement for the resident, while he holds a full-time job in the community. This can be accomplished using a nonsecure or less secure housing unit located on the same grounds of the secure treatment facility, such as the one provided by the Arizona civil commitment program (Messer, 2000), or by increasing the privileges of the resident to the point where he merely returns to the secure treatment facility after conducting a "normal" day in the community. An example of how one state, Minnesota, adapts its program to allow for transition-stage residents to use the facility in a halfway house-type manner is included in Figure 10.1 at the end of this chapter. Residents in that transition plan can live most of their day in the community, while returning to the program at night until they can secure appropriate housing, if by no other means, by saving enough money to place a down payment on the purchase of a house.

AFTERCARE ISSUES

Any "sexual predator" who is about to be discharged, particularly if he is one of the first to be released from a relatively new program, will likely become a high-profile case. Sex offender treatment providers in the community usually wish to avoid publicity, especially if their practice was not the most welcome addition to their building when they first opened. In addition, because offenders in transition were once judged to present the highest risk for reoffending, community treatment providers may assume they are still more likely to reoffend than the population the providers are currently serving, and they may become afraid of potential liability issues. Providers may be extremely reluctant to accept discharges from civil commitment programs into their aftercare groups, thereby seriously limiting the treatment options available for discharged offenders.

When a community provider does accept an offender into a treatment program, the length of time needed for aftercare services can become an issue. Some community aftercare groups serve offenders recently discharged from the Department of Corrections on terms of supervised release. Their involvement in outpatient sex offender treatment can range from a very short period of time (e.g., four months), to longer periods of time, but usually not more than eighteen months. Sex offenders discharged from civil commitment programs may require more extensive follow-up services, beginning during their transition period and continuing for a lengthy period of time after discharge. For many offenders, their aftercare group may be the most significant part of their support system; however, they may find that there is frequent "turnover" in the group's participants, which can interfere with the quality of the support they receive from the group.

One partial solution to the above-mentioned concerns is to arrange for the offenders to begin attending aftercare sessions while they are still in the transition stage prior to discharge. If the offender is clearly still a resident of the program and the state retains liability for his actions for a long enough period of time for the community provider to be assured of his readiness for discharge, it is likely that more options for aftercare will be made available. This type of arrangement also allows for the offender to experience some of the change in make-up of the members of the aftercare group while still in a familiar setting where there are other sources of support. (Figure 10.1 contains Minnesota's plan, which provides for such transition components.)

STAKEHOLDERS

Because the human cost of failure is so high if reintegration into the community of civilly committed sex offenders fails, stakeholders in the process of the transition from treatment settings to the community may hold conflicting views, policies, and roles. The treatment staff and the offender in transition may experience stress related to that phenomena in addition to the natural stresses of the transition itself.

Victims and Victim Advocates

Treatment providers for sex offenders know that the first priority is public safety, under all circumstances. Protection from harm for victims and potential victims undergirds the treatment process and implementation of transition processes. The treatment team must formally introduce victims' perspectives into the review of the plan for the offender's movement into community life. This is not a conflict of interest, since ensuring that the offender will not reoffend is in his best interest as well. Many states provide for victim advocacy representatives, along with other community representatives, to review and decide the level of community notification required for public safety. During the end of the confinement review process, they assess the offender's progress, assurance of risk reduction, and responsible planning. In Minnesota, for example, this review occurs per statute prior to pass-eligible status.

Some treatment programs include victim advocates in advisory groups to ensure inclusion of those perspectives. Sometimes a victims' advocate may perceive a lack of certainty that an offender will put into practice what he has learned in treatment, and may experience a conflict between wanting to support successful treatment and wanting to oppose any discharges.

Policy-Makers

State governments, legislators, and human services and corrections officials are responsive to the public demand for safety and the containment of criminal behavior. Indeed, the "politics" of sexual offending has changed dramatically over the past fifteen years. In many states, criminal sentences for sexual offending have become longer and the use of the civil commitment process has dramatically increased during the past few years. Inevitable tensions develop between the dual policies of offender containment and the provision of credible treatment for civilly committed offenders.

Officials must balance the public's demand for secure containment with the need to ensure ethical treatment practices for sex offenders, including the earned opportunity for monitored return to community life. They must also balance the public's concern about the unavoidable high cost for such programs. Public reaction to sex offenses and sex offenders tends to be strong and immediate. Treatment providers understand that a civilly committed sex offender's reoffense while in the community can have a strong impact on treatment and transition programs for other offenders, making it more difficult for offenders in the future to be released even after successful completion of treatment.

County Government

Civil commitment judges, county attorneys, defense attorneys, and county social services officials invest significant human and financial resources into screening, evaluation, legal proceedings, and appeals processes for civil commitments of sex offenders. Even in civil commitment cases, state and county legal officials tend to focus their attention on issues of public safety and detention, as opposed to planning for the sex offender's reintegration into society. Ironically, corrections systems have developed sophisticated and effective responses for supervision of sex offenders diverted from prison and placed in community settings, taking into account the need for ongoing effective treatment (Scott, 1997; English et al., 1996).

Historically, social services and case management functions in the mental health and public social services arena have not served areas defined as problems of criminal behavior. There are no statewide or national public systems of social services/case management design that would serve as effective models for the supervision of civilly committed sex offenders, yet these departments are often assigned to civilly committed sex offenders. When this occurs, individual counties must develop and maintain discrete systems for monitoring sex offenders in treatment programs without the benefit of experience in this area.

Counties will also demonstrate a range of philosophical and practical differences in the task of assisting with the transition of civilly committed sex offenders into their home communities. Those differences will likely range from active assistance and support for the transition process, to active resistance to the idea of the offender moving to a less secure environment. For example, some county social services officials refuse to expend social services dollars for the sex offender's case management needs or to provide for community-based sex offender aftercare services. Such variances in attitudes and services provide special challenges for the inpatient service provider, which as a critical element of a credible treatment program, must provide an effective transition program for the civilly committed sex offender.

The Media

The media plays a significant role in both providing the public with information and shaping public opinion. Because sex offenses elicit strong emotional reaction in people, there are few compelling reasons for the media to attend to the nuances related to the management of sex offenders. The American public appears to have a dual response to sex offenders—it both abhors their deeds and also sometimes harbors fascination with the idea of the "outlaw" or "psychopath." While nothing is inherently wrong with either attitude, the media's response to this abhorrence/fascination mutes any discussion of more complex ideas and perceptions. Treatment providers can become quickly subject to the effects of sensationalized reporting related to individual offenders or policy issues. This can create special pressures for offenders in transition to community life. Treatment programs need to foster an informed media, in the interest of sound public policy and the well-being of offenders making genuine attempts to successfully complete the requirements of treatment. This can be extremely difficult, especially since those offenders making a good adjustment in the community are not likely to be willing to call extra attention to their identity.

The Sex Offender

Civilly committed sex offenders need gradual, well-supported practice in their newly learned life skills to impede any regression to old behaviors. They need to demonstrate to themselves and to others that they have taken on an internalized self-control and can live responsibly with gradually reduced external structures of control. They need safe ways to apply the principles of relapse prevention, share fears, express apprehension, and discuss their small failures. Their families and friends need time to accommodate to their safe introduction into home environments, and the marital and/or parental roles they must assume there. Offenders need ways to acclimate and be accountable to new providers and systems of monitoring upon discharge from the treatment program. Conflicts can emerge for the sex offender when he balances his personal needs with his fears about community notification. A conflict can arise, for example, when he begins to feel a newly developed empathy for society or considers the possibility of telling a new acquaintance about his history of offending, but fears the personal effect of such a disclosure.

The Treatment Program

Treatment programs and staff need opportunities to validate the sex offender's progress in a way that protects public safety, avoids revictimization or new victims, and enhances the offender's ability to function without incident in less restrictive environments. Gradual, incremental, transitional experiences through work, recreation, and self-care for the offender are an effective process to those ends. The treatment program must assure all other interested parties that the offender has made real and enduring changes in his social and sexual behaviors and thus has an interest in the extended and carefully monitored transition to less secure environments. To achieve this, the program developers and directors must be sure their programs have been developed thoughtfully enough to ensure that a resident who completes the program's expectations can reasonably be expected to make a successful transition despite potentially unexpected stressors. In addition, treatment staff need to deal with their own fears about an offender having unsupervised time in the community despite the strides he may have made in treatment. Given the extensiveness of their offense histories and the fact that an offender is not "cured" but is instead in recovery, staff may find themselves struggling against a desire to err "on the side of caution" and delay discharge despite evidence of clearly met goals on the part of the offender.

TRANSITION AND TECHNOLOGY

Stakeholders in the management of sex offenders could easily wish for simple and certain systems of containment and supervision. In truth, no single method or technology has yet been demonstrated as a single effective intervention. Those offenders who demonstrate successful responses to treatment are likely to have engaged in a protracted and arduous treatment effort, using the information and support afforded by the treatment program.

Sex offenders are held in low regard by society and are subject to negative stereotyping as a group. It is thus especially important that intrusive methods and technologies (1) are based on well-thought-out protocols, (2) are research based, (3) are not intrinsically harmful, (4) are congruent with professional ethics, and (5) are effective for the offender as well as the treatment staff or monitoring authorities. Some methods to assist with assessment and monitoring of offenders in transition that trigger some controversy are described below:

- **Polygraphs.** Polygraph examinations can be an extremely helpful tool throughout both the inpatient stage(s) of treatment and during transition. A reoffense prevention plan is only helpful to the offender if he has been fully honest about his offense history, including victim pool, paraphilias, and various aspects of his build-up phases. Polygraph examinations can assure the treatment staff that an essential part of his offense history has not been overlooked when he developed his reoffense prevention plan. Polygraph examinations during transition are particularly important since it is during this stage of treatment that the offender may first come into contact with some external high-risk factors or with stresses that could lead to certain internal high-risk factors. With increased privileges, his reactions to such high-risk factors may be less observable by staff. In addition, regular and random urinalysis is useful to the offender in maintaining abstinence from alcohol and/or drug use, in conjunction with other transition and chemical dependency aftercare services.

- **The penile plethysmograph and the Abel Assessment of Sexual Interest.** The penile plethysmograph, which measures physiological arousal to various sexual stimuli, and the Abel Assessment of Sexual Interest (Abel, 1996), which provides a comparison chart of level of interest in deviant versus appropriate themes, are both useful sources of information. Although disordered arousal is not expected to disappear following participation in treatment, staff would obviously question the readiness of an offender for discharge if he continued to demonstrate an overwhelming interest in deviant themes and minimal arousal to appropriate stimuli.

- **Pharmacological agents.** Pharmacological agents may also play an important role during a transition stage and following discharge. Offenders who are dually diagnosed with major mental illnesses may have become used to having consistent reminders for their medications while in the treatment center and should be monitored to ensure that they are adequately accepting responsibility for the management of their medications. Some offenders may also find it necessary to remain on medications such as selective serotonin reuptake inhibitors (SSRIs) or Provera/Depo-Provera (medroxyprogesterone acetate) to control symptoms of sexual compulsivity.

- **Global positioning systems.** A global positioning system (GPS) is a tracking system in which the offender wears a twenty-four-hour per day electronic bracelet and must keep a signal pack close to himself at all times. These systems were originally designed for short-term use for criminals on diversion from jail, but some stakeholders may be interested in using a GPS for offenders released after completing civil commitment programs and may see it as an easy way to assure a worried community. It should be noted, however, that the use of these systems as a factor in clinically based aftercare services has not been researched regarding psychological impact or long-term effect.

The Association for the Treatment of Sexual Abusers has included provisions for the use of the polygraph, penile plethysmography, and pharmacological agents in its Code of Ethics; however, neither protocols for the use of GPSs nor codes of ethics for its use are currently in place.

ETHICAL ISSUES

Ethical considerations regarding the transition of civilly committed sexual offenders into the community are several and essential. Civil commitment treatment programs must have clear goals and expectations for completion of the program. Each resident must be made aware of these expectations from the day of his admission. The program's clinical director and treatment team must evaluate a resident's progress toward those goals as objectively as possible.

Because these offenders likely have quite extensive offense histories and multiple paraphilias, it may be difficult for the treatment staff to ignore a "gut feeling" that they are not ready to return to the community regardless of the evidence that the resident has made significant changes and has met expectations. For that reason, the criteria for program completion should be very carefully developed, so that staff can assure themselves that anyone consistently meeting those expectations has earned the opportunity for increased privileges in the community. Then staff must put aside their subjective emotions and analyze each resident's progress as objectively as possible. Similarly, treatment staff need to be aware of the possibility of a loss of objectivity concerning an offender in the form of over-investment in the resident's success. This can be particularly likely to occur in civil commitment programs given the extensive period of time a resident might work with the same staff members.

For the above-mentioned reasons, it is vital that decisions concerning discharge be team decisions and not left to the recommendation of one therapist. It can also be particularly helpful to have an outside agency conduct a review of discharge decisions, in order to add an additional objective analysis of the offender's progress. Figure 10.1, Part IV-C, describes the role of an outside review board in this process.

When the time comes for a program completer to be discharged, other stakeholders may need to remind themselves of their earlier-held positions concerning civil commitment treatment programs. In arguing for the need for such programs, judges, prosecutors, and victims' advocates may have verbalized their commitment to having a program that includes the ability of the offender to complete treatment and return to the community, but these same people may find that once discharges actually start to occur, they are less certain of their convictions. Although they might be aware that commitment to a program with no chance of release would be considered unconstitutional, their fearful emotions may take over when the discharge is planned to occur in their own community.

The high cost of civil commitment programs also touches on ethical issues. Treatment providers may experience some outside pressure to release residents more quickly due to complaints about the high cost and also to provide assurances of their program's effectiveness. Staff must constantly remind themselves that overlooking a resident's deficits and prematurely releasing him is negligent, has a devastatingly high cost to society, and is also not in the best welfare of the offender.

SUMMARY

Many agencies have devoted extensive effort to the development of statutes allowing for the civil commitment of sexual offenders, defending the constitutionality of those statutes and the development of treatment programs to house the offenders selected by those statutes. Those efforts began several years ago and continue to this day. However, the same amount of effort has not always been devoted toward planning for their eventual return to the community. There are numerous concerns regarding the discharge of a civilly committed sexual offender, and for this process to be a success, all stakeholders need to begin to devote equal attention to this area.

Figure 10.1
Plan for Transition Stage (Used in the Minnesota Sex Offender Program)

I. **Orientation Week**

   A. **Required Activities**

   Prior to beginning the Transition Stage, the resident will have completed his Pre-Discharge Plan, which includes having staff witness the offender educate his main support people regarding his offense cycle. He will also have passed a polygraph examination and an assessment using the Abel Assessment of Sexual Interest.

   A resident beginning the Transition Stage will have one week during which he will be oriented to the facility, given a job assignment, and assessed for his adjustment to the move. During this week, he will not have additional privileges. He is required to complete an On/Off Grounds Privileges Plan that meets staff approval before moving to the next level of privileges.

   B. **Treatment Issues**

   Upon beginning the Transition Stage, the resident will attend therapy sessions three times per week. These sessions will be either group or individual sessions, depending on the number of residents in the Transition Stage. During these sessions, staff will assess issues including the resident's decision-making, distress tolerance, ability to delay gratification, identification of high-risk factors, use of coping interventions, openness to feedback, and relationships with support persons.

   In addition, staff will review the resident's short-term and long-term plans. A resident with identified chemical dependency issues will develop an acceptable plan specific to this need area. In addition, he will develop his "Supervised On-Grounds Privilege Plan" to be submitted to the Clinical Director for signature.

   C. **Legal Issues**

   Victim notification of the resident's plan to earn gradually increasing privileges will occur according to current guidelines.

II. **On-Grounds, Supervised Privileges**

   A. **Required Activities**

   After the "orientation" week, the resident will be given the opportunity to demonstrate increased responsibility through the use of On-Grounds, Supervised Privileges ("supervised" means supervised by staff). During this time he is expected to demonstrate a willingness to accept direction and supervision at work, to show initiative in seeking out assistance for treatment issues, and to continue to meet all goals and expectations for the four earlier phases of treatment (see Schlank et al., 1999).

   After a **minimum** of two months and a **minimum** of sixteen non-work-related On-Grounds, Supervised activities, the resident will be considered for the next level of privileges. The resident is expected to engage in a wide range of available activities that address his specific treatment needs. Before moving to the next level of privileges, he is required to develop a two-month Off-Grounds, Supervised Privilege Plan that meets staff approval.

B. Treatment Issues

The resident will continue to attend his therapy sessions three times each week. Any plan to address chemical dependency issues will also continue. The resident will also develop an acceptable two-month Off-Grounds, Supervised Privilege Plan to be submitted to the Clinical Director for signature.

C. Legal Issues

None.

III. Off-Grounds, Supervised Privileges

A. Required Activities

The resident is expected to demonstrate responsible use of Off-Grounds, Supervised Privileges for a **minimum** of two months and a **minimum** of sixteen non-work-related Off-Grounds, Supervised activities before he will be considered for the next level of privileges. He is expected to engage in a wide range of available activities that address his specific treatment needs.

Before moving to the next level, the resident is required to develop a two-month, "On-Grounds, Unsupervised Privilege Plan" that meets staff approval.

B. Treatment Issues

The resident will continue to attend his therapy sessions three times each week. Any plan to address chemical dependency issues will also continue. In addition, the resident will develop an acceptable On-Grounds, Unsupervised Privilege Plan to be submitted to the Clinical Director for signature.

C. Legal Issues

Victim notification will occur in accordance with time lines established by the Victim Notification policy prior to implementation of the On-Grounds, Unsupervised Privilege Plan.

IV. On-Grounds, Unsupervised Privileges

A. Required Activities

The resident is expected to demonstrate responsible use of On-Grounds, Unsupervised Privileges for a **minimum** of four months and a **minimum** of thirty-two non-work related, On-Grounds, Unsupervised activities. He is expected to engage in a wide range of available activities that address specific treatment needs.

The resident is also required to develop a two-month Pass Plan (Off Grounds, Unsupervised) that meets staff approval before staff will give sixty-day notice to all interested parties, including the victim, via the Victim Notification policy.

B. Treatment Issues

After the first month of successful use of On-Grounds, Unsupervised privileges, the resident's therapy sessions will decrease from three times per week to twice per week. Chemical Dependency treatment will continue as approved by staff. The resident will also develop his two-month Off Ground, Unsupervised Pass Plan to be submitted to the Clinical Director for signature. Treatment staff will make frequent, unannounced checks on the resident at various times during the use of his unsupervised privileges. The resident will also be administered additional polygraph examinations.

C. Legal Issues

Staff will give sixty-day notice to all interested parties of the facility's intention to grant the resident pass-eligible status (the privilege of having unsupervised passes off-grounds). If there are objections to this plan, a Special Review Board (SRB) hearing will be scheduled. The SRB is a panel of members who are not employed by the Department of Human Services who can make an objective decision concerning the readiness of the offender for these privileges. The board consists of a psychiatrist, a lawyer, and a mental health professional, often a social worker.

The pass-eligible status will not be implemented until a final determination is reached through any subsequent appeals process. Victim notification of the proposed change in status will occur according to the provisions of the victim notification policy. If the SRB approves Off-Grounds, Unsupervised Passes but the county of commitment wants to appeal the decision, the case is referred to a Three-Judge Panel for final determination. The resident will also be scheduled for an End-of-Confinement Review Committee (ECRC) hearing, in which his community notification level will be assigned. Community notification will occur prior to granting the Off-Grounds, Unsupervised Passes.

V. Passes (Off-Grounds, Unsupervised)

A. Required Activities

Each resident reaching this level of privileges will have an individualized, four-level pass plan, with increased Unsupervised, Off-Grounds time at each level. Residents are expected to demonstrate responsible use of privileges for a **minimum** of eight weeks AND a **minimum** of eight passes **at each level of the pass plan**.

> **Level 1**—During Level 1, the resident may earn gradually increasing Off-Grounds, Unsupervised Passes, beginning with one hour and progressing to two-, four-, and eight-hour passes. Staff will transport the resident to the destinations of these passes.
>
> **Level 2**—During Level 2, the resident may earn Off-Grounds, Unsupervised Passes up to twelve hours in duration, including travel time. There will be no overnight passes during this level. The resident will be considered for "driving privileges" during this level.
>
> **Level 3**—During Level 3, the resident may earn Off-Grounds, Unsupervised Passes up to thirty-six hours, including travel time. Only one overnight will be included per pass.
>
> **Level 4**—During Level 4, the resident may earn Off-Grounds, Unsupervised Passes ranging up to seven days (six nights) in duration. Every pass exceeding two days requires explicit approval by the Clinical Director, and in no case will the pass exceed seven days.

B. Treatment Issues

Therapy sessions will continue twice weekly at first, gradually decreasing to once weekly after the resident begins attending aftercare sessions in the community, which occurs after the resident has begun holding full-time employment in the community. Chemical Dependency treatment plans will continue as approved by staff. The resident will continue to develop acceptable two-month pass plans as needed.

C. Legal Issues

Treatment staff will petition the SRB for the resident's provisional discharge. Victim notification of the proposed change in status will occur according to the provisions of the victim notification policy. If the SRB approves provisional discharge, but the county of commitment wants to appeal the decision, the case is referred to a Three-Judge Panel for final determination.

VI. Provisional Discharge

Before a SRB hearing requesting provisional discharge will be supported by staff, the resident will be expected to demonstrate increased responsibility, increased competency in work and social situations, and increased self-management in all problem areas. In addition, he will be expected to demonstrate that he is appropriately taking control of his life situation without requiring prompts. After a **minimum** of two months and a **minimum** of eight passes on Level 4 of his Pass Plan, he may be considered for referral to the SRB for Provisional Discharge. Copies of the Provisional Discharge plan, with an attached Risk Management Plan and Chemical Dependency Aftercare Plan (where applicable), will be provided to the SRB. The conditions of the provisional discharge plan allow for the possibility that an offender's discharge can be revoked if he begins to show signs of regression toward old behaviors, prior to the commission of a new sexual offense. The Clinical Director has the ability to revoke a resident's provisional discharge; however, the resident has the right to request a speedy hearing by the SRB of any revocation.

References

Abel, G. G., (1996). *Abel assessment for sexual interest: Adult offenders.* Atlanta, GA: Abel Screening, Inc.

English, K. Pullen, S. & Jones, L. (1996). *Managing adult sex offenders on probation and parole: A containment approach.* Lexington, KY: American Probation and Parole Association.

Messer, G. (June 1, 2000). Roundtable discussion of transition issues, SVP Conference: Summit 2000, Oshkosh, WI.

Schlank, A., Harry, R. & Farnsworth, M. (1999). The Minnesota sex offender program. In A. Schlank & F. Cohen (Eds.), *The sexual predator: Law, policy, evaluation, and treatment.* Kingston, NJ: Civic Research Institute.

Scott, L. K. (1997). Community management of sex offenders. In B. Schwartz & H. Cellini (Eds.), *The sex offender: New insights, treatment innovations, and legal developments.* Kingston, NJ: Civic Research Institute.

Steele, N. (1995). Aftercare treatment programs. In B. Schwartz. & H. Cellini (Eds.), *The sex offender: Corrections, treatment, and legal practice.* Kingston, NJ: Civic Research Institute.

Chapter 11

Dangerousness and Sex Offenders—Assessing Risk for Future Sex Offenses

by Harry M. Hoberman, Ph.D., L.P.

The Three Basic Factors Governing Commitment 11-3
    Role of the Mental Health Professional 11-3
    Constitutional Basis for Mental Health Professionals' Role 11-4
Definitional Issues: Just What Is It That Is Being Predicted? 11-5
Relative Ability of Mental Health Professionals to Predict
    Dangerousness for Legal Matters 11-6
Prediction of Dangerousness, General Criminal and Violent Recidivism 11-7
Evidentiary Standards for Admissibility of Expert Witness Testimony 11-8
    Admissibility of Expert Testimony 11-9
    The *Daubert* Standard 11-9
Statistical Aspects of Prediction 11-10
    Significance of Base Rate 11-11
    ROC Analysis 11-12
    The Confidence Interval 11-13
The Methodology of Prediction of Future Dangerousness 11-13
    Unstructured ("Pure") Clinical Judgment 11-13
    Structured or Guided Clinical Judgment 11-14
    Pure Actuarial Methods 11-15
        Limitations 11-16
        Specificity Problem 11-17
    Actuarial Plus Expert Modifiers—Adjusted Actuarial Methods 11-17
Elements and Issues Involved in the Methodology of Risk Prediction 11-18
    Population Sample Variables 11-18
    Predictor Variables—Identifying and Defining Potential
        Risk Factors 11-19
    Criterion Variables—Identifying and Defining Sex Offense
        Recidivism 11-20
        Self-Reports and Collateral Sources 11-20
        Processes in the Justice System 11-20

        Number of Actual Offenses 11-21
        Police and Parole Office Records 11-21
        No Correlation Between Variable and Potential Offense 11-22
    Length of Follow-Up Period 11-22
        Survival Analysis 11-22
        Types of Sex Offenders 11-23
        Increased Recidivism With Increased Follow-Up Period 11-23
    The Base Rate of Sexual Offense Recidivism 11-24
Obtaining Information for Risk Assessment 11-25
Individual and Combinations of Risk Factors That Differentiate
    Recidivists 11-25
    Static and Historical Factors 11-26
    Deviancy and Psychopathy 11-26
    Meta-Analysis 11-27
    Dynamic Risk Factors 11-28
    Two General Types of Risk Factors 11-29
Specific Risk Assessment Measures and Guidelines 11-30
    The Psychopathy Checklist—Revised 11-30
        Inter-Rater Reliability 11-30
        Meta-Analysis 11-30
        Psychopathy and Recidivism 11-31
        PCL Screening Version 11-31
        Misuse of PCL-R 11-32
    The ASSESS-LIST 11-32
    Violence Risk Appraisal Guide (VRAG) 11-33
        Violent Behavior Predictions 11-34
        Limitations 11-35
    Minnesota Sex Offender Screening Tool (MnSOST) 11-35
    Rapid Risk Assessment for Sexual Offense Recidivism
        (RRASOR) 11-37
    Sex Offender Risk Appraisal Guide (SORAG) 11-39
    Minnesota Sex Offender Screening Tool—Revised (MnSOST-R) 11-40
    Structured Anchored Clinical Judgment (SACJ/SACJ-Min) 11-42
    Static-99 11-43
    Sex Offender Need Assessment Rating (SONAR) 11-44
    Structured Risk Assessment (SRA) 11-45
    Historical Clinical Risk Management-20 11-46
    Sexual Violence Rating Scale 11-47
    Risk for Sexual Violence Protocol (RSVP) 11-48
    Relationships Among the Different Recidivism Measures 11-48

Communicating Information Regarding the Level of Risk of
    Future Dangerousness 11-50
Conclusion 11-50

THE THREE BASIC FACTORS GOVERNING COMMITMENT

The assessment of future dangerousness, typically defined as the likelihood of sex offense recidivism, is the central issue in civil commitment matters for persons petitioned for commitment as sexual predators in the United States. Civil commitment procedures involving a person petitioned as a sexual predator (referred to herein as a PPSP) can result in indeterminate commitment for the purpose of treatment. Typically, three offender factors appear common to the different states' statutes governing such civil commitment processes:

- A history of one or more sexual offenses;
- The presence of a condition of "mental abnormality or dysfunction"; and
- A determination of the degree of risk of a specific type of dangerousness—future sexual offending—for persons with similar characteristics to the PPSP.

The statutory language states either explicitly or implicitly that the risk of future danger relative to sexual offending is understood to be a function of the characteristics of a PPSP's history of sexual offending and of his type and range of mental abnormality and/or dysfunction. Determining a history of sexual offending is usually relatively straightforward in most specific commitment matters. However, the other two common elements of these statutes require particular judgments. The first, a judgment as to whether one or more mental abnormalities or dysfunctions are present, is predominantly a dichotomous one. As discussed previously (e.g., Hoberman, 1999), this determination is not a simple one and requires rigorous methods of assessment to achieve an acceptable level of reliability and validity. The second, a judgment of a risk of future dangerousness, is central to civil commitment proceedings for PPSPs. This judgment can be conceptualized in different ways and is associated with a significant set of issues regarding the ability of mental health professionals to offer meaningful risk assessments and predictions of future behavior. The focus of this chapter is to discuss both the issues and the currently available methods of risk assessment regarding sexually violent recidivism among adult males.

Role of the Mental Health Professional

Clearly, mental health professionals are frequently requested to provide both information and judgments to judicial officers and/or to jurors—to triers of fact (TF) or of law (TL), or of both (TFL). Regarding particular matters, such professionals are often obligated to supply such information to the court. The relative value and admissibility of their information as presented to the judicial system has long been a matter of controversy (see Melton et al., 1997). This controversy can be found across virtually all areas of so-called forensic mental health, including criminal competency issues, child custody issues, personal injury matters, and workplace harassment and discrimination.

In each of these domains, evaluations and opinion testimony by mental health professionals are almost always part of the case-related material presented to the TFL.

The judicial system is called on to make decisions about the so-called dangerousness of individuals in a number of areas, including both criminal law (e.g., orders for protection related to allegations of domestic abuse, conditional release on bail prior to criminal matters, parole, and probation) and civil law (e.g., the civil commitment of mentally incompetent individuals, the discharge of such individuals from institutions, and stated threats of harm to specific individuals). In the majority of such cases, forensic evaluations and opinion testimony as to dangerousness of an individual are involved, as may be more specific expert witness testimony regarding the dangerousness of particular groups of individuals. The courts or parties typically invite mental health professionals to conduct such evaluations and provide opinion/expert witness testimony. Moreover, both clinical and forensic mental health professionals are at times *required* by law to perform such evaluations, reach conclusions, offer opinions and/or take actions, as seen in the cases *Addington v. Texas* (441 U.S. 418 (1979)); *Tarasoff v. Regents of the University of California* (551 P.2d 334 (1976)); and *Currie v. United States* (664 F.Supp. 1074 (1986)). In *Lipari v. Sears, Roebuck & Co.* (497 F. Supp. 185 (1980)), a duty was imposed on mental health professionals to protect society at large from potentially dangerous clients, even where a client does not specify who may be the future victim of his actions.

Constitutional Basis for Mental Health Professionals' Role

The constitutional basis of the admissibility of expert witness testimony regarding the domain of future dangerousness has been established in the United States. In *Barefoot v. Estelle* (463 U.S. 880 (1983)), the U.S. Supreme Court acknowledged the current limits of future dangerousness predictions; however, despite recognizing the potential unreliability of clinical predictions of that time, the Court allowed for expert testimony on that topic. The decision was based in part upon the belief that TFLs could sift reliable from unreliable expert testimony and that differences among experts regarding future dangerousness go to the weight, not the admissibility, of expert testimony. In *United States v. Salerno* (481 U.S. 739 (1987)), the Court held that "there is nothing inherently unattainable about the prediction of future criminal conduct" (481 U.S. at 751). In Canada, the Dangerous Offender Legislation originally passed in 1948 (for sex offenders) and modified in 1977 (broadened to include others in addition to sex offenders) provided for the determination of the dangerousness of sex offenders based on the expert witness testimony of psychiatrists. Thus, relevant judicial decisions have provided the basis for the mental health professional's ability to provide opinion or testimony regarding predictions of future dangerousness.

Regarding the judicial perspective of such professionals' ability to offer opinion testimony as to dangerousness, Monahan (1996) has noted that the courts have upheld the constitutionality of laws that relied on prediction by mental health professionals even when confronted with older empirical evidence of the potential for low accuracy of many of those predictions. Further, it has been argued that "courts have seemed more, not less, interested in recruiting mental health professionals to assess the future risk of violent behavior" (Douglas & Webster, 1999, p. 178). As Janus and Meehl (1997) conclude:

[I]t seems well established that there is no constitutional impediment to using predictions of dangerousness in legal proceedings up to and including those that result in a loss of liberty or death. As a legal matter, prediction is not, in all of its forms and for all purposes, so inaccurate as to violate the due process clause." (p. 36)

DEFINITIONAL ISSUES: JUST WHAT IS IT THAT IS BEING PREDICTED?

"Danger" generally is defined as harm or damage as well as exposure or liability to injury, pain, harm, or loss; while "violence" is defined as an exertion of physical force so as to injure or abuse. "Sexual violence" has been defined as actual, attempted, or threatened sexual contact with a person who is nonconsenting or is unable to provide consent and can include communications of a sexual nature (Hart, 2000). "Dangerous" refers to something or someone that may cause harm or loss unless dealt with carefully; its synonym, "risky," means involving the chance of loss or injury. Risk refers to the possibility of loss or injury, the chance of loss, or the degree of probability of such events. Since risk is a possibility, a risk determination is always an estimate. "Dangerousness" is then the risk or probability of injury, pain, or harm, assessed over some period of time; the risk of violent injury or abuse by physical acts is a subset of dangerousness. The risk of sexual violence is that of the probability of injury or abuse, of a sexual nature, caused by an individual's action.

Monahan and Steadman (1994) have argued that the legal concept of "dangerousness" confounds or confuses the variables on which a prediction is based, the type of event being predicted, and the likelihood of the event occurring. For research purposes, they advocate that "dangerousness" be disaggregated into three components:

- Risk factors (variables used to predict violence);
- Harm (the amount and type of violence being predicted); and
- Risk level (the probability that harm will occur).

In addition, they suggest that harm be scaled in terms of relative seriousness and that risk level be viewed as a *continuous* probability statement, not a dichotomous variable. Finally, they note that estimates of risk should be in the form of a "risk assessment" (as opposed to a static, one time prediction) given that risk levels may not be stable but fluctuate over time and context.

In cases involving PPSPs, the issue is the *relative probability* that a sex offender with certain characteristics similar to a particular PPSP will commit a future sex offense. Further, in all of the current states that have legislated civil commitment of sex offenders, the apparent length of time of risk to be considered is the offender's lifetime. Consequently, the actual task is not to predict whether the specific sex offender will reoffend. Rather, the apparent task at hand is to determine whether sex offenders with certain characteristics exceed a particular threshold of probability to commit an additional sex offense for the remainder of their lives. That is, as Doren (1999) has stated regarding the concept of accuracy:

> In all of the "new generation" sex offender civil commitment laws currently existing in the USA, the statutes do not require a differentiation, or a designation of which offender will or will not sexually recidivate. *Evaluators instead need to determine whether or not a subject is above a certain likelihood threshold for sexual re-offending, not whether he will or will not reoffend.* Certainly these two concepts are related, but they are not the same things. (p.1, emphasis added)

In short, evaluators are not typically asked to predict an individual's "absolute" degree of risk, but his degree of risk (higher or lower) relative to a specified threshold for risk (Doren, 2000).

RELATIVE ABILITY OF MENTAL HEALTH PROFESSIONALS TO PREDICT DANGEROUSNESS FOR LEGAL MATTERS

Early studies of the prediction of dangerousness were characterized by two issues—low base rates for the occurrence of violent behavior and unguided, asystematic clinical judgment. Both of these factors interacted to produce high rates of overprediction as to which individuals would be violent. Further, they attempted dichotomous classifications as to whether an individual was dangerous or not dangerous. Based largely on such studies, Monahan (1981), most prominently among other writers, offered a pessimistic view of mental health professionals' then-current ability to predict future dangerousness. Monahan did suggest that clinical prediction might stem from a lack of knowledge or understanding and not from an essential lack of ability. He discussed what he believed to be the most common sources of clinical error. Among these, he included:

- The lack of specificity in defining a criterion of violent or dangerous behavior;

- The overwhelming tendency for clinicians to ignore the base rates of violence;

- The reliance of clinicians on so-called "illusory correlations" (This refers to the phenomenon of clinicians believing that a predictor is associated with some outcome when in fact there is little or no (or even an opposite) positive empirical relationship between predictor and outcome variables. Garb (1998) notes that clinicians frequently report and opine on correlations between characteristics of individuals and behaviors when there is no scientific evidence to establish such a relationship.); and

- The failure to incorporate environmental or contextual information.

However, it has been argued that " . . . in the past 5 or 10 years, improved research methodology has demonstrated that, while risk assessments remain far from perfect, they may be appreciably better than previous studies may have led us to believe" (Douglas & Webster, 1999, p. 176). These writers go on to state that currently available research in the prediction of violence has demonstrated that while far from perfect, risk assessments can be performed at levels notably better than chance and that a sense of "guarded optimism" has emerged from research regarding the ability of mental health professionals to offer useful predictions of future dangerousness.

Despite Monahan's early pessimism, it had been shown that some clinicians are also more able predictors than others (e.g., Webster et al., 1994). A variety of studies have demonstrated that a variety of violent behaviors occur at much higher rates among a variety of populations (e.g., Borum, 1996). Further, a major shift has occurred in which mental health professionals have begun considering future dangerousness in terms of conditional risk and not as a simple dichotomous determination; probabilistic statements are offered as a preferable method of presenting information about prediction because they more accurately reflect current ability to identify the possibility of future violence. Slobogin (1996) concludes that the improved success of more recent studies relates to their use of better methodologies, including less narrow outcome criteria and improved outcome data. He also discusses the possibility that increased accuracy rates could be related to improvements in predictive science, particularly the growing development of actuarial methods of prediction and their use in "hybrid" form with clinical prediction. Mossman (1994) reevaluated fifty-eight data sets from forty-four published studies of violence prediction involving over 16,000 subjects and found sufficient heterogeneity among these studies to opine that no simple conclusion can be reached regarding clinicians' prediction of violence. However, he also concluded that for 81 percent of the data sets studied, prediction accuracy was *significantly* greater than chance and, in some cases, far better. Litwack and Schlesinger (1987; 1999) have consistently argued that certain conditions for mental health professionals' predictions of dangerousness could satisfy judicial standards.

Slobogin (1996) argues that expert opinion regarding dangerousness should follow two principles. The first is that facts regarding an individual's history should be corroborated with collateral or documentary sources of data to serve as the basis for the expert's opinion; the second is that in the absence of good actuarial data, experts should be limited to stating factors that might increase or decrease an individual's future risk of violence or dangerousness. Slobogin also opines that at the present time, "it appears that 'good' clinical prediction is better than chance" (p. 378) and thus such predictions, as well as actuarial data on prediction, should be admissible under the contemporary judicial standards regarding the introduction of evidence.

PREDICTION OF DANGEROUSNESS, GENERAL CRIMINAL AND VIOLENT RECIDIVISM

As Quinsey et al. (1998) state, "Considerable evidence demonstrates that a disproportionately large amount of violence is committed by a small group of persistently violent individuals whose history of violent and aggressive behavior extends back through childhood" (p. 183).

Litwack and Schlesinger (1999) enumerate a number of conclusions based on available research concerning the broad area of dangerousness risk assessments. They note that

> Even when an individual's history of violence is a somewhat distant history of serious violence, which led to a continuing confinement, it can be reasonably assumed that the individual remains at risk for violence, if released from confinement, if it can be shown that he or she maintains the same complex attitudes and personality traits (and physical abilities) that led to violence in the

past and that, if released, the individual would confront circumstances quite similar to those that led to violence in the past. (p. 191)

Several particular studies demonstrate that mental health professionals were able to predict future violence among psychiatrically disturbed patients. Lidz et al. (1993) found that patients who elicited professional concern regarding future violence were significantly more likely to be violent after release than patients who did not elicit such concerns. The accuracy of the clinician's predictions substantially exceeded chance levels. Similarly, McNiel and Binder (1991) and Klassen and O'Connor (1988) have identified actuarial predictors of institutional and community violence, respectively, among psychiatric patients.

Hanson (1999) states that "There is no longer any serious debate about whether general criminal recidivism can be predicted among general criminal populations" (p. 8-2). He also notes, "there is agreement that it is possible to predict general criminal recidivism with at least moderate accuracy" (1997, p. 2). Such accuracy has been achieved by specifying which risk factors to consider and assigning relative weights to these variables based on research. Hanson notes, "Those offenders most likely to reoffend have been identified by risk factors such as a history of criminal behavior, antisocial personality/psychopathy, a young age, antisocial peers, and pro-criminal attitudes. . . . Most of the risk factors that predict general recidivism have also been noted to predict violent recidivism . . ." (1999, p. 8-2). Bonta et al. (1998) conducted a meta-analysis that shows that the major predictors of criminal and violent recidivism are the same for mentally disordered criminal offenders as for non-mentally disordered offenders. Criminal history variables were the best predictors, as were juvenile delinquency variables and "clinical" variables (clinical symptoms or psychopathology).

However, Hanson (1999) has also argued and demonstrated (e.g., see Hanson & Bussière, 1998) that certain factors that predict sex offense recidivism are distinct from factors that predict other forms of violent crime. This suggests that sex offense recidivism should be studied both separately and in conjunction with other types of violent recidivism.

EVIDENTIARY STANDARDS FOR ADMISSIBILITY OF EXPERT WITNESS TESTIMONY

Before considering specific issues and instruments related to the prediction of sexual recidivism, we must consider the basis or criteria for the admissibility of so-called expert witness testimony, including that of forensic mental health evaluators. These professionals must understand there are legal standards inherent in judicial rules of evidence that are determinant in all jurisdictions and that establish criteria governing their ability to offer opinion testimony. Any risk assessment measures must be considered within the context of specific legal criteria that govern the admissibility of testimony. Moreover, state appellate court decisions and the U.S. Supreme Court have continued to dismiss challenges to the constitutionality of the civil commitment of PPSPs. Consequently, it seems reasonable to believe that such courts will increasingly encounter issues of evidentiary reliability and relevance and, thus, the admissibility of testimony or other evidence based on risk assessment measures.

Admissibility of Expert Testimony

For many years, the basis for the admissibility of expert testimony was rooted in the determination that the subject of that testimony lay outside the normal experience of the average TF or TFL. An early decision involving the admissibility of polygraph evidence, *Frye v. United States* (293 F. 1013 (D.C. Cir. 1923)), advocated as the principle for admissibility that the information provided by the expert "must be sufficiently established to have gained general acceptance in the particular field in which it belongs." This standard for admissibility was known as that of "general acceptance" within the relevant "scientific community."

Some fifty years later, Article VII of the Federal Rules of Evidence (FRE), "Opinions and Expert Testimony," was developed to provide mandates for cases in federal court; Rules 702, Testimony by Experts, and 703, Bases of Opinion Testimony by Experts, have also been used by many states as models or guidelines for the admissibility of such testimony. It is useful to review these rules. Per Federal Rule 702:

> If scientific, technical or other specialized knowledge will assist the trier of fact to understand the evidence or determine a fact in issue, a witness qualified as an expert by knowledge, skill, experience, training, or education, may testify thereto in the form of an opinion or otherwise.

Further, per Federal Rule 703:

> The facts or data in the particular case upon which an expert bases an opinion or inference may be those perceived or made known to the expert at or before the hearing. If of a type reasonably relied upon by experts in the particular field in forming opinions or inferences upon the subject, the facts or data need not be admissible in evidence.

Relative to the so-called *Frye* test of general acceptance within the scientific community, FRE Rules 702 and 703 have been viewed as broadening the potential scope of expert testimony, which creates a potential conflict between the FRE and the *Frye* precedent.

The *Daubert* Standard

In *Daubert v. Merrell Dow Pharmaceutical, Inc.* (509 U.S. 579, 597 (1993)), the U.S. Supreme Court ruled in favor of the FRE as applied to matters in Federal Court. This decision has often been viewed as broadening the admissibility of expert opinion. However, this decision actually articulates a middle ground where new research not yet generally accepted could be permitted and poor-quality science and nonscientific clinical perspectives having "general acceptance" could be excluded. Under the *Daubert* standard, the credentials of the expert witness go to the credibility of both the witness and the relative quality of the scientific basis for the witness's testimony.

Further, the value of expert witness testimony is to be determined on the basis of direct and cross-examination by the attorneys for the parties and the presentation of contrary evidence, including other expert opinion. Thus, *Daubert* represents a trend toward a more demanding level of scrutiny by courts, one where scientific evidence of research supports a forensic expert's evaluation methods and procedures, the opinions resulting from that evaluation, and the larger body of knowledge and practice in the particular area.

According to the *Daubert* rule, the trial court must determine whether the expert testimony presented has a *reliable foundation* and is *relevant* to the proceeding. The "evidentiary reliability" of proposed evidence is to be evaluated on the basis of four stepwise criteria:

1. A trial court must determine whether the proposed evidence has been subjected to empirical testing and has

2. Received peer review or been published in peer-reviewed journals;

3. The known or potential error rates must be able to be identified; and

4. General acceptance of the substance of the expert testimony in the field may then be considered.

The potential relevance of the expert testimony is that the information the expert provides must have a valid scientific connection to the key issues in the legal matter. In fact, the U.S. Supreme Court's decision in *Kumho Tire, Inc. v. Carmichael* (119 S. Ct. 1167 (1999)) expanded the scope of the *Daubert* decision by holding that the trial judge must determine whether proposed expert testimony, including clinical opinion, "reflects scientific, technical or other specialized knowledge" that has a reliable basis in the knowledge and experience of a particular discipline. (See also Petrila, Chapter 3, this volume, regarding the *Frye* and *Daubert* standards.)

Clearly, whether a jurisdiction relies on the so-called *Frye* or *Daubert/Kumho* tests, the key issue for admissibility is acceptance within some portion of the scientific community and (at least generally) *not* the clinical community.

STATISTICAL ASPECTS OF PREDICTION

It is useful to discuss the statistical basis for prediction. Predictive validity concerns the degree to which actual outcomes are matched by outcomes predicted by a particular method. Correlations have long been used to determine the association of a variable or procedure with a characteristic or outcome, such as recidivism. Correlations provide information about the relative strength of the association between a variable or set of variables and a chosen outcome. Hanson (1998) has stated that in general, the magnitude of a correlation coefficient can be interpreted as the relative difference in the recidivism base rate between a person with or without the particular characteristic.

According to Cohen (1992), a moderate-sized correlation is $r = +/- .30$ and a large correlation is $r = +/- .50$. The size of a correlation diminishes when the base rate (the occurrence of a phenomenon in a sample) of the outcome variable is less than 50 percent (e.g., Douglas et al., 1999). In such cases, correlational techniques may not be the most effective means of estimating the predictive efficiency of a risk assessment instrument (Rice & Harris, 1995).

Significance of Base Rate

Most commonly in the past, a "2x2" contingency table provided the mechanism for discussing the accuracy of prediction; on one axis is the dichotomous predicted outcome (e.g., will commit a future offense versus will not commit a future offense), and on the other is the actual outcome (committed a future offense versus did not commit a future offense). As Webster et al. (1994) stated, "There are two ways of being right and two ways of being wrong." Thus, there will be true positives ("hits") and true negatives; these constitute the two ways of "being right." Conversely, one can predict that an offender will not recidivate but he does commit another offense (a false negative, or "miss"), or one can predict that an offender will recidivate but he does not commit another offense (a false positive, or "false alarm"). These are the two ways of being wrong—the types of errors that accompany any prediction procedure. However, as with correlation coefficients, the percentage correct identified via a contingency table is significantly influenced by the base rate. Consequently, for events with a low base rate, the likelihood of error in prediction rises greatly, particularly for false alarms.

In the medical and epidemiological literature, particular terms are traditionally used to describe the performance (i.e., relative accuracy) of diagnostic tests. *Sensitivity* refers to the ability of a test or prediction to identify true positives (and is sometimes referred to as the hit rate); the sensitivity of a test is the proportion of true cases detected by a test within a sample. Regarding a test for future dangerousness, sensitivity refers to the proportion of people who are found to be violent who were previously predicted to display violent behavior.

Specificity refers to the prediction instrument's ability to correctly classify true negatives, or the proportion of people found to be nonviolent who were previously predicted to be nonviolent. To measure the accuracy of prediction, one can compute the positive predictive power (PPP) by dividing the number of true positives by the sum of the true positives and false positives and multiplying by 100. In this manner, the PPP provides the percentage of individuals predicted to be violent in the future and who actually were violent at follow-up.

Prediction with a given method invariably involves a trade-off between "false alarms" and "hits." Statistically, reductions in one group cannot be accomplished without increases in the other. The so-called sensitivity-specificity tradeoff refers to the problem that enhancing the "hit rate" of a predictive method will always lead to a lower sensitivity and increase the identification of false positives. Consequently, the selection of a specific cut-off for a particular predictive method will always involve value judgments about the consequences of those cutoffs—is it better for a given method to minimize "false alarms" or to maximize "hits?" As Mossman (1994) has indicated, clinicians/evaluators may well have preferences about avoiding certain types of prediction errors.

Further, the sensitivity and specificity obtained with a particular predictive method are highly influenced by the base rate (the occurrence, in this case, of sexual reoffending) and the selection ratio (the proportion of a sample predicted to reoffend by some value or level of the method).

ROC Analysis

A method exists for describing detection (hits) and false alarm rates at different decision thresholds. For each threshold, one can graph the true positive rate as a function of the false positive rate and create a curve of the predictive qualities of a particular method. The tradeoff from plotting the graph of the "hit" rate as a function of "false alarms" based on different cutoffs is referred to as the receiver operating characteristic (ROC). As Douglas et al. (1999) state, "The ROC took its name because it describes the detection or prediction 'characteristics' of the test and the 'receiver' of data can 'operate' at any given point on the curve." (p. 922).

ROC analyses are meant to be applied to data that are comprised of a continuous predictor variable and a dichotomous dependent measure or criterion. In ROC methodology, the space or *area under the curve* (AUC) (or graph) of the ratio of "hits" to "false alarms" provides a measure of the relative value of a particular method of prediction. The AUC can be taken as an index for interpreting the overall predictive accuracy of the predictor variable or method. AUCs can range from 0 (a perfect negative prediction) to .50 (a chance prediction) to 1.00 (a perfect positive prediction). The results of a ROC are expressed as the AUC for the cut-off for a particular measure/method, or as the common language effect size (CLES). Regarding a sex offender released from a facility, a given AUC represents the probability that a randomly selected released sex offender who reoffended had a higher score on the chosen method of prediction than a randomly selected released sex offender who did not reoffend. That is, an AUC of .70 would mean that there is a 70 percent chance that a sexual recidivist would score above the cutoff for additional sexual violence on the predictor method and a 70 percent chance that a sexual nonrecidivist would score below that cutoff (see Douglas & Webster, 1999).

Rice and Harris (1995) have demonstrated that the tradeoff of "hits" to "false alarms" for the ROC of a given test remains largely unchanged over significant variations in both base rates and selection ratios. Thus, ROCs permit an estimate of the accuracy of a method or test by providing a measure of effect size that is relatively unaffected by variations in base rate and selection ratio. Given a determination of the relative cost of errors of different types, the best selection ratio can be identified for different base rates.

Thus, in Mossman's (1994) reevaluation of published studies of violence prediction, he found the median AUC for all fifty-eight data sets was .73 and the weighted average was .78, both well above a chance level. These results can be taken as indicating the probability or chance that a randomly selected individual who commits a future act of violence is rated more highly by clinicians than a randomly selected individual who does not commit a future act of violence.

Doren (1999b; 2000) has argued that the relative utility of the ROC as a measure of accuracy in civil commitment procedures may be misconstrued. In these procedures, the key differentiation relative to risk is whether an individual is above or below a particular threshold for recidivism. The ROC is computed across the full range of predicted/obtained scores for all individuals who are studied for recidivism. Doren (1999b) argues that much of the existing ""error" for ROC scores is found at the lower end of scale scores; he suggested that if one were to restrict the range over which the ROC is computed for specific instruments to the higher range of scores, "then the ROC will typically go up dramatically . . . the prediction of sexual recidivism by a restricted use of high scale scores can be remarkably accurate" (p 4).

Doren (2000) notes that the concept or definition of accuracy can be construed in a number of different ways. It can be viewed as a dichotolous term—an opinion or determination is completely correct or it is not. In contrast, accuracy can be understood as *the degree* to which something is correct or, more specifically, the degree to which a determination (e.g., a probability) falls along a continuum, potentially one with particular thresholds that have some particular meaning.

The Confidence Interval

Doren (1999b) has called attention to the value of the confidence interval (CI) as a statistic that is most specifically related to the accuracy of probabilistic assessment. The CI applies to the particular scale score computed for an individual as opposed to the scale as a whole. A CI is expressed as a particular percentage likelihood that a particular score is the true score for a particular event or characteristic present; typically, CI scores (e.g., the statistically probable outcome) are expressed as having a 95 percent chance of being within a range of scores around that identified score. If CIs were available for particular risk assessment measures, Doren argues that an evaluator could offer an opinion about the accuracy of a risk assessment based on an actuarial instrument by offering a statement to the effect that there is a 95 percent likelihood that the PPSP's risk level is within a specific range of scores of the specified risk probability. For example, if a PPSP receives a score of 5 or greater on the Static-99, this would place him in a "high risk" category for sexual recidivism. Based on data provided by Doren (1999b), using the CI, an evaluator could express the fifteen-year sex offense recidivism rate as 52 percent, with a 95 percent CI of +/-8.6 percent. This means there is a likelihood of 95 percent that the PPSP's risk of sex offense recidivism over a fifteen-year period would range from 43.4 percent to 60.6 percent. However, it remains for investigators to identify CIs for almost all of the current risk measures.

THE METHODOLOGY OF PREDICTION OF FUTURE DANGEROUSNESS

Unstructured ("Pure") Clinical Judgment

A substantial body of data has accumulated in the areas of both cognitive and clinical psychology that significant problems exist when lay persons and clinicians make subjective judgments about probabilities. Rice and Harris (1995) report that practicing mental health clinicians possess no particular expertise in the predictions of violence and that reliance on subjective clinical judgment alone can result in inaccurate predictions of dangerousness. Goldberg (1968; 1970) has demonstrated that clinical experience was unrelated to accuracy but was related to (false) confidence in predictions. Further, he found that using statistical models based on clinicians' reports of how they made judgments provided more accurate predictions about new cases than the clinicians' particular subjective judgments regarding those cases. This research has suggested that clinicians are typically asystematic in how they both collect and value, or "weigh," information and that this can lead to less accurate judgments.

Clinical judgment is also likely affected by well-established findings that practicing clinicians often fail to stay current on new research or even ignore new research in preference of their previous beliefs; both of these tendencies also appear likely to reduce the accuracy of clinicians' prediction of future behavior. Overall, then, subjective or unstructured judgment by clinicians tends to lack consistency or agreement across evaluators with respect to the process and content of evaluations and the means by which decisions are made. Clinical evaluators typically fail to specify why or how they reached a decision.

Further, it is well known that humans, both lay persons and professionals, are susceptible to a variety of errors in cognition and judgment in particular (Garb, 1998). As noted by Grove et al. (2000), these errors include ignoring base rates, assigning nonoptimal weights to cues, failing to take into account regression toward the mean, and failing to properly assess covariation. Decision-making heuristics such as representativeness or availability can similarly reduce accuracy of judgment.

Particularly with regard to dangerousness, various studies (cited in Quinsey et al., 1998) have demonstrated that clinicians tend to ignore base rates of violent behavior and offense history while overemphasizing more general clinical factors (e.g., symptoms or life history events), both of which contribute to inaccurate predictions of future violence. Similarly, clinicians appear to confuse perceived treatability with prognosis, which can also lead to inaccurate predictions of future dangerousness.

In a recent meta-analysis of risk factors for sex offense recidivism, Hanson and Bussiere (1998) found that the average of predictive accuracy for pure or subjective clinical judgment for this outcome was only slightly better than chance (average $r = .10$).

Structured or Guided Clinical Judgment

As noted, Goldberg (1970) demonstrated that when clinical methods of judgment are "standardized" into a multiple regression equation, accuracy of prediction is improved. This suggests that when clinical judgments are made according to a structured formula, both information and method variance decrease, which can lead to improved professional judgment and prediction.

Following specific and defined procedures for conducting an assessment improves the consistency and accuracy of the information collected and the decisions made using that information. However, the issue arises of specifying the best way to combine and weigh information about the different variables. Without uniformity of method, different evaluators could reach different conclusions when assessing the same individual. Further, without an explicit method or procedure for combining information, it is impossible to determine specific recidivism probabilities. As Hanson (1999) states, "Offenders who rate highly on many risk factors can reasonably be considered 'more dangerous' than offenders having a few risk factors, but the absolute, or even relative, recidivism rates are difficult to determine with the guided clinical approach" (p. 8-14).

One of the most problematic aspects of unaided clinical judgment is the expression of confirmatory bias, namely the selective collection and overinterpretation of information that supports an initial hypothesis. Borum (1996) cites several studies in the larger medical literature that indicate that using structured data-gathering tools can lead to greater comprehensiveness and, consequently, more reliable and accurate judgments. Rogers (1995) reviewed several studies in the area of psychiatric diagnosis which indicate that unstandardized methods of collecting information have a negative effect on the diagnostic process, "particularly in the underdiagnosis and omission of many mental disorders from classification . . ." (p. 4). The lack of structured assessment procedures leads to information variance as well as criterion variance, the asystematic application of standards for relevant classification of variables. In turn, such characteristics reduce both the reliability and validity of the clinical process. Conversely, Rogers (1995) presents the results of a number of studies that indicate substantial improvements in both the reliability and validity of psychiatric diagnosis when structured and semistructured information-gathering techniques are applied. Moreover, Melton et al.'s (1985) study showed that mental health professionals with specific training in forensic mental health performed better in their knowledge of forensic issues relative to mental health professionals who lacked specific training in forensic mental health.

Hart (2000) advocates for the utility of structured clinical guidelines for assessing sex offenders when legal decisions are to be made regarding them. He advocates for the consideration of a fixed and explicit set of risk factors with a specific process for information gathering; the instructions for such guidelines are precise enough to permit reliable assessments and the content of the identified risk factors are reasonably sufficient to assess risk.

To this end, Hanson (1999) reports that not all clinical assessments of sex offense recidivism are "equally poor." Rather, the most accurate of such assessments are those that require the evaluators to review a standard list of risk factors before making their assessments. He notes that a reanalysis of the Hanson and Bussiere (1998) sex offense recidivism studies indicates that the average correlation in the studies that used guided risk assessments ($r = .23$) is more than three times those that involve unstructured risk assessments.

Pure Actuarial Methods

Actuarial methods of prediction are also referred to as statistical or mechanical methods. Grove and Meehl (1996) state that actuarial prediction "involves a formal, algorithmic, objective procedure (e.g., equation) to reach the decision" (p. 293), while unaided clinical prediction "relies on an informal, 'in the head,' impressionistic, subjective conclusion, reached (somehow) by a human clinical judge" (p. 294). Generally, actuarial scales specify both the particular items to be considered in prediction as well as explicit direction as to the relative importance of each item (e.g., the relative weighting of individual items). In a seminal article, Meehl (1954) condemned so-called clinical judgment as subjective and therefore less accurate and less consistent than statistical prediction.

According to Grove & Meehl (1996), multiple studies demonstrate that subjective, unaided clinical judgment is at best equal to, but often worse than, actuarial methods of prediction. In their meta-analysis of 136 studies, sixty-four studies show that a "mechanical" or actuarial method of prediction is superior to clinical judgment, while sixty-four show no difference between clinical and mechanical prediction; and in only eight studies was subjective clinical judgment superior to mechanical predictions. Mossman (1994) found that for predictions longer than one year, the average AUC was greater for predictions based on discriminant functions (statistical methods) than for all types of clinical judgment.

In a recent updated meta-analysis of the accuracy of clinical versus mechanical data-combination techniques in the area of human health and behavior, however, Grove et al. (2000) found that:

> On average, mechanical-prediction techniques were about 10% more accurate than clinical predictions . . . mechanical predictions substantially outperformed clinical predictions in 33%-47% of studies examined. Although clinical predictions were often as accurate as mechanical predictions, in only a few studies (6%-16%) were they substantially more accurate. . . . These data indicate that mechanical predictions of human behaviors are equal to or superior to clinical predictions methods for a wide range of circumstances. (p. 19)

Nonetheless, the authors conclude:

> [O]ur results qualify overbroad statements in the literature opining that such superiority [of mechanical prediction] is completely uniform; it is not. In half of the studies we analyzed, the clinical method is approximately as good as mechanical prediction, and in a few scattered instances, the clinical method was notably more accurate. (p. 25)

Limitations. Actuarial methods have several limitations. First, such instruments typically involve the consideration of a small number of risk factors. They also typically begin with identifying a larger number of factors that demonstrate significant correlations with the outcome of interest (e.g., recidivism). Multiple regression is generally used as a primary data-analytic method to reduce a number of (relatively independent) scale items to a final set, with each item contributing some unique information to the prediction equation. However, in multiple regression, when variables are highly inter-correlated with one another, it is common for the investigators to drop the items with lower correlations from the final scale. Consequently and as a result of particular data-combination practices, certain factors that are in fact empirically associated with outcomes like recidivism do not appear as final predictors of those outcomes in order to maintain a set of relatively independent predictors.

Hanson (1999) notes that existing multivariate analyses include between three and nine items with no single item common to all available studies. Regarding more formal actuarial measures, he states, "The major vulnerability of the current actuarial scales is their lack of comprehensiveness. . . . The existing actuarial scales cannot even claim to address all the relevant static risk factors" (p. 17). Further, some actuarial measures have identified variables shown to be linked to future violence that do not appear to make common sense (e.g., offenders who had seriously injured their victims reoffended less frequently than other offenders, as found by Webster et al., 1994).

With a pure actuarial model, low probability variables are unlikely to enter an empirical prediction because of their low base rate of occurrence. Nonetheless, such variables may be highly predictive of future violence; examples of such factors are the belief that an adult is entitled to be sexual with any person he or she may simply desire or that an adult has an imperative to socialize a child into sexual functioning. The actuarial method emphasizes the characteristics of *groups* of individuals who reoffend and is relatively insensitive to idiographic or rare characteristics of persons who subsequently commit additional sex offenses. In addition, as Boer et al. (1997a) point out, actuarial instruments constructed using an empirical approach are "high fidelity" predictors; they are "optimized" to predict a specific outcome over a specific period of time in a specific population. Further, it is the case that available actuarial measures are not truly, or a least not completely, actuarial in nature in that they may be influenced by cohort effects (e.g., changes in the types of sex offenders incarcerated or released) and almost no such measures have been cross-validated on a range of samples of sex offenders (e.g., are Canadian offenders different from American offenders? Are offenders in the southern United States different from those in northern states?).

Specificity Problem. As we just mentioned, a pure actuarial model is not likely to include low probability variables with a low base rate of occurrence. Lidz et al. (1993) have stated that actuarial predictions demonstrate greater sensitivity (higher hit rates), but poorer specificity (fewer true negatives), than clinical predictions. Litwack and Schlesinger (1999) caution that actuarial tools based upon ROCs while allowing researchers to better evaluate the relative validity and utility of particular assessment tools can be misleading if such analyses view and rate assessments as if they were predictions. More specifically, these writers point out that that it is not clear that ROC analyses can effectively take into account different time periods that subjects are available for follow-up or adequately take into account the relative seriousness of particular forms of violence. They further argue that "there are no validated actuarial bases for determining dangerousness in many circumstances. And actuarial predictions may not sufficiently specify the possible severity or temporal closeness of predicted violence to be meaningful for use in actual decision-making" (p. 188). Existing actuarial instruments may predict the likelihood of any act of sexual violence but ignore the nature, severity, or frequency of the violence; such variables may be of particular importance in policy or legal decisions regarding future violence.

While they acknowledge that using a formula to combine empirically identified risk factors and applying a standard cut-off may maximize predictive accuracy, Boer et al. (1997a) argue that "it may be unreasonable, unethical and illegal for professionals to make decisions using such a procedure, that is, without considering the totality of circumstances in a given case" (p. 20). Similarly, Borum (1996) writes, "At a minimum, these devices can serve as a checklist for clinicians to ensure that essential areas of inquiry are recalled and evaluated. At best, they may be able to provide hard actuarial data on the probability among persons (and environments) with a given set of characteristics, circumstances, or both" (p. 948).

Actuarial Plus Expert Modifiers—Adjusted Actuarial Methods

The available evidence clearly demonstrates that "scientific" or actuarial methods of predicting relative risk of future dangerousness are superior or equal to unstructured clinical judgment, but that they are also characterized by a lack of comprehensiveness and an insensitivity to idiographic or rare characteristics of persons who are likely to commit additional violent or sexual offenses. Quinsey and Lalumiere (1996) originally recommended that an actuarial estimate of risk be used to anchor clinical judgment, advising clinicians "to start with an actuarial estimate of risk and then to conservatively adjust that estimate upward or downward" by considering salient variables such as dynamic predictors (e.g., progress in treatment) or idiographic characteristics of particular offenders or their history. As they viewed matters at the time, the "art" of prediction involved this adjustment of the scientifically based estimate of risk to particularly relevant aspects of particular, individual cases. Similarly, Hanson (1998) argued that an "adjusted" actuarial approach, which begins with actuarial predictions but allows for "expert evaluators" to adjust (or not) the actuarial prediction based on consideration of potentially important factors not included in the actuarial measure. In particular, he argued that clinical adjustments to recidivism estimates have the least chance of introducing error when the factors employed to adjust the probabilities have strong empirical support. Conversely, he cautions evaluators not to dilute actuarial predictions with irrelevant information not supported by empirical research.

Given the evidence for the improved accuracy of clinical judgment in general (e.g., Grove et al., 2000) and for structured professional judgment regarding sex offenders specifically (e.g., Hanson, 1999), it seems apparent that a combination of both approaches offers the strongest likelihood of accurate professional judgment. Consequently, it is recommended that risk assessment and prediction involve both structured clinical judgment and actuarial prediction measures. Further, the basis for adjusting actuarial estimates down or up should be explicit, nonduplicative of the items included in the actuarial measures, and rooted in the results of empirical studies.

ELEMENTS AND ISSUES INVOLVED IN THE METHODOLOGY OF RISK PREDICTION

Population Sample Variables

An often neglected issue regarding follow-up studies of reoffending by sex offenders concerns the sample variables in those studies. The available samples possess significant limitations. The studies typically track individuals who have been incarcerated in penal institutions or hospitalized in forensic psychiatric settings. This means that a variety of persons are not included in those samples. As Quinsey et al. (1998) note, samples of offenders are, in effect, often chosen by convenience or availability to the particular investigators.

In addition, there is a problematic bias built into most studies based largely on "sample censoring." This refers to the fact that certain individuals are not released into the community because of the "severity" of their criminal behavior—their frequency of offending or the more heinous nature of their crimes (e.g., murder); such individuals may serve very long sentences or may be hospitalized for an indeterminate length of time. Monahan and Steadman (1994) note that "patients whom clinicians assess as having a very high likelihood of imminent violence are, for that reason, unlikely to be released (and thus are unavailable for community follow-up) . . ." (p. 5). Perhaps the most dangerous sex offenders—serial rapists and child molesters—often escape detection by any authorities and so their reoffending is never captured by existing follow-up studies. *Consequently, many of the most serious offenders have not been available for study.* The "inability" to follow such offenders likely lowers recidivism rates because such persons have lacked the opportunity to commit new sex offenses. In short, a variety of factors affects the likely inclusion of actual sexual offending in studies of reoffending by known offenders. This phenomenon may also dilute the strength of the association between risk factors and true potential for recidivism.

A further issue concerns what is meant by a sample of sex offenders. For example, it is common in sex offender literature to distinguish between groups labeled "rapists" versus "child molesters." Most (if not all) studies of sexual recidivism do not uses diagnostic categories such as paraphilias to distinguish subgroups of sex offenders, but rather simply refer to whether the target victims were (predominantly) non-consenting adults or minors. Available research indicates that a significant percentage of sex offenders may by characterized by coerced sex offenses against both children and adults.

It has generally been considered important to separate so-called "pure incest offenders" from other types of rapists or child molesters because of evidence that their recidivism rates are lower than those of other rapists or child molesters. However, Rice and Harris (2000) have recently demonstrated that father-daughter incest offenders share similar risk factors for sex offense recidivism with other types of child molesters, including deviant sexual arousal to children. In general, it must be noted that a number of the studies used for the most common risk assessment measures refer simply to samples of sex offenders and do not specify the proportion of rapists or extra-familial child molesters contained within their samples.

Predictor Variables—Identifying and Defining Potential Risk Factors

Several issues exist regarding the identification, measurement, and analysis of the potential risk factors to be evaluated with respect to sex offense recidivism. It is critical to point out that the ability of psychology and related fields (1) to measure and quantify variables of interest and (2) to establish their validity is quite limited. For example, it is quite difficult to meaningfully quantify such commonly discussed variables as self-esteem. This is true for most variables or characteristics of interest within the social and behavioral sciences. These limitations on the capacity to measure the various constructs of interest necessarily affect the identification of risk factors and interfere with their relative contribution to predicting particular outcomes.

In addition, most studies of sex offenders are designed retrospectively. Consequently, they must rely on information that may have been collected years previously. Many studies are forced to rely on the available material regarding a particular offender; this creates more studies and results based on those variables of convenience—that is, based on information that is currently available or in a form that can be measured. Of course, available research indicates that *pre-treatment* measures are more highly correlated with violent and sexual recidivism than post-treatment measures (Quinsey et al., 1998).

Moreover, the failure of a particular risk factor to predict violence may be related to whether its predictive value is contingent on the presence of situational factors. It is quite intuitively apparent that a risk factor may not be potentiated unless one or more other factors are also present; risk factors may be context-dependent. Unfortunately, from a statistical perspective, it is extremely difficult to scientifically demonstrate the interaction of multiple variables.

It may also be the case that the predictors of first acts of sexual violence may be somewhat different from those that predict more chronic patterns of offenders. Finally, available studies are typically limited in terms of the number of variables that they are able to consider; thus, the available knowledge of risk factors may be characterized by "impoverished predictor variables" (Monahan & Steadman, 1994).

Criterion Variables—Identifying and Defining Sex Offense Recidivism

The criterion variable in the civil commitment of a PPSP is the likelihood of future sexual offenses or sexual offense recidivism. However, determining the true incidence of sexual offenses is generally quite difficult. Offenses must first be reported, an alleged perpetrator identified and charged, and that offender must be found and arrested. Offenders are typically charged with the most serious alleged offense for a particular alleged victim, even where it is alleged there are multiple criminal sexual acts over a period of time (e.g., repeated sexual perpetration of the same victim to whom the offender has ongoing access and opportunity to offend against), and then the charges must be resolved by the legal system. Problems in identifying sex offenses can occur at many points along this pathway.

Self-Reports and Collateral Sources. Regarding future violent behavior, studies that have obtained apparently genuine self-report of violent behavior indicate that more than 25 percent of "false positive" risk identifications may be true positives when accurate self-report is available (e.g., Klassen & O'Connor, 1987). Similarly, obtaining reports of the number of violent situations by collateral sources of information produced a 26 percent increase in the number of violent incidents (Monahan & Steadman, 1994). As Bonta and Hanson (1994), among others, have noted, when known criminal offenders are questioned about criminal activity for which they were not apprehended, they report an "extraordinary level of crime" (p. 17). Specifically with regard to sex offenders, a study of a sample of such a group seeking treatment found a very high incidence of sex offenses that never resulted in criminal charges. It is estimated that only 10 percent of all actual rapes come to the attention of authorities, while the likelihood of getting arrested for child molestation is approximately only 3 percent (Abel et al., 1987). In other words, multiple sources of evidence indicate that at least 90 percent of sex offenses committed in the community go undetected!

Processes in the Justice System. Further, the criminal justice system obfuscates the true nature of sexual offending by virtue of how an alleged sex offense is charged and by the plea bargain process. When such arrangements are made (ostensibly to protect alleged victims or to relieve the demands on crowded criminal court dockets), there may be several consequences to accurate reports of actual sex crimes. First, a particular offender's record of the number of actual sex offenses committed may be reduced both at the time of charging and in plea bargains. Frequently, multiple acts against a single victim are reduced to a single count of a particular degree of sexual misconduct (e.g., multiple molestations of a particular child are charged as one count for the most serious alleged behavior). Second, in certain cases, the actual sexual nature of the offense may be eliminated (e.g., when an alleged sexual assault is pleaded down to a nonsexual offense such as a simple assault). In addition, it is likely that some percentage of truly guilty offenders are not proved to be guilty in court.

Number of Actual Offenses. Regarding sexual offense recidivism, it is worth emphasizing that determining the rate of actual offenses committed by identified sexual offenders is even more problematic. To be forthright and honest about the actual number of such offenses places the offender at risk of more extensive incarceration or institutionalization. The self-report of sex offenders, particularly in adversarial proceedings, is highly problematic and subject to gross dissimulation regarding both proximal and distal sexual offenses (Sewell & Salekin, 1997). Marshall and Barbaree (1989) note that relying on the self-report of sex offenders regarding later offenses is unwise because such reports are so unreliable when compared to other data sources.

Abel and Rouleau (1990) cite a unique study in which sexual offenders voluntarily sought assessment for their paraphilias and in which their anonymity was guarded by a Federal Certificate of Confidentiality. The investigators determined that in the criminal justice system, offenders report only *5 percent* of the sex crimes that they admit to within the mental health system. Further, Abel and Osborn (1992) report in a controlled study that 62 percent of paraphilics confronted with their physiologic measurements admitted to paraphilic diagnoses that they had previously denied or kept hidden. Indeed, the self-report of new offenses by released offenders appears extremely limited. Since original records are often not available to evaluators, an offender's dissimulated self-report regarding his sexual history may become memorialized into official records as "fact." Where the only source of information in a record regarding a potential past offense is the offender himself, then as in any other forensic context, it must be regarded with great scrutiny.

Police and Parole Office Records. The most conservative measure of recidivism is the number of reconvictions for sexual offenses relative to a judicial determination of an individual's responsibility for a particular offense(s). However, a person who has actually committed a sexual offense will not necessarily receive a conviction for such an offense. Marshall and Barbaree (1989) point out that "official" police records of charges indicate a rate of reoffending 42 percent less than that obtained via "unofficial" records (e.g., reports to child protection or the police). Similarly, Marques et al. (1994) show that the review of parole office records produced a 33 percent increase in estimates of the number of serious crimes committed by sex offenders. Further, it is possible that particularly driven or compulsive sex offenders may be arrested at earlier stages of their offense chain (e.g., by exhibiting their genitals to children or abducting adult victims); consequently, the official charge may be a nonsexual charge or for a lesser sexual offense (e.g., a "hands-off" offense).

Given the inaccuracy of official and offender-reported past and later sexual offending, it has been argued that using arrests or charges (as opposed to convictions) for any sexual offense may provide a better estimate of true sex offense recidivism. There is empirical support for the association between the number of arrests for sexual offenses and sexual reoffending (Hanson & Bussiere, 1998; Hanson, 1999); in fact, certain studies indicate a stronger relationship between prior criminal *charges* and violent recidivism than criminal *convictions* (Quinsey et al., 1998). Further, Quinsey et al. (1998) argue that measuring general violent recidivism provides a more accurate measure of sex offense recidivism, particularly given the nature of plea bargains. They state, "Although overinclusive, violent recidivism is likely to capture significantly more sexual reoffenses than the more commonly used sexual recidivism definition" (p. 129).

No Correlation Between Variable and Potential Offense. In short, there will be unavoidable error in the measurement of sexual offenses, even relative to the broader category of violent offenses. This fact affects the utility and strength of the relationship between a history of sexual offenses and later offenses as well as the relationship between any other variable or factor and future sex offenses. Consequently, there will always be an upper limit to the degree of possible improvement in predictive accuracy.

Finally, it is worth noting that the available studies simply provide estimated rates for some violent or sexual recidivism. That is, current studies and available methods provide no information as to whether the potential future offense will be similar to past offenses or if available information indicates that an individual's trajectory of sexual violence may be changing. It is a common finding that many sex offenders are heterogeneous and have committed multiple types of offenses in the past. Further, as laws increasingly provide for the possibility of lengthy sentences for additional sex offenses or reconvictions, the possibility of escalation to more extreme violence (e.g., sexual homicide) must be considered. That is, the possibility of longer sentences for additional sex offenses raises the concern that repeat offenders may be more likely to kill their victims to reduce the possibility of being identified as the perpetrator.

Length of Follow-Up Period

Still another factor that affects the recidivism rate is the length of the follow-up period. Longer follow-up periods provide greater "opportunity" for released offenders to potentially commit further crimes. Unfortunately, most available studies of recidivism of sex offenders have relied on relatively short follow-up periods. It has been empirically demonstrated that the longer the opportunity to recidivate, the greater the rate of recidivism among sex offenders. Further, simply calculating the percentage of individuals who reoffend during a specified study period actually *underestimates* the rate of recidivism because it does not factor in the time available for an individual to have potentially committed a new offense (Prentky et al., 1997b).

Survival Analysis. Most studies of recidivism have not controlled for the relative opportunity to commit offenses among offenders who were studied; obviously, it is most useful to obtain information regarding the amount of time that each offender was in the community and thus able to reoffend. Survival analysis is a type of statistical procedure that allows for the estimation of risk (year-by-year recidivism rates) across a range of follow-up periods (e.g., samples in which offenders have been in the community for various lengths of time) and provides recidivism rates on a year-by-year basis. Survival analysis calculates the probability of recidivism for each time period given that an offender has not yet offended; once offenders recidivate, they are removed from the analysis of subsequent time periods. Thus, Prentky et al. (1997b) found that just calculating a simple percentage of recidivism (e.g., not using survival analysis) would result in significant under-estimations of sexual reoffending (e.g., 20 percent for child molesters and 13 percent for rapists).

Types of Sex Offenders. Despite the lack of survival analysis, several studies have reported particularly higher rates of recidivism among child molesters. Rice et al. (1991) found of their subjects who were child molesters that in only a six-year follow-up period, 31 percent were convicted of a new sex offense, 43 percent committed a violent or sexual offense, and 58 percent were arrested for some offense or returned to an institution. Hanson et al. (1993) found that 42 percent of their sample of child molesters were eventually reconvicted for sexual crimes, violent crimes, or both; the rate of reconviction was highest within five years of release. Quinsey et al. (1995) found that over almost five years, 28 percent of sex offenders were convicted of a new sex offense and 40 percent were arrested, convicted, or returned to the psychiatric facility for a new violent (including sexual) offense. However, rapists were more likely to recidivate in this study relative to child molesters.

Increased Recidivism With Increased Follow-Up Period. Clearly, existing data reveal increasing recidivism over an extended follow-up period, particularly for untreated child molesters (Barbaree & Marshall, 1988). Romero and Williams (1985) found that 27 percent of their sample were not identified as beginning to recidivate until four years or more after their release from prison. Marshall et al. (1991) concluded that "some untreated child molesters and rapists do not reoffend until more than 20 years after release from prison" (p. 468). In Hanson et al.'s (1993) study, 10 percent of the sample were reconvicted of additional sexual offenses as long as ten to thirty-one years postrelease. As Hanson et al. state, "Our results support previous research that child molesters are at risk for reoffending for many years. . . . The greatest risk appears to be the first 5–10 years, but child molesters appear to be at significant risk for reoffending throughout their life" (p. 650).

Using survival analysis, Prentky et al. (1997a) examined the cumulative recidivism rates for child molesters over a twenty-five-year period; 52 percent of the child molesters followed in the study eventually were arrested for another sexual offense. Prentky et al. (1997b) suggest that the failure rate for charges that they report is comparable to the figures presented by Hanson et al. for reconvictions, indicating that Hanson's rates are underestimates of actual sexual recidivism by child molesters. Moreover, in contrast to Hanson et al., Prentky et al. (1997b) found that the failure rate for child molesters was stable (the same rate) for the third to fifteenth year of the twenty-five year follow-up.

Regarding rapists, Rice et al. (1990) report that 28 percent of rapists released from a maximum-security psychiatric hospital over a forty-six-month follow-up period were convicted for a sexual offense, and 43 percent were convicted for some type of violent offense. This study too found higher recidivism rates for rapists than reported in previous reviews and concluded that "a high proportion will reoffend." Marques et al. (1994) found that 28 percent of rapists who did not receive treatment but had expressed interest in such treatment committed a new sex offense within three years of follow-up. Quinsey et al. (1995) report that over a nearly five-year period, rapists showed no deceleration in the rate of recidivism over time and were actually characterized by a higher rate of recidivism than child molesters (despite a shorter follow-up period). Prentky et al. (1997b) used survival analysis to identify a failure rate for sexual offense recidivism of 39 percent over a twenty-five-year period among released rapists (as defined by charges). Moreover, they found that the failure rate for rapists was stable (the same rate) for the third to fifteenth year of the twenty-five-year follow-up.

Thus, although Beck and Shipley (1989) found in a study of general recidivism of convicted felons that rearrest rates in general declined with age, the results of several studies have found both that pedophilic behavior may continue into the late decades of life and that rapists do not always cease sexual offending with increasing age.

The Base Rate of Sexual Offense Recidivism

The so-called base rate concerns the proportion of the sample(s) that have the expected characteristic (e.g., a new sexual offense). Base rates of recidivism are derived by follow-up studies of offenders to determine the rates of recidivism among the group of offenders or among particular subgroups of such offenders. The base rate is the likelihood or probability that a particular sexual offender will reoffend in a sexual manner within some period of time. As noted earlier, the base rate of the behavior being predicted has significant implications for prediction methods, with lower base rates leading to higher error rates. Further, the base rate is highly influenced by the length of time over which a sample is studied. Offenders in such studies are those deemed fit to be released from penal or forensic psychiatric institutions, based on either the end of their sentence or a larger set of factors.

Quinsey et al. (1998) note that base rates close to .50 offer optimal opportunities to discover predictors of violent behavior. The authors further note that higher base rates inevitably occur in institutions with stable selection ratios and even slightly better-than-chance accuracy of release decisions. Doren (1998), in a discussion of base rates and predictions of sex offender recidivism, provides a review of a number of factors that he argues have produced underestimates of base rates for recidivism in child molesters and rapists. In particular, he compared studies of sex offense recidivism based on the studies' definition of the criterion variables (charge, rearrest, or reconviction) and length of follow-up and attempts to show that the result of these studies largely converge. Doren concludes: "The overall conservative approximation for the long-term sexual recidivism base rates for child molesters and rapists were 52% and 39%, respectively" (p. 108). On this basis, he opines that these base rates demonstrate that sexual violence is not a rare event but rather in the mid-range of probability.

Doren also points out that a high degree of selectivity (1 to 12 percent) exists among state screening systems for referring repeat sex offenders for consideration for civil commitment. PPSPs are individuals who typically have been screened and determined to possess certain characteristics associated with a greater likelihood of future reoffense. By definition they are characterized by some combination of factors that indicates elevated risk for future sexual violence. Given the base rates for sexual reoffending for all incarcerated sex offenders and the selectivity of referral rates for potential civil commitments, it seems likely that the base rate for the selected group would be higher than for the average sex offender. Using this reasoning, Doren argues that *many* actual sexual recidivists (true positives) will be inaccurately predicted as nonrecidivists:

> In this scenario, the over-prediction of recidivism would equal zero while the under-prediction of recidivism would be very great . . . there is a very significant *under-prediction* of sexual predation when it comes to the commitment of sexual offenders within the sexual predator laws as they are currently implemented. (p. 109–110)

Doren claims that given the information currently known regarding risk factors for sexual reconvictions within a five-year period, the prediction could reasonably be made that a person with a significant number of identified risk factors will likely be reconvicted of a sexual offense within five years post-incarceration.

Overall, the strong consensus is that specifically regarding sex offense recidivism, currently available figures concerning base rates are regarded as underestimates by most mental health professionals. Brooks (1992) has argued the behavior of violent sex offenders tends to be more predictable than that of mentally ill persons in general. Certainly, the above-noted figures for recidivism for rapists and child molesters suggest that the base rate for later sex offending is much higher than the rate of criminal or violent behavior in the general public or among the mentally ill.

OBTAINING INFORMATION FOR RISK ASSESSMENT

A number of authors (see Boer et al., 1997a; 1997b; Hoberman, 1999) have advocated principles and practices in conducting risk assessment for sexual violence. Such assessments should collect information about multiple domains of an individual's functioning given the heterogeneity and complexity of sex offenders and sexual offending. Multiple methods (record review, psychological tests, structured interviews, and the like) should be used to gather data regarding the individual. Self-report is most useful as a source of particular clinical rating schemes and as a potential indicator of change; however, as in any forensic context, self-report must be carefully evaluated, particularly if there is a lack of measure of social desirability and other measures of potential validity.

Third-party or collateral sources are particularly useful. It is almost always more valuable to rely on such sources of information compared to an offender's self-report or its archival derivatives. The veracity or accuracy of all information obtained should be explicitly evaluated. In addition, risk assessments should attempt to gather information regarding both static/historical and dynamic factors potentially related to future sexual violence.

INDIVIDUAL AND COMBINATIONS OF RISK FACTORS THAT DIFFERENTIATE RECIDIVISTS

As indicated above, guided professional judgment or adjusted actuarial judgments should rely on those risk factors for sexual recidivism that are rationally or empirically justified. It is, of course, assumed that persons who agree to serve as evaluators or expert witnesses in civil commitment procedures of PPSPs are well acquainted with the extensive recent literature regarding risk factors for violent and sexual recidivism. The following review is therefore intentionally brief.

Static and Historical Factors

Static or historical risk factors indicate fixed attributes and mark long-term propensities to engage in criminal behavior. Regarding predictions of future violence, Mossman (1994) showed that past behavior is a particularly good predictor on its own, with average accuracy of predictions higher for past behavior alone than for subjective clinical judgments. Static and historical risk factors are limited, however, because they are enduring characteristics of a particular individual and, therefore, cannot represent the individual's potential changes that may lower his relative risk of recidivism.

In terms of specific risk factors for recidivism, McGrath (1991) summarized the essential risk factors identified by then-existing research studies and remarked that the consistency with which various risk factors emerge in this literature is particularly noteworthy. He identified such factors as:

- Denial of offenses
- Type of sexual offense
- Multiple paraphilias
- Criminality
- Deviant sexual arousal pattern
- Impulsivity
- Alcohol abuse
- Psychopathology
- Use of force
- Social support
- Employment status
- Offender age for rapists
- Grooming or attack behavior
- Victim characteristics
- Length of time at risk

Research over the past ten years has provided additional and converging empirical support for the majority of the risk factors McGrath has identified.

Deviancy and Psychopathy

Rice et al. (1991) found that offenders' *self*-report of their arousal preferences was not predictive of reconviction for child molesters; however, phallometrically measured deviant arousal was a strong predictor. Rice et al. (1990) reported that higher scores on the Psychopathy Checklist (PCL) were one of the two best predictors of which rapists reoffended, the other being phallometrically measured sexual interest in non-sexual violence. Rice et al. (1991) found that subjects convicted of a new sex offense had previously committed more sex offenses, had been admitted to correctional institutions more frequently, were more likely to have been diagnosed as personality disordered, and had shown more inappropriate sexual preferences. Quinsey et al. (1995) found psychopathy, measures of previous criminal history, and phallometric indexes of deviant sexual arousal to be useful predictors of recidivism among sex offenders. Rice and Harris (1997) showed that sexual recidivism rates for sex offenders were substantially higher among identified psychopaths; the combination of deviant sexual arousal and psychopathy produced the most pronounced rates for sexual recidivism.

Quinsey et al. (1995) present a description of a risk assessment procedure (e.g., stepwise multiple regression) developed specifically for sex offenders. The variables included for study were:

- Prior convictions for sex offenses
- Prior violent convictions
- Never married
- Previous child victim
- Sexual deviance index
- Previous admissions to corrections
- Previous male victim
- Previous admissions to their particular forensic/correctional facility
- Previous female victim
- The PCL
- Number of male victims
- Prior convictions for other offenses
- Previous adult victim

Using a prediction equation based on weighted values assigned to each of these factors, Quinsey et al. were able to obtain 77 percent correct classifications regarding true sexual recidivists and nonrecidivists. The probability of sexual reoffending was found to be a linear function of the number of predictors, with persons with a large number of predictors reoffending at a rate of nearly 80 percent.

Meta-Analysis

A meta-analysis is a set of statistical procedures that allow investigators to combine or compare the results from different studies. This type of comparison, in turn, permits statistically derived conclusions about the strength of association between a particular characteristic and an outcome. In their meta-analysis of sixty-nine potential predictors of sex offense recidivism involving multiple studies with a total of nearly

29,000 sex offenders, Hanson and Bussière (1998) identify the most reliable predictors of such recidivism across studies (based on at least five studies and an average correlation with sex offense recidivism greater than .10) as follows:

- Any deviant sexual preferences (r = .22)
- Prior sexual offenses (r = .19)
- Failure to complete treatment (r = .17)
- Anti-social personality disorder/psychopathy (r = .14)
- Any prior offenses (r = .13)
- Younger age (r = .13)
- Never married (r = .11)
- Any unrelated victims (r = .11)
- Any male child victims (r = .11)

Factors unrelated to future sexual reoffending were low self-esteem, denial of offending, or a history of sexual abuse as a child. Summarizing their findings, Hanson and Bussière (1998) demonstrate that sexual offense recidivism is best predicted by sexual deviancy variables (deviant sexual interests and victim choices such as boys or strangers, prior sexual offenses), general criminological factors (younger age, total prior offenses), and failure to complete treatment. Personality disorders were also related to sexual recidivism, particularly antisocial personality disorder (ASPD).

Prentky et al. (1997a) identify three risk factors associated with recidivism among extra-familial child molesters: a degree of sexual preoccupation with children, more paraphilias, and number of prior sexual offenses. These three factors predicted a high percentage of child molesters who committed future offenses when released from a treatment center for sexually dangerous persons. Proulx et al.'s (1997) findings show that child molesters reconvicted for a sexual offense have higher pedophilic indices, have more previous sexual charges, are younger, more frequently have male victims, more frequently have extrafamilial victims, and are more likely to live alone. Their findings also show that rapists reconvicted of a sexual offense are younger and have more previous convictions.

Dynamic Risk Factors

Investigators have recently begun to examine and consider the role of potentially dynamic risk factors in the prediction of future sexual and other violence. Dynamic characteristics have the potential of changing or of being modified (i.e., in response to interventions) and, when changed, may be associated with related changes in relative probability of recidivism. Hanson (1999) and Hanson and Harris (1998; 2000) distinguish two types of dynamic risk factors:

- *Stable risk factors*—Stable dynamic risk factors are viewed as states that have the potential to change but that typically endure for long periods of time (e.g., deviant sexual preferences, alcoholism).

- *Acute risk factors*—Acute dynamic risk factors are viewed as states that may change quickly, such as sexual arousal or intoxication, that immediately precede sexual offenses.

However, very little information exists regarding such factors. Gendreau et al. (1996) found in their meta-analysis that dynamic factors predicted general criminal recidivism as well as or better than static risk factors. Hanson and Harris (2000) compared 208 sexual offense recidivists who committed a sex offense while on community supervision with 201 nonrecidivists and found that the two groups were matched on victim type, criminal history, and other variables. They collected information after the recidivists had reoffended from file reviews and interviews with community supervision officers, and they found substantial differences between the two groups. The recidivists were characterized by:

- Poor social supports;
- Attitudes tolerant of sexual assault (including low remorse for victims and feelings of entitlement to act on sexual urges);
- Antisocial lifestyles;
- Poor self-management strategies (e.g., they viewed themselves as posing little risk for new offenses, took few precautions to avoid high-risk situations, and engaged in socially deviant sexual activities); and
- Poor cooperation with supervision and increased anger and subjective distress just before reoffending.

The recidivists were also more likely to be unemployed and have substance abuse problems. In general, shortly before reoffending, they were viewed as demonstrating increased acute maladjustments of the types listed above. Unfortunately, the relative utility of these results is qualified by the fact that they were obtained postdictively (and were not the result of a true prospective study) and have yet to be cross-validated.

Two General Types of Risk Factors

Overall, the risk factors for sexual reoffending can be seen as being of two types. The first involves psychopathy, antisocial personality characteristics and/or criminal history. The second involves deviant sexual arousal, sex offense history and/or sex offense-permissive cognitions. As Hanson (1999) points out, deviant sexual arousal can be identified and assessed by self-report, offense history, or phallometric assessment; he notes that repeatedly selecting non-normative or unusual sexual targets or repeatedly engaging in deviant sexual activities can serve as suggestions of deviant sexual interests.

Simply because a sex offender may not show strong characteristics of one type of risk does not place him at low risk overall; certain child molesters are primes examples of this. As a group, child molesters tend to score lower on the PCL-R and/or show low rates of general criminal history—the prevalence of relative psychopathy is lower among child molesters than among rapists. However, since a child molester may show extremely high levels of deviant sexual arousal (e.g., the respondent Hendricks in *Kansas v. Hendricks*, 117 S. Ct. 2072 (1997)), he may still carry an elevated risk of reoffending.

SPECIFIC RISK ASSESSMENT MEASURES AND GUIDELINES

The Psychopathy Checklist—Revised

The Psychopathy Checklist—Revised (PCL-R) (Hare, 1991) is a research-based, clinical rating scale designed to assess psychopathy, defined as a constellation of affective, interpersonal, and lifestyle characteristics that have been shown to predispose individuals toward aggression and violence. Psychopaths are viewed as individuals who are (relatively speaking) interpersonally manipulative and exploitative; callous, with shallow, poorly integrated affective experiences; and impulsive, typically disliking social rules and conventions. The PCL-R rates an individual for twenty areas according to the extent ("none," "some," "very") that the particular domain applies to the person being rated. Total scores reflect the degree to which the respondent matches the "prototypical psychopath." The administration of the PCL-R requires considerable training, effort, and expertise, as evaluators must make clinical judgments regarding the extent to which the person being evaluated manifests particular traits.

Inter-Rater Reliability. The violence of persons classified as psychopaths tends to be more instrumental, dispassionate, and predatory than that of other offenders; the propensity toward such instrumental violence appears to decrease very little with age (Hare, 1999). The PCL-R has been demonstrated in multiple investigations to be a reliable and valid instrument (Hare, 1991). In particular, inter-rater reliability for the total twenty items included in PCL-R is .83; consequently, despite being a instrument rated according to clinical judgment it is highly likely that two independent evaluators will agree on total PCL-R scores approximately 80 percent of the time. Hare (1998) states that the available evidence indicates that two independent raters will almost always rate an individual similarly. The PCL-R's standard error of measurement, a variant of the standard deviation, is 3.25. According to Hare (1997), the mean scores for prison inmates is approximately 2, while that for the general population of males is 6. The PCL-R has been studied for its ability to predict future violent behavior. Using a dichotomous or categorical cutoff score of 30 or more on the PCL-R alone produced a sensitivity of .72 and a specificity of .93 (Hare, 1991); the positive predictive power was .86 and the negative predictive power was .84.

Meta-Analysis. In their meta-analysis of studies involving the PCL and PCL-R, Salekin et al. (1996) demonstrate that aggregating the mean "effect size" across eighteen studies using the PCL-R or its earlier version, the PCL produces an overall mean effect size of .79 for violent recidivism and a mean effect size of .55 for general recidivism. As Salekin et al. note, the classification rates derived from the research on the PCL/PCL-R are "unprecedented in predictions of dangerousness." They note that the mean Negative Predictive Power across studies is .59, meaning that 41 percent of non-violent reoffenders were incorrectly classified as violent; but they fail to point out that most of the studies they reviewed looked at short and moderate lengths of time for potential recidivism. Longer periods of follow-up would likely produce both higher rates of violent recidivism and heightened predictive accuracy. Further, the Salekin et al. meta-analysis includes studies that used overlapping and nonindependent samples.

More recently, Hemphill et al. (1998a; 1998b) published a meta-analysis of the PCL-R and its relationship to recidivism that relies only on predictive studies and calculated effect sizes from independent samples of subjects. For example, for single databases reanalyzed several times, they selected only one statistical value per database based on the largest sample size for the particular types of recidivism. Results demonstrate that the PCL-R was consistently among the best predictors of recidivism, whether used as a continuous or as a categorical measure. In fact, surprisingly, survival analyses for "medium" and "high" PCL-R groups are not clearly differentiated from one another; both of these groups show similar recidivism rates and patterns. Hemphill and his colleagues found the average correlation between the PCL-R and violent recidivism and sexual recidivism to be .27 and .23, respectively, across combined samples of more than 1300 individuals. The PCL-R score was typically the strongest (or one of the strongest predictors) of violent and sexual recidivism.

The Hemphill et al. study further shows that in the first year of release from prison, psychopaths are three times more likely to reoffend in general and four times more likely to reoffend in a violent manner. The authors found that both PCL-R factors contribute equally to the prediction of violent recidivism and that the PCL-R routinely adds incremental validity to predictions of recidivism—for example, it makes a significant contribution above and beyond other variables studied such as criminal history and personality disorder diagnoses. The study also demonstrates that PCL-R scores are more strongly associated with violent recidivism than actuarial risk scales designed specifically to predict reoffending.

Psychopathy and Recidivism. Serin and Amos (1995) found that psychopaths reoffend significantly sooner on release from incarceration and are substantially more likely to recidivate in a violent manner. In a study of rapists and child molesters, Quinsey et al. (1995) found that within six years of release from prison, more than 80 percent of psychopaths (versus 20 percent of nonpsychopaths) had violently recidivated and that many of their offenses were sexual in nature. Rice and Harris (1997) found that violent recidivism rates for five years after release were 85 percent for persons classified as psychopaths by record review (e.g., cutoff score of 25) based on survival analysis; this rate was approximately 50 percent higher than for nonpsychopaths. A combination of higher PCL-R scores and deviant sexual arousal results in substantially faster and higher rates of sexual reoffending; sexual recidivism per survival analysis was approximately 60 percent for this group.

PCL Screening Version. The PCL-SV (Hart et al., 1995) was originally developed for use in a large risk assessment study; it is an abbreviated form of the PCL-R that consists of twelve instead of twenty items. There is rapidly accumulating evidence for this instrument's construct validity, including its ability to predict aggression and violence in offenders and civil psychiatric patients (Hare, 1999). Cooke et al. (1999) note that the PCL-SV has structural properties very similar to the PCL-R and that a total score can be considered a metrically equivalent measure of the construct of psychopathy. This study finds that the interpersonal and affective features (Part 1) are more strongly related to the construct of psychopathy. Douglas et al. (1997) show that a median split for PCL-SV scores in a sample of civil commitment patients produces results showing that psychopathic patients are approximately ten times more likely to be arrested for a violent offense.

Misuse of PCL-R. Hare (1998) calls attention to the potential misuse of the PCL-R, as virtually any licensed mental health professional can purchase a copy of it. Hare identifies the most important issues regarding the unprofessional use of the PCL-R as those concerning individuals who:

- Lack professional and legal qualifications to conduct psychological assessments;
- Lack adequate training and experience in the use of the PCL-R; and
- Fail to adhere to accepted professional standards for test administration and interpretation.

It appears common that some professionals represent their competency to administer the test based solely on having attended a workshop on psychopathy or psychopathic personality or only having read the manual that accompanies the test. Hare states that these types of workshops typically do not qualify as "appropriate training" (Hare, 2000). Both the Association for the Treatment of Sexual Abusers (ATSA) and Dr. Hare, the developer of the instrument, strongly recommend that professionals intending to use the PCL-R attend one of the authorized, formal, three-day training workshop led by Dr. Hare and/or selected colleagues. In addition, after the workshop, evaluators can register to complete a certification process that involves rating eight videotaped practice cases.

The ASSESS-LIST

As part of the development of the Violence Prediction Scheme (Webster et al., 1994) (see below), a clinically determined mnemonic device called the ASSESS-LIST was produced that covers ten areas "often considered important by experienced forensic clinicians." These areas are:

Antecedent history
Self-presentation
Social and psychosocial adjustment
Expectations
Symptoms
Supervision
Life factors
Institutional behavior
Sexual adjustment
Treatment progress

Violence Risk Appraisal Guide (VRAG)

Based on an extensive study of "mentally disordered offenders" in Canada, Harris et al. (1993) developed an actuarial instrument to measure violent recidivism, the Violence Risk Appraisal Guide (VRAG). The development and scoring of the VRAG is described in *The Violence Prediction Scheme* by Webster et al. (1994), by Rice (1997), and most recently by Quinsey et al. (1998). The primary sample of study consisted of 685 Canadian mentally disordered males, of whom 618 had an opportunity to recidivate. The term "mentally disordered" refers to a heterogeneous group of individuals that includes:

- Offenders referred by the courts for psychiatric evaluation prior to standing trial for criminal charges;

- Mentally ill criminal offenders and mentally ill patients under civil commitment referred from other less secure penal and psychiatric institutions;

- Patients originally detained as not criminally responsible on account of mental disorder; and

- A more recent group of individuals referred by the courts under civil commitment after their criminal sentences had expired.

As Quinsey et al.(1998) state, "The demographic data reveal that the admission population strongly resembles that of a prison, whereas the cross-sectional population comprises a more severely mentally disordered group" (p. 23). It is worth noting that the literature on the development of the VRAG does not specify the proportion of rapists or extra-familial child molesters contained within the samples. Currently, data is available regarding seven- and ten-year follow-up periods.

The VRAG was developed with an examination of the univariate relationship between fifty potential risk factors and any new criminal charge (rearrest) for a violent offense. Where variables were highly inter-correlated with one another, the one(s) with lower correlations with violent recidivism were dropped. The investigators used stepwise multiple regression to identify variables that added independently to the prediction of violent recidivism. They then considered nineteen variables that were correlated with such charges in at least three out of five sub-samples considered. A final stepwise multiple regression analysis identified twelve variables for the final instrument, the VRAG. Listed in order of their strength of association with recidivism, these composite variablies are:

- PCL-R score
- Elementary school maladjustment
- Younger age at index offense
- Diagnosis of personality disorder
- Separation from biological parents prior to age sixteen
- Failure on prior conditional release
- Criminal history for property offenses

- Marital status (e.g., never married)
- Lack of a diagnosis of schizophrenia
- Decreased victim injury in index offense
- History of alcohol abuse
- Male victim in index offense

Harris et al. accorded each of these variables a weight for specified differences in association with the recidivism rate from the mean recidivism rate. Specifically, they used a modified Nufield (1982) procedure as the initial step in selecting and scoring of each variable. Item levels with reoffense rates 5 percent greater than the baseline were scored +1 for each 5 percent increment and vice versa. The scores obtained by adding the weighted values for each item were then divided into nine equal-size steps or "bins"; persons with scores at the upper end of the steps are highly likely to reoffend.

The variable accounting for the greatest variance in accurate prediction was the PCL (the earlier version of the PCL-R based on clinical judgments/ratings); other items such as elementary school maladjustment also require clinical judgment to rate. As Litwack and Schlesinger (1999) state, "Indeed, *the VRAG has its predictive power in large part because it takes 'clinical' variables and assessments into account*" (p. 189, emphasis in original). While certain variables require considerable effort or expertise to rate, Webster et al. (1994) demonstrate that the VRAG retains its predictive power even when those items more difficult to rate are excluded. According to Wagner et al. (2000), the VRAG's standard error of measurement is 4.1.

Violent Behavior Predictions. The VRAG significantly predicts violent behavior in mentally disordered offenders. Persons with more of the characteristics measured by the VRAG generally have approximately twice the likelihood of future violence (Harris et al., 1993). Applying receiver operating characteristic (ROC) analysis (see earlier discussion) to the VRAG, Rice and Harris (1995) identified a large effect size for prediction, thus obtaining even greater accuracy in predicting violent behavior. Over a ten-year follow-up, they found that the base rate of severe violent recidivism for violent offenders was 29 percent compared to 57 percent for the subsample of sex offenders. In a subsequent study that attempted to cross-validate the VRAG, Rice and Harris (1997) examined child molesters and rapists followed over a period averaging ten years. The base rate of sexual recidivism was 35 percent. The VRAG identified those at greatest risk of violent recidivism; the prediction of specifically sexual recidivism was poorer than that of more general violent recidivism. The VRAG apparently predicts violent recidivism, inclusive of sex offense recidivism, much better than it predicts specific sex offense recidivism [$r = .47$ (violent recidivism) $> r = .20$ (sex offense recidivism].

Rice (1997) reports, "The correlation between the scores on the VRAG and violent recidivism was .44 and, choosing the 80th percentile of risk scores as a cutoff, classification accuracy was 74%, with a sensitivity of .40 and a specificity of .88" (p. 416). Rice and Harris (1997) found that the VRAG predicts violent recidivism in a replication sample of sex offenders; specifically, they found a correlation of .47 between VRAG scores and such recidivism and the AUC of the ROC of .77.

Hanson and Harris (2000) show that VRAG scores differentiated well between sex offenders who did reoffend and those who did not. Rice (1999) reports that the VRAG predicted violent recidivism in a new sample of 530 sex offenders released from incarceration or from forensic hospitals. Rice and Harris (2000) show that the VRAG predicted sexual recidivism among incestuous offenders (ROC area = .65) and among a larger group of child molesters (ROC area = .81).

The VRAG demonstrates the largest effect size for violent recidivism reported to date. It has been cross-validated with different and heterogeneous samples and the results have been replicated by other investigators. As Monahan (1995) states, "[F]or use with male patients with histories of serious violence, the [VRAG] is so far superior to anything previously available that not to seriously consider its use . . . would be a difficult choice to justify" (p.447).

Limitations. It should be noted that all of these studies by Rice et al. and their colleagues were conducted in Canada with offenders released from specific psychiatric institution (namely patients from Oak Ridge in Pentaguishene). Thus, individuals who were sentenced as dangerous offenders under Canadian criminal law were not necessarily among those individuals released into the community; most of the research with this instrument represents a classic example of sample censoring. As a result, those persons already deemed most likely to reoffend (and, consequently, with perhaps the greatest risk of reoffending), were not released into the community. This state of affairs has the effect of decreasing the likely base rate of reoffense and the resultant predictive accuracy. Quinsey and Maguire (1986, cited in Litwack & Schlesinger, 1999) studied a group of long-term forensic psychiatric patients who had been assigned "maximal dangerousness ratings" and who were eventually released for a variety of reasons. Within a "very short follow-up period . . . these results unambiguously confirm the dangerousness of this group" (pp. 168, 184). Consequently, the base rates and results of the VRAG should be regarded as conservative and as representing an underestimate of the accuracy of prediction.

The substantial resource requirements of the VRAG can also be considered a limitation. It requires professionally trained interviewers, careful and detailed file review, and access to information about the offender's childhood particularly to rate the PCL-R. Quinsey et al. (1998) report on the use of an alternate measure to "substitute" for the PCL-R, the Child and Adolescent Taxon Scale (CATS). Using the CATS instead of the PCL-R resulted in nearly identical predictive accuracy (AUC of the ROC = .75); VRAG scores calculated with the PCL-R and the CATS correlated .98, demonstrating that they appear virtually identical. Similarly, Looman (2000) found that the correlation between VRAG scores calculated with the PCL-R and the CATS showed a correlation of .93.

Minnesota Sex Offender Screening Tool (MnSOST)

In response to a Minnesota legislature mandate in 1991, the state Department of Corrections created a task force and began to develop an instrument for screening inmates incarcerated for sexual offenses to determine their relative risk for reoffending. This information was to be used to classify inmates into one of three levels of risk in order to identify sex offenders considered to pose the highest risk to the public. In particular, those inmates who received higher scores were to be considered for community notification on their release from prison.

As described by Huot (1999), primary considerations in the process of developing this instrument included that the items (1) be based on the extant research literature and the offenders' objective behavior and (2) lend themselves to high reliability among the DOC case managers who would be making the initial ratings on the instrument. Further, "The work group did not include items from studies focusing on information about sex offenders that could not realistically be obtained and used by correctional staff for all sex offenders, even if the relationship was known to be strong (e.g., through results from the plethysmograph testing)" (p. 6-4, Huot, 1999). The risk factors identified as having the highest degree of empirical support were (1) history of prior sexual offenses and prior nonsexual offenses, (2) number of sex offense victims, (3) presence of multiple paraphilias, (4) chemical dependency, and (5) certain victim characteristics. The original instrument consisted of fourteen items assigned weights based on clinical judgment and was known as the Psychopathic Personality Screen Test (PPST).

The original reliability and validity study was conducted using all sex offenders released in 1988. Files of these former inmates were recreated solely with information that would have been available to case managers at the time of the inmates' release. Inter-rater reliability, determined by the intra-class correlation coefficient, was .87. The criterion or outcome variable was rearrest for a "hands-on" sex offense within a five-year follow-up period. The task force identified three groups of inmates: offenders arrested for a sex offense subsequent to their release, offenders arrested for a non-sex offense subsequent to their release, and offenders for whom there was no record of any arrest for an offense subsequent to their release. The results indicated that inmates with new arrests for sex offenses had higher scores on the PPST. The base rate for the total sample for rearrest for a sex offense was 35 percent; however, for those offenders who were arrested for a sex offense subsequent to their release and who had scores greater than a cut point of 40, the rate of such rearrest was 78 percent.

Investigators eventually added additional items to the PPST (for a total of twenty-one items) and the measure was later relabeled the Minnesota Sex Offender Screening Tool (abbreviated as the MnSOST) (per Huot, 1999) or the MnSOST-Research Edition (per Epperson et al., 1999a). A second reliability and validity study was conducted starting in 1993 and reported by Epperson et al. (1995). This study involved 256 sex offenders divided into three groups. The first two groups included sex offenders released in 1988 (1) with no known arrest and who had been at risk for five years or (2) with a known arrest for a non-sex offense. However, the third group contained all sex offenders released since 1988 (i.e., 1988–1993) who were known to have been rearrested for a new sex offense. This group constituted an "enriched" or over-sample of sex offense reoffenders and its sex offense rearrest rate was 41 percent, which was not considered to represent the true base rate of the population of released sex offenders. This decision was apparently made in an attempt to maximize predictive accuracy. However, as Hanson (1997) points out, it is difficult to tell how well the MnSOST would predict recidivism given the much lower base rates found in the naturalistic contexts; he notes that it would be difficult to translate MnSOST scores into recidivism rates because the study oversampled recidivists to create artificially high base rates. Further, it is not clear as to the length of time individuals were at risk in the community before being arrested for a sex offense.

Inter-rater reliability, as determined by the intra-class correlation coefficient, was .73. The results indicated that inmates with new arrests for sex offenses had higher scores on the MnSOST. Those offenders who were arrested for a sex offense subsequent to their release and who had scores greater than a cut point of 47 (based on relative improvement over chance) showed a rate of subsequent rearrest of 62 percent. Of those released sex offenders, forty-one of the sixty-six who scored over 47 subsequently were rearrested for a sex offense. It was reported that the scale correlated .27 with sex offense rearrest; however, many of the individual MnSOST items did not correlate significantly with sexual recidivism (Hanson, 1997). The MnSOST is apparently no longer used by the Minnesota Department of Corrections. It was reportedly replaced by an updated version of the instrument in that department in September 1999.

Rapid Risk Assessment for Sexual Offense Recidivism (RRASOR)

Hanson (1997) described the development of a brief actuarial risk scale for sexual offense recidivism, noting the desirability and need for "a brief, efficient actuarial tool that could be used to assess the risk for sexual offense recidivism" (p. 4). He identified the initial pool of predictor variables based on the earlier Hanson and Bussière's (1996; see also 1998) meta-analysis as well as the three criteria used to select variables: (1) an average correlation of at least .10 with sexual offense recidivism; (2) if a variable was expected to be highly correlated with another, then only the variable with the highest correlation; and (3) variables that can be scored using commonly available information. Hanson also created common definitions to determine understandable cut-points. The predictor variables selected for initial study were:

- Prior sex offenses
- Any stranger victims
- Any prior offenses
- Age (young)
- Never married
- Any non-related victims
- Any male victims

Recidivism was defined as any new sexual offense as indexed by official records (arrests, convictions, readmissions). Hanson used data from seven different follow-up studies (from Canada and the United States) as the development sample; these studies provided 2,919 individuals who were followed an average of 8.4 years (with a range from two to twenty-three years). Recidivism rates ranged from .06 to .35. Three of the studies defined recidivism as reconvictions, while the remainder defined it as charges or readmission to a hospital. The majority of individuals followed were child molesters and some proportion of the individuals had participated in some form of sex offender treatment. However, there is no information available regarding the particular proportion of child molesters or rapists included within these samples for developing the risk scale. The resulting instrument was then cross-validated on an independent sample of 303 individuals released from Her Majesty's Prison Service in the United Kingdom who were followed for sixteen years (1979–1995), with a recidivism rate of .25 defined by convictions for a new sex offense.

Correlations were used to form an averaged correlation matrix. The results of this matrix were then analyzed using stepwise regression. Predictive accuracy was measured using both individual correlation and the AUC under the ROC curve. All of the predictors were found to be significantly correlated with sexual offense recidivism; the strongest predictors were a history of prior sexual offenses ($r = .20$) and extrafamilial victims ($r = .14$). In general, the predictor variables were not found to be highly correlated with each other.

The scale was titled the Rapid Risk Assessment for Sexual Offense Recidivism, or RRASOR. Only four variables were retained after the stepwise progression, each of which is relatively easily scored from archival records:

- Prior sexual offenses (either arrests or convictions),
- Extrafamilial victims,
- Age less than twenty-five, and
- Male child victims.

The first two variables are the strongest individual predictors of recidivism. A numerical item score is obtained for each of the four variables that allows the rater to compute a total score ranging from 0 to 6. No standard error or measurement is available for the RRASOR because a reliability coefficient is not calculated; however, given the nature of the items contained within the RRASOR, one would expect that the reliability coefficient would be high.

The RRASOR demonstrates a moderate level of predictive accuracy across all the samples, with an average correlation of .27. Similarly, the average AUC under the ROC curve (.71) indicates moderate predictive accuracy. The predictive accuracy of the RRASOR in the independent validation sample is not significantly different from the development samples.

Each increase in total of the RRASOR is associated with an orderly increase in the sex offense recidivism rate. Hanson concludes that the results suggest the possibility of identifying a small subgroup of sexual offenders (2 to 8 percent) who are at substantial risk for sexual offense recidivism (e.g., 50 percent over five years and 73 percent over ten years).

As Hanson notes, the primary weakness of the RRASOR is that it does not directly measure deviant sexual preferences (the strongest recidivism predictor in Hanson and Bussiere's meta-analysis); another weakness is that it does not assess treatment compliance or completion. In addition, his findings with the RRASOR contrast with his earlier meta-analysis results, which found that sex offense recidivism is predicted by a number of variables related to general antisocial behavior. Hanson concludes, "There is, nevertheless, sufficient recidivism research to suggest that applied risk assessments should consider more than the four basis factors covered in the RRA-SOR" (p. 19). He further states that sole reliance on actuarial risk scales can only be justified when the scale considers a sufficient number of relevant predictor variables. The RRASOR is not intended to provide a comprehensive assessment of all the factors relevant to the prediction of sexual offender recidivism. Instead, Hanson argues that the RRASOR should be used primarily to screen offenders into relative risk levels. These risk levels could then be adjusted by the consideration of other relevant information, such as deviant sexual preferences and treatment compliance.

Sex Offender Risk Appraisal Guide (SORAG)

Quinsey et al. (1998) report on the results of a modification of the VRAG to develop an instrument using variables that would predict at least one rearrest for a sexual offense. The instrument, labeled the Sex Offender Risk Appraisal Guide, or SORAG, differs somewhat from the VRAG and has fourteen items (as opposed to the VRAG's twelve). As with the VRAG, the following variables are empirically associated with sex offense recidivism:

- PCL-R scores
- Elementary school maladjustment
- Separation from biological parents prior to age sixteen
- Marital status (e.g., never married)
- Age at index offense
- Alcohol abuse history
- Personality disorder
- Schizophrenia

Unique variables to the SORAG include:

- Nonviolent offenses
- Violent offenses
- Previous convictions for sex offenses
- History of sex offense against male children or adults
- Phallometrically determined sexual deviance score

Currently, data is available regarding seven- and ten-year follow-up periods.

The original AUC under the ROC of the SORAG was .62 (lower than that obtained for the VRAG). Quinsey et al. attribute this lower predictive accuracy to the higher measurement error associated with the definition of sexual offense recidivism, the relatively narrow range of risk in their studies of sex offenders (e.g., there are few low-risk sex offenders among the patients from Oak Ridge in Pentanguishene), and the issue of additive linear relationships (or statistical interactions) among variables which compose the SORAG.

Belanger and Earls (1996) report that the SORAG yielded a CLES (common language effect size—see earlier discussion of ROC analysis) of .82 (equivalent to the AUC) for recidivism among a sample of fifty-seven federally sentenced sex offenders. Rice (1999) reports that the SORAG, like the VRAG, predicted violent recidivism in a new sample of 530 sex offenders released from incarceration or from forensic hospitals. She found that the VRAG and SORAG were highly correlated with one another (r = .93) and that both of these instruments were significantly better than the RRASOR in predicting both violent and sexual recidivism.

Hanson and Thornton (2000) found that for a subsample of 142 sex offenders for whom there were complete data available, the SORAG was equivalent to the Static-99 in predicting sex offender recidivism and better at predicting violent recidivism.

In a yet unpublished paper, Rice and Harris (2000) use the SORAG to compare recidivism rates between a group of sex offenders who had molested a daughter or step-daughter (incest perpetrators) and those who had molested extrafamilial female youth. The results demonstrate that the risk factors for incest offenders are similar to those for other sex offenders, including history of sexual and other offenses, psychopathy, and deviant sexual preferences. In predicting sex offense recidivism, the SORAG showed an AUC for the ROC of .80; the correlation of the SORAG with sex offense recidivism was .42. This study constitutes a cross-validation of the SORAG; it also produces the highest effect size to date regarding sex offense recidivism, perhaps because this sample possesses the most diverse set of risk scores to date.

A particular problem with applying the SORAG is its inclusion of phallometrically assessed "deviant sexual preferences." It appears that relatively few incarcerated sex offenders will have had one, let alone several, penile plethysmograph administrations. It is unclear whether inferring deviant sexual preferences from archival material or an offender's self-report affects the validity of the SORAG. Consequently, this variable may not be available for calculating a SORAG score.

Minnesota Sex Offender Screening Tool—Revised (MnSOST-R)

A revision of the MnSOST was undertaken in 1996 and the new instrument is known as the MnSOST—Revised, or MnSOST-R. Epperson and his colleagues (1999b) created the actual screening tool and general instructions for scoring the instrument, while Epperson et al. (1999a) authored a technical paper regarding research in the instrument. The modification of the MnSOST aimed to incorporate the results of more recent research on the prediction of sex offense recidivism as well as to reflect a change to empirical methods for both item selection and scoring. The MnSOST-R was made available for use in 1999; the items for the measure and general instructions for scoring are dated March 23, 1999. The initial sample for the MnSOST-R was composed of three groups of adult male sex offenders:

- All 221 sex offenders released in 1998;
- A stratified random sample of 150 sex offenders released in 1990; and
- Any other sex offender who had committed another sex offense upon release before May 1994, regardless of the year of offense.

This sampling approach resulted in an exhaustive sample of 123 sex offenders who committed another sex offense on release, a random sample of 120 sex offenders who committed a nonsexual offense on release, and a random sample of 144 sex offenders who did not commit any offense on release. Sex offenders who committed only intrafamilial offenses that did not involve penetration or high degrees of physical force were excluded from analyses. The remaining members of the sample were identified as either rapists or child molesters; data were available for 256 out of these 274 sex offenders through a six-year period of risk. Files were randomly assigned to forty case managers for "blind" reviews on seventeen dimensions; in addition, each file was also reviewed by a researcher on a number of research dimensions and was rated on the PCL-SV (a screening version of the PCL-R) and the RRASOR.

The specific criterion variable or follow-up period was a six-year offense rate. This was based largely on the fact that for this sample, reoffense rates clearly declined by the sixth year, as did the sample size. A reoffense was defined as an arrest for a "hands on" sex-related offense within six years of targeted release dates; those persons who had been at risk for six years without an arrest for a sex-related offense were defined as non-reoffenders. Preliminary analyses indicated that nearly all arrests resulted in convictions and that prediction rates were equivalent for arrests and for convictions.

The baseline reoffense rate was 35 percent in this sample. A modified Nufield (1982) procedure was used as the initial step in selecting and scoring each item of the MnSOST-R. Item levels with reoffense rates 5 percent greater than the baseline were scored +1 for each 5 percent increment and vice versa. In addition, items were retained if they appeared significantly related to reoffense status at the $p < .10$ level and showed statistical independence. Sixteen items were retained for inclusion in the scale.

Inter-rater reliability was determined by having eleven raters each rate the same twelve offenders; the intraclass correlation coefficient was .73. According to Wagner et al. (2000), the VRAG's standard error of measurement is approximately 2.

The MnSOST-R demonstrated a correlation with a reoffense status of .45. A large effect size characterizes the difference between the mean scores for reoffenders and non-reoffenders. The MnSOST-R was moderately correlated with the other risk assessment instruments studied, including the MnSOST; however, the other instruments all showed relatively low correlations with sex offense recidivism. Analyses indicated that MnSOST-R scores were roughly equivalent in predicting sex offense recidivism rates for rapists ($r = .47$) and extrafamilial child molesters ($r = .41$).

Using a cut-score, offenders scoring at or above that score were identified as high-risk; the relationship between MnSOST-R scores and the percentage of correct high-risk predictions for reoffense status was quite linear with a fairly steep slope. Using a particular cut score for a high-risk group identified 16 percent of the sex offenders who reoffended; 88 percent of offenders who scored at or above that cut-score (i.e., as high-risk) did reoffend.

Epperson provides information via his web-site (http://www.psych-server.iastate.edu/faculty/epperson) regarding a cross-validation study he and his colleagues (Epperson et al., 2000) did of the MnSOST-R. The sample consists of sex offenders (rapists and child molesters) released in 1992 (n =95). Sixty-six of these offenders were at risk for a full six years; of these, the base rate for sex offense recidivism (defined as a "hands-on" sexual offense) was 31 percent. Regarding predictive validity of the MnSOST-R in the cross-validation sample, the correlations between the MnSOST-R scores and reoffending were .39 (n = 95) and .51 (n = 66); the AUC of the ROC were .76 and .82 respectively for the samples.

As noted, the overall baseline recidivism rate for the development sample for the MnSOST-R was 35 percent; the authors estimate that even excluding the oversampled recidivists the base rate was 30 percent. Both of these figures are somewhat higher than what most studies have reported for a six-year period. However, the authors note that the study required that all nonrecidivists be at risk for a full six years (i.e., a minimum of six years) and that a reoffense was defined as rearrest for a sex offense or sex-related offense. Epperson et al. (1999b) provide detailed instructions for item scoring in their manual for scoring criteria and guidelines. The measure, scoring guidelines, technical paper, and updates on cross-validation studies are all available on Dr. Epperson's website (above).

Although the goal was to develop an instrument that can be scored by case managers and other nonclinical staff, Epperson et al. conclude that using the MnSOST-R requires a careful reading of the file and diligence on the part of the rater.

Structured Anchored Clinical Judgment (SACJ/SACJ-Min)

The Structured Anchored Clinical Judgment (SACJ) (Grubin, 1998) was developed to predict sexual and violent recidivism using a three-stage approach, with each stage incorporating different kinds of information. The first stage of consideration is based on an offender's official history of convictions including any current sex offenses, any prior sex offenses, any current nonsexual violent offenses, any prior nonsexual violent offenses, and/or four or more prior sentencing occasions. An offender with four or more of these initial factors is automatically considered high risk.

The second stage involves the consideration of a number of potentially aggravating factors, divided into two sets. Set A includes any stranger victims, any male victims, never married, and convictions for non-contact sex offenses. Set B includes items such as substance abuse, placement in residential care while a child, deviant sexual arousal, and psychopathy. Since some of the Set B items are difficult or resource-high items to assess, Step 1 and Step 2-Set A items are considered the minimum for a valid assessment. Using this reduced set of items produced a scale that has come to be known as the SACJ-Min (Min = minimum).

The third stage of the SACJ uses information that is likely applicable only to sex offenders who had entered treatment; consequently, it is not considered part of the SACJ-Min.

The SACJ-Min was developed through several exploratory data analyses using United Kingdom data sets. However, the SACJ-Min was validated on a sample of approximately 500 sex offenders released from Her Majesty's Prison Service in 1979 who were followed for sixteen years (this set includes the 303 individuals studied as the validation sample for the RRASOR). The criterion variable was reconviction for a sexual offense. Reportedly, the SACJ-Min correlated .34 with sex offense recidivism and .30 with any sexual or violent recidivism (Thornton, personal communication, February 10, 1999 as cited in Hanson & Thornton, 1999).

The SACJ-Min was originally tested only with samples from within the United Kingdom. When tested in three Canadian samples, it showed some degree of variability in the prediction of sex offense recidivism (Hanson & Thornton, 1999).

Static-99

Hanson and Thornton (1999; 2000) report on a comparison of the predictive accuracy of three sex offender risk assessment measures—the RRASOR, the SAC-J Min, and a new scale, the Static-99, which they created by combining the items from the two other scales studied. The combination resulted after the authors determined that the RRASOR and SACJ-Min were assessing related but not identical constructs and that each contributed unique variance to regression equations predicting recidivism. The Static-99 was so named to indicate that it only includes static factors and that the available version is a current version of a presumed work in progress. The variables in the Static-99 can be grouped across these five dimensions:

- Sexual deviance
- Range of available victims
- Persistence or lack of deterrence
- Antisocial behavior patterns
- Age

Three Canadian samples were used for analyzing the Static-99 (two from psychiatric facilities and one from a correctional facility) as well as an expanded U.K. sample (n = 563) that included a subsample previously used to cross-validate the RRASOR (n = 303). The criterion for sex offense recidivism was convictions (for three samples) and charges/readmissions (for one sample). However, there is no information available regarding the particular proportion of child molesters or rapists included within these samples for developing the Static-99.

The authors use survival analyses to calculate recidivism probabilities. The AUC under the ROC provides the primary measure of predictive accuracy. The four samples were combined for a total of 1,208 subjects. The Static-99 showed moderate predictive accuracy for both sexual recidivism (r = .33) and violent (including sexual) recidivism (r = .32). For the prediction of sex offense recidivism, the Static-99 was marginally more accurate (AUC = .71) than the RRASOR (A = .68) or the SACJ-Min (AUC = .67). The RRASOR and the SACJ-Min were not significantly different from one another in their accuracy in predicting such recidivism. Regarding the prediction of violent recidivism, the Static-99 was more accurate than either the RRASOR or the SACJ-Min. Again, the RRASOR and the SACJ-Min were not significantly different from one another in their accuracy in predicting violent recidivism. All of the scales show similar predictive accuracy for both rapists and child molesters.

The Static 99 identified a subsample of incarcerated/hospitalized sex offenders (approximately 12 percent) whose long-term risk for reoffending (defined predominantly by later convictions for sex offenses) was greater than 50 percent. Most of the offenders with elevated scores on the Static-99 are also at substantial risk for any violent recidivism over a fifteen-year follow-up period.

Phenix et al. (2000) developed coding rules in California for use of the Static-99, and Hanson and Thornton (1999; 2000) provided the coding rules for the individual variables.

In a May 8, 2000 e-mail, Hanson (2000) wrote, "I believe that Static-99 contains new information not contained in RRASOR, and that there is no evidence to suggest that RRASOR provides information not already contained in Static-99." Given this, Hanson indicates that the Static-99 should be used in place of, not in addition to, the RRASOR.

As Hanson and Thornton (1999) write, the Static-99 is intended to be a measure of long-term risk potential. Yet they note that:

> [A]ctuarial scales are accurate to the extent that they consider all relevant risk factors. Static-99 does not claim to be comprehensive, for it neglects whole categories of potentially relevant variables (e.g., dynamic factors). As well, prudent evaluators would want to consider whether there are special features of individual cases that limit the applicability of actuarial risk scales . . . . (p. 16)

Sex Offender Need Assessment Rating (SONAR)

Most of the variables identified in previous studies associated with sex offense recidivism are static or historical items. Hanson and Harris (2000) developed the Sex Offender Need Assessment Rating, or SONAR, to evaluate the possibility of *change* in risk among sexual offenders, based on the results of their 1998 study of dynamic risk factors for sex offense recidivism. This constitutes an attempt to examine how identified dynamic risk factors can be organized into a structured risk assessment. Because they used the same data base that they used in 1998 to identify variables and items associated with reoffense to test the SONAR's validity, it was not possible to establish the predictive validity of the SONAR.

The SONAR includes dimensions viewed as "stable" (expected to persist for months or years, including intimacy deficits, negative social influences, attitudes tolerant of sex offending, sexual self-regulation) and viewed as "acute" (expected to last for minutes or days, including substance abuse, negative mood, anger, and victim access).

Subjects were nonincestuous, hands-on sexual offenders who had received community supervision (parole, probation) from the Canadian provincial or federal correctional systems. Thus, this sample does not entirely consist of formerly incarcerated sex offenders. The subjects were divided into two groups: those who had committed a new sexual offense while on community supervision (n = 208) and those who had not committed either a sexual or other serious violent offense. In addition, the entire subject sample was composed of roughly equal numbers of boy-victim child molesters and girl-victim child molesters/rapists. The members of the two comparison groups were matched on offense history, index victims, and jurisdiction.

Most of the information used to create the items of the SONAR was drawn from one-hour structured interviews with the sample's supervision officers. Information was collected for recidivists with regard to whether particular problems had ever been a concern and whether the problem was worse in the month before recidivism (for those who had reoffended) or the previous month (for those who had not reoffended). Interrater reliability for the information collected and coded was consistently high (e.g. > 90%).

The ability of the SONAR to differentiate between the two groups was moderately high (r = .43) with an AUC under the ROC of .74. The SONAR also correlated with VRAG scores (computed on 267 of the subjects for whom sufficient data was available) at a statistically significant level (r = .40, p <.001). The dimension of the SONAR that most strongly differentiated recidivists from nonrecidivists was that of general self-regulation.

Recidivists differed from nonrecidivists on a number of static risk factor variables, including diverse types of victims, paraphilias, prior nonsexual offenses, lower IQ, and PCL-R definitions of psychopathy. After controlling for these preexisting differences on known risk factors, the SONAR still demonstrated an association with risk for recidivism.

As Hanson and Harris (1998) state, "The results suggest that dynamic factors are important in risk assessment, but the current study does not support any direct translation of SONAR scores into expected recidivism rates" (p. 12) because the study used an artificial base rate of 50 percent by virtue of its subject selection. The authors did suggest that an assessment of an offender's dynamic characteristics could be justified as a useful consideration in determining whether that offender's risk level (as determined by actuarial measures) should be increased or decreased.

Structured Risk Assessment (SRA)

The Structured Risk Assessment is a three-step framework for a structured approach to combining actuarial risk scales with other empirically based risk factors (Thornton, 2000). The current version uses the Static-99 as the first step in risk assessment to measure static risk factors. This provides an actuarial risk classification (low, medium-low, medium-high, or high).

The second step is to rate an offender's relative functioning on five dynamic risk factors (DRFs) to revise the risk level identified by the Static-99. Each DRF is a psychological factor that contributes to or sustains relative risk; each DRF area examines domains that could potentially change, usually in response to intensive treatment. The evaluator considers "relative deviance" in each area in terms of the range and intensity of the psychological processes that might underlie an offender's sexually violent behavior. The five DRFs include:

- Sexual interests
- Distorted attitudes
- Socio-affective functioning
- Self-management

- Criminogenic significant others

An individual is viewed as "low" on a factor if it is a weak or isolated component of his functioning or "high" if it is a pervasive or dominant component. Each of the five DRFs is considered in terms of whether the factor has played a part in the offender's typical offense pattern or chain. As Thornton (2000) indicates, this second step can be accomplished using various psychological tests (a nomothetic model):

> Psychometrics can be an extremely efficient way of investigating a comprehensive range of potential dynamic risk factors . . . SRA therefore uses psychometrics as one channel through which to investigate the density of risk factors applying to a particular offender. (p. 26)

The SRA calls for the use of "acceptable indicators" in the five DRF areas. The subject offender is compared to norms for "high" and "low" rated sex offenders. Alternatively, Thornton notes the usefulness of behaviorally based idiographic assessment methods where offenders are unwilling to complete psychological tests or where local norms may not be available. An offender is characterized by high deviance if his functioning is considered strongly problematic in at least two of the five domains. This second step ends with a determination of the offender's "deviance categorization," to modify the initial Static-99 assessment; a "revised risk" categorization then follows using the same category labels as the first step.

The third step is based on information regarding the offender's relative response to treatment. The SRA is viewed as a system that reflects the complexity of the actual situations in which risk assessment takes place. As Hanson and Thornton (1999) note, "At each stage, the system is empirically based, becoming actuarial where practical and elsewhere using lesser, although still credible, forms of analysis" (p.7). Hanson and Thornton (2000) indicate that the results of two prospective studies found that the key dynamic components of the SRA improved upon assessments using simply static factors.

Historical Clinical Risk Management-20

The Historical Clinical Risk Management (HCR-20) (Webster et al., 1997) was designed to provide domain guidelines to assist evaluators in considering the assessment of risk for future violence. Originally developed in 1995, the authors published an updated version 1997. Their intention was to create a guide for assessing future violence, not a formal psychological test. They defined violence as actual, attempted, or threatened harm to a person or person involving acts serious enough to result in criminal or civil sanctions. Based on a manageable number of items and constructs, the HCR-20 was not designed specifically to evaluate recidivism in sex offenders. The authors suggest its main value might lie "in the general principles it espouses rather than its detail" (p. 5).

The HCR-20 checklist of risk factors for violent behavior contains twenty items organized around ten past (historical) factors, five present (clinical) issues, and five future (risk management) issues. Each item is coded on a three-point scale similar to that of the PCL-R:

0 = risk factor is absent;

1 = risk factor is possibly or partially present (some but not conclusive evidence); and

2 = risk is definitely or clearly present.

After rating all twenty items, the assessors make a final decision regarding risk for violence using a simple scale of low (no or low risk), moderate (somewhat elevated risk), and high (at high or very elevated risk). The authors state, "it is reasonable for assessors to conclude that the more factors present in a given case, the higher the risk for violence" (p. 22). However, they also note that risk likely depends on the specific combination and not simply the number of risk factors present.

Douglas et al. (1999) studied the predictive validity of the HCR-20. ROC analyses yielded "strong associations" with violence, with AUCs ranging from .76 to .80. Persons scoring above the HCR-20 median were six to thirteen times more likely to be violent than those scoring below the median. The internal consistency and inter-rater reliability were both reported to be good. Further, HCR-20 scores were found to add incremental validity to PCL-SV scores.

Sexual Violence Rating Scale

The Sexual Violence Rating Scale (SVR-20) (Boer et al., 1997a; 1997b) is another instrument recently developed to provide assistance in conducting risk assessments for future sexual violence. The authors' purpose was to provide information that might distinguish the relative risk of sex offenders for sexual recidivism from more general violent recidivism. The authors suggest that the SRV-20 is particularly useful for identifying high-risk sexual offenders who might not be prone to more general types of violent behavior. They define "sexual violence" as actual, attempted, or threatened sexual contact with a person who is nonconsenting or unable to give consent.

The authors associate twenty variables in three domains with a higher risk of sex offense recidivism. In identifying the variables, the authors considered the item's empirical relation to future sexual violence, its practical utility in making decisions about sex offenders, and parsimony in balancing brevity and comprehensiveness. The three areas and associated variables are:

1. *Psychosocial adjustment*—Sexual deviations or paraphilias; victim of child abuse; relative psychopathy; cognitive impairment; substance abuse; suicidal or homicidal ideation; relationship problems, including the absence of a relationship; employment problems, including instability in employment; prior nonsexual violent offenses; prior nonviolent offenses; past violation of conditional release.

2. *The nature of sexual offending*—High density offenses; multiple offense types; physical harm to others; the use of weapons or threats of death; escalation in frequency or severity of offenses; extreme minimization or denial of offenses; attitudes that support or condone offenses.

3. *Future plans*— Lacks realistic plans; a negative attitude toward intervention.

Risk for Sexual Violence Protocol (RSVP)

Most recently, Kropp (2000) presented information regarding an updated version of the SVR-20, now entitled the Risk for Sexual Violence Protocol (RSVP). The RSVP covers four areas: social adjustment, psychological adjustment, sexual adjustment, and management. Kropp recommends that multiple sources of information be used to determine ratings for the items in these areas, including interviews with the offender and with relevant others, standardized testing, specialized assessment techniques (e.g., polygraph and plethysmograph), and collateral records. In addition to rating the relative presence of each item for a lifetime and for the past year (e.g., recent period), the rater is also asked to indicate (1) whether the item is considered criminogenic to sex offending for the individual and (2) the relative imminence of the overall risk for both sexual and general violence for the individual.

Based on two small samples (one of incarcerated offenders and the other of sex offenders referred to a community clinic), Kropp demonstrates that the RSVP has concurrent validity and that RSVP ratings for sexual violence have a stronger correlation (.40) with sex offense recidivism than the PCL-R, Static-99, MnSOST-R and the SORAG. Logan (2000) conducted a preliminary study of the RSVP with a small sample of English sex offenders determined to have Dangerous and Severe Personality Disorders. She shows that the RSVP had adequate internal reliablity and inter-rater reliablity. She also demonstrates some degree of concurrent validity of the RSVP with actuarial measures.

Regarding structured clinical judgment measures such as the HCR-20, the SVR-20, and the RSVP, it is worth noting that such instruments offer particular utility to the consideration of risk management. More specifically, because they include variables related to management, some of which are dynamic variables (such as treatability, supervisability and plans for release), these measures provide an opportunity to assess whether demonstrable change has occurred for a particular sex offender. In turn (and in contrast to actuarial measures, which contain almost exclusively static or historical variables), structured clinical judgment measures may be of great value in considering the issue of risk relative to decisions to discharge a sex offender who has already received a civil commitment as a sexual predator.

Relationships Among the Different Recidivism Measures

Epperson et al. (1999a) have recently reported on the inter-correlations of the MnSOST-R with other risk assessment measures based on the sample used to develop the MnSOST-R. They obtained the following associations with these measures:

MnSOST (.57)

PCL-SV (.20)

RRASOR (.45)

The MnSOST was correlated .48 with the RRASOR and .03 with the PCL-SV. The PCL-SV was correlated .04 with the RRASOR.

Packard and Gordon (1999) present information on a factor analysis of the items contained in the PCL-R, VRAG, RRASOR, and MnSOST as well as the inter-correlations among these scales. Their sample consists of 523 individuals who had participated in prison-based sex offender treatment in the state of Washington. The PCL-R correlated .72 with the VRAG but only .16 with the RRASOR. The VRAG correlated .31 with the RRASOR. The MnSOST dynamic items correlated .14 with the RRASOR although the total score of the MnSOST correlated .59 with the RRASOR.

Doren (1999a) compared various risk measures in a sample of 103 sex offenders who were detained, pre-civil commitment trial. The Static-99 demonstrated the following correlations:

RRASOR (.69);

MnSOST (.59);

MnSOST-R (.51);

SACJ (.70);

VRAG (.40); and

PCL-R (.42).

The RRASOR demonstrated the following correlations:

MnSOST (.26);

MnSOST-R (.21);

SACJ (.34);

VRAG (.19); and

PCL-R (.04).

The MnSOST demonstrated the following correlations:

MnSOST-R (.66);

SACJ (.42);

VRAG (.64); and

PCL-R (.56).

The MnSOST-R demonstrated the following correlations:

SACJ (.41);

VRAG (.63); and

PCL-R (.56).

Recently, Kropp (2000) showed that the RSPV demonstrates the following correlations with other risk assessment instruments:

MnSOST-R (.53);

Static-99 (.53); and

PCL-R (.75).

COMMUNICATING INFORMATION REGARDING THE LEVEL OF RISK OF FUTURE DANGEROUSNESS

Most state statutes provide that the risk of future dangerousness shall be determined to be above some specific legal standard. Typically that standard is "more likely than not," but in certain states the standard is by "clear and convincing evidence." Information can be presented to the TFL in different ways. Some writers advocate that information be presented in a simple fashion, namely by stating that the individual appears to exceed the level specified by the statute; others argue that a set of information should be presented concerning the specific estimates of risk provided by different measures or methods, with or without the expert's conclusion as to whether the PPSP's level of risk equals or exceeds that specified by the statute. Still others recommend that the role of the mental health professional is to provide both specific estimates of risk provided by the set of different measures or methods and a conclusion as to whether a person with characteristics like the PPSP is characterized by a level of risk equal to or exceeding that specified by the statute.

CONCLUSION

The prediction of violent behavior, including sexual offending, is a complex and controversial area. Clearly significant gains have been made in the accuracy of predictions of such violence in general and, most specifically, relative to the commission of future sex offenses by persons with a history of sex offenses. The quality of the research in the area of sex offense recidivism has been the target of extensive effort over a relatively brief period of time. As a result of these efforts and their advances in research quality, substantial improvements in predictive accuracy have been achieved. It can be argued that relative to other areas of forensic psychology and other areas of mental health specialties, the ability to offer credible information to TFL regarding the future dangerousness of sex offenders exceeds the capacity to offer predictions in other areas such as child custody decisions or personal injury evaluations.

The development of the various measures for predicting future dangerousness in identified sex offenders demonstrates a number of methodological advances: the inclusion of valid risk factors; the relative ease of scoring for many of these risk factors, as demonstrated by high reliability; explicit rules for combining those risk factors and, in certain instances, other relevant information; explicit probability estimates derived from survival analysis; increasing evidence that the risk factors and risk assessment procedures are relatively robust across settings and samples; and, finally, the clear relationships that have been found between ratings on such measures and the predicted outcome of sexual reoffending.

Existing instruments and rating scales are not definitive. Overall, they demonstrate what is referred to as moderate predictive accuracy; nonetheless, their predictive accuracy is greater than that for most aspects of human behavior. Specific measures each possess weaknesses. Some do not incorporate important factors (such as direct or indirect measures of sexual arousal), and most do not permit the evaluation of so-called dynamic risk factors. Certain available measures are based on items that apparently offer no apparent contribution to the general understanding of sex offenders—they are atheoretical. Much of the available research on risk for violent and sexual recidivism has been conducted in Canada, in part because such studies are greatly facilitated by a centralized data system that enables investigators to track an offender's contacts with the criminal justice system across provinces. It will be important for risk assessment instruments to be studied with broader samples, particularly those that include typical offenders from particular regions and even from specific states within the United States. The study of the prediction of future sex offending is just beginning with female and adolescent sex offenders.

Practically speaking, it makes sense to use multiple actuarial instruments to obtain the most comprehensive set of estimates of the probability for sexual reoffending applicable for a person with the particular set of characteristics identified in a case at hand. Based on a knowledge of the particular instruments selected, an evaluator must be prepared to discuss the likely differences that result from using instruments normed on different samples and based on different sets of variables. At this point, a report or testimony could provide a summary of the ranges of violence or sex offense recidivism estimates obtained via pure actuarial measures; obviously, the matter of interest is whether these estimates place an individual with a particular set of characteristics at or above the threshold specified by a particular statute necessary for civil commitment. Since all existing risk assessment measures offer risks for specified time periods, the evaluator must be prepared to discuss the implications for a person with characteristics similar to the PPSP for the period of the remainder of his life. Further, if one intends to offer an adjusted actuarial assessment, an evaluator must clearly specify the empirically based characteristics or the particular fact(s) of a case (e.g., stated behavioral intent to reoffend) that have directed a modification of the obtained estimates.

Pollock et al. (1989) argued that the assessment of dangerousness has "come to be regarded as having a single purpose—accurate prediction." They suggested that while accuracy in prediction is clearly a worthwhile aim, it should not be the only consideration for forensic mental health professionals. They advocated for an emphasis on accountability over accuracy where "the test of clinical prediction is not in its overall accuracy or "hit rate" but rather how defensible the prediction is in terms of social realities and the current state of scientific knowledge" (p. 90). Such a position continues to have significance in its recommendation of the explicit integration of all meaningful sources of information available to the forensic mental health professional with a broad awareness of the limitations of existing knowledge and the context of the application and results of risk assessment procedures.

Regarding the broad area of dangerousness risk assessments, Litwack and Schlesinger (1999) state:

> A hopeful sign for the future is that the advantages and limits of both actuarial and clinical methods of risk assessments are increasingly being recognized throughout the field. Indeed, in recent years, there has been a refreshing absence from the literature of the polemical and unjustified attacks on clinical assessments that characterized many earlier writings. However, there

remains, among academic observers, a strong preference for actuarial instruments that is neither realistic (because validated and legally useful actuarial means of assessment are not, and may never be, available regarding many important risk assessments) nor justified by actual data (because actuarial risk assessment formulas have yet to be proven to be superior to many of the risk assessments that clinicians actually make). On the other hand, there is now a widespread recognition that both actuarial and clinical contributions can be useful in making dangerousness risk assessments, at least in many cases. (p. 209)

In considering the specific prediction of future sexual dangerousness, it seems apparent that investigators have made particularly impressive strides in developing and studying instruments (with demonstrated reliability and predictive validity) and particular characteristics that can be used to consider whether certain types of offenders appear to exceed legal thresholds for the likelihood or probability of future sexual violence. Clearly, there can be no basis for the admission of pure or unguided clinical judgments; there is neither reliability nor relevance to such opinions.

Quinsey et al. (1998) have declared a change from their previous recommendations and now advocate the complete replacement of existing clinical practice with actuarial methods, stating, "Actuarial methods are too good and clinical judgments too poor to risk contaminating the former with the latter" (p. 171). However, as Hanson (1999) notes, guided clinical, pure actuarial, and adjusted actuarial approaches are all plausible sources of information regarding risk assessment. As he explains, the research on actuarial measures for sexual offense recidivism has yet to demonstrate a clear superiority to the best clinical assessment measures. Moreover, given the blurred distinctions between most clinical and actuarial assessments, assessors of the dangerousness of known sex offenders should be willing to consider all apparently relevant and useful sources of information (including both actuarial and clinical data) in offering opinions regarding the relative risk of dangerousness of sex offenders being considered for civil commitment.

In conclusion, the available evidence as of this date provides only stronger support for opinions offered previously (e.g., Hanson, 1999) that all of the plausible risk assessment procedures:

can be expected to reliably identify a small subgroup of offenders with an enduring propensity to sexually reoffend. The rate at which this highest risk subgroup actually offends with another sexual offense could conservatively be estimated at 50 percent and could reasonably be estimated at 70 to 80 percent. (p. 8-20).

References

Abel, G. G., Becker, J. V., Mittelman, M., Cunningham-Rathner, J., Rouleau, J. L. & Murphy, W. D. (1987). Self-reported sex crimes of nonincarcerated paraphiliacs. *Journal of Interpersonal Violence, 2,* 3–25.

Abel, G. G. & Osborn, C. A. (1992). Stopping sexual violence. *Psychiatric Annals, 22,* 301–306.

Abel, G. G. & Rouleau, J. L. (1990). The nature and extent of sexual assault. In W. L. Marshall, D.

R. Laws & H. E. Barbaree (Eds.), *Handbook of sexual assault: Issues, theories, and treatment of the offender.* New York: Plenum Press.

Addington v. Texas, 441 U.S. 418 (1979).

Barbaree, H. E. & Marshall, W. L. (1988). Deviant sexual arousal, offense history, and demographic variables as predictors of reoffense among child molesters. *Behavioral Sciences and the Law, 6,* 267–280.

Barefoot v. Estelle, 463 U.S. 880 (1983).

Beck, A. J. & Shipley, B. E. (1989). *Recidivism of prisoners released in 1983.* U.S. Department of Justice: Bureau of Justice Statistics, 1–13.

Belanger, N. & Earls, C. (1996). Sex offender recidivism prediction. *Forum on Correctional Research, 8,* 22–24.

Boer, D. P., Hart, S. D., Kropp, P. R. & Webster, C. D. (1997a). *Manual for the sexual violence risk-20: Professional guidelines for assessing risk of sexual violence.* Burnaby, British Columbia: Mental Health, Law and Policy Institute, Simon Fraser University.

Boer, D. P., Wilson, R. J., Gauthier, C. M. & Hart, S. D. (1997b). Assessing risk for sexual violence: Guidelines for clinical practice. In C. D. Webster & M. A. Jackson (Eds.), *Impulsivity: Theory, assessment, and treatment.* New York: Guilford Press.

Bonta, J. & Hanson, K. (1994). *Gauging the risk for violence: Measurement, impact and strategies for change.* Ottawa, Canada: Department of the Solicitor General of Canada.

Bonta, J., Law, M. & Hanson, K. (1998). The prediction of criminal and violent recidivism among mentally disordered offenders: A meta-analysis. *Psychological Bulletin, 123,* 123–142.

Borum, R. (1996). Improving the clinical practice of violence risk assessment: Technology, guidelines and training. *American Psychologist, 51,* 945–956.

Brooks, A. D. (1992). The constitutionality and morality of civilly committing violent sexual predators. *University of Puget Sound Law Review, 15,* 709–754.

Cohen, J. (1992). A power primer. *Psychological Bulletin, 112,* 155–159.

Cooke, D. J., Michie, C., Hart, S. D. & Hare, R. D. (1999). Evaluating the screening version of the Hare Psychopathy Checklist—Revised (PCL-R): An item response theory analysis. *Psychological Assessment, 11,* 3–13.

Currie v. United States, 644 F. Supp. 1074 (1986).

Daubert v. Merrell Dow Pharmaceutical, Inc., 509 U.S. 579, 597 (1993).

Doren, D. M. (1998). Recidivism base rates, predictions of sex offender recidivism, and the sexual predator commitment laws. *Behavioral Science and the Law, 16,* 97–114.

Doren, D. M. (1999a, September). *A comprehensive comparison of risk assessment instruments to determine their relative value within civil commitment evaluations.* Paper presented at the annnual meeting of the Association for the Treatment of Sexual Abusers, Orlando, FL.

Doren, D. M. (1999b). *The issue of accuracy of the risk assessment instruments within the context of sex offender civil commitment evaluations.* Unpublished draft paper, Mendota Mental Health Institute, Madison, WI.

Doren, D. M. (2000, November). *Being accurate about accuracy of risk assessment instruments.* Paper presented at the annual meeting of the Association for the Treatment of Sexual Abusers, Orlando, FL.

Douglas, K. S., Ogloff, J. R. P., Grant, I. & Nicholls, T. L. (1999). Assessing risk for violence among psychiatric patients: The HCR-20 violence risk assessment scheme and the psychopathy checklist: Screening version. *Journal of Consulting and Clinical Psychology, 67,* 917–930.

Douglas, K. S., Ogloff, J. R. P. & Nicholls, T. L. (1997). *Personality disorders and violence in civil psychiatric patients.* Paper presented at the International Congress on Disorders of Personality, Vancouver, British Columbia.

Douglas, K. S. & Webster, C. D. (1999). Predicting violence in mentally and personality disordered individuals. In R. Roesch, S. D. Hart & J. R. P. Ogloff (Eds.), *Psychology and the law: The state of the discipline.* New York: Plenum Press.

Epperson, D. L., Kaul, J. & Hesselton, D. (1999a). *Minnesota sex offender screening tool—Revised*

(MnSOST-R): Development, performance, and recommended risk level cut scores. Iowa State University, Department of Psychology.

Epperson, D. L., Kaul, J. & Hesselton, D. (2000). *Minnesota sex offender screening tool—revised (MnSOST-R): Development, performance, and recommended risk level cut scores; Description of cross-validation sample.* Iowa State University, Department of Psychology.

Epperson, D. L., Kaul, J. & Huot, S. (1995, October). *Predicting the risk of recidivism for incarcerated sex offenders: Updated development of the Minnesota sex offender screening tool (MnSOST).* Paper presented at the fourteenth annual research and treatment conference of the Association for the Treatment of Sexual Abusers, New Orleans, LA.

Epperson, D. L., Kaul, J., Huot, S. J., Hesselton, D., Alexander, W. & Goldman, R. (1999b). *Minnesota sex offender screening tool—Revised (MnSOST-R).* St. Paul: Minnesota Department of Corrections.

Federal Rules of Evidence, art. III, Rules 702, 703 (1974, 2000).

Frye v. United States, 293 F. 1013 (D.C. Cir. 1923).

Garb. H. N. (1998). *Studying the clinician: Judgment research and psychological assessment.* Washington, DC: American Psychological Association.

Gendreau, P., Little, T. & Goggin, C. (1996). A meta-analysis of the predictors of adult offender recidivism: What works! *Criminology, 34*, 575–597.

Goldberg, L. R. (1968). Seer over sign: The first "good example"? *Journal of Experimental Research in Personality, 3*, 168–171.

Goldberg, L. R. (1970). Man versus model of man: A rationale, plus some evidence, for a method of improving on clinical inferences. *Psychological Bulletin, 73*, 422–432.

Grove, W. M. & Meehl, P. E. (1996). Comparative efficiency of informal (subjective, impressionistic) and formal (mechanical, algorithmic) prediction procedures: The clinical-statistical controversy. *Psychology, Public Policy, and Law, 4*, 293–323.

Grove, W. M., Zald, D. H., Lebow, B. S., Snitz, B. E. & Nelson, C. (2000). Clinical versus mechanical prediction: A meta-analysis. *Psychological Assessment, 12*, 19–30.

Grubin, D. (1998). *Sex offending against children: Understanding the risk.* Police Research Series Paper 99. London: Home Office.

Hanson, R. K. (1997). The development of a brief actuarial risk scale for sexual offender recidivism (User Report No. 1997-04). Ottawa, Canada: Department of the Solicitor General of Canada.

Hanson, R. K. (1998). What do we know about sex offender risk assessment? *Psychology, Public Policy and Law, 4*, 50–72.

Hanson, R. K. (1999). What do we know about risk assessment? In A. Schlank & F. Cohen (Eds.), *The sexual predator: Law, policy, evaluation, and treatment.* Kingston, NJ: Civic Research Institute.

Hanson, R. K. & Bussière, M. T. (1996). *Predicting relapse: A meta-analysis.* (User Report No. 96-04). Ottawa: Department of the Solicitor General of Canada.

Hanson, R. K. & Bussière, M. T. (1998). Predicting relapse: A meta-analysis of sexual offender recidivism studies. *Journal of Consulting and Clinical Psychology, 66*, 348–362.

Hanson, R. K. & Harris, A. (1998). *Dynamic predictors of sexual recidivism.* Ottawa: Department of the Solicitor General of Canada.

Hanson, R. K. & Harris, A. (2000). *The sex offender need assessment rating (SONAR): A method for measuring change in risk levels.* Ottawa, Canada: Department of the Solicitor General of Canada.

Hanson, R. K., Steffy, R. A. & Gauthier, R. (1993). Long-term recidivism of child molesters. *Journal of Consulting and Clinical Psychology, 61*, 646–652.

Hanson, R. K. & Thornton, D. (1999). *Static-99: Improving actuarial risk assessments for sex offenders* (User Report No. 99-02). Ottawa: Department of the Solicitor General of Canada.

Hanson, R. K. & Thornton, D. (2000). Improving risk assessments for sex offenders: A comparison of three actuarial scales. *Law and Human Behavior, 24*, 119–136.

Hare, R. D. (1991). *The Hare Psychopathy Checklist—Revised Manual.* Toronto: Multi-Health Systems.

Hare, R. D. (1997, November). *Assessing psychopathy: Clinical and forensic applications of the PCL-R*. Presentation of Minnesota Association for the Treatment of Sexual Abusers.

Hare, R. D. (1998). The Hare PCL-R: Some issues concerning its use and misuse. *Legal and Criminological Psychology, 3*, 101–122.

Hare, R. D. (1999). Psychopathy as a risk factor for violence. *Psychiatric Quarterly, 70*, 181–197.

Hare, R. D. (2000, January). Personal communication.

Harris, G. T.., Rice, M. E. & Quinsey, V. L. (1993). Violent recidivism of mentally disordered offenders: The development of a statistical prediction instrument. *Criminal Justice and Behavior, 20*, 315–335.

Hart, S. D., Cox, D. N. & Hare, R. D. (1995). *The Hare PCL:SV*. Toronto: Multi-Health Systems.

Hemphill, J. F., Hare, R. D. & Wong, S. (1998a). Psychopathy and recidivism: A review. *Legal and Criminological Psychology, 3*, 139–170.

Hemphill, J. F., Templeman, R., Wong, S. & Hare, R. D. (1998b). Psychopathy and crime: Recidivism and criminal careers. In D. Cooke, A. E. Forth & R. D. Hare (Eds.), *Psychopathy: Theory, research, and implications for society*. Amsterdam: Kluwer, 375–399.

Hoberman, H. M. (1999). The forensic evaluation of sex offenders in civil commitment proceedings. In A. Schlank & F. Cohen (Eds.), *The sexual predator: Law, policy, evaluation, and treatment*. Kingston, NJ: Civic Research Institute.

Huot, S. (1999). The referral process. In A. Schlank & F. Cohen (Eds.), *The sexual predator: Law, policy, evaluation, and treatment*. Kingston, NJ: Civic Research Institute.

Janus, E. S. & Meehl, P. E. (1997). Assessing the legal standard for predictions of dangerousness in sex offender commitment proceedings. *Psychology, Public Policy, and Law, 3*, 33–64.

Kansas v. Hendricks, 117 S. Ct. 2072 (1997).

Klassen, D. & O'Connor, W. A. *Predicting violence among mental patients: A cross validation of an actuarial scale*. Paper presented at the American Society of Criminology.

Klassen, D. & O'Connor, W. A. (1988). A prospective study of predictors of violence in adult mental health admission. *Law and Human Behavior, 12,* 143–148.

Kropp, P. R. (2000, November). *The risk for sexual violence protocol (RSVP)*. Paper presented at the annual meeting of the Association for the Treatment of Sexual Abusers, San Diego, CA.

Kumho Tire Co. v. Carmichael, 119 S. Ct. 1167 (1999).

Lidz, C. W., Mulvey, E. P. & Gardner, W. (1993). The accuracy of predictions of violence to others. *Journal of the American Medical Association, 269*, 1007–1011.

Lipari v. Sears, Roebuck & Co., 497 F. Supp. 185 (1980).

Litwack, T. R. & Schlesinger, L. B. (1987). Assessing and predicting violence: Research, law, and applications. In I. Weiner & A. Hess (Eds.), *Handbook of forensic psychology*. New York: Wiley.

Litwack, T. R. & Schlesinger, L. B. (1999). Dangerousness risk assessments: Research, legal, and clinical considerations. In I. Weiner & A. Hess (Eds.), *Handbook of forensic psychology*. New York: Wiley.

Logan, C. (2000, November). *Risk for sexual violence protocol: Applications in a sample of English mentally disordered offenders*. Paper presented at the annual meeting of the Association for the Treatment of Sexual Abusers, San Diego, CA.

Looman, J. (2000). ATSA-List communication.

Marques, J. K., Day, D. M., Nelson, C. & West, M. A. (1994). Effects of cognitive-behavioral treatment on sex offender recidivism: Preliminary results of a longitudinal study. *Criminal Justice and Behavior, 21*, 28–54.

Marshall, W. L. & Barbaree, H. E. (1988). The long-term evaluation of a behavioral treatment program for child molesters. *Behaviour Research and Therapy, 26*, 499–551.

Marshall, W. L. & Barbaree, H. E. (1989). Sexual violence. In K. Howells & C. R. Hollin (Eds.), *Clinical approaches to violence*. New York: Wiley.

Marshall, W. L., Jones, R. Ward, T., Johnston, P. & Barbaree, H. E. (1991). Treatment outcome with sex offenders. *Clinical Psychology Review, 11*, 465–485.

McGrath, R. J. (1991). Sex-offender risk assessment and disposition planning: A review of empirical and clinical findings. *International Journal of Offender Therapy & Comparative Criminology, 35*, 328–350.

McNiel, D. E. & Binder, R. L. (1991). Clinical assessment of the risk of violence among psychiatric inpatients. *American Journal of Psychiatry, 148*, 1317–1321.

Meehl, P. E. (1954). *Clinical versus statistical prediction.* Minneapolis: University of Minnesota Press.

Melton, G. B., Petrila, J., Poythress, N. G. & Slobogin, C. (1997). *Psychological evaluations for the courts: A handbook for mental health professionals and lawyers* (2d ed.). New York: Guilford Press.

Melton, G. B., Weithorn, L. A. & Slobogin, C. (1985). *Community based mental health centers and the courts: An evaluation of community-based forensic services.* Lincoln: University of Nebraska Press.

Monahan, J. (1981). *The clinical prediction of violent behavior.* Monograph of the National Institute of Mental Health, Washington, DC.

Monahan, J. (1995). *The clinical prediction of violent behavior.* Northvale, NJ: Jason Aronson.

Monahan, J. (1996). Violence prediction: The last 20 and the next 20 years. *Criminal Justice and Behavior, 23*, 107–120.

Monahan, J. & Steadman, H. J. (1994). Toward a rejuvenation of risk assessment research. In J. Monahan & H. J. Steadman (Eds.), *Violence and mental disorder: Developments in risk assessment.* Chicago: University of Chicago Press.

Mossman, D. (1994). Assessing predictions of violence: Being accurate about accuracy. *Journal of Consulting and Clinical Psychology, 62*, 783–792.

Nufield, J. (1982). *Parole decision-making in Canada: Research towards decision guidelines.* Ottawa: Department of the Solicitor General of Canada.

Packard, R. & Gordon, A. (1999, September). *An investigation of actuarial risk scales: Concordance and factor analysis.* Paper presented at the annual meeting of the Association for the Treatment of Sexual Abusers, Orlando, FL.

Phenix, A., Hanson, R. K. & Thornton, D. (2000). *Coding rules for the Static-99.* Ottawa: Department of the Solicitor General of Canada.

Pollock, N., McBain, I. & Webster, C. D. (1989). Clinical decision-making and the assessment of dangerousness. In K. Howells & C. R. Hollin (Eds.), *Clinical approaches to violence.* New York: Wiley.

Prentky, R. A., Knight, R. A. & Lee, A. F. S. (1997a). Risk factors associated with recidivism among extrafamilial child molesters. *Journal of Consulting and Clinical Psychology, 65*, 141–149.

Prentky, R. A., Lee, A. F. S., Knight, R. A. & Cerce, D. (1997b). Recidivism rates among child molesters and rapists: A methodological analysis. *Law and Human Behavior, 21*, 635–659.

Proulx, J., Pellerin, B., Paradis, Y., McKibben, A., Aubut, J. & Ouiment, M. (1997). Static and dynamic predictors of recidivism in sexual aggressors. *Sexual Abuse: A Journal of Research and Treatment, 9*, 7–27.

Quinsey, V. L., Harris, G. T., Rice, M. E. & Cormier, C. A. (1998). *Violent offenders: Appraising and managing risk.* Washington, DC: American Psychological Association Press.

Quinsey, V. L. & Lalumiere, M. L. (1996). *Assessment of sexual offenders against children.* Thousand Oaks, CA: Sage.

Quinsey, V. L., Lalumiere, M. L., Rice, M. E. & Harris, G. T. (1995). Predicting sexual offenses. In J. C. Campbell (Ed.), *Assessing dangerousness: Violence by sexual offenders, batterers, and child abusers.* Thousand Oaks, CA: Sage.

Quinsey, V. L. & Maguire, A. (1986). Maximum security psychiatric patients: Actuarial and clinical predictions of dangerousness. *Journal of Interpersonal Violence, 1*, 143–171.

Rice, M. E. (1997). Violent offender research and implications for the criminal justice system. *American Psychologist, 52*, 414–423.

Rice, M. E. (1999). *A multi-site followup study of sex offenders: The predictive accuracy of risk assessment instruments.* Presented at the third annual Forensic Psychiatry Program Research Day, University of Toronto.

Rice, M. E. & Harris, G. T. (1995). Violent recidivism: Assessing predictive validity. *Journal of Consulting and Clinical Psychology, 63,* 737–748.

Rice, M. E. & Harris, G. T. (1997). Cross-validation and extension of the Violence Risk Appraisal Guide for Child Molesters and Rapists. *Law and Human Behavior, 21,* 435–448.

Rice, M. E. & Harris, G. T. (2000). *Sexual preferences and risk of recidivism among father-daughter incest offenders and other child molesters.* (Manuscript submitted for publication).

Rice, M. E., Harris, G. T. & Cormier, C. A. (1992). An evaluation of a maximum security therapeutic community for psychopaths and other mentally disordered offenders. *Law and Human Behavior, 16,* 399–412.

Rice, M. E., Harris, G. T. & Quinsey, V. L. (1990). A follow-up of rapists assessed in a maximum-security psychiatric facility. *Journal of Interpersonal Violence, 5,* 435–448.

Rice, M. E., Quinsey, V. L. & Harris, G. T. (1991). Sexual recidivism among child molesters released from a maximum security psychiatric institution. *Journal of Consulting and Clinical Psychology, 59,* 381–386.

Rogers, R. (1995). *Diagnostic and structured interviewing: A handbook for psychologists.* Odessa, FL: Psychological Assessment Resources.

Romero, J. J. & Williams, L. M. (1985). Recidivism among convicted sex offenders: A 10-year follow-up study. *Federal Probation, 47,* 58–64.

Salekin, R. T., Rogers, R. & Sewell, K. W. (1996). A review and meta-analysis of the psychopathy checklist and psychopathy checklist—revised: Predictive validity of dangerousness. *Clinical Psychology: Science and Practice, 3,* 203–215.

Serin, R. C. & Amos, N. L. (1995). The role of psychopathy in the assessment of dangerousness. *International Journal of Law and Psychiatry, 18,* 231–238.

Sewell, K. W. & Salekin, R. T. (1997). Understanding and detecting deception in sex offenders. In R. Rogers (Ed.), *Clinical assessment of malingering and deception* (2d ed.). New York: Guilford Press.

Slobogin, C. (1996). Dangerousness as a criterion in the criminal process. In B. D. Sales & D. W. Shuman (Eds.), *Law, mental health, and mental disorder.* Pacific Grove, CA: Brooks/Cole.

Tarasoff v. Regents of the University of California, 551 P.2d 334 (1976).

Thornton, D. (2000). *SRA—Initial deviance assessment* (unpublished manuscript). London: Her Majesty's Prison Service.

United States v. Salerno, 481 U.S. 739 (1987).

Wagner, D. E., Van Nort, J. J., Scanish, J. D., Barnes, J. M., Hallman, J. L., Thomas, K. W. & Smith, N. L. (2000). Daubert *hearing information: Sex offender risk assessments.* LaGrange, KY: Kentucky Department of Corrections.

Webster, C. D., Douglas, K. S., Eaves, D. & Hart, S. D. (1997). *Manual for the HCR-20: Assessing risk for violence* (version 2). Burnaby, British Columbia: Mental Health, Law and Policy Institute, Simon Fraser University.

Webster, C. D., Harris, G. T., Rice, M. E., Cormier, C. & Quinsey, V. L. (1994). *The violence prediction scheme: Assessing dangerousness in high-risk men.* Toronto: University of Toronto, Centre of Criminology.

Part 3

Special Populations

When SVP laws were first being passed, little attention was paid to the special needs of some subgroups affected by these statutes. For example, few clinicians were aware that juveniles might also be included in this type of legislation, and yet several states now allow for the civil commitment of juveniles. Similarly, other states provide for civil commitment beginning with the day a person reaches majority, despite the fact that his or her offense history occurred entirely during adolescence. Several states that adopted SVP statutes have also noted that developmentally disabled sexual offenders often "fall through the cracks" of standard programs. At times they present too high a risk for existing facilities designed for people with developmental disabilities, yet their placement in standard SVP programs has also been found to be inappropriate. In addition, the provision of treatment to address chemical dependency needs in sex offender treatment programs has often been only an afterthought. Part 3 addresses the needs of these three special populations.

In Chapter 12, Ted Shaw, Amy Heesacker, and Edward Delgado-Romero discuss the special needs of the juvenile or very young adult offender. Their suggestions should be considered carefully by any state that is adopting an SVP statute and has not yet considered whether the commitment criteria could be interpreted to be inclusive of juveniles.

In Chapter 13, Jim Haaven and Anita Schlank describe the inappropriateness of attempts to merge developmentally disabled sex offenders into existing SVP programs. The specialized approach required for the treatment of this population is also outlined.

Finally, Bill Plum notes in Chapter 14 that historically, sex offender treatment programs have separated the treatment for chemical dependency from the sex offender-specific groups, when a well-integrated approach is actually preferred. With the potential dangerousness of this population being so great, it seems particularly important to adequately address the high-risk factor of substance abuse in a manner that clearly identifies for the offender its relevance to his choice to reoffend. The author describes one method for integrating substance abuse groups in a standard civil commitment program and offers a new assessment tool that will help in the identification of specific treatment needs for this subgroup.

Chapter 12

Implications of Sexually Violent Predator Laws for Youthful Offenders

by Ted Shaw, Ph.D., Amy K. Heesacker, Ph.D., and Edward A. Delgado-Romero, Ph.D.

Overview	12-1
Brief Review of the Development of SVP Laws	12-2
Assessment of Dangerousness	12-3
Traditional Assessment Tools	12-3
Juvenile Data	12-4
Housing Issues	12-4
Quality of Treatment	12-5
Financial Implications of Civil Commitment	12-6
Specific Costs	12-6
Political Capital	12-8
Summary	12-9

OVERVIEW

The stated purpose of sexually violent predator (SVP) laws is to provide long-term care and confinement to convicted sex offenders who are determined, initially by "experts" and subsequently by judges and/or juries, to be at significant risk to sexually reoffend without such treatment and confinement. The standard for determining the threshold for risk and dangerousness in regard to the likelihood for sexual recidivism differs from state to state, but in general it can be defined as somewhere between "likely" and "more likely than not" to reoffend sexually. Generally, these SVP laws have been interpreted by the agencies responsible for implementing them and the courts that enforce them as targeting essentially the "worst of the worst" sex offenders in terms of risk and dangerousness.

These SVP laws have contributed significantly to the impetus to create more reliable means of determining dangerousness for sex offenders and effectively treating the most dangerous. However, while much progress has been made recently towards developing reliable and valid measures of recidivism prediction (Quinsey et al., 1998), there is still much work to be done, particularly with special populations such as juvenile offenders. Alas, youthful and juvenile sex offenders, while included in the SVP legislation of several states, have generally been excluded from empirical research concerning recidivism risk.

BRIEF REVIEW OF THE DEVELOPMENT OF SVP LAWS

On June 23, 1997, the U.S. Supreme Court upheld a Kansas state law that established procedures for the civil commitment of "sexually violent predators" (SVPs) who have completed their prison sentences. The case of *Kansas v. Hendricks* (521 U.S. 346 (1997)) tested the constitutionality of this law with particular attention to issues of due process, double jeopardy, and ex post facto. In a 5-4 decision the Court found that the SVP law was not unconstitutional, a finding that implicitly validated SVP laws in other states and opened the door for the adoption of similar laws across the country. Seventeen states as of the time of this writing have authorization to involuntarily commit sexually violent predators once their criminal sentence is complete. These states include Arizona, California, Florida, Illinois, Iowa, Kansas, Kentucky, Maine, Minnesota, Missouri, New Jersey, North Dakota, South Carolina, Texas, Virginia, Washington, and Wisconsin. Four of these states (Illinois, South Carolina, Washington, and Wisconsin) include juveniles under their respective statutes (Mercer, 1999), and it appears that many of the states will allow for the civil commitment of individuals who committed their sex offenses when they were juveniles under specific conditions. For example, in Florida individuals age eighteen and over with a sexual offense conviction, whether instant (the most recent) or prior, are considered for civil commitment under the SVP statute, even if they were adjudicated as juveniles and are incarcerated in juvenile facilities. In addition, individuals whose sexual offenses were committed exclusively as juveniles but who are in adult facilities under adult sanctions, either due to a subsequent adult conviction or because their original juvenile offenses were of such a nature that they were waived to adult court at the time and sentenced as adults, are included in the Florida statute (Fla. Stat. ch. 394.912(2c), 394.912(11) (1999)). Minnesota's statute also allows for individuals to be committed once they turn age eighteen, even if their history of sexual offenses occurred when they were juveniles.

These statutes are variations of the laws that permit the civil commitment of mentally ill individuals who have been determined to be unable to care for themselves or who are at imminent risk for harming themselves or others. Most of the SVP statutes are based on those originally developed by the State of Washington (NASMHPD, 1999). They generally define an SVP as a person who has been convicted of or charged with a "sexually violent offense," which is essentially any offense included in a statute by the legislature (e.g., sexual battery), and who suffers from a "mental abnormality" or personality disorder (e.g., antisocial personality disorder, pedophilia) that makes the person likely to engage in predatory acts of sexual violence if not confined in a secure facility for treatment. A "mental abnormality" has generally been defined as a congenital or an acquired condition that affects the emotional or volitional capacity of an individual, predisposes him to commit sexually violent offenses, and thereby causes him to be a menace to the health and safety of others. The SVP laws are intended to provide a legal mechanism to identify, confine, and treat the most serious sexual predators for an indeterminate period of time. This time period lasts, in effect, until it is determined that the individual is not likely to engage in further acts of sexual violence by whatever process is defined under the statute. For example, the Florida statute includes provisions for annual reviews by the court with consideration of whether the individual continues to meet criteria for commitment or not (Fla. Stat. ch. 394.918 (1999)).

With regard to identification, the statutes stipulate that prior to completion of their criminal sentences, potential candidates for civil commitment (i.e., those who have committed sexual crimes) will be evaluated to determine whether they meet the criteria for consideration under the SVP statute of their respective state. That is, mental health professionals, primarily psychologists, are being asked to assess dangerousness and/or the potential risk of recidivism in order to determine whether an individual should be civilly committed for this indeterminate length of time.

ASSESSMENT OF DANGEROUSNESS

Traditional Assessment Tools

Assessing dangerousness has traditionally been a daunting task, and the average predictive accuracy of clinical judgment has been shown to be only slightly better than chance (Hanson & Bussiere, 1998). Moreover, a meta-analytic study (Hanson & Bussiere, 1998; Hanson, 1997) that combined the data from numerous outcome studies of over 20,000 subjects demonstrated that many of the factors once believed to predict recidivism are not necessarily useful in this regard. Consequently, a number of actuarial assessment instruments such as the Rapid Risk Assessment for Sexual Offense Recidivism (RRASOR) (Hanson, 1997), its recent "replacement" the Static-99 (Hanson & Thornton, 1999-02), and the Minnesota Sex Offender Screening Tool-Revised (MnSOST-R) (Epperson et al., 1998) have been developed to assist in more accurately predicting sexual recidivism among sex offenders. These actuarial instruments are now commonly being used to help evaluators make decisions with regard to SVP assessments in most states that have SVP statutes.

In an effort to create reasonably valid and reliable tools, the developers of these instruments used measures that would likely be found in available records so that scoring could be based primarily on reviews of records rather than the often unreliable self-report of offenders. As a result, these instruments cannot predict actual reoffending; such documentation is not expected to be found in the records. These instruments must rely instead on estimates of sexual reoffending, using rearrest and reconviction data for their risk values to produce an estimate of the risk of reoffending. These studies identify "factors" that predict rearrest and reconviction and that may be considered similar to factors that predict actual reoffending. The studies use a variety of follow-up periods, such as six years and five, ten, and fifteen years respectively. Hanson (1997) has referred to his recidivism predictions as "estimates," and anyone who has worked with sex offenders will recognize that sex offenders rarely have been arrested and/or convicted of every sex offense they committed. This leads to the dilemma that factors that predict rearrest and reconviction for sex offenses may not be the same as factors that predict actual reoffense (Sreenivasen et al., 2000). Moreover, while these instruments make predictions for five, six, ten, and fifteen years, the SVP laws refer to lifetime risk, which is likely to be significantly greater than for the length of time studied.

Juvenile Data

Unfortunately, these instruments are not based on data collected from juvenile sex offenders or specifically on individuals who committed their sex offenses only as juveniles; therefore, they cannot be expected to provide valid and reliable predictions (even of rearrest and reconviction risk) for this population. Instruments such as the Hare Psychopathy Checklist for Adolescents (Hare, 1999) are currently being developed, though they remain unavailable. A version of the MnSOST-R for juveniles reportedly is under development and may soon be ready for use (Epperson, 2000), and other researchers purport to be developing additional instruments targeting juveniles. The current potential is quite high for SVP evaluators to make inaccurate and/or misinformed dangerousness predictions in the cases of juvenile sex offenders or those adult offenders whose sex offenses were committed exclusively as juveniles.

In regards to determining appropriate actuarial instruments for prediction of recidivism in juvenile sex offenders, the demographics of the samples used to develop the instruments essentially govern their applicability. The samples used for the RRASOR, for example, included adult incarcerated sexual offenders whose offenses were committed before age eighteen, provided they had been continuously incarcerated for those offenses at the time of the SVP evaluation (Doren, 2000). In other words, a sex offender who committed his last sex offense at age sixteen, was incarcerated in a secure facility continuously since adjudication for that offense, and is now age eighteen or older would have been included in the Hanson study. On the other hand, an adolescent sex offender who committed a sex offense at age sixteen, was incarcerated until age seventeen and subsequently released on juvenile probation, and then violated his probation (not a new sex offense) would have been dropped from the study. The developers of the MnSOST-R were even more restrictive in that they only included offenders who had a sex offense charge since age eighteen or who were waived to adult court and sentenced to adult sanctions (Epperson, 2000).

The significant consequence of the exclusion of juvenile sex offenders and offenders whose sex offenses occurred exclusively before age eighteen from the current actuarial assessments is that for the present, the clinician providing an opinion to the court concerning recidivism risk must depend primarily on clinical judgment. As noted above, the average predictive accuracy of these clinical judgments has been shown to be only slightly better than chance, and many of the factors once believed to predict recidivism have not been shown to be useful in this regard (Hanson & Bussière, 1998).

HOUSING ISSUES

In addition to the problem of making rationally based prediction decisions concerning juvenile sex offenders, the enormous dilemma of safely housing these youth in a therapeutic environment that minimizes the opportunities for abuse is cause for great concern. Generally, the Departments of Health Services, Human Services, Children and Family Services, Mental Health, and Social and Rehabilitation Services are responsible for the commitment of SVPs (Mercer, 1999). These offenders are required to be placed in a hospital or secure facility, and often it is stipulated that they must be housed separately from other types of offenders. However, it is conceivable that juvenile sex offenders or offenders who committed their sex offenses as juveniles and are still young and/or immature will be housed with older adult offenders who have been incarcerated for many years and offenders who committed their offenses as adults. This, in fact, has been the case in some states where incidents arise, leading to internal sanctions or charges with law enforcement.

The possibility of abuse while in treatment is made more likely by the current trend in the United States for juvenile courts to use a more adult-like criminal justice model, and more juveniles are being adjudicated and tried as adults in response to public outcry for community protection (CSOM, 1999). Questions arise as to the safety of the younger offenders who will be held in confinement in SVP programs and the seemingly punitive nature of potentially unlimited confinement for juvenile offenders, despite the stated rehabilitation goals of these statutes. For example, in one program, a nineteen-year-old mentally retarded sex offender convicted of sex offenses as a juvenile and placed in a juvenile facility was screened for civil commitment and placed in a facility while progressing through the SVP legal proceedings. While housed at the facility he reported that an older "predatory" sex offender had been pressuring him for sex, and the case was sufficiently serious to warrant a police report.

QUALITY OF TREATMENT

Similar questions arise when considering the realistic potential for effective treatment of juvenile offenders confined to SVP programs with adult offenders and confined individuals who have committed very different crimes (e.g., exhibitionism versus rape). Civilly committed offenders have already begun litigation about the treatment they are receiving in these programs. The U.S. Supreme Court heard arguments in October 2000 regarding the treatment received by rapist Andre Brigham Young in the State of Washington (*Seling v. Young*, 121 S. Ct. 727 (2001)). Young claimed that his confinement in the SVP program was punitive because he was being denied the "adequate care and individualized treatment" the statute mandates (Porterfield, 2000). The litigation pointed out the problems inherent in the treatment component of the SVP statutes, and it suggested that the individual treatment needs of the diverse population of confined offenders may need to be more adequately addressed.

On the other hand, the quality of treatment issue may be more related to the resistance of sex offenders to actively participate in and successfully complete treatment because of the involuntary nature of the treatment setting. No doubt all treatment providers, whether treating adults or juveniles, inpatient or outpatient, have experienced their clients misrepresenting the nature of the treatment and its applicability to any one offender. The NASMHPD Medical Directors Council Technical Report (1999) suggests principals governing the treatment of SVPs, including standards specific to individual treatment. While it may very well be prudent and even necessary to separate the youngest and most vulnerable (including mentally retarded) sex offenders from the general population of adult sex offenders, under controlled conditions there could be therapeutic advantages to exposing juvenile offenders to adult sex offenders. Experts in the sex offender treatment field have long suggested that treating different types of sex offenders together, specifically rapists and child molesters, especially in group, intensifies and improves the treatment experience, in part because the rapists and child molesters have such difficulty relating to each other's pathology.

This foments the very essence of conflict in the group process that can, in turn, lead to therapeutic change (Barnard et al., 1989).

According to an article produced by the Center for Sex Offender Management, "It is estimated that juveniles account for up to one-fifth of the rapes and one-half of the cases of child molestation committed in the United States each year" (CSOM, 1999). The article reports that between 1986 and 1992 the number of juvenile sex offender treatment programs doubled, and increased societal concerns about rising rates of juvenile sex offenses is cited as one reason for program growth in recent years. As the trend toward the civil commitment of SVPs coincides with the trend to adjudicate and try juveniles as adults, it is becoming more relevant to address the issue of juvenile sex offender treatment, particularly as the SVP statutes will affect this issue. One very important related issue is the nature of the juvenile justice system and its significant differences from the adult criminal justice system. In a recent case pending before a county court in Florida (Cohen, 2000, re: *In re T.B.B.*, No. 99-0214 (Hillsborough County Ct. Fla. 2000)), the attorney argued that juveniles:

- Are not afforded a right to trial by jury;
- Endure statutory periods of jurisdiction until age nineteen or above "regardless of the age of the juvenile or the crime charged"; and
- Are subject to violation of community sanctions and subsequent incarceration without due process as is afforded to adults.

The attorney also noted that in the juvenile system unproven allegations and "mental health" issues may be considered in sentencing, citing *In re T.B.B.* as a case in which a juvenile who was convicted of a property offense was sentenced to a residential sex offender treatment program due to a mental health-related history of sexual offending for which he was never charged (Cohen, 2000).

FINANCIAL IMPLICATIONS OF CIVIL COMMITMENT

Civil commitment programs involve extensive evaluation, assessment, and long-term treatment, all of which involve considerable expense. Annual per offender costs of from $65,000 to more than $100,000 have been reported. Because of this great expense, it is important to consider the cost to society of providing earlier interventions, including prevention and intermediate care, along with this deep-end treatment for nonvoluntary clients.

Specific Costs

In exploring the true (long-term) costs of civil commitment and considering the effect on adolescent sex offender funding, it is important to consider numerous factors. The process of civil commitment begins with the evaluation of the offender by specified professionals. Each state has defined the qualification requirements of the evaluators as well as the procedures they must follow. The first phase of evaluation is usually a review of the offender's record to determine whether he meets the criteria for a civil commitment evaluation. If the first phase indicates that the offender is to be formally evaluated, then specified mental health professionals will evaluate him for civil commitment. Some states specify that the offender must be evaluated by more than one mental health professional. These findings are then defended in court to establish whether civil commitment is warranted. If the offender is determined to need civil commitment, he is then assigned to a treatment center where he will undergo treatment with annual evaluations of his continued civil commitment. Several states do not provide for conditions of release (see, e.g., Fla. Stat. ch. 394.918 (1999)).

In this process there are many costs. In the first phase there are some costs associated with reviewing cases as they are presented; however, the first significant costs occur when the offender needs to be evaluated. Some states mandate more than one evaluator and others specify the qualifications of the examiners. At any rate, experts are not cheap. For one evaluation that includes travel, review of department of corrections records, time spent doing the evaluation and time spent preparing the report, costs could run from $90 to $250 per hour. The authors estimate that each evaluation averages fifteen hours, with some taking as much as forty hours.

If a case is pursued by the state and a court hearing is necessary, then numerous events—including interrogatories, depositions, adversarial probable cause hearings and trials as well as travel and preparation costs—are involved for the prosecution as well as the defense. These costs run many thousands of dollars and may involve six or more expert witnesses for several days.

If an offender is civilly committed, secure treatment facilities must be available to house the offender. States have either constructed new facilities or adapted existing facilities; Mercer (1999) provides examples of facilities built or adapted to house and treat SVPs. The average construction cost per bed is $136,000, with a range from $50,000 to $253,000 cost per bed. As Mercer points out, there are no national specifications for treatment facilities for SVPs.

The cost of treatment is yet an additional financial factor. Estimates of the cost of treating an SVP for one year range from $30,000 to $125,000. The cost of housing, feeding, and security alone is about $30,000 per offender, so in the case of the low estimate, pressure is exerted on the government to fund these programs. Of great concern is the likely need to cut corners, and given that food, shelter, and security will not be compromised, the area of treatment is left as the area to cut. For example in Texas, when the cost of a $17 million facility for civil commitment became public knowledge, politicians were moved to introduce an alternative outpatient monitoring system with a more politically acceptable price tag of $3.9 million. The politicians agreed that the outpatient monitoring system was not the preferred treatment setting, yet the financial and political costs were too high to move them to do otherwise.

As the reader can surmise, the costs of these programs add up quickly, and despite best estimates it seems that demand for civil commitment outstrips the best predictions, and sexual offenders are being civilly committed at a significantly higher rate than projected. For example, in 1997 state officials in Wisconsin had projected that from 1994 to 1997, thirty offenders would be civilly committed. Instead, they were faced with 179 commitments in that period, 600 percent more than predicted! At that rate, the $30 million treatment facility will be full in less than five years (half the predicted time), and the costs to continue the program will be astronomical.

Why would mental health professionals endorse civil commitment at such high rates? Common belief is that psychologists tend to overestimate the likelihood of violent behavior and recidivism and might be cautious about endorsing what might be a lifelong civil commitment. Doren (1998) calculated what he claims are "true" recidivism rates for sex offenders of from 39 to 52 percent. Consequently, in accordance with sexual predator law guidelines, clinicians may actually be underpredicting recidivism rates rather than overpredicting them, as has been widely believed. Doren's findings support a high rate of civil commitment for offenders.

The number of offenders eligible for a civil commitment is considerable. For example, Mercer (1999) projected that as many as 7,216 inmates in the custody of the Florida Department of Corrections on November 30, 1999 will be referred to the Florida SVP program in the future. Mercer attempted to estimate the number of juveniles who might be referred to commitment programs from the Department of Juvenile Justice, but found that this was a difficult task. It was estimated that there would be six to seven new referrals per month based on previous data, but this estimate did not take into account the effect that civil commitment might have on the treatment of juvenile sex offenders. Therefore, it is likely that this number is a severe underestimate of the juvenile "pipeline" into the civil commitment program.

Political Capital

As the example from Texas (above) shows, the political value of being tough on SVPs has to be weighed against the reality of the required funding. This introduces another type of cost as real as financial—political cost. The ascension of civil commitment legislation can be seen as a politically motivated phenomenon that has risen to prominence in states with conservative leadership. The political fear is being perceived as "soft on crime," and SVPs can provide high profile examples of tough attitudes toward criminals. The political capital of civil commitment is gained at the expense of rehabilitation, prevention, and diversion of adolescent offenders. For example, money that might have been used for diversion programs may be reallocated to centers that handle dangerous and repeat offenders. This reallocation is typical of what has been referred to as the "tough love" approach to juvenile justice (Fisher, 2000), and it shares the ideological base with civil commitment that resources should be allocated to the most dangerous members of society. Consequently, prevention is deemphasized in favor of detention.

Unfortunately this is not a new phenomenon. Prentky and Burgess (1990) traced the trend towards what Pacht (1976) noted as preventive detention and not rehabilitation. In attempts to operationalize the benefits of rehabilitation, they performed a cost-benefit analysis of the treatment of child molesters. Their research indicated that it was cost effective to treat sex offenders and that the cost to society for untreated sex offenders was substantial. The authors suggested that sex offenders should be treated for the sake of their victims (i.e., preventing future victims). Civil commitment programs treat offenders *after* they have committed their various offenses rather than *before*, yet there still is an opportunity to prevent additional victims.

Other than funding issues, civil commitment laws may have another profound effect on juvenile sex offender treatment. Part of the risk assessment for recidivism (MnSOST-R) (Epperson et al., 1998) includes whether or not the offender has "successfully completed" a treatment program. In addition, many civil commitment laws provide for data collection regarding the demographics of SVPs. Given these two factors, it becomes apparent that civil commitment provides an unprecedented evaluation of the effectiveness of treatment programs. Providers who have tailored their programs to meet unrealistic demands of agencies, for example, may find themselves facing their program inadequacies in court. For example, many contracts in Florida require providers to maintain a certain percentage of successful completers in a specific period of time while not having control over their intake or discharge criteria. Those programs with poorly defined criteria for "successful completion" of treatment or with admission/treatment/discharge criteria beyond their control may find themselves under scrutiny and in danger of losing state funding should the reality of their situation come under the scrutiny of the courts.

SUMMARY

If we believe that treatment works, that primary prevention works, and that treatment and prevention are cost effective, then developing civil commitment laws and programs seems an extreme step in the prevention process. The authors have examined the political reasons for these laws and programs in this chapter, but find that even political gains have their limits. We know that prejudice and hatred against violent sexual predators runs high. It is widely believed that human beings make rational economic decisions (Howard, 1997), and rational thoughts are the cornerstone of treating sex offenders. Yet civil commitment for juveniles appears to represent an irrational and short-sighted position that ignores the long-term costs to society and the benefits of prevention in favor of a "tough" stance on crime. At the very least, juvenile sexual offender specialists must become informed about the true costs of civil commitment and the long- and short-term effects that civil commitment can have on juvenile treatment, and they must struggle to provide necessary interventions for juveniles while they are juveniles in order to keep them from falling into the civil commitment system.

References

Barnard, G., Fuller, A., Robbins, L. & Shaw, T. (1989). *The child molester: An integrated approach to evaluation and treatment.* New York: Bruner/Mazel.

Center for Sex Offender Management (CSOM) (1999, December). *Understanding juvenile sexual offending behavior: Emerging research, treatment approaches and management practices.* Silver Spring, MD: Author.

Cohen, J. L (2000). Motion filed in a commitment case currently pending before Hillsborough County Court, regarding: In re Commitment of T.B.B., No. 99-0214 (Hillsborough County Ct. Fla. 2000).

Doren, D. M. (1998). Recidivism base rates, predictions of sex offender recidivism, and the "sexual predator" commitment laws. *Behavioral Sciences and the Law, 16*, 97–114.

Doren, D. M., (2000, January 5). Personal communication regarding In re Commitment of L.R., No. 99-9902 (Hillsborough County Ct. Fla. 2000).

Epperson, D. L. (2000, October). *The assessment of the sexually violent predator using the Minnesota sex offender screening tool—Revised.* Workshop presented on behalf of the Florida Department of Children and Families, Orlando, Fl.

Epperson, D. L., Kaul, J. D. & Hesselton, D. (1998, October). *Final report on the development of the Minnesota sex offender screening tool—Revised* (MnSOST-R). Paper presented at the seventeenth annual research and treatment convention of the Association for the Treatment of Sexual Abusers, Vancouver, British Columbia.

Fisher, L. (2000). Cuts leave few options for judges, *The Gainesville Sun*, June 28, 2000, at A1.

Fla. Stat. ch. 394.910–394.931 (1999).

Hanson, R. K. (1997). *The development of a brief actuarial risk scale for sexual offense recidivism.* (User Report 97-04). Ottawa: Department of the Solicitor General of Canada.

Hanson, R. K. & Bussière, M. T. (1998). Predicting relapse: A meta-analysis of sexual offender recidivism studies. *Journal of Consulting and Clinical Psychology, 66,* 348–362.

Hanson, R. K. & Thornton, D. (1999). *Static 99: Improving actuarial risk assessments for sex offenders* (User Report No. 99-02). Ottawa: Department of the Solicitor General of Canada.

Hare, R. D. (1999, September). *Assessing psychopathy with the HARE psychopathy checklist—Revised (PCL-R).* Workshop presented in conjunction with the eighteenth annual training and research conference of the Association for the Treatment of Sexual Abusers, Orlando, FL.

Howard, G. S. (1997). *Ecological psychology: Creating a more earth-friendly human nature.* Notre Dame, Indiana: University of Notre Dame Press.

Kansas v. Hendricks, 521 U.S. 346 (1997).

Mercer, W. M. (1999, December 20). *Study of the programmatic and facility needs of the Florida sexually violent predator program: Final report.* A report presented to the State of Florida Department of Children and Families, Tallahassee, FL.

National Association of State Mental Health Program Directors (NASMHPD) (1999, April 25–27). *Medical directors counsel technical report*, Portland, OR.

Pacht, A.R. (1976). The rapist in treatment: Professional myths and psychological realities. In M. J. Walker & S. L. Brodsky (Eds.), *Sexual assault: The victim of the rapist.* Lexington, MA: Lexington Books.

Porterfield, E. (2000). High court to take up sexual-predator law: Justices to weigh rapist's case against state statute, *Seattle Post-Intelligencer*, Mar. 21, 2000, at B1.

Prentky, R. & Burgess, A. W. (1990). Rehabilitation of child molesters: A cost-benefit analysis. *American Journal of Orthopsychiatry, 60,* 108–117.

Quinsey, V. L., Harris G. T., Rice M. E. & Cormier, L. A. (1998). *Violent offenders: Appraising and managing risk.* Washington, DC: American Psychological Association Press.

Seling v. Young, 121 S. Ct. 727 (2001).

Sreenivasen, S., Kirkish, P., Garrick, T., Weinberger, L. E. & Phenix, A. (2000, November). Actuarial risk assessment models: A review of critical issues related to violence and sex offender recidivism. *Journal of the Academy of Psychiatry and the Law, 28,* 438–448.

Chapter 13

The Challenge of Treating the Sex Offender With Developmental Disabilities

by James Haaven, M.A. and Anita Schlank, Ph.D., L.P.

Elements of the Challenge 13-1
    Safety and Management Issues 13-2
    Population Characteristics 13-2
Assessment Considerations 13-5
    Interview/Sexual History 13-5
    Psychometric Testing 13-6
    Plethysmograph 13-7
    Abel Assessment for Sexual Interest 13-7
Treatment Approaches 13-8
    Overall Strategies 13-8
        Milieu/Motivation 13-8
        Effective Teaching 13-9
        Community Transition 13-10
    Specific Components 13-11
        Adapting the DDSO's Relapse Prevention Model 13-11
        Approach Skills—The "New Me" 13-13
        Avoidance Skills—"What-to-Dos" 13-14
        Medication 13-15
Civil Commitment Programs 13-16
Summary 13-17

ELEMENTS OF THE CHALLENGE

Civil commitment statutes for sexual offenders often use broad language when referring to the disorders that must be present to meet the criteria for commitment. Most statutes refer to a requirement for the presence of a "mental disorder," which can include nearly any diagnosis (e.g., substance dependence disorder, personality disorder). Because of the latitude of the language in these statutes, sexual offenders with developmental disabilities are increasingly being placed in civil commitment programs (SVP Conference, 2000). They present unusual challenges with regard to the appropriateness of their placement and treatment. This phenomenon may be yet another negative consequence of deinstitutionalization, which Haaven and Coleman (2000) note has already resulted in more developmentally disabled sexual offenders (DDSOs) being redirected to correctional and psychiatric settings that are not designed to meet their needs.

Safety and Management Issues

From a treatment perspective, the most basic need of safety is complicated when DDSOs are placed in correctional settings. The prison environment and experience is naturally more punitive for them than for nondisabled inmates (Santamour & West, 1982).

They are often victimized (Bright, 1989), as the other inmates quickly detect their signs of weakness. Their vulnerability greatly increases the likelihood that they will be taken advantage of (Garcia & Steele, 1988), including the likelihood they will be sexually abused. They may interpret the sexual advances of nondisabled inmates as signs they are accepted and cared about.

Simply managing the behavior of DDSOs in correctional settings may require facility modifications, specialized staff training, and programmatic changes addressing rules, procedures, and protocols. DDSOs are generally very different from commitees receiving treatment in institutions for the mentally retarded. The DDSO, while handicapped, is nevertheless more sophisticated and better able to mask his limitations, and when placed in an institution for retarded persons, he can victimize the other residents and disrupt routine. It is generally accepted among professionals who work with the institutionalized retarded that DDSOs should not be placed in institutions for developmentally disabled nonoffenders (Santamour & West, 1982). Ideally, civil commitment programs would have separate DDSO facilities, but with so few DDSOs in each program, the cost becomes prohibitive.

Civil commitment programs with only a few developmentally disabled residents may try to integrate these persons with the nondisabled population and attempt to just simplify the material in the standard program. This, however, will not constitute adequate treatment for DDSOs. In addition to the offense-specific treatment needed, DDSOs often need specific habilitation training and maintenance. "It is well documented that mentally retarded people institutionalized without proper habilitation will regress and lose vitally important life skills they previously possessed" (Ellis & Luckasson, 1985, p. 482). This loss of social skill competencies only compounds the problems of DDSOs trying to integrate into the community and maintain appropriate self-control.

Population Characteristics

If we compare the DDSO with other sexual offenders, we will find there are actually more similarities than differences (Haaven & Coleman, 2000; Coleman & Haaven, 1998). For example, most sexual offenders, regardless of intellectual abilities, hold cognitive distortions that justify and minimize their offending behavior. Their cognitive scripts are similar and often unsophisticated ("She wants me"; " I'm teaching her about sex"). As with nondisabled sex offenders, the presence of disordered arousal can also play a significant role for offenders who are developmentally disabled. DDSOs also have deviant fantasies to which they masturbate, although their fantasies generally are more simple and focused on the sexual act or a specific physical characteristic of the victim. However, significant differences do exist in these two populations, as outlined below.

1. *Fewer consequences for offenses.* One difference might manifest in how society has dealt with the DDSO in the past—he may have a history of little or no consequences for many of his offenses. Caregivers and professionals involved in his case may have minimized his behavior because they saw him as childlike, with no power differential (e.g., as compared to his child victim), or as without control over his behavior (Coleman & Haaven, 1998). Swanson and Garwick (1990) also note the tendency for offenses of low-functioning sexual offenders to be ignored or only scolded, rather than directed to any involvement with legal proceedings or a referral for treatment. These offenders may be gradually desensitized to the seriousness of their offenses and then unexpectedly punished.

2. *Behavioral traits.* Of course, most non-DD offenders (average IQ and above) have similar characteristics, but the DD offender differs in the degree and frequency exhibited. Santamour and West (1982) list the following DDSO traits: low frustration tolerance, inability to delay gratification, poor impulse control, low level of motivation, anxiety about being accepted, demanding of attention, and easily persuaded or manipulated. While such traits easily apply to nondisabled offenders, recognizing such behaviors in DDSOs can help correctional and treatment personnel to identify them and to better understand them. This recognition can have significant impact on the behavior management of DDSOs within both correctional and treatment settings. In their need to be accepted, DDSOs will mask their limitations, causing staff to overestimate their abilities. It's common to hear a staff member say, for example, "He's smarter than he acts." Correctional settings demand order and a consistent routine. Any disruption of this order due to the unpredictable nature of the developmentally disabled offender is met with a strong reaction by both inmates and staff (Stacken & Shevich, 1999). This is why in correctional settings this type of offender often is harrassed and the victim of physical and sexual assault and also why he receives more discipline violations, spends more time in solitary confinement, and serves longer sentences (Buser et al., 1987).

3. *Need for acceptance.* The DDSO's desire to be accepted may cause him to assume and embrace the prison culture even more readily than other inmates. Civil commitment programs have a treatment focus and a more therapeutic environment, but many traditional correctional characteristics still exist and the committed offenders have spent significant time in prison settings. Therefore, directors of civil commitment programs housing DDSOs must not only modify treatment programming, they must make adaptations in the routine functioning of the program. This is necessary to ensure no resources are wasted or misused trying to manage DDSOs' disruptive behavior arising from environmental influences. It is necessary to have a staff member(s) who understands the unique needs of DDSOs and who in a systematic way can functionally evaluate the environment as to the supports needed. This requires not only an assessment of the programs's existing systems, but a walk through every

aspect of a DDSO's daily routine to learn which adaptations are needed to meet his basic needs.

For example, what provision exists for the DDSO to seek help or share concerns when necessary? A program's communication system usually requires literacy skills, an ability to learn events in sequence, a level of confidence, and the interpersonal skills to initiate communication, all of which are usually significant barriers for a developmentally disabled person. To communicate simplified procedures and supports—such as daily briefings with staff and basic institutional survival skills training—you may need to install visual aids, for example. Adjustment to any change, including schedule changes of activities, can be difficult for these individuals.

4. *Lack of social skills.* Another deficit that both nondisabled and disabled offenders share but that is more exaggerated in the latter is a lack of social skills, which impairs their ability to learn life skills such as stress management, assertiveness, and anger control (Coleman & Haaven, 1998). They have difficulty meeting their needs through appropriate means, so they act out their frustrations, unable to control their negative affective states (Haaven & Coleman, 2000). Due to the anxiety they feel and the amount of deprivation they experience, their high incidence of mental health problems is not surprising. Garcia and Steele (1988) estimated that 30 percent of the inmate population with intellectual impairment also exhibit symptoms of mental illness (p. 817). While stress management skills and knowing appropriate ways to get their needs met are critical for this group, their deficits in social skills makes it extra hard for them to develop support systems, to "fit in," and to gain a healthy recognition within their own environment. This contributes to their attention-seeking behavior, which especially in a correctional setting can be disruptive and misunderstood. Therefore, the development of interpersonal relationship skills for DDSOs is necessary not only for treatment purposes, but also for institutional adjustment.

5. *Sensitivity to criticism.* DDSOs generally have lower self-esteem than their nondisabled peers because they have had fewer real and perceived life successes. They generally exaggerate their accomplishments, are sensitive to criticism, and are resistant to change or to trying new experiences (Haaven & Coleman, 2000; Haaven et al., 1990). It is important in working with DDSOs not to overreact to their embellishments and tactics. Instead, give attention to providing initial successes in the treatment process so that momentum for change can be fostered.

6. *Little capacity for empathy.* Another area of difference is that DDSOs can be limited in their capacity to empathize (Haaven et al., 1990). This is not to say that they cannot care or be sensitive to others, but their mental processing abilities—most notably, being able to sense what others feel—are compromised. The clinician may have unrealistic expectations for the clinician when addressing issues of empathy, especially since the development of empathy is a requirement for successful completion of a program. In addition, due to lack of any research, we should not assume that a DDSO's limited cognitive empathic processing is a recidivism factor.

7. *Rigid attitudes.* DDSOs generally have incorrect or inadequate knowledge of sexuality and hold rigid attitudes regarding gender roles (Coleman & Haaven, in

press). Their knowledge about human sexuality and myths about sexual practices may more resemble those held by children and adolescents.

8. *Frequent misdiagnoses by professionals.* DDSOs also are frequently misdiagnosed. Personality disorders, substance abuse disorders, and depressive illnesses are often missed during diagnostic interviews. Schizophrenia may tend to be over diagnosed due to the low-functioning offender's potential for unusual sensory misperceptions (Coleman & Haaven, 1998), but mental retardation also may partially mask mental disorders (Luckasson, 1988). Depression, especially, can significantly affect a DDSO's social skill competencies, thereby causing stress and disruption in his life. Most affected is his ability to meet basic activities of daily living and maintaining healthy relationships.

9. *Difficulty learning.* A difficulty in learning new information is the greatest difference between the developmentally disabled offender and others. High anxiety and low frustration tolerance are usually present in learning situations. DDSOs therefore need to be taught at a slower pace, using simple vocabulary, breaking tasks into smaller increments, and repeating concepts to increase the effectiveness of the learning process (Brown & Pond, 1999).

10. *Unique use of denial mechanism.* DDSOs present a unique challenge to treatment providers because they may use denial in a manner that differs from other sexual offenders. Compared to the nondisabled offender, the DDSO may use denial as a general defense mechanism to avoid painful differences rather than as a discrete self-protective maneuver in response to committing a sexual offense (Haaven & Coleman, 2000; Coleman & Haaven, 1998; Coleman & Haaven, in press). DDSOs may cling to their denial more rigidly to protect themselves from anything that may be threatening or embarrassing. Therefore, DDSOs may take longer to risk self-disclosure and openly share details of their offenses.

ASSESSMENT CONSIDERATIONS

A sex offender-specific evaluation designed for a DDSO is the first step in the treatment process. To be effective, the evaluator needs to be familiar with and understand the unique differences of the DDSO compared to the non-DDSO. He or she must respect the DDSO and be mindful of his limitations, but also understand his ability to manipulate, deceive, and divert responsibility. The following evaluation practices are often used with DDSOs (Haaven & Coleman, 2000; Coleman & Haaven, in press).

Interview/Sexual History

After reviewing third-party information and completing the informed consent procedure, general history, and mental status exam, the evaluator takes a sexual history. Obtaining an accurate sexual history from a DDSO can be more difficult than doing so with nondisabled offenders. DDSOs have greater difficulty being open about sexuality, particularly their own offending history. Due to their embarrassment and performance anxiety, they have difficulty self-disclosing; they also have difficulty focusing and paying attention even when the evaluator is nonthreatening. They often try to give information that they believe is expected. All of these factors can interfere with obtaining information and an accurate sexual history.

The physical setting can affect the DDSO's ability to respond and, thus, the accuracy of the information given. The room in which the interview takes place should be private, with no unplanned interruptions. This desirable setting is often not available in correctional settings, where finding privacy is difficult and where interview rooms are often stark, with few pictures on the walls or items of interest to provide healthy distraction for the DDSO to make himself feel comfortable. Interviews need to be paced so that less threatening information is initially requested and then interspersed with more personal and probing questions as the interview proceeds. More breaks are usually needed during the interview process.

The evaluator should be aware of his or her own demeanor and reactions to the DDSO's responses. Developmentally disabled offenders are hyper-vigilant about detecting any reaction by the evaluator that indicates disapproval or ridicule, and the whole interview process winds up being affected. It is important to use the DDSO's sexual vocabulary to maximize accuracy and avoid rapid fire questioning that will only frustrate, confuse, and exhaust the client. Sometimes a DDSO's responses may be interpreted as a function of his denial syndrome when in fact it is part of his cognitive deficit. When a DDSO says "I don't remember," he may be speaking the truth. Difficulty in accurately disclosing time periods, ages, or other specifics may be primarily due to cognitive or memory deficits. Completing a sexual history provides the evaluator an opportunity to reinforce the DDSO in initiating the change process and assuming responsibility for his actions.

Psychometric Testing

Few psychometric tests are designed for DDSOs; usually, tests used to evaluate nondisabled offenders are adapted for use with DDSOs. Three such tests are the Adult Self Expression Scale (ASES), the Sexual Interest Cardsort, and the Pedophile Cognition Scale. Some tests can be adapted by simplifying the language or changing the response style (e.g., from a 1 to 5 rating to a "yes" or "no" response). Ideally, the DDSO completes the questionnaire, thereby reducing the influence of the person assisting, but in many cases the questions have to be read to the DDSO. While such alterations to the tests affect their standardization and perhaps therefore their reliability, they can still provide useful information.

One questionnaire specifically developed for sexual offenders with DDSO characteristics who may not be verbally proficient is the Socio-Sexual Knowledge and Attitude Test (SSKAT) (Edmonson et al., 1977). This test provides information regarding sexual knowledge and attitudes including body parts, masturbation, dating, and intimacy. Another sexual interest/attitudes questionnaire about pedophilia and rape of adult women adapted for DDSOs is the Modified Cognition Scale for the Developmentally Disabled (Haaven, 1995). Assessment of interpersonal skills, sexual interests and attitudes, thinking errors, and mental health problems like depression should be evaluated through as many methods as possible, including gathering information from third-party interviews, psychometrics, and plethysmography.

Plethysmograph

For the past seventeen years, the penile plethysmograph (PPG) has been used in the assessment and treatment of DDSOs. It has been a useful assessment instrument, especially in providing information with which to confront the offender's denial, identifying arousal problems, and perhaps most important, monitoring treatment progress. While there is research to support the effectiveness of the PPG in separating sex offenders from non-sex offenders (although with some limits on reliability and validity) (Murphy & Barbaree, 1994), there is no research addressing a similar comparison between DDSOs and nondisabled offenders. Therefore, data must be interpreted more conservatively. Certain adjustments are also necessary in using this instrument on DDSOs.

Due to performance anxiety, DDSOs may need more time to desensitize to the laboratory. They have difficulty accurately perceiving the stimuli and understanding the self-report procedure. Audio tapes should be clearly sexual or clearly violent, not mixed. The DDSO should be asked to explain the *content* to which he is responding. DDSOs often over-respond to stimuli presented in a laboratory. This may be due to their limited cognitive suppression skills or to a less perceived need to conform to societal expectations. It could also simply be the arousing aspect of the lab experience, including placing the gauge on their penis. Either way, their over-response can result in over-interpretation.

The only stimuli specifically designed for this population is the MONARCH DDMR Projective Audio/Visual VHS set, version 2. This stimuli is available from Behavioral Technology Incorporated in Salt Lake City, Utah, and it has been adapted for the comprehension level of DDSOs. The audiotapes use simple language and less abstraction, and at a slower pace. To increase the DDSO's ability to discriminate age and gender of each presentation in the assessment, nonpornographic visuals are presented simultaneously with the auditory tapes.

Abel Assessment for Sexual Interest

An increasing number of evaluators are using the Abel Screen, or Abel Assessment for Sexual Interest (Abel, 1996) in place of the PPG. The Abel Screen is based on visual attention research. This instrument uses self-report of attraction to various categories of possible sexual stimuli as well as a healthy measure of sustained attention to photographs of the stimuli. A questionnaire regarding sexual behavior (relapse prevention score) is included.

The stimuli used in the Abel Screen, like that of the MONARCH series, does not use sexually explicit materials. The relapse prevention score (RPS) designed to assess risk, as part of the Abel Screen, is currently not validated for either DDSOs or nondisabled offenders. The questions on this test are also at a level higher than what most DDSOs can comprehend. Currently, the research is not conclusive as to the Abel Screen's test-retest reliability, screening validity, and diagnostic validity. Although similar concern has been expressed regarding the use of the PPG, the Abel Screen is still new in the field and less researched than the PPG. There is no published research to date on the efficacy of the Abel Screen with regard to DDSOs. However, the Abel

Screen has the advantage over the PPG of being more user friendly. With the Abel Screen, the client may feel less anxiety or embarrassment than with the PPG, which requires him to partially undress and place a gauge on his penis. Due to this potential discomfort for some clients, advocates for persons with developmental disabilities may discourage the use of the PPG.

The Abel Screen provides ease of use and there is less political resistance regarding its administration. If it is capable of providing useful assessment information regarding sexual interest, it would be of significant benefit to DDSOs. Ideally, the PPG and the Abel Screen would both be used for best results in discriminating paraphilic profiles (Seghorn & Weigal, 1999).

TREATMENT APPROACHES

Overall Strategies

Certain strategies or philosophies should guide the design of a therapeutic program for DDSOs. To increase treatment effectiveness, it is important to incorporate DDSO-specific strategies to address these offenders' treatment needs.

Milieu/Motivation. The role of the milieu is often overlooked in program design. *This is especially true in correctional settings, where greater barriers exist for modifying and changing the physical setting.* Still, it is important that the treatment environment suggests to the DDSO that this is a safe place, both respectful and humane (Ferguson & Haaven, 1990). Developmentally disabled people are extra-sensitive to their surroundings, and the physical environment can have a significant effect on facilitating healthy social interaction (Haaven & Coleman, 2000; Coleman & Haaven, 1998; Haaven et al., 1990). The treatment environment should also be designed to provide motivation for change and to foster both behavioral and cognitive change (Willis, 1980). Finding a balance between security and treatment within correctional programs is an ongoing challenge. From a security perspective, changes in the physical environment can significantly reduce disruptive behavior. Safety and security are enhanced by a milieu that reinforces in the offender-residents some level of pride in and ownership of their surroundings.

Numerous things can be done to the environment to increase security and enhance treatment. Ideally, a range of physical spaces should provide a continuum from private areas to larger areas for active group interaction. Walls can be painted a variety of color schemes and soft furniture can be provided, along with carpeting, plants, curtains, and hand-made bedspreads. Activity areas should provide opportunities for a variety of leisure activities, including board games, puzzles, crafts, and music. It is best not to have tavern-like activities (e.g., no pool tables or foos-ball) because they only reinforce tavern-like behavior and skills.

If DDSOs share living space with nondisabled offenders, it is preferable that the DDSOs have their own group room (Stacken & Shevich, 1999). Group rooms should be comfortable and decorated using an abundance of visual stimuli such as posters, bulletin boards, mobiles, and collages. Creating visual representations of treatment themes and having the DDSOs personally associated with such projects reinforces their treatment efforts, accomplishments, and life skills being learned. Universal values such as honesty, helping others, and standing up for what's right can be visually and experientially represented throughout the milieu.

Remember that the physical environment is active twenty-four hours per day, a fact that can have significant effects on how behavior is managed and change facilitated (Coleman & Haaven, in press). Facilitating a sense among DDSOs of their own "group" helps foster the motivation to change. DDSOs should work cooperatively on projects using a buddy or sponsor system. They should be recognized for treatment successes that are not part of a specific plan; small rituals of appreciation can be quite motivating. "Most importantly, a culture in which status is gained by participation in the program needs to be nurtured and a sense of responsible self-identity encouraged" (Haaven & Coleman, 2000, p 281).

Habilitation of developmentally disabled offenders has been guided extensively by the principles of behavioral psychology (Denkowski et al., 1983), and level systems (token economy) are commonly used in treatment programs. While this approach may be useful initially in treatment, it has the disadvantage of relying on external control rather than reinforcing the internal locus of control of the DDSO. The guidelines presented above aim to reinforce that internal locus.

Effective Teaching. Most of what is accomplished in treatment is education. Treatment providers teach clients how to think about issues, to identify feeling states, and to learn new skills. We come to this challenge as clinicians who understand what needs to be done and why, but with little or no experience or training to achieve our goals. We have not learned to teach effectively. Our effectiveness is sometimes compromised when we impart new information to sex offenders, and the problem is greatly compounded in teaching a DDSO. The developmentally disabled person may have limited learning capacity, but it is important to keep in mind that his ability to learn is significantly more compromised by our inability to teach effectively then by his learning disabilities.

In addition to the traditional teaching methods for such individuals (slower pace, smaller steps, etc.), what we need is engagement in the learning process. We must link emotion with the learning process. Learning activities should have a component of being "fun, dramatic or bizarre" (Haaven et al., 1990). Many methods can be used to increase engagement in learning, such as art, music, poems, riddles, and drama. (Coleman, 1997). Other useful experimental activities are role plays, board games, and using passive and active sports activities in prescriptive ways. One of the most useful teaching tools is videotape—rarely have developmentally disabled people seen themselves on video, and it can be a very engaging and illuminating process.

All of these techniques comprise a multisensory approach to teaching and learning. Important points or themes can be reinforced by visual reminders throughout the milieu. All surface areas are potential billboards of information—eating placemats, inside the doors of toilet stalls, and ceilings over residents' beds. Nor should the clinicians and teachers unwittingly allow themselves to do most of the work. The DDSO must take the initiative, and the teacher must coach. Like other programs for sexual offenders, a DDSO-specific program should incorporate ways to assess the DDSO's learning maintenance and retention. One way to do this is to provide for periodic reviews in a time-sequence fashion (e.g., after one session, one day, one month, and so forth).

Community Transition. The transition of sex offenders in civil commitment programs into the community is a critical phase of programming. Not only does it present significant clinical and risk management problems, but the political implications can be daunting. Monat (1982) and Edgerton & Dingman (1964) showed that adults with mild mental retardation are not significantly different from people without mental retardation in the exploration and control of their sexual impulses, yet many myths exist about how the developmentally disabled express sexuality. The developmentally disabled individual is already considered by some to be impulsive, out-of-control, and oversexed, one to whom nothing sexual in nature should ever be introduced. Conversely, others see the individual as one with no sexual expression or intimacy in his or her life and no need for it.

The DDSO is a feared individual whose release to the community is greatly challenging. He will need support services. There is some data to indicate that disabled offenders who do not receive close supervision on parole recidivate more quickly and more frequently than nondisabled parolees (Santamour & West, 1977). But the disabled offender on parole or probation does as well as or better than the nondisabled parolee when appropriate programming is provided (Myers, 1976).

Certainly, without adequate support in the transition process, DDSOs can become overwhelmed by the change in structure and routine and regress to previous offending patterns. The kind of setting they transition to and the way they are received is important. Even nonoffending developmentally disabled people adjust best when they are met with positive regard on entering a group home (Belcher, 1994). But finding adequate housing in a community for a DDSO will be one of a civil commitment program's most difficult tasks. Where a DDSO qualifies for state services for the developmentally disabled, a more extended network of service options, including housing (foster care, group homes) and vocational services, becomes available. The problem is that such state agencies are often reluctant to assume any responsibility for sex offenders.

It would also be inappropriate to integrate many DDSOs into group homes or other facilities with nonoffenders. Where a DDSO is not eligible for such services (e.g., because he has borderline intelligence or adequate adaptive skills), the problem is compounded as to what facility can provide housing and necessary support services. His disabilities and consequent support needs are similar to those of eligible developmentally disabled offenders, but he is denied the traditional "safety net" for the developmentally disabled community.

DDSOs have an additional problem when it comes to generalizing their newly learned skills to the community setting. This problem requires prescriptive approaches to training and monitoring as clients are introduced to situations that could lead to regression. Only after demonstrating competency of avoidance/escape skills in specific potential risk situations should they be allowed to be in situations with lessening supervision (Haaven & Coleman, 2000). An example of this would be where a client who is being staff escorted takes the bus to work. The client must demonstrate his ability to identify risk situations, such as children getting on a bus, and use appropriate avoidance strategies, such as changing his seat or leaving the bus altogether. Demonstrating competency in avoidance/escape strategies in role-play situations alone is not adequate. In vivo demonstration of appropriate skills under observation is necessary before supervision gets reduced (e.g., before allowing unescorted bus trips).

Consistency, continuity of treatment, and monitoring is essential in the transition process. From a clinical perspective, treatment, planning, vocabulary, techniques, and approaches should be tailored to be easily understood so they can be effectively used by all the community providers (Coleman & Haaven, 1998). This easily-understood approach also applies to vocational, housing, financial, mental health, and conditional release supervision support services. Additionally, communication systems among providers regarding changes in treatment plans or supervision as well as potential problems require formats and protocols understood by all parties and streamlined to provide timely exchange of necessary information. The comprehensive relapse prevention plan should clearly indicate risk situations and should be given to all providers, especially for monitoring purposes. The plan may be more sophisticated than the DDSO can understand or needs to know, but this does not diminish its usefulness for providing supervision by all support systems.

The DDSO needs a more extensive support system in the community than the nondisabled offender. He is not unlike any person with developmental disabilities who needs additional support, and his extra need does not mean that he is a more serious threat to the community in general. Expanding his support system and including individuals and organizations such as friends, volunteers, churches, and other advocates will increase the effectiveness and safety of the community transition (Haaven & Coleman, 2000). You may also find it necessary to provide direct training for all providers about basic sex offender treatment and supervision. Complacency is one of the biggest problems facing providers, especially those who are not used to working with offender populations (Coleman & Haaven, 1998; Ward & McElwee, 1995). Follow-up training and discussions and an informational twenty-four-hour hotline to the parent civil commitment program could be established to provide immediate access to assistance.

Specific Components

Adapting the DDSO's Relapse Prevention Model. As with the population characteristics, the methods for treating DDSOs are similar in many ways to the methods used to treat other groups of sexual offenders. For example, group is the preferred modality, and treatment programming must be comprehensive, addressing both sex offender-specific issues and habilitation deficit areas. The deficit areas can be addressed within the Relapse Prevention Model (Pithers et al., 1983), which provides an effective theoretical framework on which to base the treatment program. But with low-functioning offenders such as DDSOs, modifications are required in each of these areas.

1. *Group sessions.* Group sessions are an important element in DDSO treatment for many reasons, including the opportunities they provide for social skills training. Through the group discussions, offenders learn how to give appropriate feedback, practice effective nonverbal communication, and demonstrate care and concern for their peers. Group is also important for the opportunities it provides for the DDSO to receive challenging feedback. Peers can challenge the DDSO on inconsistencies between what he presents in group and how he acts on the living unit. Peers also often recognize manipulation efforts that the therapist might miss. The group experience

provides an offender suffering from isolation the chance to see that he is not alone in his efforts to address his sex-offending behavior. It gives him a forum to learn to relate and, more important, to respect his own peers. Groups for low-functioning offenders, however, should be relatively small, ideally no larger than eight participants. More frequent and shorter sessions are preferable. "Four groups a week for thirty minutes are more effective than two groups a week for an hour . . ."(Haaven & Coleman, 2000, p. 379).

For group work to be effective, the therapist(s) needs to have a wide array of techniques available to maintain attention, engagement, and recall of information being learned (Prout & Cale, 1994). Some helpful methods include:

- Use of videotaping
- Visuals that facilitate verbal expression and feeling states
- Relaxation exercises, some silent and some with music
- Use of experiential activities such as drama, competitions, show and tell exercises

The therapist will need to take a more active role when facilitating groups for DDSOs. He or she will need to identify themes and then make those themes relevant to the individual DDSO and then to the group as a whole. The therapist also needs to protect the often fragile defenses of DDSOs to keep them from shutting down. Always important in group therapy with developmentally disabled persons is to check repeatedly that the participants understand what is being discussed and what is at issue. When a developmentally disabled person is facing a difficult concept and is asked whether he understands, he will often will give the "nod of incomprehension"—nodding his head yes even when he is totally confused (Brown & Pond, 1998).

2. *Individual counseling.* Although group therapy can be effective with most developmentally disabled people, individual counseling is useful in some cases. A client who has a great deal of performance anxiety in a group setting may need to be desensitized and coached individually to get the most benefit from the group experience. He can be told what to anticipate in group, given some training on how to share personal information, and respond to questions in preparation for self-disclosure in a group setting. In some instances, gathering self-disclosure information and teaching new concepts is simply better accomplished in an individual format with this population.

3. *Relapse Prevention Model.* The Relapse Prevention Model (Pithers et al., 1983) has been adopted in many programs for DDSOs. This model is considered quite compatible with past learning models typically used with developmentally disabled people (such as self-management, use of behavioral antecedents, a psychoeducational focus) (Haaven & Coleman, 2000). However, some problems have arisen in the application of this model to this special population. For example, developmentally disabled persons are deficient in their ability to identify and understand the links in a behavior chain. This is especially true where the precursors are more subtle. Also, while DDSOs can usually identify and understand the importance of avoiding external high-

risk factors (e.g., environments in which the presence of children is likely), they may experience extreme difficulty in identifying internal high-risk factors. In addition, DDSOs often have more difficulty in controlling their negative emotional states (Haaven & Coleman, 2000), which affects their ability to retrieve and use the information and skills they have learned to effectively remove themselves from risk behaviors. Support systems are necessary to assist DDSOs in their relapse management. What supports are needed, how they are to be used, and how they are to be maintained are all necessary parts of a comprehensive relapse plan. You need specific prescriptive planning to ensure that the plan facilitates and maintains the DDSO's use of his new skills and fulfills his expectations.

In adapting a relapse prevention model for a DDSO, an important area to focus on is the development of self-efficacy—a success identity—for the offender (Haaven & Coleman, 2000). The developmentally disabled often feel discounted, disenfranchised, and looked down upon. As we noted, they generally have low self-esteem and correspondingly are more prone to accept failure in the face of adversity. Therefore, developing goals to achieve a distinct and unique identity is central to adapting relapse prevention to this population. This sense of self in turn will increase their efforts to succeed and meet their expectations (Haaven & Coleman, 2000).

4. *Overview of DDSO relapse prevention model.* The following is an overview of the developmentally disabled sex offender relapse prevention (DDSO-RP) model (Haaven & Coleman, 2000). There are three important components in this model:

- New Me—the person they want to become;

- Setups—barriers to attaining the life they want and setups to offending behavior; and

- What-to-dos—how to attain the "good life" envisioned and how to take action when in danger of offending.

There is a distinction made between Setups that limit the client achieving his New Me goals and Setups that indicate high-risk offending situations.

Several tenets of the DDSO-RP model are important especially for this group. First, the development of a success identity provides the direction and motivation in the change process. Aquisitional goals involving approach behavior fuels the change process. Personal responsibility and accountability are central characteristics of the new identity (New Me). This model provides no attempt to teach a specific chain of events to reoffense. Although you may be able to teach the DDSO to recite his offense cycles, the usefulness of this exercise as an intervention tool in real life situations is questionable.

Approach Skills—The "New Me." The first step in introducing the DDSO-RP model is to have the client construct his Old Me and New Me, as described above (Haaven et al., 1990; Haaven & Coleman, 2000; Coleman & Haaven, 1998; Coleman & Haaven, in press). DDSOs begin by identifying their New Me goals (the person they want to become and life they want to live). Their New Me goals regarding the behaviors required to reach this new life ("good life") need to be realistic. In contrast, they also identify the characteristics (thoughts and behaviors) of their Old Me, the way they are or, as they often perceive it, the way they were. This Old Me/New Me project can be done in various ways. One such way is to make collages depicting various Old Me/New Me characteristics and then doing a show and tell in the group session. DDSOs find this Old/New Me approach both understandable and motivating. It is a nonthreatening approach that allows the therapist and offender to be active partners in the treatment process. Using terms such as Old Me/New Me as labels for thoughts and behaviors provides a common language to use throughout treatment. Developmentally disabled persons generally are sensitive to labels, so having the opportunity to develop new identities/labels is empowering. This initial positive treatment experience can motivate a DDSO to take on new treatment challenges.

The next step is to discuss how life imbalance can lead to offending behavior. The therapist begins the discussion with how the DDSO might meet his New Me goals and how various Setups can potentially create barriers to achieving these goals. The DDSO is taught that he must take action and use his new skills (What-to-dos), that even if things are going well in his life, Setups (high-risk situations) will present themselves and if he does not take control (What-to-dos), he will reoffend. The two points introduced here and throughout the treatment process are "make smart choices" and "hang in when the going gets tough." The DDSO can identify Setups (risky situations) that disrupt desired lifestyle and Setups for offending behavior either as individual homework or as a group participation project.

Identifying What-to-dos is the next step in the treatment process. The DDSO learns the What-to-dos that lead to becoming a New Me and the What-to-dos to manage sexual deviant urges. There are a number of important generic skills (What-to-dos) to learn to maintain the "good life," including interpersonal skills, problem-solving skills, and the ability to seek help when needed. DDSOs are capable of learning problem-solving skills and need specific training in how and when to seek help and in overcoming fears associated with seeking help. Learning interpersonal skills is especially important. They allow the DDSO the opportunity to develop and maintain support systems, which are so critical in relapse prevention with this population. Interpersonal skill training areas include communication, anger and stress management, and relationships. It is within the context of relationships that sex education and therapy is presented. Sex education includes traditional topics such as male/female anatomy, birth control, safe sex, sexual dysfunctions, heterosexuality, and homosexuality.

The therapist's central focus should be on the DDSO's attitude toward sexuality and values clarifications. The DDSO needs to be reminded about the relevance of sexual knowledge and relationships to his sex offending behavior. Developmentally disabled people generally have been isolated from opportunities to develop healthy sociosexual practices. Significant attention needs to be given to this area. Another important area, often not addressed, is to identify and address the skill area or characteristic that has a significant effect on the DDSO's sense of identity (New Me). A habit like poor hygiene or a tendency to stand too close when talking to others can significantly affect how others relate to the developmentally disabled, thereby affecting their ability to maintain relationships and a positive self identity.

Avoidance Skills— "What-to-Dos." Acquiring skills to manage deviant impulses is the final area of treatment focus. Unlike the approach skills in becoming a New Me, What-to-do skills are avoidance techniques used to escape external high-risk factors, to cognitively restructure deviant thoughts, and to control deviant sexual arousal.

The DDSO must have his high-risk situations identified. Avoidance skills are taught by having the DDSO develop escape techniques from the identified situations. He can make collages visually depicting these new What-to-do skills and present them to the group. Since DDSOs have a very difficult time identifying high-risk emotional states, having him focus on identifying the physical symptoms that represent his feeling states is most effective. The skills to avoid and/or remove oneself from these situations are best learned using role plays with drama and exaggeration. As mentioned previously, the videotaping of DDSOs demonstrating avoidance and escape skills and allowing them to review and critique their skills is an effective learning tool. Avoidance of alcohol and drugs should also be a focus for all DDSOs.

Similar to nondisabled sexual offenders, DDSOs develop cognitive distortions or thinking errors to justify their sexual offending behavior. They absorb teachings that encourage rigid male and female stereotypes and sexual beliefs (Coleman & Haaven, in press). DDSOs can have very fixed attitudes that can fuel and justify the abuse cycle. They can confuse thoughts and feelings, but cognitive restructuring can be of benefit. It is best to introduce New Me statements that are concrete and behavioral to replace or refute Old Me thoughts (Haaven et al., 1990; Haaven & Coleman, 2000; Coleman & Haaven, in press). The group and the therapist may need to help the DDSO identify new language to stop the Old Me thoughts, but the DDSO must be able to feel that he personally owns his New Me cognitions. Generally it is most effective if the therapist and/or group focus on no more than one or two critical distortions (Haaven & Coleman, 2000). The technique of having the therapist debate or argue the Old Me distortions against the DDSO using his New Me cognitions can be effective, especially so if it is done within the group setting using some emotional intensity. It is not advisable, however, to allow other DDSO group members to assume the role of the Old Me distortions in such role plays.

DDSOs should be provided access to the full range of sexual arousal control techniques offered to non-DDSOs in treatment (Coleman & Haaven, 1998). Methods that have been used with DDSOs include covert sensitization, assisted covert sensitization, satiation techniques, hormonal drug therapy, and the use of serotonin selective reuptake inhibitors (SSRIs). The aversive conditioning techniques have been used sparingly, primarily due to ethical issues raised and the difficulty in maintaining ongoing inoculation regimes. Verbal satiation is difficult to implement due to this group's poor verbal/memory skills and their difficulty in outlining in detail their deviant fantasies. Covert sensitization can be effective with some DDSOs, but the steps of the covert intervention still need to be short with simple descriptions and concrete language (Haaven et al., 1990). DDSOs practicing covert sensitization also need a high level of emotional intensity to make this technique effective.

Medication. The antiandrogen most used with sex offenders, including DDSOs, is medroxyprogesterone acetate (MPA or DepoProvera). Although this drug can be an effective adjunct to sex offender treatment in some cases, it can also have significant side effects. Grubin (2000) recommends that if it is used, it should be for a relatively brief period, about a year. The long-term effects of MPA are unknown. Lower doses in oral form (Provera) have been used with some success (Gotestein & Schubert, 1993). An antiandrogen recently getting attention for its use in controlling aberrant sexual behavior is leuprolide (Lupron). It too has side effects, with the long-term risk of osteoporosis (Reilly et al., 2000). SSRIs such as Prozac, Zoloft, and Paxil are being used to reduce sexually compulsive paraphilic behavior. Because the known side effects of these drugs appear to be minimal and their use appears beneficial where an offender's behavior has an obsessive-compulsive quality, SSRIs are being used with DDSOs.

CIVIL COMMITMENT PROGRAMS

Civil commitment programs throughout the nation are reporting an increasing frequency of admissions of DDSOs. These admissions create many problems for the professionals attempting to best meet the treatment needs of the entire population. One such problem is due to the vulnerability of such offenders. DDSOs referred for civil commitment are often "street-wise" enough and predatory enough to be too risky for placement in a traditional program for developmentally disabled persons; however, these same offenders can be quite vulnerable when placed in a civil commitment program where the participants tend to be free of major mental illness, are of at least low-average intellectual functioning, and may have a diverse criminal background. Some SVP programs have noted that the lower functioning offenders fall victim to financial scams from the other offenders, while others have observed them learning more deviant behaviors from the general population (SVP Conference, 2000). The general population in an SVP program may inappropriately amuse themselves by deliberately reinforcing negative behaviors in the lower functioning subgroup.

It is important for SVP programs to provide clear, attainable goals that all residents must meet in order to be released (Schlank, 1999); however, these goals may actually require skills not achievable by a low-functioning offender. Program directors then face the dilemma of deciding when and how these offenders should be transitioned into the community. The validity of risk asessment tools is also questionable when these tools are used to assess the developmentally disabled. Therefore, risk assessment with DDSOs must not only look at individual characteristics and treatment progress, but also at what support systems are needed and available in the community.

SVP programs are not typically staffed with professionals experienced in treating a developmentally disabled population. In fact, it is often difficult to find "a mental health professional who is familiar with both sexual offender and mental retardation issues. Yet knowledge and proficiency in both arenas is needed to work effectively with this population" (Haaven & Coleman, 2000, p. 278). Staff experienced only with standard sex offender treatment may attempt to merely simplify the program format used for the nondisabled population. Staff with mental retardation experience but no sex offender experience may be trained to focus solely on reinforcing the positive and may have difficulty adjusting to the necessity to directly challenge the offenders. In addition, staff working with this special population must be comfortable both with sexual topics and with nontraditional therapeutic methods. For example, a staff member may need to rely on the use of art or drama therapy, and it is important that he or she is the type of person who "does not feel sorry for their client, but feels respect, is aware of limitations, and is able to follow through on consequences" (Haaven & Coleman, 2000, p. 279).

Adding to the problem is that SVP programs need to include procedures regarding informed consent applicable for developmentally disabled people. The program may need to have an ethical practice review committee, including advocate representation for review of treatment procedures that may be called into question; such procedures may include the use of chemotherapy, aversive conditioning, the polygraph, and physiological assessments. A civil commitment program may have to consider psychopharmacological options with DDSOs to address their mental health problems and issues of control over sexual urges, which means they will need greater medical/psychiatric services if DDSO populations grow.

Exacerbating all of the above-mentioned problems is the fact that despite the recent increase in admissions of developmentally disabled offenders committed to SVP programs, they still make up quite a small minority of the entire population. Their small numbers make it impossible for programs to effectively separate these offenders from the more predatory offenders. In addition, there are not sufficient numbers to effectively develop a special "track" of the program to address their unique treatment needs.

SUMMARY

States are increasingly faced with dilemmas regarding the issue of dangerous sexual offenders who are also developmentally disabled. Such offenders may have proven themselves to be too high a risk for placement in traditional programs for the developmentally disabled, particularly since such programs tend not to have a very high level of security. However, placement in the highly secure SVP programs may put these vulnerable offenders at risk for predation from others. In addition, the format, treatment techniques, and goals of an SVP program may be inappropriate for the low-functioning offender.

Currently, there are no ideal answers to address these problems. States considering the adoption of SVP statutes may wish to plan ahead for the special needs this population presents. One option might be for one state to house a civil commitment program specifically for developmentally disabled offenders; however, there still must be provisions for slow and supervised return of these offenders to the community from which they were committed. Continuity of programming could easily be lost. Therefore, states may wish to consider an alternative of establishing a high security unit within one of their standard programs that already treats persons with developmental disabilities. This solution would meet the safety concerns of the community without forcing the low-functioning offender into an inappropriate placement. This problem is best addressed by a collaborative inter-agency SVP program, a developmental disability services agency, advocates, and community participation. What SVP programs can do is to continue to increase their understanding of the unique issues associated with this population. It is important not to allow DDSOs, although few in number, to be gradually immersed and then "lost" within the program. Significant limitations do exist, but a continued effort to make modifications to make treatment relevant and effective for this population can make a difference.

References

Abel, G. G. (1996). *Abel assessment for sexual interest: Adult offenders*. Atlanta, GA: Abel Screening, Inc.

Abrams, S. (1989). *The complete polygraph handbook*. Lexington, MA: Lexington Books.

Belcher, T. L. (1994, April). Movement to the community: Reduction of behavioral difficulties. *Mental Retardation, 2*, 32.

Bright, Jenny (1989). Intellectual disability and the criminal justice system: New developments. *Law Institute Journal, 63*, 933–935.

Brown, J. & Pond, A. (1999). "They just don't get it"—Essentials of cognitive behavioral treatment for intellectually disabled sexual abusers. In B. Schwartz (Ed.), *The sex offender: Theoretical advances, treating special populations, and legal developments*. Kingston, NJ: Civic Research Institute.

Buser, C., Leone, P. & Bannon, M. (1987, June). Segregation —Does educating the handicapped stop here? *Corrections Today, 49*, 17–18.

Coleman, E. M. & Haaven, J. (1998). Adult intellectually disabled sexual offenders: Program considerations. In W. M. Marshall (Ed.), *Sourcebook of treatment programs for sexual offenders*. New York: Plenum Press.

Coleman, E. M. & Haaven, J. (in press). Assessment and treatment of the intellectually disabled sex offender. In M. S. Carich & J. Mussack (Eds.), *Handbook on sex offender treatment*. Brandon, VT: Safer Society Press.

Denkowski, G., Denkowski, K. & Mabli, J. (1983). A 50 state survey of the current status of residential treatment programs for mentally retarded offenders. *Mental Retardation, 21*, 197.

Edgerton, R. B. & Dingman, H. (1964). Good reasons for bad supervision: Dating in a hospital for the mentally retarded. *Psychiatric Quarterly Supplement Part 2*, 221–223.

Edmonson, B., Wish, J. & Fiechtl, K. (1977). Development of a sex knowledge and attitude test for the moderately and mildly retarded. Final Report, HEW Project 6007500382, Columbus, OH: Nisonger Center, Ohio State University.

Ellis, J. W. & Luckasson, R. A. (1985). Mentally retarded criminal defendants. *Washington Law Review, 53*, 444–493.

Ferguson, E. W. & Haaven, J. (1990). On the design of motivating learning environments for intellectually disabled offenders. *Journal of Correctional Education, 41*, 32–34.

Garcia, S. A. & Steele, H. (1988). Mentally retarded offenders in the criminal justice and mental retardation services systems in Florida: Philosophical, placement and treatment issues. *Arkansas Law Review, 41*, 809–859.

Gotestein, H. G. & Schubert, D. S. P. (1993). Low-dose oral medroxy projesterone acetate in the management of paraphilias. *Journal of Clinical Psychiatry, 54*, 182–188.

Grubin, D. (2000). Complimenting relapse prevention with medical intervention. In D. R. Laws, S. M. Hudson & T. Ward (Eds.), *Remaking relapse prevention with sex offenders: A sourcebook*. Thousand Oaks, CA: Sage.

Haaven, J. (1995, October). Treatment of intellectually disabled sex offenders. Paper presented at the training workshop at the fourteenth annual research and treatment conference of the Association for the Treatment of Sexual Abusers, New Orleans, LA.

Haaven, J. L. & Coleman, E. M. (2000). Treatment of the developmentally disabled sexual offender. In D. R. Laws, S. M. Hudson & T. Ward (Eds.), *Remaking relapse prevention with sex offenders: A sourcebook*. Thousand Oaks, CA: Sage.

Haaven, J. L., Little, R. & Petre-Miller, D. (1990). *Treating intellectually disabled sex offenders*. Brandon, VT: Safer Society Press.

Luckasson, R. A. (1988). The dually diagnosed client in the criminal justice system. In J. Stark, F. Menolascino, M. Albarelli & V. Gray (Eds.), *Mental retardation and mental health: Classification, diagnosis, treatment, services*. New York: Springer-Verlag.

Monat, R.K. (1982). *Sexuality and the mentally handicapped*. San Diego: College Hill Press.

Murphy, W. D. & Barbaree, H. E. (1994). *Assessments of sex offenders by measures of erectile response: Psycometric properties and decision making.* Brandon, VT: Safer Society Press.

Myers, D. (1976). Supported work for mentally retarded parolees. In M. Santamour (Ed.), *The mentally retarded citizen and the criminal justice system: Problems and programs.* Newport, RI: James Maher Center.

Pithers, W. D., Marques, J. K., Gibat, C. C. & Marlatt, G. A. (1983). Relapse prevention with sexually aggressive persons: A self-control model of treatment and maintenance of change. In J. G. Greer & I. R. Stuart (Eds.), *The sexual agressor: Current perspective on treatment.* New York: Van Nostrand Reinhold.

Prout, H. T. & Cale, R. L. (1994). Individual counseling approaches. In D. C. Strohmer & H. T. Prout (Eds.), *Counseling and psychotherapy with persons with mental retardation and borderline intelligence.* Brandon, VT: Clinical Psychology Publishing.

Reilly, D., Delva, N. J. & Hudson, R. W. (Aug. 2000). Protocols for the use of cyproterone, medroxyprogesterone, and leuprolide in the treatment of paraphilia. *Canadian Journal of Psychiatry, 45*, 559–563.

Santamour, M. & West, B. (1977, August). *The mentally retarded offender and corrections.* Washington, DC: National Institute of Law Enforcement and Criminal Justice.

Santamour, M. & West, B. (Eds.) (1982). The mentally retarded offender: Presentation of the facts and a discussion of the issues. *The retarded offender.* New York: Praeger.

Schlank, A. (1999). Guidelines for the development of new programs. In A. Schlank & F. Cohen (Eds.), *The sexual predator: Law, policy, evaluation, and treatment.* Kingston, NJ: Civic Research Institute.

Seghorn, T. K. & Weigel, M. (1999, September). Comparative use of Abel assessments and penile plethysmograph laboratory assessments in an outpatient forensic practice. In S. Johnson (Chair), *Current research comparing plethysmography with the Abel assessment for sexual interest.* Symposium conducted at the annual meeting of the Association for the Treatment of Sexual Abusers, Orlando, FL.

Stacken, N. M. & Shevich, J. (1999). Working with the intellectually disabled/socially inadequate sex offender in a prison setting. In B. Schwartz (Ed.), *The sex offender: Theoretical advances, treating special populations, and legal developments.* Kingston, NJ: Civic Research Institute.

SVP Conference: Summit 2000. May 31–June 2, 2000. Oshkosh, WI.

Swanson, C. K. & Garwick, G. B. (1990). Treatment for low-functioning sex offenders: Group therapy and interagency coordination. *Mental Retardation, 28*, 155–161.

Ward, K. & McElwee, D. (1995, May). Supporting individuals with inappropriate sexual behaviors in community based settings. Paper presented at the training workshop at the ANCOR Conference on Intellectually Disabled Sex Offenders, New York.

Willis, V. (July 1980). Design considerations for mental health facilities. *Hospital and Community Psychiatry, 31*, 483–490.

Chapter 14

Sex Offender and Chemical Dependency Treatment

by William Plum, L.A.D.C.

Introduction	14-1
Philosophy (Program Statement)	14-1
Core Clinical Concepts	14-2
Sex Offender-Specific CD Model	14-3
CA Component Design	14-3
Assessment and Education	14-5
Recovery Structure and Support System	14-5
Application of the Relapse Prevention Model	14-6
Transition Issues and Aftercare Planning	14-7
Conclusion	14-8

INTRODUCTION

In 1998, the Minnesota Sex Offender Program (MSOP) invited me to consult on the chemical dependency (CD) component of their program. The results of that work are outlined in this chapter. While the chemically dependent population as a group shares many characteristics, I was struck by the clinical challenges associated with working with the chemically dependent sex offender, namely the potential of one orthodox clinical approach to hamper another. It is unfortunate that undue separation and compartmentalization of CD treatment from sex offender treatment occurs in many programs. Perhaps this is a developmental issue for both fields. It appears that the complex interrelationship between an individual's chemical abuse and his choice to sexually offend needs to be fully appreciated by all clinicians involved.

The gradual introduction and integration of CD treatment services into mainstream mental health and medical services has already challenged the CD field to modify its orthodox modalities to fit new settings and populations. With regard to sex offender treatment, CD components must develop techniques that can uncover how a client's sexual offending is interrelated with his substance abuse. This chapter describes the model used by the MSOP, whose CD component is free from compartmentalization and suggests the extent to which allied disciplines can work together.

PHILOSOPHY (PROGRAM STATEMENT)

The abuse of mood altering chemicals among the sex offender population is well documented (Langevin & Lang, 1990). Valliere (1997) found that the incidence of alcohol use and alcohol dependence in sex offenders exceeds that in the general population. Because relapse to chemical use signals a very high risk of reoffending, it is of great importance that sex offenders receive CD treatment services. Therefore, the development of a CD treatment service that takes into account the core issues of sex offenders is of paramount importance. The key clinical and administrative task is to design protocols that integrate chemical dependency treatment services into sex offender programs. Every effort must be made to design CD services that will be congruent with the sex offender treatment program.

Because of the intense nature of the MSOP and the high degree of integration of its treatment modules, it was of key importance to develop a clear program statement and clinical vision for its chemical abuse (CA) component. The MSOP chose to use the term "chemical abuse" rather than "chemical dependency" because the substance use history of some offenders did not meet criteria for an actual diagnosis of *dependence*, and yet their use of substances was significantly related to the build-up phase of their sex offending cycle. This necessary first step provided a framework to create a component with clinical assignments that were relevant both to the clients' chemical use and their sex offense history. CA and CD are bio-psycho-social phenomena that have multiple etiologies and varying degrees of severity. The goal of the CA component within the MSOP is for clients to develop insight into their chemical use pattern and consequences and how their chemical use pattern has interrelated with their sex offense history.

Core Clinical Concepts

In addition to the program statement above, three core clinical concepts were developed that became the basis for the development of clinical assignments within the CA component:

1. Alcohol and/or drug abuse has either intensified the offenders' behavior or served as a means to support the offenders' behavior.

2. Alcohol and/or drug abuse presents a high-risk factor that can promote relapse in offending behavior.

3. Treatment for chemical abuse or dependency must focus on the interrelationship of the offenders' chemical use pattern and their offense history.

This approach of coordinating CA treatment services under the umbrella of sex offender treatment may seem counterintuitive to the traditionally trained CD professional, who may view a client's addiction as the primary disorder. However, there is an increasing body of literature that questions this viewpoint. Mee-Lee (1995) cites a number of studies that argue for multifactorial and integrative approaches in the assessment and treatment of chemical dependency (Donovan, 1986; Brower et al., 1989). Because of the wide variety and marked differences between groups of substance abusers, a uniform approach to substance abuse treatment may be inadequate (Nace et al., 1991). When sex offending and CD are present in the same person, it is illustrative to think of them as operating within a complex matrix of bio-psycho-social factors that defy simple generalizations (Miller & Rollnick, 1991).

The standard definition of chemical addiction is that it is a primary progressive illness. While this definition has some utility in uncomplicated cases of chemical addiction, it falls apart when there are two or more serious disorders coexisting in a client. Treating clients with comorbid disorders requires a high degree of flexibility, continuous efforts to design mutually supportive clinical interventions, and a view to long-term outcomes. The addition of CA treatment services to a sex offender treatment program requires significant modification of standard CD treatment interventions and concepts. Figure 14.1 outlines a structured interview that clinicians may use as part of their chemical use assessment and review. Figure 14.2 is a questionnaire for use with sex offenders with chemical abuse histories.

Sex Offender-Specific CD Model

A careful review of CA clinical assignments, treatment materials, and methods is required before a sex offender program director creates and implements CA treatment services within the program. Taking wholesale packages of CD treatment materials without making a critical analysis may cause a number of problems for the unit.

First, CD treatment is a specific vernacular that may or may not fit well with the sex offender program. Second, most CD materials are designed for people who have not been incarcerated for long periods of time. Third, there are several models of relapse prevention used within the CD treatment profession, some of which may be antagonistic with the model used in sex offender treatment. For instance, one popular relapse prevention model used in the CD field conceptualizes internal processes of relapse as neurologically based cognitive dysfunctions termed post-acute withdrawal syndrome (PAW). PAW is thought be an expression of the long-term effects of chronic alcohol and drug poisoning. Psychosocial stressors, in this model, aggravate internal brain dysfunctions and eventually lead to loss of control over behavior (Chiauzzi, 1991). The application of this model with chemically dependent sex offenders may reinforce their thinking errors by allowing them to blame their relapses on their brain dysfunction and perhaps deflect responsibility for their sex offenses by placing it on their chemical dependency. Fourth, the use of unreviewed or unmodified CD treatment materials may cause unintentional compartmentalization of treatment. It was for all of these reasons that the MSOP took the time to review, modify, and design clinical CA materials that were congruent with the philosophy of its sex offender program.

CA COMPONENT DESIGN

The MSOP-CA treatment component is divided into the following four phases:

1. Assessment and education
2. Recovery structure and support system
3. Application of the relapse prevention model
4. Transition issues and aftercare planning

Each phase of the component is one trimester (one trimester = four months), with participants meeting once per week. Group therapy is the main modality of treatment.

Figure 14.1
Chemical Use Assessment

The chemical use assessment is a structured interview to gather as much relevant information as possible regarding a client's chemical use pattern. The following outlines a multidimensional risk assessment developed by Dr. David Mee-Lee (1995) and modified by the author.

Dimension One: Acute Intoxication/Withdrawal
- Last chemical used and in what amount
- Chemical use pattern during the six months prior to last use (frequency, types, and amounts)
- Onset of chemicals: age for each, types, frequency, and amounts
- History of progression of symptoms: tolerance, loss of control, withdrawal syndrome
- Prior diagnosis of addiction; prior treatment history

Dimension Two: Biomedical Conditions
- Client's current biomedical conditions
- Medications prescribed by physicians
- Does the client suffer from biomedical conditions that were caused by his/her chemical addiction or exacerbated by chemical abuse?
- Client's general health history

Dimension Three: Mental Health
- Client's current mental health status
- Medications prescribed for diagnosed mental health disorders
- Does the client admit to a history of using nonprescribed mood-altering chemicals to medicate mental health symptoms?
- Does the client have a history of mixing psychotropic medication with nonprescribed mood altering chemicals?

Dimension Four: Treatment Acceptance
- Does the client identify a chemical use problem?
- What is the client's characterization of his chemical use history?
- Can the client identify any consequences associated with his chemical use pattern?
- Does the client believe he needs CA treatment?
- Does the client express ambivalence about chemicals, believing that some chemicals are still safe to use while others are not?

Dimension Five: Relapse/Continued Use Potential
- If the client was not in a supervised setting, what is his relapse/continued use potential?
- How aware is the client of external/internal high risk factors?
- What coping skills does the client currently have that would support a change in his chemical use pattern?

Dimension Six: Recovery Environment
- What is the client's current environment?
- Does this environment support change?
- If the client were not in a supervised setting, what type of environment would he return to?
- Can the client identify support people or not?
- What is the client's relationship and family history?
- How prevalent is chemical abuse among his family and friends?

In addition to the clinical interview, the use of testing can be helpful. The Substance Abuse Subtle Screening Inventory (SASSI) (Miller, 1994) is an excellent tool that tests for both alcohol and drug abuse. It is divided into face valid items and empirically based scales. The SASSI also tests for defensiveness and random answering patterns.

Clinical goals and outcomes for each phase are clearly stated. Clients need to achieve and maintain the goals for each phase before they can move to the next; the therapist must keep in mind that the group sessions are not "classes" and that mere attendance is not sufficient for progression to the next phase. The offenders must demonstrate progress within each phase by completing assignments and relating personal accountability for their chemical use pattern and sex offenses.

Assessment and Education

The goals of Phase 1, assessment and education, are for the clients to receive a basic education on substance abuse issues and to make a comprehensive assessment of their chemical use history. The intent in Phase 1 is twofold—to help offenders understand the historical relationship between their chemical use pattern and their sexual offending, and to help them surrender their cognitive distortions about this relationship (e.g., to let go of their tendency to blame the sex offenses on the chemical dependency). It is important for Phase 1 clients to have an opportunity to find for themselves meaningful consequences associated with their chemical use pattern and sex offending. Therefore, the core clinical assignments of Phase 1 are structured in such a manner as to allow clients the opportunity to find out for themselves meaningful relationships between their chemical use pattern and sexual offending. The clinical assignments of Phase 1 are:

1. Complete a comprehensive chemical use history.
2. Identify twenty chemical-related consequences.
3. Identify twenty examples of how your chemical use pattern was interrelated with your sex offense pattern (i.e., supported your sexual abuse cycle).

In support of these clinical assignments, Phase 1 includes discussions that address substance issues. The discussion topics are:

- Use, abuse, and dependency
- The bio-psycho-social model of addiction
- Defenses and thinking errors
- Alcohol and drugs of abuse

Phase 1 group work frequently focuses on helping clients identify a substance abuse problem, resolving clients' ambivalence about their chemical use, challenging any cognitive distortions such as blaming their choice to commit sexual offenses on their history of chemical abuse, and/or dealing with their compartmentalization of their substance abuse from their sexual offending.

Recovery Structure and Support System

The goal of Phase 2, recovery structure and support system, is for clients to identify the need for two critical elements in their relapse prevention plans—a recovery structure that will give them the means and resources to avoid a relapse, and a recovery support system that is comprised of the people who will support their relapse prevention plan. To accomplish this goal, the client is asked to evaluate his cycle of relapse and reoffending. The clinical assignments of Phase 2 are:

1. Complete the chemical relapse and offense pattern calendar.

2. Identify criminal thinking and lifestyles.

3. Identify external high-risk factors.

4. Identify behavior styles that promote recovery.

The group discussions that extend from these assignments often center around the themes of dishonesty, withdrawal, isolation, and hopelessness. Clients need time to work through their resistance to talking to others about their thoughts of using chemicals or reoffending, their fears of not being able to abstain, and their reluctance to give up an exciting and secretive lifestyle. Central to Phase 2 is helping clients recognize the need for supportive relationships and realistic recovery plans. Clients are challenged during this phase to examine their willingness to develop supportive relationships. Clients need to confront their "us versus them" attitude and their sense that "everyone is out to get them" and is waiting to see them "fail."

During Phase 2 it can be helpful to introduce clients to twelve-step programs and their basic concepts such as honesty, open mindedness and willingness, personal accountability for one's recovery, and the acronym HALT (hungry, angry, lonely, tired). This acronym gives a framework to define common internal high-risk factors for chemically abusive clients; they are taught not to allow themselves to become too hungry, angry, lonely, or tired.

In addition to providing clients with information about recovery programs, clinicians must challenge clients to find ways to practice recovery programs within the institution. Frequently, CA offenders separate recovery as something that happens outside of the institution. They often state that since they are not tempted to use chemicals because of the difficulty accessing them in the controlled environments, they do not really need to practice a recovery program within their current circumstances. This emphasis on "temptation" and the "outside" allows the offenders to avoid confronting their current high-risk behavior. Furthermore, they become overfocused on whether or not they feel tempted to use chemicals. They mistake the absence of craving to use for a full recovery. This thinking error generally leads them to develop inadequate recovery/relapse prevention plans (i.e., they will seek help when they feel like they "need it"). The clinician working with clients in Phase 2 must take the time to challenge them to develop recovery plans they can practice currently and that will lay the foundation for the skills they will need during the transition phase of the sex offender treatment program.

Application of the Relapse Prevention Model

Phase 3 is the application of the relapse prevention model. The goal of this phase is for clients to integrate what they have learned about their sexual offending high-risk factors with their chemical dependency treatment. External high-risk factors are not ignored, but the emphasis in this phase is on the client's internal high-risk factors. The clinical assignments in Phase 3 are:

1. Compare the six internal high-risk factors associated with your sex offending with the internal high-risk factors associated with your chemical use patterns.
2. Develop an integrated list of internal/external high-risk factors.
3. Develop coping interventions for each high-risk factor.

Phase 3 focuses on the offenders' mindfulness of their internal high-risk factors and their ability to challenge their deviant/chemical relapse thinking. A cursory list of general high-risk factors is not sufficient to complete this phase. Each offender must be given the opportunity to develop a highly individualized hierarchy of his high-risk factors. To accomplish this level of individuality, the offender must view his CA treatment and his sexual offending treatment as mutually supportive. It should be a routine assignment for a client to share his CA assignments in his sex offender core group, particularly in Phase 3. Coping interventions should also be shared in both groups so the client can receive ongoing feedback on the efficacy of his interventions.

Transition Issues and Aftercare Planning

Phase 4 provides for discussion of transition and aftercare issues. A client participating in this phase will develop a chemical abuse aftercare plan that can be fully integrated into his over-all aftercare/transition plan. In Phase 4, the client needs to be able to realistically appraise his transition and aftercare needs. Discussion of these needs should take place within the context of his awareness of his internal and external high-risk factors. The clinical assignments in Phase 4 are:

1. Review your high-risk factors.
2. Develop a list of community resources that will support your relapse prevention plan.
3. Identify your specific transition issues (freedom, paying bills, living alone, and similar considerations).
4. Role play your coping interventions for specific high-risk situations.

In addition to reviewing the client's clinical assignments and doing role plays, Phase 4 group work should deal with any unrealistic expectations about freedom he may have as well as his fears about being released. In the past, release from prison or treatment programs represented the first step back to a client's reoffending or relapsing on chemicals. Clients in Phase 4 cannot simply be allowed to outline plans for the future; they also need to directly confront the dilemmas that the new plans will create. For instance, clients through the course of their sex offender treatment have worked on developing relationships with their family members, but through the process of reunification, they may become involved with some family members who have chemical use problems themselves. A client may feel torn between an obvious high-risk factor and his fear of being rejected by the family member if he sets up a boundary about chemical use. This is just one example of the dilemmas facing the Phase 4 client. Issues of honesty, trust, and accountability will need to be balanced with the client's concerns about being accepted and staying free in a society that may always fear him.

CONCLUSION

In summary, the CA treatment component in a civil commitment sex offender program is considered a necessary adjunct to the overall sex offender program. The CA service is designed to offer the client an opportunity to understand the interrelationship between his chemical abuse history and his sexual offending history. The four phases of the CA component are constructed to be mutually supportive of the other phases of the clients' sex offender treatment program. It is of paramount importance that clients are never allowed to blame their sexual offending on their chemical abuse. The CA component of a civil commitment program should provide a means for clients to recognize how their substance abuse is interrelated with their choice to commit sexual offenses. The goal is for the client to develop an integrated relapse prevention plan that incorporates elements of his sex offense and chemical abuse history.

Figure 14.2
Plum Sex Offender Inventory for Chemical Abuse

This questionnaire is an inventory that was developed for sexual offenders with chemical abuse histories. Although norms are not yet available for this assessment tool, it has been found to be helpful in assisting the offenders to see the connection between their chemical abuse and their choice to commit sex offenses.

Name: _____

Date: _____

Answer the following questions only if you have used alcohol or other drugs at some time in your life.

	Strongly Agree	Somewhat Agree	Strongly Disagree	Somewhat Disagree
1. I have used many different mood-altering chemicals.	1	2	3	4
2. I have family members who abuse alcohol and/or drugs.	1	2	3	4
3. My substance abuse is not related to any of my sex offending.	1	2	3	4
4. I believe that if my victim/s were drunk or high that s/he is somewhat responsible for the crime.	1	2	3	4

	Strongly Agree	**Somewhat Agree**	**Strongly Disagree**	**Somewhat Disagree**
5. I use mood-altering chemicals as a "weapon" or as a means to "control" my victims.	1	2	3	4
6. I coerced my victims by supplying them with alcohol or other drugs.	1	2	3	4
7. My sexual fantasies increase when I use mood-altering chemicals.	1	2	3	4
8. I like to use mood-altering chemicals alone and watch X-rated movies or read sexually explicit magazines.	1	2	3	4
9. Drinking or drug taking often gave me the courage to do what was on my mind.	1	2	3	4
10. I used criminal behavior to intensify my "high" from mood-altering chemicals.	1	2	3	4
11. I believe that if I did not use mood-altering chemicals I would not have offended.	1	2	3	4
12. I often use mood-altering chemicals while I sexually offended.				
13. I often used mood-altering chemicals after I sexually offended.	2	2	3	4
14. I used different substances when I sexually offended than when I was not sexually offending.	1	2	3	4
15. I used my substance abuse as an "excuse" or "reason" to explain my behavior to my victim/s.	1	2	3	4
16. I think that only some types of chemicals are a problem for me.	1	2	3	4
17. I used only a certain type/s of mood-altering chemical/s before my sexual offending.	1	2	3	4

	Strongly Agree	**Somewhat Agree**	**Strongly Disagree**	**Somewhat Disagree**
18. I believe that my chemical use has nothing to do with my sexual offending.	1	2	3	4
19. I believe that if I am successful in sex offender treatment, I will be able to safely use mood-altering chemicals.	1	2	3	4
20. I understand that use of mood-altering chemicals could influence my choice to sexually offend.	1	2	3	4
21. I frequently used mood-altering chemicals to cover up my feelings, particularly after I sexually offended.	1	2	3	4
22. I used mood-altering chemicals to stop me from thinking about sexually offending.	1	2	3	4
23. My use of mood-altering chemicals helped me control my behavior by relaxing me.	1	2	3	4
24. Thinking about using mood-altering chemicals is as exciting sometimes as having sexual fantasies.	1	2	3	4
25. It is hard for me to think of any consequences associated with my alcohol and/or drug use.	1	2	3	4
26. I have committed sexual offenses when I have been sober.	1	2	3	4
27. I have committed sexual offenses while in or after completing treatment for chemical dependency.	1	2	3	4
28. I think that my sexual offenses were more violent when I was under the influence of alcohol and/or drugs.	1	2	3	4

	Strongly Agree	Somewhat Agree	Strongly Disagree	Somewhat Disagree
29. I only started to abuse alcohol and/or drugs after I went to prison.	1	2	3	4
30. I have used alcohol and/or drugs while going through outpatient sex offender treatment.	1	2	3	4
31. I am confused about the role of my alcohol and/or drug use in my sexual offending.	1	2	3	4

References

Brower, K. J., Blow, F. C. & Beresford, T. P. (1989). Treatment implications of chemical dependency models: An integrative approach. *Journal of Substance Abuse Treatment, 6,* 147–157.

Chiauzzi, E. J. (1991). *Preventing relapse in the addictions: A biopsychosocial approach.* New York: Pergamon Press.

Donovan, J. M. (1986). An etiologic model of alcoholism. *American Journal of Psychiatry, 143,* 1–11.

Langevin, R. & Lang, R. A. (1990). Substance abuse among sex offenders. *Annals of Sex Research, 3,* 397–424.

Mee-Lee, D. (1995). Matching in addictions treatment: How do we get there from here? *Alcoholism Treatment Quarterly Special Issue: Treatment of the Addictions—Applications of Outcome Research for Clinical Management, 12,* 113–127.

Miller, G. (1994). *Substance abuse subtle screening inventory (SASSI-3).* Available by calling 1-888-297-2774.

Miller, W. & Rollnick, S. (1991). *Motivational interviewing: Preparing people to change addictive behavior.* New York: Guilford Press.

Nace, P., Davis, C. & Gaspari, J. (1991). Axis II comorbidity in substance abusers. *American Journal of Psychiatry, 148,* 118–120.

Valliere, V. N. (1997). Relationships between alcohol use, alcohol expectancies, and sexual offenses in convicted offenders. In B. K. Schwartz & H. R. Cellini (Eds.), *The sex offender: New insights, treatment innovations, and legal developments.* Kingston, NJ: Civic Research Institute.

Appendix 1

Bibliography

Abel, G. G. (1996). *Abel assessment for sexual interest: Adult offenders.* Atlanta, GA: Abel Screening, Inc.

Abel, G. G., Becker, J. V. & Cunningham-Rathner, J. C. (1984). Complications, consent and cognitions in sex between children and adults. *International Journal of Law and Psychiatry, 7*, 89–103.

Abel, G. G., Becker, J. V., Mittelman, M., Cunningham-Rathner, J., Rouleau, J. L. & Murphy, W. D. (1987). Self-reported sex crimes of nonincarcerated paraphiliacs. *Journal of Interpersonal Violence, 2*, 3–25.

Abel, G. G. & Osborn, C. A. (1992). Stopping sexual violence. *Psychiatric Annals, 22*, 301–306.

Abel, G. G. & Rouleau, J. L. (1990). The nature and extent of sexual assault. In W. L. Marshall, D. R. Laws & H. E. Barbaree (Eds.), *Handbook of sexual assault: Issues, theories, and treatment of the offender.* New York: Plenum Press.

Abrams, S. (1989). *The complete polygraph handbook.* Lexington, MA: Lexington Books.

Alexander, M. A. (1999). Sexual offender treatment efficacy revisited. *Sexual Abuse: A Journal of Research and Treatment, 11,* 101–116.

American Educational Research Association, American Psychological Association, National Council on Measurement in Education (1999). *Standards for educational and psychological testing* (3d ed.). Washington, DC: American Educational Research Association.

American Psychiatric Association (1982). *Statement on the insanity defense.* Washington, DC: Author.

American Psychiatric Association (1994). *Diagnostic and statistical manual of mental disorders* (4th ed.). Washington, DC: American Psychiatric Press.

American Psychiatric Association (1999). *Task force on sexually dangerous offenders.* Washington, DC: Author.

American Psychological Association (1992). Ethical principles of psychologists and code of conduct. *American Psychologist*, 47, 1597–1611.

Associated Press. (1999, December 17). Sex predator accused of getting Viagra prescription while at halfway house. *Milwaukee Journal Sentinel*, available online at http://www.onwis.com/wi/121799.

Association for the Treatment of Sexual Abusers (ATSA) (1997). *Ethical standards and principles for the management of sexual abusers.* Beaverton, OR: Author.

Association for the Treatment of Sexual Abusers (ATSA) (1998). *Civil commitment of sexually violent offenders.* Position paper adopted Nov. 6, 1998.

Bakersfield Californian. (1998, December 10). Tehachapi proposed as site for new state mental hospital.

Bannister, A. (1997). *The healing drama: Psychodrama and dramatherapy with abused children.* London: Free Association Books. (New York: N.Y.U. Press).

Barbaree, H. E. & Marshall, W. L. (1988). Deviant sexual arousal, offense history, and demographic variables as predictors of reoffense among child molesters. *Behavioral Sciences and the Law, 6,* 267–280.

Barnard, G., Fuller, A., Robbins, L. & Shaw, T. (1989). *The child molester: An integrated approach to evaluation and treatment.* New York: Bruner/Mazel.

Bays, L. & Freeman-Longo, R. (1989). *Why did I do it again? Understanding my cycle of problem behaviors: A guided workbook for clients in treatment.* Brandon, VT: Safer Society Press.

Beck, A. J. & Shipley, B. E. (1989). *Recidivism of prisoners released in 1983.* U.S. Department of Justice: Bureau of Justice Statistics, 1–13.

Belanger, N. & Earls, C. (1996). Sex offender recidivism prediction. *Forum on Correctional Research, 8,* 22–24.

Belcher, T. L. (1994, April). Movement to the community: Reduction of behavioral difficulties. *Mental Retardation, 2,* 32.

Berlin, F. S. (1989). Special considerations in the psychiatric evaluation of sexual offenders against minors, in R. Rosner & H. I. Schwartz (Eds.), *Critical issues in American psychiatry and the law,* vol. 4. New York: Plenum Press.

Billbrey, R. (1999). Civil commitment of sexually violent predators: A misguided attempt to solve a serious problem. *Journal of the Missouri Bar, 55,* 321–329.

Blatner, A. (1991). Role dynamics: An integrative psychology. *The Journal of Group Psychotherapy, Psychodrama & Sociometry, 44,* 33–40.

Blatner, A. (1997). *Acting-in: Practical applications of psychodramatic methods* (3d ed.). London: Free Association Books.

Blatner, A. (1999). Psychodrama. In D. J. Wiener (Ed.), *Beyond Talk Therapy: Action Approaches in Treatment.* Washington, DC: Heldref, www.heldref.org (subscription included in membership in ASGPP, 301 North Harrison St., Ste 508, Princeton, NJ 08540).

Blatner, A. & Blatner, A. (1997). *The art of play: Helping adults reclaim imagination & spontaneity.* Philadelphia: Brunner/Mazel-Taylor & Francis.

Boer, D. P., Hart, S. D., Kropp, P. R. & Webster, C. D. (1997). *Manual for the Sexual Violence Risk-20: Professional guidelines for assessment of risk of sexual violence.* Burnaby, British Columbia: Mental Health Law and Policy Institute, Simon Fraser University.

Boer, D. P., Wilson, R. J., Gauthier, C. M. & Hart, S. D. (1997). Assessing risk for sexual violence: Guidelines for clinical practice. In C. D. Webster & M. A. Jackson (Eds.), *Impulsivity: Theory, assessment, and treatment.* New York: Guilford Press.

Bonta, J. & Hanson, K. (1994). *Gauging the risk for violence: Measurement, impact and strategies for change.* Ottawa: Department of the Solicitor General of Canada.

Bonta, J., Law, M. & Hanson, K. (1998).

The prediction of criminal and violent recidivism among mentally disordered offenders: A meta-analysis. *Psychological Bulletin, 123*, 123–142.

Borum, R. (1996). Improving the clinical practice of violence risk assessment: Technology, guidelines and training. *American Psychologist, 51*, 945–956.

Borum, R., Otto, R. K. & Golding, S. (1993). Improving clinical judgment and decision making in forensic evaluation. *Journal of Psychiatry & Law, 21*, 35–76.

Bradford, J. M. W. (1990). The antiandrogen and hormonal treatment of sex offenders. In W. L. Mashall, D. R. Laws & H. E. Barbaree (Eds.), *Handbook of sexual assault: Issues, theories, and treatment of the offender*. New York: Plenum.

Brakel, S. J. & Cavanaugh, J. L. (2000). Of psychopaths and pendulums: Legal and psychiatric treatment of sex offenders in the United States. *New Mexico Law Review, 30*, 69–94.

Brakel, S. J. & Weiner, B. A. (1986). *The mentally disabled and the law* (3d ed.). Washington, DC: American Psychiatric Association.

Bright, Jenny (1989). Intellectual disability and the criminal justice system: New developments. *Law Institute Journal, 63*, 933–935.

Brooks, A. D. (1992). The constitutionality and morality of civilly committing violent sexual predators. *University of Puget Sound Law Review, 15*, 709–754.

Brower, K. J., Blow, F. C. & Beresford, T. P. (1989). Treatment implications of chemical dependency models: An integrative approach. *Journal of Substance Abuse Treatment, 6*, 147–157.

Brown, J. & Pond, A. (1999). "They just don't get it"—Essentials of cognitive behavioral treatment for intellectually disabled sexual abusers. In B. Schwartz (Ed.), *The sex offender: Theoretical advances, treating special populations, and legal developments*. Kingston, NJ: Civic Research Institute.

Browne, A. & Finkelhor, D. (1986). *A sourcebook on child sexual abuse*. London: Sage.

Bumby, K. M. (1996). Assessing the cognitive distortions of child molesters and rapists: Development and validation of the MOLEST and RAPE scales. *Sexual Abuse: A Journal of Research and Treatment, 8*, 37–54.

Burt, M. (1980). Cultural myths and supports for rape. *Journal of Personality and Social Psychology, 38*, 217–230.

Buser, C., Leone, P. & Bannon, M. (1987, June). Segregation—Does educating the handicapped stop here? *Corrections Today, 49*, 17–18.

California Legislative Analyst's Office (1999). A "containment" strategy for adult sex offenders on parole. *Cross-cutting issues: Judiciary and criminal justice*. Sacramento: Author.

Campbell, T. W. (2000). Sexual predator evaluations and phrenology: Considering issues of evidentiary reliability. *Behavioral Sciences and the Law, 18*, 111–130.

Center for Sex Offender Management (CSOM) (1999, December). *Understanding juvenile sexual offending behavior: Emerging research, treatment approaches and management practices*. Silver Spring, MD: Author.

Chiauzzi, E. J. (1991). *Preventing relapse in the addictions: A biopsychosocial approach*. New York: Pergamon Press.

Clark, D. (1994). Evaluation of behavioural changes after intervention. *Inside Psychology: The Journal of Prison Service Psychology, 2,* 2–43.

Clark, D. (2000). *Offender Assessment System.* Unpublished paper, to be submitted for publication.

Cleckley, H. (1982). *The mask of sanity* (4th ed.). St. Louis, MO: Mosby.

Cohen, J. (1992). A power primer. *Psychological Bulletin, 112,* 155–159.

Cohen, J. L. (2000). Motion filed in a commitment case currently pending before Hillsborough County Court, regarding: *In re Commitment of T.B.B.,* No. 99-0214 (Hillsborough County Ct. Fla.).

Colboum-Faller, K. (1988). *Child sexual abuse: An interdisciplinary manual for diagnosis, case management and treatment.* London: Macmillan.

Coleman, E. M. & Haaven, J. (1998). Adult intellectually disabled sexual offenders: Program considerations. In W. M. Marshall (Ed.), *Sourcebook of treatment programs for sexual offenders.* New York: Plenum Press.

Coleman, E. M. & Haaven, J. (in press). Assessment and treatment of the intellectually disabled sex offender. In M. S. Carich & J. Mussack (Eds.), *Handbook on sex offender treatment.* Brandon, VT: Safer Society Press.

Colorado Sex Offender Management Board (1996). *Standards and guidelines for the assessment, evaluation, treatment and behavioral monitoring of adult sex offenders.* Denver: Colorado Department of Public Safety.

Colorado Sex Offender Management Board (1999). *Standards and guidelines for the assessment, evaluation, treatment and behavioral monitoring of adult sex offenders* (rev. ed.). Denver: Colorado Department of Public Safety.

Committee on Ethical Guidelines for Forensic Psychologists (1991). Specialty guidelines for forensic psychologists. *Law and Human Behavior, 15,* 655–665.

Cook, J. H. (1999). Civil commitment of sex offenders: South Carolina's Sexually Violent Predator Act. *South Carolina Law Review, 50,* 543–563.

Cooke, D. J., Michie, C., Hart, S. D. & Hare, R. D. (1999). Evaluating the screening version of the Hare psychopathy checklist—Revised (PCL-R): An item response theory analysis. *Psychological Assessment, 11,* 3–13.

Copas, J. B. & Marshall, P. (1998). The offender group reconviction scale. *Journal of the Royal Statistical Society, 47,* 159–171, Series C.

Courtois, C. (1988). *Healing the incest wound: Adult survivors in therapy.* New York: W.W. Norton & Co.

Cumming, G. F. & McGrath, R. J. (2000). External supervision: How can it increase the effectiveness of relapse prevention? In D. R. Laws, S. M. Hudson & T. Ward (Eds.), *Remaking relapse prevention with sex offenders: A sourcebook.* Thousand Oaks, CA: Sage.

Dawes, R., Faust, D. & Meehl, P. (1989). Clinical versus actuarial judgment. *Science, 243,* 1668–1674.

Deblinger, E., Hathaway, C., Lippman, J. & Steer, R. (1993). "Psychosocial characteristics and correlates of symptom distress in non-offending mothers of sexually abused children." *Journal of Interpersonal Violence, 8,* 155–168.

Deblinger, E. & Heft, A. H. (1996). *Treating sexually abused children and their nonoffending parents: A cognitive behavioral approach.* London: Sage.

Denkowski, G., Denkowski, K. & Mabli, J. (1983). A 50 state survey of the current status of residential treatment programs for mentally retarded offenders. *Mental Retardation, 21*, 197.

Dempster, R. (1998). *Prediction of sexually violent recidivism: A comparison of risk assessment instruments.* Unpublished master's thesis, Simon Fraser University, Burnaby, British Columbia.

DesLauriers, A. T. & Gardner, J. (1999). The sexual predator treatment program of Kansas. In A. Schlank & F. Cohen (Eds.), *The sexual predator: Law, policy, evaluation, and treatment.* Kingston, NJ: Civic Research Institute.

Doege, D. (1999, December 31). Most predators find a place, attorney argues. *Milwaukee Journal Sentinel*, available online at: http://www.jsonlive.com/news/metro.

Donovan, J. M. (1986). An etiologic model of alcoholism. *American Journal of Psychiatry, 143,* 1–11.

Doren, D. M. (1998). Recidivism base rates, predictions of sex offender recidivism, and the "sexual predator" commitment laws. *Behavioral Sciences and the Law, 16,* 97–114.

Doren, D. M. (1999, September). *A comprehensive comparison of risk assessment instruments to determine their relative value within civil commitment evaluations.* Paper presented at the annnual meeting of the Association for the Treatment of Sexual Abusers, Orlando, FL.

Doren, D. M. (1999). *The issue of accuracy of the risk assessment instruments within the context of sex offender civil commitment evaluations.* Unpublished draft paper, Mendota Mental Health Institute, Madison, WI.

Doren, D. M. (2000, November). *Being accurate about accuracy of risk assessment instruments.* Paper presented at the annual meeting of the Association for the Treatment of Sexual Abusers, Orlando, FL.

Douglas, K. S., Cox, D. N. & Webster, C. D. (1999). Violence risk assessment: Science and practice. *Legal and Criminological Psychology, 4,* 149–184.

Douglas, K. S., Ogloff, J. R. P., Grant, I. & Nicholls, T. L. (1999). Assessing risk for violence among psychiatric patients: The HCR-20 violence risk assessment scheme and the psychopathy checklist: Screening version. *Journal of Consulting and Clinical Psychology, 67,* 917–930.

Douglas, K. S., Ogloff, J. R. P. & Nicholls, T. L. (1997). *Personality disorders and violence in civil psychiatric patients.* Paper presented at the International Congress on Disorders of Personality, Vancouver, British Columbia.

Douglas, K. & Webster, C. (1999). Predicting violence in mentally and personality disordered individuals. In R. Roesch, S. D. Hart & J. R. P. Ogloff (Eds.), *Psychology and law: The state of the discipline.* New York: Kluwer Academic/Plenum.

Duran, S. (2000, April 22).Three sexual predators may soon be freed. *The News Tribune*, available online at: http://www.search.tribunet.com/archive.

Edgerton, R.B. & Dingman, H. (1964). Good reasons for bad supervision: Dating in a hospital for the mentally retarded. *Psychiatric Quarterly Supplement Part 2,* 221–223.

Edmonson, B., Wish, J. & Fiechtl, K. (1977). Development of a sex knowledge and attitude test for the moderately and mildly retarded. Final Report, HEW

Project 6007500382, Columbus, OH: Nisonger Center, Ohio State University.

Eldridge, H. & Saradjian, J. (2000). Replacing the function of abusive behaviors for the offender: Remaking relapse prevention in working with women who sexually abuse children. In D. R. Laws, S. M. Hudson & T. Ward (Eds.), *Remaking relapse prevention with sex offenders.* Newbury Park, CA: Sage.

Ellis, J. W. & Luckasson, R. A. (1985). Mentally retarded criminal defendants. *Washington Law Review, 53,* 444–493.

English, K. (1998). The containment approach: An aggressive strategy for the community management of adult sex offenders. *Psychology, Public Policy, and Law, 4,* 218–235.

English, K. Pullen, S. & Jones, L. (1996). *Managing adult sex offenders on probation and parole: A containment approach.* Lexington, KY: American Probation and Parole Association.

Ennis, B. & Emery, R. (1978). *The rights of mental patients.* New York: Free Press.

Ennis, B. & Litwack, T. (1974). Flipping coins in the courtroom: Psychiatry and the presumption of expertise. *California Law Review, 62,* 693–723.

Epperson, D. L. (2000, October). *The assessment of the sexually violent predator using the Minnesota sex offender screening tool—Revised.* Workshop presented on behalf of the Florida Department of Children and Families, Orlando, Fl.

Epperson, D. L., Kaul, J. D. & Hesselton, D. (1998, October). *Final report on the development of the Minnesota Sex Offender Screening Tool—Revised* (MnSOST-R). Paper presented at the seventeenth annual research and treatment convention of the Association for the Treatment of Sexual Abusers, Vancouver, British Columbia.

Epperson, D. L., Kaul, J. & Hesselton, D. (1999). *Minnesota sex offender screening tool—Revised (MnSOST-R): Development, performance, and recommended risk level cut scores.* Iowa State University, Department of Psychology.

Epperson, D. L., Kaul, J. & Hesselton, D. (2000). *Minnesota sex offender screening tool—revised (MnSOST-R): Development, performance, and recommended risk level cut scores; Description of cross-validation sample.* Iowa State University, Department of Psychology.

Epperson, D. L., Kaul, J. D. & Huot, S. J. (1995, October). *Predicting risk of recidivism for incarcerated sex offenders: Updated development of the Minnesota Sex Offender Screening Tool (MnSOST).* Paper presented at the fourteenth annual research and treatment conference of the Association for the Treatment of Sexual Abusers, New Orleans, LA.

Epperson, D. L., Kaul, J., Huot, S. J., Hesselton, D., Alexander, W. & Goldman, R. (1999). *Minnesota sex offender screening tool—Revised (MnSOST-R).* St. Paul: Minnesota Department of Corrections.

Faigman, D. L. (1995). The evidentiary status of social science under Daubert: Is it "scientific," "technical" or "other" knowledge? *Psychology, Public Policy, and Law, 1,* 960–979.

Faigman, D. L., Kaye, D. H., Saks, M. J. & Sanders, J. (1997). *Modern scientific evidence: The law and science of expert testimony.* St. Paul, MN: West Publishing.

Falk, A. J. (1999). Sex offenders, mental illness and criminal responsibility: The constitutional boundaries of civil commitment after *Kansas v. Hendricks*. *American Journal of Law and Medicine, 25,* 117–147.

Federal Rules of Evidence, art. III, Rules 702, 703 (1974, 2000).

Federoff, J. P. (1993). Serotonergic drug treatment of deviant sexual interests. *Annals of Sex Research, 6,* 105–121.

Ferguson, E. W. & Haaven, J. (1990). On the design of motivating learning environments for intellectually disabled offenders. *Journal of Correctional Education, 41,* 32–34.

Findings of fact, conclusions of law, and order re motions heard April 18-21, 2000. Turay v. Seling, No. C91-664WD (unpublished opinion, 1997), Washington, May 5, 2000.

Finkelhor, D. (1984). *Child sexual abuse: New theory and research.* London: Macmillan.

Fisher, L. (2000). Cuts leave few options for judges, *The Gainesville Sun,* June 28, 2000, at A1.

Fitch, L. (1998). Sex offender commitment in the United States. *Journal of Forensic Psychiatry, 9,* 237–240.

Fitch, L. (1999, October). *Sex offender commitment in the United States.* Presentation at the Annual Meeting of the State Mental Health Program Directors—Forensic Section, Tarrytown, New York.

Freeman-Longo, R. E., Bird, S. L., Stevenson, W., & Fiske, J. (1995). *1994 nationwide survey of treatment programs and models.* Brandon, VT: Safer Society Press.

Freeman-Longo, R. E., Bird, S., Stevenson, W. & Fiske, J. A. (1995). *1994 nationwide survey of treatment programs & models serving abuse-reactive children and adolescent & adult sex offenders.* Brandon, VT: Safer Society Press.

Garb, H. (1994). Toward a second generation of statistical prediction rules in psychodiagnosis and personality assessment. *Computers in Human Behavior, 10,* 377–394.

Garb, H. (1998). *Studying the clinician: Judgment research and psychological assessment.* Washington, DC: American Psychological Association.

Garcia, S. A. & Steele, H. (1988). Mentally retarded offenders in the criminal justice and mental retardation services systems in Florida: Philosophical, placement and treatment issues. *Arkansas Law Review, 41,* 809–859.

Gendreau, P., Little, T. & Goggin, C. (1996). A meta-analysis of the predictors of adult offender recidivism: What works! *Criminology, 34,* 575–597.

Goldberg, L. R. (1968). Seer over sign: The first "good example"? *Journal of Experimental Research in Personality, 3,* 168–171.

Goldberg, L. R. (1970). Man versus model of man: A rationale, plus some evidence, for a method of improving on clinical inferences. *Psychological Bulletin, 73,* 422–432.

Gotestein, H. G. & Schubert, D. S. P. (1993). Low-dose oral medroxy projesterone acetate in the management of paraphilias. *Journal of Clinical Psychiatry, 54,* 182–188.

Gough, G. H. (1960). Theory and measurement of socialization. *Journal of Consulting Psychology, 24,* 23–30.

Grisso, T. (1981). *Juveniles' waivers of Miranda rights: Legal and psychological competence.* New York: Plenum.

Grisso, T. (1998). *Manual for understanding and appreciation of Miranda rights tests.* Sarasota: Professional Resource Press.

Grove W. & Meehl, P. (1996). Comparative efficiency of informal (subjective, impressionistic) and formal (mechanical, algorithmic) prediction procedures: The clinical-statistical controversy. *Psychology, Public Policy, and Law, 2,* 293–323.

Grove, W. M., Zald, D. H., Lebow, B. S., Snitz, B. E. & Nelson, C. (2000). Clinical versus mechanical prediction: A meta-analysis. *Psychological Assessment, 12,* 19–30.

Grubin, D. (1998). *Sex offending against children: Understanding the risk.* Police Research Series Paper 99. London: Home Office.

Grubin, D. (2000). Complimenting relapse prevention with medical intervention. In D. R. Laws, S. M. Hudson & T. Ward (Eds.), *Remaking relapse prevention with sex offenders: A sourcebook.* Thousand Oaks, CA: Sage.

Haaven, J. (1995, October). *Treatment of intellectually disabled sex offenders.* Paper presented at the training workshop at the fourteenth annual research and treatment conference of the Association for the Treatment of Sexual Abusers, New Orleans, LA.

Haaven, J. L. & Coleman, E. M. (2000). Treatment of the developmentally disabled sex offender. In D. R. Laws, S. M. Hudson & T. Ward (Eds.), *Remaking relapse prevention with sex offenders: A Sourcebook.* Thousand Oaks, CA: Sage.

Haaven, J. L., Little, R. & Petre-Miller, D. (1990). *Treating intellectually disabled sex offenders.* Brandon, VT: Safer Society Press.

Hagler, H. H. (1995). Polygraph as a measure of progress in the assessment, treatment and surveillance of sex offenders. *Sexual Addiction and Compulsivity, 2,* 98–111.

Haley, J. (2000, April 26). Sex predators won't be housed at Indian Ridge. *The Everett Herald,* available online at http://www.heraldnet.com/stories/00/4/26/12546925.htm.

Hall, G. C. N. (1995). Sexual offender recidivism: A meta-analysis of recent treatment studies. *Journal of Consulting and Clinical Psychology, 63,* 802–809.

Hanson, R. K. (1997). *The development of a brief actuarial risk scale for sexual offense recidivism* (User Report No. 1997-04). Ottawa: Department of the Solicitor General of Canada.

Hanson, R. K. (1998). What do we know about sex offender risk assessment? *Psychology, Public Policy, and Law, 4,* 50–72.

Hanson, R. K. (1999). What do we know about risk assessment? In A. Schlank & F. Cohen (Eds.), *The sexual predator: Law, policy, evaluation, and treatment.* Kingston, NJ: Civic Research Institute.

Hanson, R. K. & Bussière, M. T. (1996). *Predicting relapse: A meta-analysis.* (User Report No. 96-04). Ottawa: Department of the Solicitor General of Canada.

Hanson, R. K., & Bussière, M. T. (1998). Predicting relapse: A meta-analysis of sexual offender recidivism studies. *Journal of Consulting and Clinical Psychology, 66,* 348–362.

Hanson, R. K. & Harris, A. (1998).

Dynamic predictors of sexual recidivism. Ottawa: Department of the Solicitor General of Canada.

Hanson, R. K. & Harris, A. (2000). *The sex offender need assessment rating (SONAR): A method for measuring change in risk levels.* Ottawa: Department of the Solicitor General of Canada.

Hanson, R. K., Steffy, R. A. & Gauthier, R. (1993). Long-term recidivism of child molesters. *Journal of Consulting and Clinical Psychology, 61,* 646–652.

Hanson, R. K. & Thornton, D. (1999). *Static 99: Improving actuarial risk assessments for sex offenders* (User Report No. 99-02). Ottawa: Department of the Solicitor General of Canada.

Hanson, R. K. & Thornton, D. (2000). Improving risk assessments for sex offenders: A comparison of three actuarial scales. *Law and Human Behavior, 24,* 119–136.

Hare, R. D. (1991). *The Hare Psychopathy Checklist—Revised Manual.* Toronto: Multi-Health Systems.

Hare, R. D. (1997, November). *Assessing psychopathy: Clinical and forensic applications of the PCL-R.* Presentation of Minnesota Association for the Treatment of Sexual Abusers.

Hare, R. D. (1998). The Hare PCL-R: Some issues concerning its use and misuse. *Legal and Criminological Psychology, 3,* 101–122.

Hare, R. D. (1998). Psychopaths and their nature: Implications for the mental health and criminal justice systems. In T. Millon, E. Simonsen, M. Birket-Smith, & R. Davis, R. (Eds.), *Psychopathy: Antisocial, criminal, and violent behavior.* New York: Guilford Press.

Hare, R. D. (1999, September). *Assessing psychopathy with the HARE psychopathy checklist—Revised (PCL-R).* Workshop presented in conjunction with the eighteenth annual training and research conference of the Association for the Treatment of Sexual Abusers, Orlando, FL.

Hare, R. D. (1999). Psychopathy as a risk factor for violence. *Psychiatric Quarterly, 70,* 181–197.

Hare, R. D., Hart, S. D. & Harpur, T. J. (1991). Psychopathy and DSM-IV criteria for antisocial personality disorder. *Journal of Abnormal Psychology, 100,* 391–398.

Harris, G. T., Rice, M. E. & Cormier, C.A. (1991). Psychopathy and violent recidivism. *Law and Human Behavior, 15,* 625–631.

Harris, G. T., Rice, M. E. & Quinsey, V. L. (1993). Violent recidivism of mentally disordered offenders: The development of a statistical prediction instrument. *Criminal Justice and Behavior, 20,* 315–335.

Hart, S. D., Cox, D. N. & Hare, R. D. (1995). *The Hare PCL:SV.* Toronto: Multi-Health Systems.

Heilbrun, K. (1998). Sexual offending: Linking assessment, intervention, and decision making. *Psychology, Public Policy, and Law, 4,* 138–174.

Heilbrun, K., O'Neill, M. L., Strohman, L. K., Bowman, Q. & Philipson, J. (2000). Expert approaches to communicating violence risk. *Law & Human Behavior, 24,* 137–148.

Held, A. (1999). The civil commitment of sexual predators—Experience under Minnesota's law. In A. Schlank & F. Cohen (Eds.), *The sexual predator: Law, policy, evaluation, and treatment.*

Kingston, New Jersey: Civic Research Institute.

Hemphill, J. F., Hare, R. D. & Wong, S. (1998). Psychopathy and recidivism: A review. *Legal and Criminological Psychology, 3,* 139–170.

Hemphill, J. F., Templeman, R., Wong, S. & Hare, R. D. (1998). Psychopathy and crime: Recidivism and criminal careers. In D. Cooke, A. E. Forth & R. D. Hare (Eds.), *Psychopathy: Theory, research, and implications for society.* Amsterdam: Kluwer, 375–399.

Hennessy, M. T. (1999). *A survey of the nation's sexual predator treatment programs.* Doctoral dissertation, University of Denver.

Hoberman, H. M. (1999). The forensic evaluation of sex offenders in civil commitment proceedings. In A. Schlank & F. Cohen (Eds.), *The sexual predator: Law, policy, evaluation, and treatment.* Kingston, NJ: Civic Research Institute.

Home Office & Department of Health (1999). *Managing dangerous people with severe personality disorder.* Available from Department of Health, P.O. Box 777, London, SE1 6XH, England.

Hornby, R. L. (2000). New Jersey Sexually Violent Predator Act: Civil commitment of the sexually abnormal. *Seton Hall Legislative Journal, 24,* 473–508.

Howard, G. S. (1997). *Ecological psychology: Creating a more earth-friendly human nature.* Notre Dame, Indiana: University of Notre Dame Press.

Huot, S. (1999). The referral process. In A. Schlank & F. Cohen (Eds.), *The sexual predator: Law, policy, evaluation, and treatment.* Kingston, NJ: Civic Research Institute.

International Classification of Diseases (10th ed.) (1992). Geneva, Switzerland: World Health Organization.

James, B. & Nasjleti, M. (1983). *Treating sexually abused children and their families.* Palo Alto, CA: Consulting Psychologists Press.

Janus, E. S. (2000). An empirical study of Minnesota's sex offender commitment program. *Sex Offender Law Report, 1,* 49–63.

Janus, E. S. (2000). Sex offender commitments in Minnesota: A descriptive study of second generation commitments. *Behavioral Sciences and the Law, 18,* 343–374.

Janus, E. S. (2000). Sexual predator commitment laws: Lessons for law and the behavioral sciences. *Behavioral Sciences and the Law, 18,* 5–21.

Janus, E. S. & Meehl. P. (1997). Assessing the legal standard for predictions of dangerousness in sex offender commitment proceedings. *Psychology, Public Policy, and Law, 3,* 33–64.

Jensen, S. H. (Ed.) (1993). *The ATSA practitioner's handbook.* Beaverton, Or: Association for the Treatment of Sexual Abusers.

Kesler, R. A. (1999). Running in circles: Defining mental illness and dangerousness in the wake of *Kansas v. Hendricks. Wayne Law Review, 44,* 1871–1898.

Klassen, D. & O'Connor, W. A. *Predicting violence among mental patients: A cross validation of an actuarial scale.* Paper presented at the American Society of Criminology.

Klassen, D. & O'Connor, W. A. (1988).

A prospective study of predictors of violence in adult mental health admission. *Law and Human Behavior, 12,* 143–148.

King, C. A. (1999). Fighting the devil we don't know: *Kansas v. Hendricks*, a case study exploring the civilization of criminal punishment and its effectiveness in preventing child sexual abuse. *William & Mary Law Review, 40,* 1427–1469.

Knopp, F. H. (1984). *Retraining adult sex offenders: Methods and models.* Brandon, VT: Safer Society Press.

Kropp, P. R. (2000, November). *The risk for sexual violence protocol (RSVP).* Paper presented at the annual meeting of the Association for the Treatment of Sexual Abusers, San Diego, CA.

Kropp, P. R., Hart, S. D., Webster, C. D. & Eaves, D. (1995). *Manual for the Spousal Assault Risk Assessment Guide* (2d ed.). Vancouver: British Columbia Institute on Family Violence.

La Fond, J. Q. (2000). The future of involuntary civil commitment in the U.S.A. after *Kansas v. Hendricks. Behavioral Sciences & the Law, 18,* 153–167.

La Fond, J. Q. & Winick, B. (1998). Introduction to the special issue on sex offenders. *Psychology, Public Policy and Law, 3,* 4.

Landy, Robert J. (1993). *Persona and performance: The meaning of role in drama, therapy, and everyday life.* New York: Guilford Press.

Landy, Robert J. (1994). *Drama therapy: Concepts and practices* (2d ed). Springfield, IL: Charles C. Thomas.

Langevin, R. & Lang, R. A. (1990). Substance abuse among sex offenders. *Annals of Sex Research, 3,* 397–424.

Laws, D. R. (Ed.) (1989). *Relapse prevention with sex offenders.* New York: Guilford Press.

Levy, R. M. & Rubenstein, L. S. (1996). *The rights of people with mental disabilities: The authoritative ACLU guide to the rights of people with mental illness and mental retardation.* Carbondale, Ill: Southern Illinois University Press.

Lidz, C. W., Mulvey, E. P. & Gardner, W. (1993). The accuracy of predictions of violence to others. *Journal of the American Medical Association, 269,* 1007–1011.

Litwack, T. R. & Schlesinger, L. B. (1987). Assessing and predicting violence: Research, law, and applications. In I. Weiner & A. Hess (Eds.), *Handbook of forensic psychology.* New York: Wiley.

Litwack, T. R. & Schlesinger, L. B. (1999). Dangerousness risk assessments: Research, legal, and clinical considerations. In I. Weiner & A. Hess (Eds.), *Handbook of forensic psychology.* New York: Wiley.

Logan, C. (2000, November). *Risk for sexual violence protocol: Applications in a sample of English mentally disordered offenders.* Paper presented at the annual meeting of the Association for the Treatment of Sexual Abusers, San Diego, CA.

Luckasson, R. A. (1988). The dually diagnosed client in the criminal justice system. In J. Stark, F. Menolascino, M. Albarelli & V. Gray (Eds.), *Mental retardation and mental health: Classification, diagnosis, treatment, services.* New York: Springer-Verlag.

Maller, P. (2000, February 1). Even at

95, molester is a threat, jury told. *Milwaukee Journal Sentinel*, available online at: http://www.onwis.com/news/state/jan00/oldpred01013100.asp.

Marlatt, G. A. (1985). Relapse prevention. New York: Guilford Press.

Marques, J. K. (1984). *An innovative treatment program for sex offenders: Report to the Legislature.* Sacramento: California Department of Mental Health.

Marques, J. K. (1998, May 14). *Thirteenth report of the special master, Turay v. Seling,* No. C91-664WD (unpubl. op. W.D. Wash.).

Marques, J. K. (1999, September 9). *Sixteenth report of the special master, Turay v. Seling,* No. C91-664WD (unpub. op. W.D. Wash.).

Marques, J. K. (2000). Seventeenth report of the special master, *Turay v. Seling,* No. C91-664WD (unpub. op. W.D. Wash.).

Marques, J. K., Becker, J. V., Messer, G. A., Nelson, C. & Schlank, A. (1999). *Treatment of sexual predators: Essential elements of successful civil commitment programs.* Paper presented at the eighteenth annual research and treatment conference, Association for the Treatment of Sexual Abusers, Orlando, FL.

Marques, J. K., Becker, J. V., Nelson, C. & Schlank, A. (2000). *The evolution of civil commitment programs: New ideas for solving common problems and developing programs that work.* Presented at the nineteenth annual research and treatment conference, Association for the Treatment of Sexual Abusers, San Diego, CA.

Marques, J. K., Day, D. M., Nelson, C. & West, M. A. (1994). Effects of cognitive-behavioral treatment on sex offender recidivism: Preliminary results of a longitudinal study. *Criminal Justice and Behavior, 21,* 28–54.

Marques, J. K., Nelson, C., Alarcon, J. M. & Day, D. M. (2000). Preventing relapse in sex offenders: What we learned from SOTEP's experimental treatment program. In D. R. Laws, S. M. Hudson & T. Ward (Eds.), *Remaking relapse prevention with sex offenders.* Thousand Oaks, CA: Sage.

Marsh, V. (1998). Sexually violent predators may soon prey on Virginia's public hospitals. *Network Newsletter.* Virginia Alliance for the Mentally Ill, available online at: http://www.216.156.111.229/articles/svp_crisis/svp-06-17-98.htm.

Marshall, W. L. & Barbaree, H. E. (1988). The long-term evaluation of a behavioral treatment program for child molesters. *Behaviour Research and Therapy, 26,* 499–551.

Marshall, W. L. & Barbaree, H. E. (1989). Sexual violence. In K. Howells & C. R. Hollin (Eds.), *Clinical approaches to violence.* New York: Wiley.

Marshall, W. L. & Barbaree, H. E. (1990). Outcome of comprehensive cognitive-behavioral treatment programs. In W. L. Marshall, D. R. Laws & H. E. Barbaree (Eds.), *Handbook of sexual assault: Issues, theories and treatment of the offender.* New York: Plenum.

Marshall, W. L., Jones, R., Ward, T., Johnston, P. & Barbaree, H. E. (1991). Treatment outcome with sex offenders. *Clinical Psychology Review, 11,* 465–485.

Marshall, W. L., Laws, D. R. & Barbaree, H. E. (1990). *Handbook of sexual assault: Issues, theories, and treatment of the offender.* New York: Plenum.

McGrath, R. J. (1991). Sex-offender risk assessment and disposition planning: A review of empirical and clinical findings. *International Journal of Offender Therapy & Comparative Criminology, 35,* 328–350.

McGuire, J. (Ed.) (1995). *What works: Reducing re-offending.* New York: John Wiley & Sons.

McNiel, D. E. & Binder, R. L. (1991). Clinical assessment of the risk of violence among psychiatric inpatients. *American Journal of Psychiatry, 148,* 1317–1321.

Medical Directors Council, National Association of State Mental Health Program Directors (NASMHPD) (1999). *Issues pertaining to the development and implementation of programs for persons civilly committed for treatment under sexually violent predator statutes.* Alexandria, VA: Author.

Meehl, P. E. (1954). *Clinical versus statistical prediction.* Minneapolis: University of Minnesota Press.

Meehl, P. E. (1970). Psychology and the criminal law. *University of Richmond Law Review, 5,* 1–30.

Meehl, P. E. (1996). *Clinical versus statistical prediction: A theoretical analysis and a review of the literature.* Northvale, N.J.: Jason Aronson. (Original work published in 1954.)

Mee-Lee, D. (1995). Matching in addictions treatment: How do we get there from here? *Alcoholism Treatment Quarterly Special Issue: Treatment of the Addictions—Applications of Outcome Research for Clinical Management, 12,* 113–127.

Melton, G. B., Petrila, J., Poythress, N. & Slobogin, C. (1997). *Psychological evaluations for the courts: A handbook for attorneys and mental health professionals* (2d ed.). New York: Guilford Press.

Melton, G. B., Weithorn, L. A. & Slobogin, C. (1985). *Community based mental health centers and the courts: An evaluation of community-based forensic services.* Lincoln: University of Nebraska Press.

Mercer, W. M. (1999, December 20). *Study of the programmatic and facility needs of the Florida sexually violent predator program: Final report.* A report presented to the State of Florida Department of Children and Families, Tallahassee, FL.

Messer, G. (June 1, 2000). Roundtable discussion of transition issues, SVP Conference: Summit 2000, Oshkosh, WI.

Miller, G. (1994). *Substance abuse subtle screening inventory (SASSI-3).* Available by calling 1-888-297-2774.

Miller, W. & Rollnick, S. (1991). *Motivational interviewing: Preparing people to change addictive behavior.* New York: Guilford Press.

Millon, T., Simonsen, E., Birket-Smith, M. & Davis, R. (Eds.) (1998). *Psychopathy: Antisocial, criminal, and violent behavior.* New York: Guilford Press.

Monahan, J. (1981). *The clinical prediction of violent behavior.* Monograph of the National Institute of Mental Health, Washington, DC.

Monahan, J. (1995). *The clinical prediction of violent behavior.* Northvale, NJ: Jason Aronson.

Monahan, J. (1996). Violence prediction: The last 20 and the next 20 years. *Criminal Justice and Behavior, 23,* 107–120.

Monahan, J. & Steadman, H. J. (1994). Toward a rejuvenation of risk assessment research. In J. Monahan & H. J. Steadman (Eds.), *Violence and mental disorder: Developments in risk assessment*. Chicago: University of Chicago Press.

Monat, R.K. (1982). *Sexuality and the mentally handicapped.* San Diego: College Hill Press.

Morse, S. (1978). Law and mental health professionals: The limits of expertise. *Professional Psychology, 9,* 389–399.

Mossman, D. (1994). Assessing predictions of violence: Being accurate about accuracy. *Journal of Consulting and Clinical Psychology, 62,* 783–792.

Murphy, W. D. & Barbaree, H. E. (1994). *Assessments of sex offenders by measures of erectile response: Psycometric properties and decision making.* Brandon, VT: Safer Society Press.

Murphy, W. D., Marques, J. K. & Jensen, S. (1997). *ATSA's revised ethical standards and principles.* Presented at the sixteenth annual research and treatment conference, Association for the Treatment of Sexual Abusers, Arlington, VA.

Murphy, W. D. & Peters, J. M. (1992). Profiling child sexual abusers: Psychological considerations. *Criminal Justice and Behavior, 19,* 24–37.

Myers, D. (1976). Supported work for mentally retarded parolees. In M. Santamour (Ed.), *The mentally retarded citizen and the criminal justice system: Problems and programs.* Newport, RI: James Maher Center.

Nace, P., Davis, C. & Gaspari, J. (1991). Axis II comorbidity in substance abusers. *American Journal of Psychiatry, 148,* 118–120.

National Association of State Mental Health Program Directors (NASMHPD) (1997). *Position statement on sexually violent offenders.* Alexandria, VA: Author.

National Association of State Mental Health Program Directors (NASMHPD) (1999, April 25–27). *Medical directors counsel technical report*, Portland, OR.

National Association of State Mental Health Program Directors (NASMHPD). (1999). *Third technical report by the Medical Directors Council.* Alexandria, VA: Author. Available online at: http://www.nasmhpd.org/svpfinal.htm.

Nelson, C., Miner, M., Marques, J., Russell, K. & Achterkirchen, J. (1988). Relapse prevention: A cognitive behavioral model for treatment of the rapist and child molester. *Journal of Social Work and Human Sexuality, 7,* 125–143.

Nichols, H. R. & Molinder, I. (1984). *Multiphasic sex inventory manual: A test to assess psychosexual characteristics of the sexual offender.* Tacoma, WA: Authors.

Nufield, J. (1982). *Parole decision-making in Canada: Research towards decision guidelines.* Ottawa: Department of the Solicitor General of Canada.

O'Connell, M. A. (2000). Polygraphy: Assessment and community monitoring. In D. R. Laws, S. M. Hudson & T. Ward (Eds.), *Remaking relapse prevention with sex offenders: A sourcebook.* Thousand Oaks, CA: Sage.

Ogloff, J. R. P., Wong, S. & Greenwood, A. (1990). Treating criminal psychopaths in a therapeutic community program. *Behavioral Sciences and the Law, 8,* 181–190.

Order and Injunction (1997). *Turay v. Weston,* later known as *Turay v. Seling.* No. C91-664WD (unpub. op. W.D. Wash.).

Order on plaintiff's renewed motion for injunctive relief and contempt, and defendants' motion for release from injunction. (1997, Feb. 4). *Turay v. Weston,* No. C91-664WD (unpub. op. W.D. Wash.).

Otto, R. K. (1992). The prediction of dangerous behavior: A review and analysis of "second generation" research. *Forensic Reports, 5,* 103–133.

Otto, R. K. (1994). On the ability of mental health professionals to "predict dangerousness": A commentary on interpretations of the "dangerousness" literature. *Law and Psychology Review, 18,* 43–68.

Otto, R. K. (2000). Assessing and managing outpatient violence risk in outpatient settings. *Journal of Clinical Psychology, 56,* 1239–1262.

Otto, R. K., Borum, R. & Hart, S. (2000). *Professional issues concerning the use of actuarial instruments in sexually violent predator evaluations* (unpublished manuscript submitted for publication).

Otto, R. K. & Butcher, J. (1995). Computer-assisted psychological assessment in child custody evaluations. *Family Law Quarterly, 29,* 79–96.

Otto, R. K., Poythress, N., Borum, R. & Petrila J. (1999). *Assessing risk in sex offenders.* Tampa: Florida Mental Health Institute.

Pacht, A. R. (1976). The rapist in treatment: Professional myths and psychological realities. In M. J. Walker & S. L. Brodsky (Eds.), *Sexual assault: The victim of the rapist.* Lexington, MA: Lexington Books.

Packard, R. & Gordon, A. (1999, September). *An investigation of actuarial risk scales: Concordance and factor analysis.* Paper presented at the annual meeting of the Association for the Treatment of Sexual Abusers, Orlando, FL.

Paitich, D. R., Langevin, R. Freeman, R., Mann, I. & Handy, L. (1977). The Clarke SHQ: A clinical sex history for males. *Archives of Sexual Behavior, 6,* 421–436.

Pearman, B. C. (1998). *Kansas v. Hendricks*: The Supreme Court's endorsement of sexually violent predator statutes unnecessarily expands state civil commitment power. *North Carolina Law Review, 76,* 1973–2015.

Phenix, A., Hanson, R. K. & Thornton, D. (2000). *Coding rules for the Static-99.* Ottawa: Department of the Solicitor General of Canada.

Pithers, W. D. (1997). Maintaining treatment integrity with sexual abusers. *Criminal justice and Behavior, 24,* 34–51.

Pithers, W. D., Marques, J. K., Gibat, C. C. & Marlatt, G. A. (1983). Relapse prevention with sexually aggressive persons: A self-control model of treatment and maintenance of change. In J. G. Greer & I. R. Stuart (Eds.), *The sexual aggressor: Current perspectives on treatment.* New York: Van Nostrand Reinhold.

Pollock, N., McBain, I. & Webster, C. D. (1989). Clinical decision-making and the assessment of dangerousness. In K. Howells & C. R. Hollin (Eds.), *Clinical approaches to violence.* New York: Wiley.

Porterfield, E. (2000). High court to take up sexual-predator law: Justices to weigh rapist's case against state statute, *Seattle Post-Intelligencer*, March 21, 2000, at B1.

Pratt, J. (1998). Sex offenders: Scientific, legal, and policy perspectives. *Psychology, Public Policy, and Law, 4,* 25–49.

Prentky, R. A. (1997). Arousal reduction in sexual offenders: A review of antiandrogen interventions. *Sexual Abuse: A Journal of Research and Treatment, 9,* 335–347.

Prentky, R. A. & Burgess, A. W. (1990). Rehabilitation of child molesters: A cost-benefit analysis. *American Journal of Orthopsychiatry, 60,* 108–117.

Prentky, R. A., Knight, R. A. & Lee, A. F. S. (1997). Risk factors associated with recidivism among extrafamilial child molesters. *Journal of Consulting and Clinical Psychology, 65,* 141–149.

Prentky, R. A., Lee, A. F. S., Knight, R. A. & Cerce, D. (1997). Recidivism rates among child molesters and rapists: A methodological analysis. *Law and Human Behavior, 21,* 635–659.

Proulx, J., Pellerin, B., Paradis, Y., McKibben, A., Aubut, J. & Ouiment, M. (1997). Static and dynamic predictors of recidivism in sexual aggressors. *Sexual Abuse: A Journal of Research and Treatment, 9,* 7–27.

Prout, H. T. & Cale, R. L. (1994). Individual counseling approaches. In D. C. Strohmer & H. T. Prout (Eds.), *Counseling and psychotherapy with persons with mental retardation and borderline intelligence.* Brandon, VT: Clinical Psychology Publishing.

Quinsey, V. L. (1992). *Review of the Washington State Special Commitment Center Program for Sexually Violent Predators.* Reprinted as Appendix I in LaFond, J. Q., Washington's sexually violent predator law: A deliberate misuse of the therapeutic state for social control. *University of Puget Sound Law Review, 15,* 655–708.

Quinsey, V. L. (1999). Comment on Fallon, P., et al. Report of the committee on inquiry into the personality disorder unit, Ashworth Special Hospital, vol. 1. *The Journal of Forensic Psychiatry, 10,* 631–644.

Quinsey, V. L. & Earls, C. M. (1990). The modification of sexual preferences. In W. L. Marshall, D. R. Laws & H. E. Barbaree (Eds.), *Handbook of sexual assault: Issues, theories, and treatment of the offender.* New York: Plenum.

Quinsey, V. L., Harris, G. T., Rice, M. E. & Cormier, C. A. (1998). *Violent offenders: Appraising and managing risk.* Washington, DC: American Psychological Association Press.

Quinsey, V. L. & Lalumiere, M. L. (1996). *Assessment of sexual offenders against children.* Thousand Oaks, CA: Sage.

Quinsey, V. L., Lalumiere, M. L., Rice, M. E. & Harris, G. T. (1995). Predicting sexual offenses. In J. C. Campbell (Ed.), *Assessing dangerousness: Violence by sexual offenders, batterers, and child abusers.* Thousand Oaks, CA: Sage.

Quinsey, V. L. & Maguire, A. (1986). Maximum security psychiatric patients: Actuarial and clinical predictions of dangerousness. *Journal of Interpersonal Violence, 1,* 143–171.

Quinsey, V. L., Rice, M. E. & Harris, G. T. (1995). Actuarial prediction of sexual recidivism. *Journal of Interpersonal Violence, 10,* 85–105.

Rainey, J. & Turene, V. D. (2000, June 1). Poor areas pin hopes on facility for sex offenders. *Los Angeles Times.*

Ramsey, C. B. (1999). California's Sexually Violent Predator Act: The role of psychiatrists, courts, and medical determinations in confining sex offenders. *Hastings Constitutional Law Quarterly, 26,* 469–504.

Reilly, D., Delva, N. J. & Hudson, R. W. (2000, August). Protocols for the use of cyproterone, medroxy-progesterone, and leuprolide in the treatment of paraphilia. *Canadian Journal of Psychiatry, 45,* 559–563.

Reisner, R., Slobogin, C. & Rai, A. (1999). *Law and the mental health systems: Civil and criminal aspects* (3d ed.). Minneapolis, MN: West Publishing.

Rice, M. E. (1997). Violent offender research and implications for the criminal justice system. *American Psychologist, 52,* 414–423.

Rice, M. E. (1999). *A multi-site followup study of sex offenders: The predictive accuracy of risk assessment instruments.* Presented at the third annual Forensic Psychiatry Program Research Day, University of Toronto.

Rice, M. E. & Harris, G. T. (1995). Violent recidivism: Assessing predictive validity. *Journal of Consulting and Clinical Psychology, 63,* 737–748.

Rice, M. E. & Harris, G. T. (1997). Cross-validation and extension of the Violence Risk Appraisal Guide for Child Molesters and Rapists. *Law and Human Behavior, 21,* 435–448.

Rice, M. E. & Harris, G. T. (2000). *Sexual preferences and risk of recidivism among father-daughter incest offenders and other child molesters.* (Manuscript submitted for publication).

Rice, M. E., Harris, G. T. & Cormier, C. A. (1992). An evaluation of a maximum security therapeutic community for psychopaths and other mentally disordered offenders. *Law and Human Behavior, 16,* 399–412.

Rice, M. E., Harris, G. T. & Quinsey, V. L. (1990). A follow-up of rapists assessed in a maximum-security psychiatric facility. *Journal of Interpersonal Violence, 5,* 435–448.

Rice, M. E., Quinsey, V. L. & Harris, G. T. (1991). Sexual recidivism among child molesters released from a maximum security psychiatric institution. *Journal of Consulting and Clinical Psychology, 59,* 381–386.

Rogers, R. (1995). *Diagnostic and structured interviewing: A handbook for psychologists.* Odessa, FL: Psychological Assessment Resources.

Romero, J. J. & Williams, L. M. (1985). Recidivism among convicted sex offenders: A 10-year follow-up study. *Federal Probation, 47,* 58–64.

Salekin, R. T., Rogers, R. & Sewell, K. W. (1996). A review and meta-analysis of the psychopathy checklist and psychopathy checklist—revised: Predictive validity of dangerousness. *Clinical Psychology: Science and Practice, 3,* 203–215.

Salter, A. (1988). *Treating child sex offenders and victims: A practical guide.* London: Sage.

Santamour, M. & West, B. (1977, August). *The mentally retarded offender and corrections.* Washington, DC: National Institute of Law Enforcement and Criminal Justice.

Santamour, M. & West, B. (Eds.) (1982). The mentally retarded offender: Presentation of the facts and a discussion of the issues. *The retarded offender.* New York: Praeger.

Schlank, A. (1995). The utility of the MMPI and MSI for identifying a sexual offender typology. *Sexual Abuse: A Journal of Research and Treatment, 7,* 185–194.

Schlank, A. (1999). Guidelines for the development of new programs. In A. Schlank & F. Cohen (Eds.), *The sexual predator: Law, policy, evaluation, and treatment.* Kingston, NJ: Civic Research Institute.

Schlank, A. & Cohen, F. (Eds.) (1999). *The sexual predator: Law, policy, evaluation, and treatment.* Kingston, NJ: Civic Research Institute.

Schlank, A., Harry, R. & Farnsworth, M. (1999). The Minnesota sex offender program. In A. Schlank & F. Cohen (Eds.), *The sexual predator: Law, policy, evaluation, and treatment.* Kingston, NJ: Civic Research Institute.

Schwartz B. K. (1999). The case against involuntary commitment. In A. Schlank & F. Cohen (Eds.), *The sexual predator law: Law, policy, evaluation, and treatment.* Kingston, NJ: Civic Research Institute.

Schwartz, B. K. & Cellini, H. R. (1995). Female sex offenders. In B. K. Schwartz & H. R. Cellini (Eds.), *The sex offender: Corrections, treatment, and legal practice.* Kingston, NJ: Civic Research Institute.

Scott, L. K. (1997). Community management of sex offenders. In B. Schwartz & H. Cellini (Eds.), *The sex offender: New insights, treatment innovations, and legal developments.* Kingston, NJ: Civic Research Institute.

Seghorn, T. K. & Weigel, M. (1999, September). Comparative use of Abel assessments and penile plethysmograph laboratory assessments in an outpatient forensic practice. In S. Johnson (Chair), *Current research comparing plethysmography with the Abel assessment for sexual interest.* Symposium conducted at the annual meeting of the Association for the Treatment of Sexual Abusers, Orlando, FL.

Serin, R. C. & Amos, N. L. (1995). The role of psychopathy in the assessment of dangerousness. *International Journal of Law and Psychiatry, 18,* 231–238.

Seto, M. C. & Barbaree, H. E. (1999). Psychopathy, treatment behavior, and sex offender recidivism. *Journal of Interpersonal Violence, 14,* 1235–1248.

Sewell, K. W. & Salekin, R. T. (1997). Understanding and detecting deception in sex offenders. In R. Rogers (Ed.), *Clinical assessment of malingering and deception* (2d ed.). New York: Guilford Press.

Sgroi, S. (1982). *Handbook of clinical intervention in child sexual abuse.* Lexington, MA: Lexington Books.

Shuman, D. W. (1994 & Supp. 1997). *Psychiatric and psychological evidence.* New York: McGraw-Hill.

Sink, L. (2000, Feb. 2). Molester won't be freed. *Milwaukee Journal Sentinel,* available online at www.jsonline.com/news/state/feb00/oldpred02r020100.asp.

Slobogin, C. (1988). The ultimate issue issue. *Behavioral Sciences and the Law, 7,* 259–266.

Slobogin, C. (1996). Dangerousness as a criterion in the criminal process. In B. D.

Sales & D. W. Shuman (Eds.), *Law, mental health, and mental disorder.* Pacific Grove, CA: Brooks/Cole.

Slobogin, C. (1999). A prevention model of juvenile justice: The promise of *Kansas v. Hendricks* for children. *1999 Wisconsin Law Review*, 185–226.

Solomon, J. & George, Carol (1999). The measurement of attachment security in infancy and childhood. In J. Cassidy & P. Shaver (Eds.), *Handbook of attachment.* New York: Guilford Press.

Sreenivasen, S., Kirkish, P., Garrick, T., Weinberger, L. E. & Phenix, A. (2000, November). Actuarial risk assessment models: A review of critical issues related to violence and sex offender recidivism. *Journal of the Academy of Psychiatry and the Law, 28*, 438–448.

Stacken, N. M. & Shevich, J. (1999). Working with the intellectually disabled/socially inadequate sex offender in a prison setting. In B. Schwartz (Ed.), *The sex offender: Theoretical advances, treating special populations, and legal developments.* Kingston, NJ: Civic Research Institute.

Steele, N. (1995). Aftercare treatment programs. In B. Schwartz. & H. Cellini (Eds.), *The sex offender: Corrections, treatment, and legal practice.* Kingston, NJ: Civic Research Institute.

Stephenson, S. (1993). Use of drama. In K. N. Dwivedi (Ed.), *Group work with children and adolescents.* London: Jessica Kingsley.

SVP Conference: Summit 2000. May 31–June 2, 2000. Oshkosh, Wisconsin.

Swanson, C. K. & Garwick, G. B. (1990). Treatment for low-functioning sex offenders: Group therapy and interagency coordination. *Mental Retardation, 28*, 155–161.

Taylor, R. (1999). *Predicting reconvictions for sexual and violent offenses using the revised offender group reconviction scale.* Research Findings 104. Home Office Research, Development and Statistics Directorate. Available from Information and Publications Group, Room 201, Home Office, Queen Anne's Gate, London, SW1H 9AT, England.

Thompson, R. (1999). Early attachment and later development. In J. Cassidy & P. Shaver (Eds.), *Handbook of attachment.* New York: Guilford Press.

Thornton, D. (2000). *SRA—Initial deviance assessment* (unpublished manuscript). London: Her Majesty's Prison Service.

Thornton, D. (2000, December). *Static and dynamic components of risk.* Paper presented to Her Majesty's Prison Service Treatment Managers Conference, Harrogate, England.

Turay v. Weston (1994, June 3). No. C91-664WD (unpub. op. W.D. Wash.).

Valliere, V. N. (1997). Relationships between alcohol use, alcohol expectancies, and sexual offenses in convicted offenders. In B. K. Schwartz & H. R. Cellini (Eds.), *The sex offender: New insights, treatment innovations, and legal developments.* Kingston, NJ: Civic Research Institute.

van der Kolk, B. (1988). The trauma spectrum: The interaction of biological and social events in the genesis of the trauma response. *Journal of Traumatic Stress, 1,* 273–290.

Wagner, D. E., Van Nort, J. J., Scanish, J. D., Barnes, J. M., Hallman, J. L.,

Thomas, K. W. & Smith, N. L. (2000). Daubert *hearing information: Sex offender risk assessments.* LaGrange, KY: Kentucky Department of Corrections.

Ward, K. & McElwee, D. (1995, May). Supporting individuals with inappropriate sexual behaviors in community based settings. Paper presented at the training workshop at the ANCOR Conference on Intellectually Disabled Sex Offenders, New York.

Ward, T. & Keenan, T. (1999, August). Child molesters' implicit theories. *Journal of Interpersonal Violence, 14*, 821–838.

Webster, C. D., Douglas, K. S., Eaves, D. & Hart, S. D. (1997). *Manual for the HCR-20: Assessing risk for violence* (version 2). Burnaby, British Columbia: Mental Health Law and Policy Institute, Simon Fraser University.

Webster, C. D., Harris, G. T., Rice, M. E., Cormier, C. & Quinsey, V. L. (1994). *The violence prediction scheme: Assessing dangerousness in high-risk men.* Toronto: University of Toronto, Centre of Criminology.

Willis, V. (July 1980). Design considerations for mental health facilities. *Hospital and Community Psychiatry, 31*, 483–490.

Ziskin, J. (Ed.) (1995). *Coping with psychiatric and psychological testimony.* Los Angeles: Law and Psychology Press.

Table of Acronyms

ANCOR	American Network of Community Options and Resources
APA	American Psychiatric Association
ASES	Adult Self Expression Scale
ASGPP	American Society of Group Psychotherapy & Psychodrama
ASPD	Antisocial personality disorder
ASSESS-LIST	Mnemonic device that covers ten risk-assessment areas for sex offense recidivism
ATSA	Association for the Treatment of Sexual Abusers
AUC	Area under the curve
AVE	Abstinence violation effect
CA	Chemical abuse
CATS	Child and Adolescent Taxon Scale
CD	Chemical dependency
CEPP	Conditional extension pending placement (resident status category, state psychiatric facility, New Jersey)
CI	Confidence interval (risk prediction statistical level)
CLES	Common language effect size (AUC cut-off for a particular risk prediction measure/method)
CSOM	Center for Sex Offender Management
CSPA	Criminal Sexual Psychopath Act (Michigan repealed in 1966)
DDMR	Developmental disabilities/Mental retardation
DDSO	Developmentally disabled sex offender
DDSO-RP	Developmentally disabled sex offender relapse prevention model
DHS	Department of Human Services
DOC	Department of Corrections
DRA	Dynamic risk factors
DSM-IV	*Diagnostic and Statistical Manual of Mental Disorders* (4th ed., 1994)
DSPD	Dangerous severe personality disorder
ECRC	End-of-Confinement Review Committee (in the MSOP)
FRE	Federal Rules of Evidence
GED	Graduate equivalent degree (high school); general education degree
GPS	Global positioning system
HALT	Hungry, angry, lonely, tired
HCR-20	Historical Clinical Risk Management
ICD-10	*International Classification of Diseases* (10th ed., 1992)
LRA	Least restrictive alternative (i.e., to secure confinement)
MCMI-III	Millon Clinical Multiaxial Inventory, 3d version, coordinated with the DSM-IV
MMPI-2	Minnesota Multiphasis Personality Inventory, 2d ed.

MnSOST	Minnesota Sex Offender Screening Tool
MnSOST–R	Minnesota Sex Offender Screening Tool—Revised
MPA	Medroxyprogesterone acetate
MSOP	Minnesota Sex Offender Program
MSPPTC	Minnesota Sexual Psychopathic Personality Treatment Center
NASMHPD	National Association of State Mental Health Program Directors
OASys	Offender Assessment System
OD	Officer of the Day (in a SO residential treatment facility, a staff person designated in charge on a twenty-four-hour per day basis)
PAW	Post-acute withdrawal (syndrome)
PCL	Psychopathy Checklist
PCL-R	Psychopathy Checklist—Revised (Hare)
PCL-SV	Psychopathy Checklist—Screening Version
PD	Personality disorder
PLRA	Prison Litigation Reform Act
PP Act	Psychopathic Personality Commitment Act (Minnesota)
PPP	Positive predictive power
PPSP	Person petitioned as a sexual predator
PPG	Penile plethysmograph
ROC	Receiver operating characteristic
RPS	Relapse prevention score (part of Abel Screen)
RRASOR	Rapid Risk Assessment for Sexual Offense Recidivism
RSVP	Risk for Sexual Violence Protocol
SASSI	Substance Abuse Subtle Screening Inventory
SCC	Special Commitment Center, State of Washington
SACJ	Structured Anchored Clinical Judgment (three-stage approach to predict sexual and violent recidivism)
SACJ-Min	The SACJ reduced-item scale
SDP Act	Sexually Dangerous Persons Act (Minnesota)
SOTP	Sex Offender Treatment Program (Hawaii)
SORAG	Sex Offender Risk Assessment Guide
SRA	Structured Risk Assessment
SRB	Special Review Board (in the MSOP)
SSKAT	Socio-Sexual Knowledge and Attitude Test
SSRIs	Selective serotonin reuptake inhibitors
SVP	Sexually violent predator
SVPA	Sexually Violent Predator Act
SVR-20	Sexual Violence Rating Scale
TF	Trier of fact
TFL	Trier of fact and law
TL	Trier of law
VRAG	Violence Risk Appraisal Guide

Table of Cases and Statutes

[References are to pages and footnotes (n.).]

CASES

A
Addington v. Texas, 11-4
Alan v. Verniero, 4-6 n.21
Ayers v. Doth, 4-7

B
Barefoot v. Estelle, 11-4
Blodgett, In re, 1-3 n.10, 1-8 n.35
Brooks, In re, 4-17 n.98
Brown, In re, 4-13

C
Care & Treatment of Hay, In re, 4-13
Carhart, Stenberg v., 4-3 n.8
Carmichael, Kumho Tire, Inc. v., 11-10
Casalvera v. Comm'r, 4-6 n.21
Civil S. Bend, Freidline v., 4-12 n.63
Clewley, In re, 4-17 n.98
C.M., State v., 4-9
Comm'r, Casalvera v., 4-6 n.21
Commonwealth, Gaffney v., 4-19 n.116
Commonwealth, Hall v., 4-18 n.109
Corcoran, Walsh v., 4-6
Crane, In re, 1-4 n.13, 1-8 nn.35, 38
Currie v. United States, 11-4
Cutshall v. Sundquist, 4-7 n.26

D
Daubert v. Merrell Dow Pharmaceutical, Inc., 11-9, 11-10
Dean, In re, 3-19 n.90
D.M., In re, 4-15
Doe v. Pataki, 4-5, 4-6
Donaghe v. Seling, 4-8
Doth, Ayers v., 4-7
Douglas, State v., 4-17, 4-18

E
E.B. v. Verniero, 4-6 n.21

Engler, Lanni v., 4-7 n.27
Estelle, Barefoot v., 11-4

F
Farquarson, Hermanowski v., 4-5
Farwell, Roe v., 4-5
Femedeer v. Haun, 4-9
Filippi, United States v., 4-5 n.10
Foucha v. Louisiana, 1-6 n.25
Francis S. v. Stone, 4-6 nn.19, 20
Freidline v. Civil S. Bend, 4-12 n.63
Frye v. United States, 11-9

G
Gaff, In re, 4-17 n.98
Gaffney, Commonwealth v., 4-19 n.116
Gallegos, In re, 4-17
Grosinger v. M.D., 4-19

H
Hall v. Commonwealth, 4-18 n.109
Haun, Femedeer v., 4-9
Hendricks, Kansas v., 1-2 n.1, 1-3 n.4, 1-4 n.17, 1-6 nn.21, 24, 4-1–4-19, 12-2
Henley, United States v., 4-6 n.23
Hermanowski v. Farquarson, 4-5
Hubbart v. Superior Court, 1-3, 4-10
Hurst, State v., 4-12 n.63

K
Kansas v. Hendricks, 1-2 n.1, 1-3 n.4, 1-4 n.17, 1-6 nn.21, 24, 4-1–4-19, 5-2, 12-2
Kumho Tire, Inc. v. Carmichael, 11-10

L
Lanni v. Engler, 4-7 n.27
Lauderdale, State v., 3-16 n.81
Lee v. Louisiana, 4-7 n.25

[References are to pages and footnotes (n.).]

Linehan, In re, 1-3 n.11, 1-6 n.20, 3-25 nn.77, 78
Linehan v. Minnesota, 4-7, 4-8 n.34, 4-15, 4-15 n.82
Lipari v. Sears, Roebuck & Co., 11-4
Louisiana, Foucha v., 1-6 n.25
Louisiana, Lee v., 4-7 n.25
Lowrey, State v., 4-18
Lyons, United States v., 1-11 n.52

M

Martin v. Reinstein, 4-10
M.D., Grosinger v., 4-19
Meinders v. Weber, 4-19 n.117
Minnesota, Linehan v., 4-7, 4-8 n.34, 4-15
Minnesota ex rel. Pearson v. Probate Court of Ramsey County, 1-3 nn.8, 9

N

Neal v. Shimoda, 4-8
Nicholas, In re, 4-17 n.98

O

O'Connor, Spencer v., 4-11
Office of Adult Probation, Roe v., 4-6 n.18

P

Page v. Torrey, 4-8
Pataki, Doe v., 4-5, 4-6
Petersen, In re, 4-16
Probate Court of Ramsey Count, Minnesota ex rel. Pearson v., 1-3, 1-4

R

Regents of the University of California, Tarasoff v., 11-4
Reinstein, Martin v., 4-10
Roe v. Farwell, 4-5
Roe v. Office of Adult Probation, 4-6 n.18

S

Salcedo, In re, 4-15

Salerno, United States v., 11-4
Samuelson, In re, 4-11
Sears, Roebuck & Co., Lipari v., 11-4
Seling, Donaghe v., 4-8
Seling, Turay v., 4-9
Seling v. Young, 4-3, 4-8, 12-5
Shaw, In re., 3-16 n.80
Shaw, State v., 4-18
Shawn D. Schulpius, In re, 5-21
Shimoda, Neal v., 4-8
S.L., In re, 4-15
Spencer v. O'Connor, 4-11
Stenberg v. Carhart, 4-3 n.8
Stone, Francis S. v., 4-6 nn.19, 20
Sundquist, Cutshall v., 4-7 n.26
Superior Court, Hubbart v., 1-3, 4-10
Superior Court of Fresno County, People v., 4-11

T

Tarasoff v. Regents of the University of California, 11-4
T.B.B., In re, 12-6
Texas, Addington v., 11-4
Thorell, In re., 3-17 n.83, 3-18 n.84
Torrey, Page v., 4-8
Turay, In re, 4-16
Turay v. Seling, 4-9
Turay v. Weston, 4-9, 5-2

U

Underdown, Zadvydas v., 4-7

V

Varner, People v., 4-11 n.61
Verniero, Alan A. v., 4-6 n.21
Verniero, E.B. v., 4-6 n.21

W

Walsh v. Corcoran, 4-6
Watson, Young v., 4-3
Weber, Meinders v., 4-19 n.117
Weston, Turay v., 4-9
Weston, Young v., 4-7–4-9
Williams, People v., 4-14
Williams, State v., 4-19

Winterhalter v. People, 4-11 n.61
Woods, State v., 4-18 n.11

Y
Young, In re, 1-4 n.12, 1-12 n. 63
Young, Seling v., 4-3, 4-8, 12-5

Young v. Watson, 4-3
Young v. Weston, 4-7, 4-8, 5-2

Z
Zadvydas v. Underdown, 4-7
Zanelli, State v., 4-18

STATUTES

Alabama
    Juvenile Justice Act
        § 12-15-1.1   4-10 n. 48
    Community Notification Act
        § 15-20-20   4-9 n.47

Arizona
    Sexually Violent Persons Act
        § 36-3707(B)   4-10 nn.51, 52
        § 36-3712(B)   4-10 n.53

California
    Welfare & Inst. Code
        § 6600(a)   3-9 n.39

Florida
    Mental Health Act
        § 394.455(18)   3-11 n.47
        § 394.912(2)(b)   3-9 n.40
        § 394.912(5)   3-11 n.46

Kansas
    Sexually Violent Predator Act
        § 559-29a02(b)   3-3 n.5
        § 59-29(c)   4-12 n.67
        § 59-29a01   1-2 n.1, 4-2 n.4
        § 59-29a06   4-13 n.70
        § 59-29a08(b)   4-16 n.96

Michigan
    Criminal Sexual Psychopath Act
        § 780-501   4-14 n.75

Minnesota
    Sexually Dangerous Persons Act
        § 253B.02(18b)   4-7 nn.30, 31
        § 253B.02(18c)   4-14 n.78

Missouri
    Revised Statutes
        § 632.480-632.513   4-15 n.83

New Jersey
    Statute Annotated
        § 30:4-27.24-30   4-15 n.85, 4-27 n.38

New York
    Sex Offender Registration Act
        §168-168v   4-5 n.15

Texas
    Health & Safety Code
        § 841.001   4-19 n.118

Virginia
    Sexual Predator Commitment Statute
        § 37.1-70.1   4-19 n.120

Washington
    Sexually Violent Predators Statute
        § 71.09   4-8 n. 37, 4-16 n.90

Wisconsin
    Sexually Violent Persons Commitments Act
        § 980.01   4-17 n.99

Index

[References are to pages.]

A

Abel Assessment of Sexual Interest
    for developmentally disabled sexual offenders, 13-7–13-8
    for transition assessment, 10-8
Abstinence violation effect, 1-19–1-20
Acceptance, developmentally disabled sexual offenders and, 13-3–13-4
Accountability, vs. accuracy of predictions, 11-51
Actuarial prediction methods, 6-3
    accuracy of, 11-15–11-16
    adjusted, 3-15, 3-18
    challenges to, 3-15–3-17
    of dangerous severe personality disorder, 6-5–6-6
    for dangerousness predictions, 11-15–11-17
    Florida's rejection of, 3-19–3-20
    instruments, 6-3
    limitations of, 11-16–11-17
    Minnesota's structured approach, 3-15–3-17
    multiple, use of, 11-51
    objections to, 6-5
    plus expert modifiers, 11-17–11-18
    specificity problem of, 11-17
    vs. clinical judgments, 11-52
Addiction
    chemical, definition of, 14-3
    as preference vs. disease, 1-15–1-16
Addictive disorders, strong impulses model and, 1-13–1-14
Adult Self Expression Scale, 13-6
Advocacy, for treatment program residents, 5-18
Aftercare issues, 10-3–10-4
Alabama
    Community Notification Act, 4-9–4-10
    Hendricks decision and, 4-9–4-10
    Juvenile Justice Act, 4-10
Alcohol use/dependence
    assessment of, 14-4, 14-5
    education, 14-5-14-6
    relapse and, 14-2
    treatment. *See* Chemical abuse, components of treatment program
American Psychiatric Association, civil commitment program standards, 2-5
Anger, pervasive, as motive for sexual offending, 1-12–1-13
Antiandrogens, 5-13
Antidepressants, 5-13
Antisocial personality disorder
    impulsivity and, 1-12–1-13
    recidivism risk and, 11-29
    of sexually violent predators, 5-5–5-6
Antisocial violence, 1-7
Appetitively driven offense, 1-13
Approach-automatic pathway, 1-18
Approach skills, for developmentally disabled sexual offenders, 13-13–13-14
Area under the curve, 6-6, 11-12
Arizona
    Hendricks decision and, 4-10
    least restrictive alternative, 5-19
    treatment program setting, 5-6, 5-7
Arousal preferences
    phallometric measures, 11-26–11-27
    self-reports, 11-26
ASES. *See* Adult Self-Expression Scale
ASSESS-LIST, 11-32
Assessment
    of nonoffending partners, 9-11–9-15
    of readiness for dyadic work, 9-23
    residential, of dangerous severe personality disorder, 6-9
    of risk. *See* Risk assessment
Assessment methods
    actuarial and adjusted, 3-7–3-8
        arguments against, 3-7–3-8
        perceived reliability of, 3-8
        variability of, 3-7
        vs. SVP evaluations, 3-8
    anamnestic, 3-6
    clinical, 3-6
    for evidentiary challenges, 3-6–3-8
    guided or structural, 3-6–3-7
    for treatment programs, 5-14–5-15
Association for the Treatment of Sexual Abusers, 2-4, 2-6, 2-10, 10-8
Attachment, sexually violent predator and, 8-3
Attention, self-regulation and, 1-17
Attitude rigidity, of developmentally disabled sexual offenders, 13-4–13-5
AUC. *See* Area under the curve
Automatic behavior, 1-19
AVE. *See* abstinence violation effect
Avoidance-active pathway, 1-18
Avoidance skills, for developmentally disabled sexual offenders, 13-14–13-15
Avoidant-passive pathway, 1-18, 1-19

[References are to pages.]

B

Base rates, of recidivism, 3-16, 11-24–11-25
   dangerousness predictions and, 11-6
   significance of, 11-11–11-12
   statistics on, 3-16
Behavior
   automatic, 1-19
   caused, inability to control and, 1-8–1-9
   of developmentally disabled offenders, 13-3
   grooming, 9-19–9-20
   offending. *See* Offending
   sexual, control of. *See* Impulse control
   sexually violent, prediction of. *See* Predictions
   staff, treatment environment and, 2-12
   standards. *See* Standards for behavior
   violent, prediction of. *See* Predictions
Behavior therapy, 5-13–5-14
   See also Cognitive-behavioral therapy
"Beyond a reasonable doubt" standard, 4-16–4-17
Boundary issues, for staff, 7-9

C

California
   Hendricks decision and, 4-10–4-11
   least restrictive alternative, 5-19
   psychiatric hospital treatment programs, staffing for, 5-9, 5-10
   Sex Offender Commitment Program, treatment programming, 5-17
   sexual offending, history of, 3-9
   treatment program setting, 5-6, 5-7
Case formulations, 6-3–6-4
CATS. *See* Child and Adolescent Taxon Scale
CBT. *See* Cognitive-behavioral therapy
CEPP. *See* Conditional extension pending placement
Challenges, to specific diagnoses, 3-12
Character model, 1-11
Character/personality model (type 3), 1-21–1-22
Chemical abuse
   assessment, of offender's use and, 14-3–14-5
   clinical concepts, core, 14-2–14-3
   defined, vs. dependency, 14-3
   components of treatment program, for sex offenders, 14-3–14-8
      application of relapse prevention model, 14-7
      education, 14-5
      recovery structure, 14-6
      transition/aftercare issues, 14-7–14-8
   Plum Sex Offender Inventory for Chemical Abuse, 14-8
Child and Adolescent Taxon Scale, 11-35

Child molesters
   extra-familial, risk factors of, 11-28
   psychopathy and, 11-30
   typology of, 1-13
CI. *See* Confidence interval
Circuit court rulings, *Hendricks* decision and, 4-5–4-9
   See also Kansas v. Hendricks
Civil commitment
   challenges, developmentally disabled offenders and, 13-1–13-2
   financial implications of, 12-6–12-8
   governing factors, 11-3–11-5
   indeterminate, 3-2
   involuntary confinement, 4-12–4-13
   laws. *See* Sexually violent predator laws
   proceedings, testimony of offender in, 4-15
   program standards, ATSA, 2-6
   trial, 4-13
Civil commitment programs
   administration, 7-1–7-10
      contact with local government, 7-4
      medical issues, 7-3
      program jurisdiction and, 7-10–7-11
      program location, 7-2–7-4
   clinical context, 2-4
   community services, for residents, 7-3–7-4
   completion criteria, 10-9
   compliance incentives, 5-18
   conditional release, 2-15
   for developmentally disabled sexual offenders, 13-16–13-17
   discharge, decision-making, 10-9
   eligibility, narrowing criteria, 1-5–1-6
   in future, 7-11
   jurisdiction, 7-10–7-11
   justification for, 1-6–1-7
   legal context, 2-3
   modifications, for developmentally disabled offenders, 13-2
   oversight, external, 2-13–2-15
   population characteristics, 5-3–5-4
      multiple diagnoses, 5-5–5-6
      previous treatment, 5-4–5-5
   professional standards, 2-15
   proper subjects for, 1-12
   as punishment, 4-6
   review, of internal procedures, 2-13–2-14
   settings, 5-6–5-8, 7-2
   site, requirements for, 7-2
   staff. *See* Staff
   standards, professional, 2-4
      of care, 4-9
      general resources, 2-5
      guidelines, 2-5–2-6

[References are to pages.]

measures of progress, 2-9–2-12
requirements of *Turay* injunction, 2-6–2-7
staff training/supervision, 2-8–2-9
state guidelines, 2-5
treatment components, 2-9–2-12
state provisions for least restrictive alternative, 5-18–5-21
transition to community. *See* Transition
treatment environment, 2-15
CLES. *See* Common language effect size
Clinical judgment
confirmatory bias and, 11-15
errors in, 11-14
factors affecting, 11-14
structured or guided, 11-14–11-15
unstructured, 11-13–11-14
vs. actuarial methods, 11-15–11-16
vs. actuarial prediction methods, 11-52
Cognitive-behavioral therapy, 2-10
interventions, for treatment programs, 5-12–5-13
rationale for, 9-8–9-11
treatment model. *See* Integrated treatment model
Cognitive distortions, identifying/challenging, 9-19
Colorado
civil commitment programs, professional standards for, 2-5
Hendricks decision and, 4-18
Commitment proceedings. *See* Civil commitment, proceedings
Common language effect size, 11-12
Communication, in joint work with offender and nonoffending partner, 9-23–9-24
Community
aftercare, failure to provide, 2-11
nonoffending partner's relationship with, 9-6
transition to. *See* Transition
Community notification laws, 2-10, 4-2, 4-11–4-12, 5-3, 5-20, 10-3–10-4, 10-6, Fig. 10-1
Conditional extension pending placement, 4-15
Conditional release
for personality disorder, 4-6
treatment progress and, 2-10–2-11
Confidence interval, 11-13
Connecticut, *Hendricks* decision and, 4-18
Constitution
mental health professional expert witness testimony, 11-4–11-5
requirements, for inability-to-control judgment, 1-5–1-8, 11-6
Control
inability to. *See* Inability to control behavior

lack of. *See* Inability to control behavior
of self. *See* Self-regulation
Counseling
group. *See* Group therapy
individual, for developmentally disabled sexual offenders, 13-12
County government, transition and, 10-5–10-6
Criminal acts, future, scrutiny of scientific prediction, 3-20
Criminal conduct, 1-6
Criminal history, recidivism risk and, 11-29
Criminal interstitiality, 1-7
Criminal justice system, processes, in identifying/defining recidivism, 11-20–11-21
Criminal recidivism prediction, accuracy of, 11-7–11-8, 11-28
Criminal sentence, suspension of, 4-6
Criminal Sexual Psychopath Act, 4-14
Criminality, history of, 11-8
Criticism, developmentally disabled sexual offenders and, 13-4
CSPA. *See* Criminal Sexual Psychopath Act

D

Dangerous severe personality disorder
assessment
actuarial, 6-5–6-6
first tribunal hearing, 6-8–6-9
of link to risk, 6-5
personality disorder, 6-4
residential, 6-9
of risk, 6-3–6-4
second tribunal hearing, 6-9
specialist instrument-based risk classification, 6-7–6-8
civil commitment, 6-1–6-2
advocates of, 6-2
objections to, 6-2
definition of, 6-2
release, 6-9–6-11
risk vs. harm and, 6-2
Dangerousness
assessment of future. *See also* Risk assessment
civil commitment matters and, 11-3
constitutional basis for mental health professional role, 11-4–11-5
mental health professional role in, 11-3–11-4
communicating information re, 11-50
as constitutional standard for commitment, 1-5
"inability to control" as mental disorder and, 1-2–1-3, 1-5

[References are to pages.]

Dangerousness *(continued)*
   court's reliance on test results, 3-17
   criminal nonresponsibility/interstitiality and, 1-7
   definitional issues, 11-5–11-6
   diminished, least restrictive alternative and, 5-18
   judicial system decisions, 11-4
   legal challenge to expert's ability to assess, 3-14, 11-6
   legal concept of, 11-5–11-6
   multiple diagnoses, combined with, 5-5, 8-2
   predictions
      actuarial methods for. *See* Actuarial prediction methods
      by adjusted actuarial methods, 11-17–11-18
      admissibility of testimony and. *See* Expert witness testimony
      clinical errors in, 11-6
      criterion variables and, 11-20–11-22
      general criminal recidivism and, 11-7–11-8
      by mental health professionals, relative ability of, 11-6–11-7
      nature of, 11-5–11-6
      by pure actuarial methods, 11-15–11-17
      by structured clinical judgment, 11-14–11-15
      by unstructured clinical judgment, 11-13–11-14
      obtaining information for, 11-25
      population sample variables and, 11-18–11-19
      predictor variables and, 11-19–11-20
      principles, for expert opinion, 11-7
      statistical aspects, 11-10–11-13
      violent recidivism and, 11-7–11-8
   qualification for civil commitment, 1-20
   risk factors for. *See* Risk factors
   under SVP laws, generally, 12-2
   state requirements
      California, 4-10
      Kansas, 4-11
      Minnesota, 4-13
      Vermont, 4-18
   statutory description, *Hendricks* and, 4-3–4-5
Daubert standard, 3-4–3-5, 11-9–11-10
DDSO. *See* Developmentally disabled sexual offenders
Deception, by sexually violent predator, 8-3
Decision-making, actuarial, 3-7–3-8
Denial mechanisms, developmentally disabled sexual offenders and, 13-5
DepoProvera (medroxyprogesterone acetate), 13-15–13-16

Detention, of deportee, 4-7
Developmentally disabled sexual offenders
   assessment
      Abel Assessment of Sexual Interest, 13-7–13-8
      interview/sexual history, 13-5–13-6
      plethysmography, 13-7
      psychometric testing, 13-6
   behavior traits of, 13-3
   civil commitment programs and, 13-16–13-17
   denial mechanisms and, 13-5
   elements of challenge, 13-1–13-2
   empathetic capacity of, 13-4
   learning difficulties of, 13-5
   management issues, 13-2
   misdiagnosis of, 13-5
   need for acceptance and, 13-3–13-4
   population characteristics, 13-2–13-5
   Relapse Prevention Model adaptations, 13-11–13-16
      approach skills—"Old Me/New Me," 13-13–13-14
      avoidance skills—"What-to-Dos," 13-14–13-15
      group sessions, 13-11–13-12
      individual counseling, 13-12
      medication, 13-15–13-16
      overview, 13-13
   rigid attitudes of, 13-4–13-5
   safety issues, 13-2
   sensitivity to criticism, 13-4
   social skills of, 13-4
   treatment
      community transition, 13-10–13-11
      effective teaching, 13-9
      milieu/motivation, 13-8–13-9
   programs for, 5-15–5-16
Deviant sexual arousal
   child molesters and, 11-30
   recidivism risk and, 11-26–11-27, 11-29
Diagnosis
   of mental disorder
      formal, 3-11
      outside DSM, 3-11
      outside relevant statutory definition, 3-12–3-13
   misdiagnosis, of developmentally disabled sexual offenders, 13-5
Diagnostic and Statistical Manual of Mental Disorders (DSM-IV)
   mental disorder diagnosis criteria, 3-11
   personality disorder criteria, 6-4
Discretionary Lifer Panel, 6-8–6-9
District Court rulings, *Hendricks* decision and, 4-5–4-9
   See also Kansas v. Hendricks

[References are to pages.]

District of Columbia Circuit rulings, *Hendricks* decision and, 4-9, 4-18
Double jeopardy, 3-2, 4-2, 4-8
Drama therapy, 8-2–8-15
    as action forum for struggle, 8-6–8-7
    client, genuineness of, 8-12–8-15
    deceptive clients, 8-8–8-12
        adult rapists, 8-11–8-12
        detached/passive, 8-8
        indignant, outraged, rigid and morally righteous, 8-9
        modified confrontation with, 8-10–8-11
        overly compliant, 8-8–8-9
        overly intellectualized, 8-8
        reality of play for, 8-10
    integrity of, 8-6
    role of therapist in, 8-2
    session
        components of, 8-12
        design of, 8-7–8-8
        remaking meaning in, 8-14–8-15
        successful, elements of, 8-12–8-14
Drug abuse/dependence
    assessment of, 14-4, 14-5
    education, 14-5–14-6
Drugs. *See* Medications
DSM-IV. *See* Diagnostic and Statistical Manual of Mental Disorders
DSPD. *See* Dangerous severe personality disorder
Dual jurisdiction issues, 7-10–7-11
Due process, 2-3
Dyadic work, for nonoffending partner, 9-22–9-23
Dynamic risk factors
    acute, 11-29
    stable, 11-28–11-29

E

Eighth Circuit court rulings, *Hendricks* decision and, 4-7–4-8
Eleventh Circuit court rulings, *Hendricks* decision and, 4-9
Empathy, developmentally disabled sexual offenders and, 13-4
Ethical issues, during transition, 10-8–10-9
Evidence
    general acceptance within the relevant scientific community, 11-9
    polygraph, admissibility of, 11-9
    reliability of, 11-9–11-10
    scientific
        admissibility of, 3-3–3-4
        relevancy of, 3-4
        validity of, 3-4–3-5
Ex post facto punishment
    Hendricks decision and, 4-2

    violations, SVP statutes and, 3-2
Experimental therapies, 8-5–8-6
Expert witness testimony
    See also Mental health professionals, as experts
    with actuarial prediction methods, 11-17–11-18
    admissibility
        Daubert standard, 11-9–11-10
        evidentiary standards for, 11-8–11-10
        general acceptance within relevant scientific community, 11-9
    attacks on, 3-17–3-19
    challenges
        evidentiary, assessments for, 3-5–3-8
        to mental disorder presence related to sexual offense, 3-11–3-13
    evidentiary requirements, 3-3–3-5
        Daubert standard, 3-4–3-5
        Federal Rules, 3-5
        Frye rule, 3-3–3-4
    of mental health professionals, constitutional basis for, 11-3–11-5
    on sexual nature of nonsexual offense, 3-9–3-10
    "special knowledge" requirement, 3-10–3-11
    statutory requirements and challenges, 3-8–3-21
        history of sexual offending, 3-9–3-10
        lack of control, 3-13–3-14
        presence of mental disorder related to sexual offending, 3-11–3-13
        risk for sexual reoffending, 3-14–3-19

F

Faith, loss of, nonoffending partner and, 9-4
False imprisonment, sexually motivated, 3-9–3-10
Female offenders, treatment programming for, 5-16
Fifth Circuit court rulings, *Hendricks* decision and, 4-7
First Circuit court rulings, *Hendricks* decision and, 4-5
Florida
    Hendricks decision and, 4-18
    rejection of actuarial instruments, 3-19–3-20
    sexual offending, history of, 3-9
    SVP law
        development, 12-2
        mental abnormality, definition, 3-11
    SVP law development in, 12-2
    treatment program setting, 5-7

[References are to pages.]

Fourteenth Amendment, 2-3
Fourth Circuit court rulings, *Hendricks* decision and, 4-6–4-7
Free-standing facility
    secure, as treatment program setting, 5-8
    treatment programs, staffing for, 5-9–5-10
Friends, of nonoffending partner, 9-6
Frye rule
    acceptance with relevant scientific community, 11-9–11-10
    general acceptance test, 3-3–3-4, 3-19
Future dangerousness predictions, 3-2
    See also Dangerousness

G

Global positioning systems, for transition monitoring, 10-8
GPS. *See* Global positioning systems
Grooming strategies, identifying/resisting, 8-14, 9-4, 9-5, 9-8, 9-10, 9-15, 9-16, 9-19–9-22, 11-26
Group home arrangements
    developmentally disabled sexual offenders and, 13-10
    least restrictive alternative, 5-20–5-21
    for transition, 10-3
Group therapy
    for developmentally disabled sexual offenders, 13-11–13-12
    for nonoffending partners, 9-15–9-22

H

Habeas corpus writ, lack of control and, 4-7
Halfway house, 10-3
HALT. *See* "Hungry, angry, lonely, tired"
Hare Psychopathy Checklist—Revised. *See* Psychopathy Checklist—Revised
Hawaii, Sex Offender Treatment Program, *Hendricks* decision and, 4-8–4-9
HCR-20. *See* Historical Clinical Risk Management
Hendricks decision. *See Kansas v. Hendricks*
Historical Clinical Risk Management, 6-4, 6-7, 11-46–11-47
Historical risk factors, 11-26
Housing issues, for transition, 10-3
"Hungry, angry, lonely, tired," high-risk factors for chemical abuse, 14-6

I

ICD-10. *See International Classification of Disease*
Illinois
    Hendricks decision and, 4-11
    least restrictive alternative, 5-19
    treatment program setting, 5-7
"Illusionary correlations," 11-6
Impaired-regulation model of offending, 1-13
Impaired self-regulation model
    description of, 1-11, 1-17–1-18
    inability to control, constitutional criteria, 1-14, 1-20–1-21
Implicit "dangerous world" theory of mind, 8-4
Impulse control disorder
    DSM-IV definition, 1-13
    strong impulses model and, 1-13
Impulses, sexual, 1-18
    See also Strong impulses model
    acquiescence to, 1-14–1-17
    as active decision, 1-16
    antisocial personality and, 1-12–1-13
    irresistibility of, 1-14–1-15
    lifestyle, 1-13, 1-20
    strength to resist
        mental, self-regulation and, 1-18
        offender acquiescence and, 1-14–1-17
        physical, self-regulation and, 1-18
"Inability to control" behavior, concept of, 1-1–1-22, 3-13–3-14, 4-14–4-15
    abstinence violation effect, 1-19
    "caused behavior" vs., 1-8–1-9
    constitutional requirements, 1-5–1-8
        criminal nonresponsibility/interstitiality, 1-7
        degraded civic status, of offender, 1-7
        justification for civil commitment, 11-6
        a narrowed class of offenders eligible for commitment, 1-5
    "inability to do otherwise" vs., 1-9
    involuntary/reflexive responses, 1-8
    judgment of, context for making, 1-22
    legal standard, criteria for, 1-4–1-8
        constitutional requirements, meeting, 1-5–1-8
        observation, as ground for judgment, 1-4
        normative component to, 1-5
    typology/classification models, 1-10–1-22
        application to sex offenders, 1-12
        type 1, irresistible impulse, 1-11–1-16
        type 2, impaired self-regulation, 1-11, 1-17–1-21
        type 3, character/personality flaw, 1-11, 1-21–1-22
    self-regulation concepts, 1-10
        "self-regulation" defined, 1-17
        physical and mental components, 1-18
        sexual offending patterns and, 1-18–1-20
"utter lack of power to control" as statutory requirement, 3-13

[References are to pages.]

burden of proof, state's, in evidentiary proceedings, 3-14
"difficult to control," vs., 4-14–4-15
modified lack of control standard, 3-13–3-14
vagueness of, 1-2–1-3
volitional dysfunction vs., 1-8
writ of habeas corpus and, 4-7
Incest, as sexual addiction, 1-14
Indiana, *Hendricks* decision and, 4-11–4-12
Information
  communication, of risk of future dangerousness, 11-50
  provision
    collateral sources, in identifying/defining recidivism, 11-20
    in joint work with offender and nonoffending partner, 9-23–9-24
    for nonoffending partner, 9-24–9-25
    for risk assessment, 11-25
Inner conflict, impaired self-regulation model and, 1-17
Instrumental conditioning, 9-11
Integrated treatment model, 9-25
  appropriate timing for, 9-7–9-8
  framework, 9-8, 9-9
  goals, 9-8
  as gradual process, 9-11
  program philosophy, 9-7
  rationale for, 9-8, 9-10–9-11
Intent-effects test, 4-11–4-12
Intention, volition and, 1-8
International Classification of Disease, personality disorder criteria, 6-4
Interview assessment, of developmentally disabled sexual offenders, 13-5–13-6
Involuntary commitment. *See* Civil commitment
Involuntary responses, inability to control and, 1-8
Iowa, treatment program setting, 5-7
Irresistible impulse model of rape, 1-16–1-17, 3-13
Irresistible impulse standard, 3-14

J
Judgment
  clinical. *See* Clinical judgment
  legal. *See* Inability-to-control behavior, legal standard, criteria for
Jurisdiction
  dual, 7-10–7-11
  MSOP experience, 7-10
Jurisprudence of difference, 1-7–1-8
Juvenile delinquency history, 11-8

Juvenile sex offenders
  civil commitment
    financial implications of, 12-6–12-8
    political capital and, 12-8–12-9
  community notification and, 4-9–4-10
  dangerousness assessments for, 12-4
  housing issues, 12-4–12-5
  quality of treatment and, 12-5–12-6

K
Kansas
  Hendricks decision, 4-12–4-13
  Sexual Predator Treatment Program, compliance incentives, 5-18
  treatment program setting, 5-6–5-8
Kansas Sexually Violent Predator Act, *Hendricks* decision and, 4-2
Kansas v. Hendricks
  See also Table of Cases
  broad reach of, 4-2–4-3
  circuit court rulings and
    District of Columbia Circuit, 4-9
    Eighth Circuit, 4-7–4-8
    Eleventh Circuit, 4-9
    Fifth Circuit, 4-7
    First Circuit, 4-5
    Fourth Circuit, 4-6–4-7
    Ninth Circuit, 4-8–4-9
    Second Circuit, 4-5–4-6
    Seventh Circuit, 4-7
    Sixth Circuit, 4-7
    Tenth Circuit, 4-9
    Third Circuit, 4-6
  District Court rulings and, 4-5–4-9
  impact of, 4-19–4-20
  impact on state SVP laws. *See specific states*
  legal issues raised by, 4-2–4-4
  Megan's Laws and, 4-2–4-3
  state court rulings. *See specific states*
  U.S. Supreme Court Rulings and, 4-3–4-5
Kentucky, *Hendricks* decision and, 4-18

L
Learning difficulties, of developmentally disabled sexual offenders, 13-5
Least restrictive alternative
  facilities for, 5-20–5-21
  state provisions, 5-18–5-21
    community notification laws and, 5-20
    transition, 5-19
Legal issues, from *Hendricks* decision, 4-2–4-3, 4-4
Leuprolide (Lupron), 13-16
Local government, contact with civil commitment program administration, 7-4
LRA. *See* Least restrictive alternative

[References are to pages.]

M

Maine, *Hendricks* decision and, 4-18
Massachusetts
   Hendricks decision and, 4-5, 4-13–4-14
   treatment program setting, 5-7
Mechanical prediction methods
   accuracy of, 11-15–11-16
   limitations of, 11-16–11-17
   specificity problem of, 11-17
Media, transition and, 10-6
Medications
   for developmentally disabled sexual offenders, 13-15–13-16
   selective serotonin reuptake inhibitors, 5-13, 10-8, 13-16
   during transition, 10-8
Medroxyprogesterone acetate (MPA; DepoProvera; Provera), 10-8, 13-15–13-16
Megan's Laws, *Hendricks* decision and, 4-5–4-6
Mental abnormality, definition of, 3-2–3-3, 3-11, 4-12, 12-2
Mental disorder, 1-6, 1-11–1-12
   caused behavior and, 1-8–1-9
   clinical diagnoses vs. legal definitions, 3-12–3-13
   connection to reoffense risk, 3-12
   diagnosis
      formal, 3-11
      outside DSM, 3-11
      outside relevant statutory definition, 3-12–3-13
   inability to control and, 1-3, 1-8
   justification for civil commitment
      criminal nonresponsibility/interstitiality, 1-7
      jurisprudence of difference, 1-7–1-8
      presence, related to sexual offending, 3-11–3-13
   specific diagnoses, challenges to, 3-12
   vs. inability to control behavior, 1-9
Mental health facility, in prison, 5-6, 5-8
Mental health professionals
   clinical, role in civil commitment procedures, 11-3–11-4
   clinical judgment of. *See* Clinical judgment
   "illusionary correlations" of, 11-6
   misdiagnosis, of developmentally disabled sexual offenders, 13-5
   prediction of dangerousness, relative ability of, 11-6–11-7
   risk assessment, ability as experts, 3-14
   sexual offender treatment, 2-4
   testimony, expert witness. *See* Expert witness testimony
Mental health treatment
   components, 2-9–2-12
   constitutionally adequate, failure to provide, 2-6–2-7
   due process, 2-3
   planning, consistency of, 2-8–2-9
   staff. *See* Staff
Mental illness, use of term, 3-3
Mental strength, self-regulation and, 1-18
Mentally ill offenders, treatment programming for, 5-16
Meta-analysis
   of dynamic risk factors, 11-29
   Psychopathy Checklist—Revised, 11-30–11-31
   of risk factors, 11-27–11-28
Michigan, *Hendricks* decision and, 4-14
Milieu/motivation, for developmentally disabled sexual offenders, 13-8–13-9
Minnesota
   actuarial risk assessments, 3-15–3-17
   civil commitment programs, professional standards for, 2-5
   Hendricks decision and, 4-14–4-15
   least restrictive alternative, 5-19
   treatment program setting, 5-7
Minnesota Commitment and Treatment Act, 7-10
Minnesota Multiphasic Personality Inventory, 3-3, 3-16, 3-17, 5-14
Minnesota Sex Offender Program
   chemical dependency treatment component, 14-1
   application of relapse prevention model, 14-6–14-7
   assessment, 14-4, 14-5
   education, 14-5–14-6
   phases, 14-3, 14-5
   Plum Sex Offender Inventory for Chemical Abuse, 14-8–14-11
   program statement, 14-1–14-3
   transition issues, 14-7–14-8
   Department of Corrections and, 7-10
   Department of Human Services and, 7-10
   free-standing secure facility, 5-8
   jurisdiction, 7-10
   program compliance incentives, 5-18
   staffing, 5-9–5-10
   transition plan, 10-12–10-13
Minnesota Sex Offender Screening Tool
   development of, 11-35–11-36
   inter-rater reliability, 11-37
   rejection of, in Florida courts, 3-19–3-20
   relationship with other assessment tools, 11-48–11-50

[References are to pages.]

reliability/validity of, 11-36
Minnesota Sex Offender Screening Tool—Revised, 3-7, 11-40–11-42, 12-3
Minnesota Sexual Psychopathic Personality Treatment Center, 7-10
Minnesota Sexually Dangerous Persons Act, 4-7
Missouri
   Hendricks decision and, 4-15
   treatment program setting, 5-7
MMPI-2. *See* Minnesota Multiphasic Personality Inventory
MnSOST. *See* Minnesota Sex Offender Screening Tool
MnSOST-R. *See* Minnesota Sex Offender Screening Tool—Revised
Modeling behaviors, 9-10
Modified Cognition Scale for the Developmentally Disabled, 13-6
MONARCH DDMR Projective Audio/Visual VHS set, version 2, 13-7
Montana, *Hendricks* decision and, 4-18
MPA. *See* medroxyprogesterone acetate
MSOP. *See* Minnesota Sex Offender Program
MSPPTC. *See* Minnesota Sexual Psychopathic Personality Treatment Center

N

NASMHPD. *See* National Association of State Mental Health Program Directors
National Association of State Mental Health Program Directors, 2-5, 5-3
Nebraska, *Hendricks* decision and, 4-18
New Jersey
   Hendricks decision and, 4-15
   least restrictive alternative, 5-19
   treatment program setting, 5-7
New York, *Hendricks* decision and, 4-5–4-6, 4-19
Ninth Circuit court rulings, *Hendricks* decision and, 4-8
Nonsexual offense, sexual nature of, 3-9–3-10
North Dakota
   Hendricks decision and, 4-19
   treatment program setting, 5-7
Notification provision, SVP statutes, 2-10, 4-2, 4-11–4-12, 5-3, 5-8–5-20, 10-3–10-4, 10-6, Fig. 10.1

O

OASys. See Offender Assessment System
Observation, as legal criterion for inability-to-control judgment, 1-4
Obsession, 1-21
Offender Assessment System, 6-5, 6-7–6-8

Offender Group Reconviction Scale, 6-3
Offenders
   acquiescence to impulses, 1-14–1-17
   attachment models, unsafe, 8-3
   change, therapy as agent of, 8-4–8-5
   chemical dependency and. *See* Chemical dependency, treatment services
   definition of, 4-12
   designation, appeal of, 4-15
   with developmental disabilities. *See* Developmentally disabled sexual offenders
   discordant lying by, 8-4–8-5
   dynamics, increased understanding of, 9-16, 9-18
   implicit "dangerous world" theory of mind, 8-4
   joint work with nonoffending partner, 9-22–9-23
      assessing readiness for, 9-23
      methods for, 9-23–9-24
   legal responsibility of, 1-16
   moral responsibility of, 1-16
   nongenuine self, classic presentation of, 8-8–8-12
   offense history, 10-1–10-2
   personality disorders of, 5-5–5-6
   population characteristics, for civil commitment programs, 5-3–5-6
   previous treatment of, 5-4–5-5
   repeat offenses, relative probability of, 11-5
   in residential treatment programs. *See* Residential treatment programs, residents
   risk factors
      external, 10-2–10-3
      internal, 10-2
   self-reports, bias in, 1-14
   transition and, 10-6–10-7
   types of, 11-23
   typology of, 1-13
Offending
   as addictive process, 1-13–1-14
   cycle of, 9-21
   as dangerous, 6-2
   deconstruction, 1-19
   developmentally disabled offenders and, 13-3
   follow-up period, length of, 11-22–11-24
   history of, 3-9–3-10
      recidivism risk and, 11-29
   impact of, addressing, in group therapy for nonoffending partner, 9-16
   impulse for. *See* Impulses, sexual
   motives, primary, 1-12–1-13

[References are to pages.]

Offending *(continued)*
   number of, recidivism and, 11-21
   patterns of sexual, 1-18–1-20
      approach-automatic pathway, 1-18–1-19
      approach-explicit pathway, 1-18–1-19
      avoidance-active pathway, 1-18
      avoidant-passive pathway, 1-18
      presence of mental disorder related to, 3-11–3-13
      providing alternative model/framework for, 9-18–9-19
Ohio, *Hendricks* decision and, 4-19
Opportunity, as motive for sexual offending, 1-12–1-13, 1-20
Oregon, *Hendricks* decision and, 4-19
Outpatient treatment, transition to, 5-19

P
Paraphilia
   challenges to, 3-12
   DSM-IV definition, 1-13
   strong impulses model and, 1-13
Parole office records, in identifying recidivism, 11-21–11-22
Parole revocation procedures, 5-17–5-18
Partner and victim alert list, 9-22
Partners, nonoffending
   assessment of, 9-11–9-15
   dyadic work, 9-22–9-23
   financial concerns of, 9-6
   group work for, 9-15–9-22
      Part A, 9-16–9-19
      Part B, 9-19–9-22
      Part C1, 9-22
      Part C2, 9-23–9-24
      therapist's role in, 9-24–9-25
   impact of abuse discovery, 9-3–9-7
      as individual, 9-4
      on relationship with community, 9-6
      on relationship with friends, 9-6
      on relationship with offender, 9-4–9-5
      on relationship with victim, 9-5–9-6
      on relationship with victim's siblings, 9-6
   reasons for working with, 9-2–9-3
   support services for, 9-7
PCL. *See* Psychopathy Checklist
PCL-R. *See* Psychopathy Checklist—Revised
PCL-SV. *See* Psychopathy Checklist—Screening Version
Pedophile Cognition Scale, 13-6
Pedophilia
   addictiveness of, 1-14
   challenges to, 3-12
   as mental illness, 4-5
Penile plethysmography. *See* Plethysmography

Pennsylvania, *Hendricks* decision and, 4-19
Personality, inability to control and, 1-11
Personality Disorder Not Otherwise Specified—Psychopathy, 3-11
Personality disorders, 1-6
   assessment
      of link to risk, 6-5
      link to risk and, 6-8
   conditional release for, 4-6
   dangerous severe. *See* Dangerous severe personality disorder
   diagnostic criteria, 6-4
   of sexually violent predators, 5-5–5-6
Phallometric evaluation, in risk prediction, 5-14, 11-26–11-27
Pharmacologic agents. *See* Medications
Physical strength, self-regulation and, 1-18
Play reality, for deceptive client, 8-10
Plethysmography
   for developmentally disabled sexual offenders, 13-7
   during transition, 10-8
PLRA. *See* Prison Litigation Reform Act
Police records, in identifying recidivism, 11-21–11-22
Policy-makers, transition and, 10-5
Political capital, 12-8–12-9
Polygraph examinations, 5-14–5-15
   admissibility of evidence, 11-9
   during transition, 10-7–10-8
Positive predictive power, dangerousness prediction accuracy and, 11-11
PPP. *See* Positive predictive power
PPST. *See* Psychopathic Personality Screen Test
Predictions
   accuracy of, 11-6–11-8, 11-11, 11-13, 11-15
      of actuarial methods, 11-15–11-16
      positive predictive power and, 11-11
      upper limits for, 11-22
      vs. accountability, 11-51
   confidence interval, 11-13
   correlation coefficients, 11-10–11-11
   elements/issues in, 11-18–11-25
      criterion variables, 11-20–11-22
      length of follow-up period, 11-22–11-24
      population sample variables, 11-18–11-19
      predictor variables, 11-19–11-20
   errors, 11-11
   group characteristics and, 11-17
   of individual recidivism, 3-17–3-18
   methodology, mechanical, 11-15–11-17
   methodology of, 11-13–11-18
      adjusted actuarial methods, 11-17–11-18
      pure actuarial methods, 11-15–11-17

[References are to pages.]

structured or guided clinical judgment, 11-14–11-15
unstructured clinical judgment, 11-13–11-14
ROC analysis, 11-12–11-13
sensitivity of, 11-11
sensitivity-specificity tradeoff, 11-11–11-12
specificity of, 11-11
statistical aspects of, 11-10–11-13
under-predictions, 11-25
validity of, 11-10
Preventive detention, 1-2
Prison, mental health facility, as treatment program setting, 5-6, 5-8
Prison-based treatment program, staffing for, 5-10, 5-11
Prison Litigation Reform Act, 4-8
Provera (medroxyprogesterone acetate), 10-8, 13-15–13-16
Psychiatric hospital
    as treatment program setting, 5-6
    treatment program staffing, 5-9, 5-10
Psychiatric services, as program component, 2-10
Psychometric testing, of developmentally disabled sexual offenders, 13-6
Psychopathic Personality Screen Test, 11-36
Psychopathy, recidivism risk and, 11-26–11-27, 11-29, 11-31
Psychopathy Checklist, 11-27
Psychopathy Checklist—Revised, 3-16, 3-19, 5-5, 11-30–11-32
    inter-rater reliability, 11-30
    meta-analysis, 11-30–11-31
    misuse of, 11-32
    psychopathy, recidivism and, 11-31
Psychopathy Checklist—Screening Version, relationship with other assessment tools, 11-31–11-32, 11-48–11-50

R

Rape
    irresistible impulse model of, 1-16–1-17
    as male entitlement, 1-19
    motives for, 1-20
    opportunistic, 1-20
Rapid Risk Assessment for Sexual Offense Recidivism, 3-7, 11-37–11-39, 12-3
    challenges to, 3-18–3-19
    development of, 11-37–11-38
    Florida's rejection of actuarial instruments, 3-19–3-20
    Frye challenge to, 3-18
    limitations of, 11-38–11-39
    predictive accuracy of, 11-38
    predictor variables, 11-37
    relationship with other assessment tools, 11-48–11-50
Rapists
    adult, drama therapy for, 8-11–8-12
    description of, 1-12
    psychopathy and, 11-30
    recidivism rate, extended follow-up period and, 11-23–11-24
Receiver operating characteristic analysis, 6-6, 11-12–11-13
Recidivism
    abstinence violation effect and, 1-19–1-20
    alcohol use/dependence and, 14-2
    base rate. *See* Base rates
    criminal, 11-7–11-8, 11-28
    cues, identification of, 9-21–9-22
    definition of, 11-37
    factors, "double-counting" of, 3-19
    identifying/defining, 11-20–11-22
    prediction, accuracy of, 11-7–11-8
    predictions of. *See* Predictions
    prevention, cognitive-behavioral interventions for, 5-12–5-13
    rate, extended follow-up period and, 11-23–11-24
    risk factors
        deviancy, 11-26–11-27
        dynamic, 11-28–11-29
        identifying/defining, 11-19–11-20
        meta-analysis of, 11-27–11-28
        psychopathy, 11-26–11-27
        static or historical, 11-26
    risk for, 3-14–3-19
        ability of expert to assess, 3-14
        legality of assessment method, 3-14–3-15
    specific mental disorders and, 3-12
    underestimation of, 11-22
    violent, general, 3-15
Recruitment, of staff, 7-3, 7-6–7-9
Reflexive responses, inability to control and, 1-8
Relapse. *See* Recidivism
Relapse Prevention Model, 9-21–9-22
    application, chemical dependency treatment service, 14-6–14-7
    developmentally disabled sex offender, for, 13-11–13-16
        approach skills—Old Me/New Me, 13-13–13-14
        avoidance skills—"What-to-Dos," 13-14–13-15
        group sessions, 13-11–13-12
        individual counseling, 13-12

[References are to pages.]

Relapse Prevention Model *(continued)*
    medication, 13-15–13-16
    overview of, 13-13
    limitations with special populations, 13-12–13-13
Release, from DSPD containment, 6-9–6-11
    prior record/current behavior scales, 6-10
    psychometric tests, 6-10–6-11
Reoffense. *See* Recidivism
Residential treatment programs
    advocacy for residents, 5-18
    assessment, of dangerous severe personality disorder, 6-9
    difficulties, management strategies for, 5-17–5-18
    residents of
        advocacy, 2-14
        furlough eligibility, 4-8–4-9
        grievances, 2-13
        housing, 4-8–4-9
        parole eligibility, 4-8–4-9
        treatment refusal, 2-13
    staff harassment, 5-17
    transition to outpatient treatment, 5-19
    treatment resistance, 5-16–5-17
Resist, normal capacity to, 1-11
Respondent conditioning, 9-10–9-11
Risk
    assessment of. *See* Risk assessment
    conditional, 11-7
    link to personality disorder, assessment of, 6-5, 6-8
    prediction of. *See* Predictions
Risk assessment, 11-50–11-52
    See also Actuarial prediction methods; Clinical judgment
    ability of expert, 3-14
    accuracy of, 11-50–11-51
    admissibility of expert witness testimony, 11-4–11-5
    in civil commitment procedures, 11-3
    of developmentally disabled sexual offenders. *See* Developmentally disabled sexual offenders, assessment
    for DSPD containment release, 6-9–6-11
    in future, 11-51–11-52
    getting beyond the appearance of scientific judgment, 3-20–3-21
    instruments, 11-30–11-50
        ASSESS-LIST, 11-32
        development of, 11-50, 11-52
        Historical Clinical Risk Management-20, 6-4, 6-7, 11-46–11-47
        MnSOST. *See* Minnesota Sex Offender Screening Tool
        MnSOST-R. *See* Minnesota Sex Offender Screening Tool—Revised
        PCL-R. *See* Psychopathy Checklist—Revised
        predictions of. *See* Predictions
        relationships between, 11-48–1150
        Risk for Sexual Violence Protocol, 11-48
        RRASOR. *See* Rapid Risk Assessment for Sexual Offense Recidivism
        samples, 11-51
        Sex Offender Need Assessment Rating, 11-44–11-45
        Sexual Violence Rating Scale, 11-47
        SORAG. *See* Sex Offender Risk Appraisal Guide
        Static-99, 11-43–11-44, 11-49–11-50
        Structured Anchored Clinical Judgment, 11-42–11-43
        Structured Risk Assessment, 11-45–11-46
        VRAG. *See* Violence Risk Appraisal Guide
    juvenile data, 12-4
    by mental health professionals, accuracy of, 11-6–11-7
    methodologies
        case formulations, 6-3–6-4
        legality of, 3-14–3-15
    methods. *See* Assessment methods
    obtaining information for, 11-25
    recidivism and, 11-7–11-8
    scientific principle, scrutiny of, 3-20
    tools for, 12-3
Risk factors, 11-25–11-26
    deviancy, 11-26–11-27
    dynamic
        acute, 11-29
        stable, 11-28–11-29
    general types of, 11-29
    meta-analysis of, 11-27–11-28
    number of, effect on clinical judgment, 11-14
    psychopathy, 11-26–11-27
    static or historical, 11-26
Risk for Sexual Violence Protocol, 11-48
Risk matrix, 6-5–6-7
RM. *See* Risk matrix
ROC analysis, 6-6, 11-12–11-13
RRASOR. *See* Rapid Risk Assessment for Sexual Offense Recidivism
RSVP. *See* Risk for Sexual Violence Protocol

S

SACJ. *See* Structured Anchored Clinical Judgment
SCC. *See* Special Commitment Center

[References are to pages.]

Second Circuit court rulings, *Hendricks* decision and, 4-5–4-6
Security, staffing level requirements, 7-4–7-5
Security counselors, recruitment of, 7-3
Selective serotonin reuptake inhibitors (SSRIs), 5-13, 10-8, 13-16
Self-monitoring mechanism, for self-regulation, 1-17
Self-regulation, 1-7
  See also Impaired self-regulation model
  definition of, 1-17
  dysfunctional, styles of, 1-18
  effective, approach-explicit pathway and, 1-18, 1-19
  failure, 1-17, 1-18
    avoidant-passive pathway and, 1-18, 1-19
    criminality and, 1-20
    as inability to control, 1-20–1-21
    mechanisms of, 1-19
  hierarchy of processes and, 1-10
  ingredients, key, 1-17
  mental strength and, 1-18
  misregulation, 1-18
    approach-automatic pathway and, 1-18
    avoidant-active pathway and, 1-18
  parallel and complex processes and, 1-10
  physical strength and, 1-18
  in sexual offending context, 1-18–1-20
Self-reports
  in identifying/defining recidivism, 11-20
  of new offenses, 11-21
Sensitivity, of dangerousness prediction, 11-11
Seventh Circuit court rulings, *Hendricks* decision and, 4-7
Sex Offender Need Assessment Rating, 11-44–11-45
Sex offender registration and notification laws (Megan's Laws), *Hendricks* decision and, 4-2–4-3
Sex Offender Risk Appraisal Guide, 3-7, 11-39–11-40
  Frye challenge to, 3-18
Sex offenders. *See* Offenders
Sex offense-permissive cognitions, recidivism risk and, 11-29
Sexual abuse
  of developmentally disabled offenders, 13-2
  discovery, impact of, on partner, 9-3–9-7
  impact on victim, 9-3
  of juvenile sex offenders, while in treatment, 12-5
Sexual compulsivity control, medications for. *See* Medications
Sexual gratification, as motive for sexual offending, 1-12–1-13

Sexual history, of developmentally disabled sexual offenders, 13-5–13-6
Sexual impulses. *See* Impulses, sexual
Sexual Interest Cardsort, 13-6
Sexual nature, of nonsexual offense, 3-9–3-10
Sexual psychopath laws, 3-2
Sexual violence
  justification for, 1-19
  "likely to engage in repeat acts of ," 4-12
  under-prediction of, 11-25
Sexual Violence Rating Scale, 6-4, 11-47
Sexually violent predator laws, 1-3–1-4, 2-2, 3-2, 4-2–4-3, 5-21, 12-1–12-4
  assessment process, 3-21
  constitutional validity of, 3-2–3-3
  development of, 12-2–112-3
  expert testimony, challenges to, 3-9–3-21
  expert witness testimony
    history of sexual offending, 3-9–3-11
    presence of mental disorder related to sexual offending, 3-11–3-13
  format of, 3-8–3-9
  implications for juvenile offenders
    assessment of dangerousness and, 12-3–12-4
    housing issues, 12-4–12-5
  justification, *Hendricks* decision and, 4-2–4-3
  lack of control, statutory requirements, 3-13–3-14
  purpose of, 12-1
  wide latitude in, 4-3–4-5
Sixth Circuit court rulings, *Hendricks* decision and, 4-7
Social skills, of developmentally disabled sexual offenders, 13-4
Socio-Sexual Knowledge and Attitude Test, 13-6
SONAR. *See* Sex Offender Need Assessment Rating
SORAG. *See* Sex Offender Risk Appraisal Guide
South Carolina, treatment program setting, 5-7
South Dakota, *Hendricks* decision and, 4-19
Special Commitment Center, 2-2
Specialist instrument-based risk classification, 6-7–6-8
Specificity
  of actuarial prediction methods, 11-17
  of dangerousness prediction, 11-11
SSKAT. *See* Socio-Sexual Knowledge and Attitude Test
SSRIs. *See* Selective serotonin reuptake inhibitors
Staff
  administrative, 7-5
  behavior, treatment environment and, 2-12

[References are to pages.]

Staff *(continued)*
    boundary issues, 7-9
    cohesion, 5-11
    cost, 5-11–5-12
    developmentally disabled sexual offenders and, 13-16
    direct care, 7-5
        recruitment, 7-5–7-6
        types of, 7-6
    expertise, 5-11–5-12
    harassment, 5-17
    levels
        security requirements, 7-4–7-5
        treatment requirements, 7-4–7-5
    levels/patterns, 5-9–5-11
    professional care, 7-5
        recruitment, 7-6
    recruitment, 7-3
    roles, definition of, 2-8
    structure of staffing and, 2-8
    supervision, 2-7, 2-8
    training, 2-8, 5-11–5-12
        new employee/refresher, 7-6–7-9
        policies and, 2-13
    transition and, 10-7
    treatment program, 5-9–5-12
        expertise, 5-11–5-12
        levels/patterns for, 5-9–5-11
        planning consistency for, 2-8–2-9
        training, 5-11–5-12
Standards for behavior
    inappropriate
        approach-automatic pathway and, 1-18
        approach-explicit pathway and, 1-19
        self-regulation and, 1-17
Standards for Educational and Psychological Testing, 3-8
State government
    See also specific states
    guidelines, for civil commitment programs, 2-5
    least restrictive alternative provisions, 5-18–5-21
        community notification issues, 5-20
        LRA facilities, types of, 5-20–5-21
        transition to outpatient setting, 5-19
Static-99, 11-43–11-44, 11-49–11-50
Static risk factors, 11-26
Statistical methods, for dangerousness predictions, 11-15–11-17
Statistical prediction methods
    limitations of, 11-16–11-17
    specificity problem of, 11-17
Strong impulses model, 1-11, 1-12–1-14
    addictive disorders and, 1-13–1-14
    antisocial personality and, 1-12–1-13
    negative affect and, 1-13
    offender acquiescence to impulses, 1-14–1-17
Structural clinical judgment, 6-4
Structured Anchored Clinical Judgment, 11-42–11-43, 11-49
Structured Risk Assessment, 11-45–11-46
Substantially probable, definition of, 4-17–4-18
Substantive due process, 1-5–1-6
Support
    network, for nonoffending partner, 9-22
    services, for nonoffending partner, 9-7
Supreme Court, treatment program provision, 5-1
Survival analysis, 11-22–11-23
SVP laws. *See* Sexually violent predator laws
SVP programs. *See* Civil commitment programs
SVR-20. *See* Sexual Violence Rating Scale

T

Teaching, of developmentally disabled sexual offenders, 13-9
Tenth Circuit court rulings, *Hendricks* decision and, 4-9
Texas
    Hendricks decision and, 4-19
    outpatient treatment, 5-18
Therapies, experimental, 8-5–8-6
Therapist
    in drama therapy, modified confrontation with deceptive client, 8-10–8-11
    role, in drama therapy, 8-2
    working with nonoffending partner, 9-24–9-25
Third Circuit court rulings, *Hendricks* decision and, 4-6
Training
    new employee/refresher, 7-6–7-9
    staff, for treatment program, 5-11–5-12
Transition, 5-20–5-21
    aftercare issues, 10-3–10-4
    from chemical dependency treatment service, 14-7–14-8
    civil commitment programs and, 10-7
    of developmentally disabled sexual offenders, 13-10–13-11
    ethical issues, 10-8–10-9
    gradual/controlled
        external risk factors and, 10-2–10-3
        housing issues for, 10-3
        internal risk factors and, 10-2
        need for, 10-1–10-2
    plan, 10–10-13
    progress, monitoring of
        need for, 10-7
        technical devices for, 10-7–10-8
    stakeholders, 10-4–10-7

[References are to pages.]

county government and, 10-5–10-6
media, 10-6
policy-makers, 10-5
sex offender, 10-6–10-7
treatment program, 10-7
victim advocates, 10-4–10-5
victims, 10-4–10-5
Traumatic experiences, of sexually violent predator, suppression of, 8-3
Treating Child Sex Offenders and Victims: A Practical Guide, 9-7
Treatment
    access, 2-10
    adequacy, 2-10
    alcohol use/dependence. *See* Chemical abuse
    community release component, failure to provide, 2-11
    conditional release and, 2-10–2-11
    constitutional requirements, 2-2
        clinical context, 2-3
        legal context, 2-3
    deception in, 8-5
    drama therapy. *See* Drama therapy
    drug abuse. *See* Chemical abuse
    environment, 2-11–2-13
        adequacy of, 2-11–2-12
        nonpunitive, 2-12
        policy enforcement, 2-12–2-13
        resident's grievances and, 2-13
        space, 2-12
        staff behavior and, 2-12
    experimental therapies for, 8-5–8-6
    See also Drama therapy
    feedback, 2-10
    genuineness in, 8-5
    goals/targets, 2-10
    lack of available, 3-2
    monitoring, 2-10
    planning
        comprehensive, standards for, 2-9–2-10
        consistency, staff and, 2-8–2-9
        individual, standards for, 2-9–2-10
    policies, enforcement of, 2-12–2-13
    population characteristics and, 5-3–5-6
    previous, of SVP population, 5-4–5-5
    programming
        See also Civil commitment programs
        ancillary, 5-15
        assessment, 5-14–5-15
        behavior therapy, 5-13–5-14
        cognitive-behavioral approaches, 5-12–5-13
        medications, 5-13
        phases, 5-15
        planning, 5-15
        for special populations, 5-15–5-16
    progress, identifiable phases of, 2-10–2-11
    provision, 5-2–5-3
    quality assurance/improvement program, 2-14
    record-keeping, 2-10
    refusal, 2-13
    residential management issues, 5-16–5-18
    resistance, 5-16–5-17
    staffing level requirements, 7-4–7-5
    standards, 5-3
Trust, loss of, nonoffending partner and, 9-4, 9-5
Twelve-step programs, 14-6

U

United States Supreme Court
    future dangerousness predictions, limits of, 11-4–11-5
    Hendricks decision and, 4-3–4-5
    unlawful confinement and, 4-3

V

Values, hierarchy of, 1-10
Vermont, *Hendricks* decision and, 4-19
Victim advocates, transition and, 10-4–10-5
Victims
    dynamics of, increased understanding of, 9-16
    relationship with nonoffending partner, 9-5–9-6
    siblings of, relationship with nonoffending partner, 9-6
    transition and, 10-4–10-5
Vindictiveness, as motive for sexual offending, 1-12–1-13
Violence reconviction rates, in Risk Matrix, 6-6, 6-7
Violence Risk Appraisal Guide, 6-5, 6-7, 11-33–11-35
    challenges to, 3-15, 3-18–3-19
    Florida's rejection of actuarial instruments, 3-19–3-20
    limitations of, 11-35
    relationship with other assessment tools, 11-49
    violent behavior predictions, 11-34–11-35
Virginia
    Hendricks decision and, 4-19
    least restrictive alternative, 5-19
    treatment program setting, 5-7
Volition, 3-13
    definition of, 1-8
    intention and, 1-8
Volitional dysfunction, inability to control and, 1-8
VRAG. *See* Violence Risk Appraisal Guide

[References are to pages.]

W

Washington
    civil commitment programs
        Hendricks decision and, 4-8, 4-9
        standard of care in, 4-9
    Hendricks decision and, 4-16–4-17
    least restrictive alternative, 5-19
    prison-based treatment program, staffing for, 5-10, 5-11
    Special Commitment Center, 2-2
    SVP law development in, 12-2
    treatment program setting, 5-6, 5-7, 5-8
Willpower, 1-8
Wisconsin
    expert testimony, "special knowledge" requirement, 3-10–3-11
    Hendricks decision and, 4-17–4-18
    sexually violent offense, 3-9
    treatment program setting, 5-7
Women offenders, treatment programming for, 5-16
Writ of habeas corpus, 4-8